THE WESTERN INTELLECTUAL TRADITION
VOLUME I

THE WESTERN INTELLECTUAL TRADITION

VOLUME I

GREECE THROUGH THE MIDDLE AGES

David C. Riede
J. Wayne Baker

The University of Akron

KENDALL/HUNT PUBLISHING COMPANY
Dubuque, Iowa, USA • Toronto, Ontario, Canada

Copyright © 1978 by David C. Riede and J. Wayne Baker

Copyright © 1980 by Kendall/Hunt Publishing Company

Library of Congress Catalog Card Number: 78-54670

ISBN 0-8403-2259-3

All rights reserved. No part of this publication may be reproduced, stored in a retrieval system, or transmitted, in any form or by any means, electronic, mechanical, photocopying, recording, or otherwise, without the prior written permission of the copyright owners.

Printed in the United States of America

Contents

I. The Greeks

A. Homer: *The Odyssey*, 4

B. Hesiod: *Works and Days*, 11

C. Sappho: *Ode to Anactoric*, 13; *Cleïs*, 14; *The Dust of Timas*, 14; *Ode to Aphrodite*, 14; *An Hymn to Venus*, 14; *Fragments of Sappho*, 15

D. Sophocles: *Oedipus Rex**, 16

E. Thucydides: *Funeral Oration*, 32

F. Plato: *Apology*, 37; *Crito**, 43; *Phaedo*, 50; *Republic*, 61

G. Aristotle: *Politics*, 73; *Nicomachean Ethics*, 82

II. The Romans

A. Vergil: *The Aeneid*, 91

B. Cicero: *The Laws*, 102

C. Ovid: *Art of Love*, 109

D. Martial: *Epigrams*, 111

E. Juvenal: *Third Satire*, 112

F. Marcus Aurelius: *Meditations*, 114

III. The Hebrews

A. The Old Testament, 121; *Genesis 17:1-14*, 121; *Exodus 3:1-12*, 121; *Exodus 6:1-8*, 122; *Exodus 19:1-8*, 122; *Exodus 20:1-20*, 122; *Amos 5:1-27*, 123; *Jeremiah 11:1-13*, 124; *The Song of Solomon 7:1-12*, 125; *Daniel 2:1-49*, 125

IV. Christianity

A. The Teachings of Christ and the Early Church: *The New Testament*, 131; *Matthew 5:1-48*, 131; *Matthew 16:13-20*, 132; *John 1:1-14*, 132; *John 3:1-21*, 132; *Acts 9:1-22*, 133; *Romans 4:1-25*, 134; *1 Corinthians 13:1-13*, 134; *Matthew 24:1-51*, 135; *Revelation 20:1-15*, 136

B. The Church and the Empire: *Eusebius—Conversion of Constantine*, **137**; *Eusebius—Edict of Milan**, **139**; *Nicene Creed**, **140**; *St. Augustine—Confessions*, **140**; *St. Augustine—City of God*, **146**

V. The Middle Ages

A. Feudalism: *The Ceremony of Homage and Fealty*, **155**; *Mutual Duties of Vassals and Lords*, **155**; *Feudal Justice*, **156**; *Condemnation by a Feudal Court*, **156**.

B. Early Scholasticism: St. Anselm of Canterbury-*Proslogium*, **157**; Peter Abelard-*Sic et Non*, **159**.

C. High Scholasticism: *University Life*, **160**; St. Thomas Aquinas-*Summa Theologica* (Usury, Stupidity, The Existence of God), **164**; William of Ockham-*Epistemological Problems* (Universals), **167**.

D. Literature from the High and Late Middle Ages: Dante-*The New Life*, **169**; *Inferno*, **171**; Chaucer-*The Canterbury Tales* (Prologue and Nun's Priest's Tale), **180**.

E. Popular Piety and Heresy in the Middle Ages: St Francis of Assisi-*Prayer*, **191**; *Will of St. Francis*, **191**; *The Conversion of Peter Waldo*, **193**; *A Description of the Albigensians*, **194**.

*Complete (others only partial)

THE GREEKS

Homer

Two of the greatest epic poems in Greek literature are Homer's *Iliad* and *Odyssey*. These two poems, extremely popular throughout Greek history, held a position somewhat similar to that of the Bible among Christian peoples. Both Vergil and Dante borrowed heavily from these poems, especially the subject of a visit to the underworld. Each of these poets uses this device to explain such things as the founding of their country, or punishments of individuals for living evil lives, or even to discuss the purpose of man in the world.

The *Iliad* is the story of the end of the Trojan War and deals mainly with Achilles, the mightiest Greek warrior. At the end of the *Iliad*, Achilles kills Hector who was the chief defender of the city of Troy—Ilius in Latin. The entire poem is full of the clash of arms and the din of battle. The characters are given a personal touch by Homer; each is seen as a man of flesh and blood with human virtues and failings.

The *Odyssey* is the story of the homeward journey of Odysseus who was known in Latin as Ulysses. Odysseus, probably the most versatile and well-known character in Greek literature had certain flaws, but his virtues outnumbered his flaws. Some have said that one of his most prominent virtues was his cleverness, since supposedly it was he who suggested the use of the wooden horse which ended the Trojan War. Odysseus could also use his hands as well as his brain, but, as is evidenced in several books of the *Odyssey*, he could be unscrupulous and merciless when the situation warranted.

Odysseus is one of the few characters whom Homer described physically. The giant Polyphemus described him as a "short, worthless looking runt" while in the *Iliad*, Odysseus was "a man who is shorter by a head than Agamemnon but broader in the chest and shoulders." Throughout the *Odyssey*, however, Odysseus is shown to be a rare individual who does the right thing at the right time. His long struggle was mainly with the sea and the appeal of the *Odyssey* to a nation of seafarers was immense.

Although little is known of Homer, it is assumed that he was a blind poet whose life was spent almost entirely on the eastern shores of the Aegean Sea. It is fairly certain that his career was within the 9th century B.C. and at the present time it is generally agreed that Homer wrote both the *Iliad* and the *Odyssey*. His importance, apart from the poems and stories which he told, lies in the fact that he gave to all Greeks an ideal of what a man should be. In addition he greatly influenced Greek notions of religion through his descriptions of the gods and goddesses, and probably did more than anyone else to foster the worship of the Olympian gods. In this particular selection, from Book XI of the *Odyssey*, Odysseus visited the underworld and met many spirits. In particular, he met his mother who, due to her intense longing for her son, had died from grief, a point clearly reflected in the reading. While in the underworld, he also saw Jocasta (Epicaste in Latin, line 271) mother of King Oedipus (Oedipodes in Latin), the subject of a play written by the famous playwright, Sophocles.

In this selection, Odysseus is relating his adventures to King Alcinous, Queen Arete and the chief princes of Phaeacia who have befriended him after he was cast upon the shores of their island, Scheria (Note the lines following 333). Scheria was a mythical island in the Mediterranean Sea although some scholars today believe that Homer might have had either the islands of Crete or Corfu in mind.

Since this particular translation uses all Latin names, here are the equivalent Greek names for the Latin ones mentioned. Zeus is the Greek name for the Latin

3

Jupiter or Jove; Poseidon is the Greek for Neptune; Herakles for Hercules; Artemis for Diana. Athene is the Greek for Minerva; Hera for Juno; Hermes for Mercury and Persephone for Proserpine.

THE ODYSSEY

BOOK XI

THEN, when we had got down to the sea shore we drew our ship into the water and got her mast and sails into her; we also put the sheep on board and took our places, weeping and in great distress of mind. Circe, that great and cunning goddess, sent us a fair wind that blew dead aft and stayed steadily with us keeping our sails all the time well filled; so we did whatever wanted doing to the ship's gear and let her go as the wind and helmsman headed her. All day long her sails were full as she held her course over the sea, but when the sun went down and darkness was over all the earth, we got into the deep waters of the river Oceanus, where lie the land and city of the Cimmerians who live enshrouded in mist and darkness which the rays of the sun never pierce neither at his rising nor as he goes down again out of the heavens, but the poor wretches live in one long melancholy night. When we got there we beached the ship, took the sheep out of her, and went along by the waters of Oceanus till we came to the place of which Circe had told us.

[23] "Here Perimedes and Eurylochus held the victims, while I drew my sword and dug the trench a cubit each way. I made a drink-offering to all the dead, first with honey and milk, then with wine, and thirdly with water, and I sprinkled white barley meal over the whole, praying earnestly to the poor feckless ghosts, and promising them that when I got back to Ithaca I would sacrifice a barren heifer for them, the best I had, and would load the pyre with good things. I also particularly promised that Teiresias should have a black sheep to himself, the best in all my flocks. When I had prayed sufficiently to the dead, I cut the throats of the two sheep and let the blood run into the trench, whereon the ghosts came trooping up from Erebus—brides, young bachelors, old men worn out with toil, maids who had been crossed in love, and brave men who had been killed in battle, with their armour still smirched with blood; they came from every quarter and flitted round the trench with a strange kind of screaming sound that made me turn pale with fear. When I saw them coming I told the men to be quick and flay the carcasses of the two dead sheep and make burnt offerings of them, and at the same time to repeat prayers to Hades and to Proserpine; but I sat where I was with my sword drawn and would not let the poor feckless ghosts come near the blood till Teiresias should have answered my questions.

[51] "The first ghost that came was that of my comrade Elpenor, for he had not yet been laid beneath the earth. We had left his body unwaked and unburied in Circe's house, for we had had too much else to do. I was very sorry for him, and cried when I saw him: 'Elpenor,' said I, 'how did you come down here into this gloom and darkness? You have got here on foot quicker than I have with my ship.'

[60] "'Sir,' he answered with a groan, 'it was all bad luck, and my own unspeakable drunkenness. I was lying asleep on the top of Circe's house, and never thought of coming down again by the great staircase but fell right off the roof and broke my neck, so my soul came down to the house of Hades. And now I beseech you by all those whom you have left behind you, though they are not here, by your wife, by the father who brought you up when you were a child, and by Telemachus who is the one hope of your house, do what I shall now ask you. I know that when you leave this limbo you will again hold your ship for the Æaean island. Do not go thence leaving me unwaked and unburied behind you, or I may bring heaven's anger upon you; but burn me with whatever armour I have, build a barrow for me on the sea shore, that may tell people in days to come what a poor unlucky fellow I was, and plant over my grave the oar I used to row with when I was yet alive and with my messmates.' And I said, 'My poor fellow, I will do all that you have asked of me.'

[81] "Thus, then, did we sit and hold sad talk with one another, I on the one side of the trench with my sword held over the blood, and the ghost of my comrade saying all this to me

---

From Homer, *The Odyssey*, translated by Samuel Butler, (London, New York, Longmans, Green and Co., 1900).

from the other side. Then came the ghost of my dead mother Anticlea, daughter to Autolycus. I had left her alive when I set out for Troy and was moved to tears when I saw her, but even so, for all my sorrow I would not let her come near the blood till I had asked my questions of Teiresias.

[90] "Then came also the ghost of Theban Teiresias, with his golden sceptre in his hand. He knew me and said, 'Ulysses, noble son of Lærtes, why, poor man, have you left the light of day and come down to visit the dead in this sad place? Stand back from the trench and withdraw your sword that I may drink of the blood and answer your questions truly.'

[97] "So I drew back, and sheathed my sword, whereon when he had drank of the blood he began with his prophecy.

[100] "'You want to know,' said he, 'about your return home, but heaven will make this hard for you. I do not think that you will escape the eye of Neptune, who still nurses his bitter grudge against you for having blinded his son. Still, after much suffering you may get home if you can restrain yourself and your companions when your ship reaches the Thrinacian island, where you will find the sheep and cattle belonging to the sun, who sees and gives ear to everything. If you leave these flocks unharmed and think of nothing but of getting home, you may yet after much hardship reach Ithaca; but if you harm them, then I forewarn you of the destruction both of your ship and of your men. Even though you may yourself escape, you will return in bad plight after losing all your men, in another man's ship, and you will find trouble in your house, which will be overrun by high-handed people, who are devouring your substance under the pretext of paying court and making presents to your wife.

[118] "'When you get home you will take your revenge on these suitors; and after you have killed them by force or fraud in your own house, you must take a well-made oar and carry it on and on, till you come to a country where the people have never heard of the sea and do not even mix salt with their food, nor do they know anything about ships, and oars that are as the wings of a ship. I will give you this certain token which cannot escape your notice. A wayfarer will meet you and will say it must be a winnowing shovel that you have got upon your shoulder; on this you must fix the oar in the ground and sacrifice a ram, a bull, and a boar to Neptune. Then go home and offer hecatombs to all the gods in heaven one after the other. As for yourself, death shall come to you from the sea, and your life shall ebb away very gently when you are full of years and peace of mind, and your people shall bless you. All that I have said will come true.'

[138] "'This,' I answered, 'must be as it may please heaven, but tell me and tell me true, I see my poor mother's ghost close by us; she is sitting by the blood without saying a word, and though I am her own son she does not remember me and speak to me; tell me, Sir, how I can make her know me.'

[145] "'That,' said he, 'I can soon do. Any ghost that you let taste of the blood will talk with you like a reasonable being, but if you do not let them have any blood they will go away again.'

[150] "On this the ghost of Teiresias went back to the house of Hades, for his prophecyings had now been spoken, but I sat still where I was until my mother came up and tasted the blood. Then she knew me at once and spoke fondly to me, saying, 'My son, how did you come down to this abode of darkness while you are still alive? It is a hard thing for the living to see these places, for between us and them there are great and terrible waters, and there is Oceanus, which no man can cross on foot, but he must have a good ship to take him. Are you all this time trying to find your way home from Troy, and have you never yet got back to Ithaca nor seen your wife in your own house?'

[163] "'Mother,' said I, 'I was forced to come here to consult the ghost of the Theban prophet Teiresias. I have never yet been near the Achæan land nor set foot on my native country, and I have had nothing but one long series of misfortunes from the very first day that I set out with Agamemnon for Ilius, the land of noble steeds, to fight the Trojans. But tell me, and tell me true, in what way did you die? Did you have a long illness, or did heaven vouchsafe you a gentle easy passage to eternity? Tell me also about my father, and the son whom I left behind me; is my property still in their hands, or has some one else got hold of it, who thinks that I shall not return to claim it? Tell me again what my wife intends doing, and in what mind she is; does she live with my son and guard my estate securely, or has she made the best match she could and married again?'

[180] "My mother answered, 'Your wife still remains in your house, but she is in great distress of mind and spends her whole time in tears both night and day. No one as yet has got possession of your fine property, and Telema-

chus still holds your lands undisturbed. He has to entertain largely, as of course he must, considering his position as a magistrate, and how every one invites him; your father remains at his old place in the country and never goes near the town. He has no comfortable bed nor bedding; in the winter he sleeps on the floor in front of the fire with the men and goes about all in rags, but in summer, when the warm weather comes on again, he lies out in the vineyard on a bed of vine leaves thrown anyhow upon the ground. He grieves continually about your never having come home, and suffers more and more as he grows older. As for my own end it was in this wise: heaven did not take me swiftly and painlessly in my own house, nor was I attacked by any illness such as those that generally wear people out and kill them, but my longing to know what you were doing and the force of my affection for you—this it was that was the death of me.'

[204] "Then I tried to find some way of embracing my poor mother's ghost. Thrice I sprang towards her and tried to clasp her in my arms, but each time she flitted from my embrace as it were a dream or phantom, and being touched to the quick I said to her, 'Mother, why do you not stay still when I would embrace you? If we could throw our arms around one another we might find sad comfort in the sharing of our sorrows even in the house of Hades; does Proserpine want to lay a still further load of grief upon me by mocking me with a phantom only?'

[215] "'My son,' she answered, 'most ill-fated of all mankind, it is not Proserpine that is beguiling you, but all people are like this when they are dead. The sinews no longer hold the flesh and bones together; these perish in the fierceness of consuming fire as soon as life has left the body, and the soul flits away as though it were a dream. Now, however, go back to the light of day as soon as you can, and note all these things that you may tell them to your wife hereafter.'

[225] "Thus did we converse, and anon Proserpine sent up the ghosts of the wives and daughters of all the most famous men. They gathered in crowds about the blood, and I considered how I might question them severally. In the end I deemed that it would be best to draw the keen blade that hung by my sturdy thigh, and keep them from all drinking the blood at once. So they came up one after the other, and each one as I questioned her told me her race and lineage.

[235] "The first I saw was Tyro. She was daughter of Salmoneus and wife of Cretheus the son of Æolus. She fell in love with the river Enipeus who is much the most beautiful river in the whole world. Once when she was taking a walk by his side as usual, Neptune, disguised as her lover, lay with her at the mouth of the river, and a huge blue wave arched itself like a mountain over them to hide both woman and god, whereon he loosed her virgin girdle and laid her in a deep slumber. When the god had accomplished the deed of love, he took her hand in his own and said, 'Tyro, rejoice in all good will; the embraces of the gods are not fruitless, and you will have fine twins about this time twelve months. Take great care of them. I am Neptune, so now go home, but hold your tongue and do not tell any one.'

[253] "Then he dived under the sea, and she in due course bore Pelias and Neleus, who both of them served Jove with all their might. Pelias was a great breeder of sheep and lived in Iolcus, but the other lived in Pylos. The rest of her children were by Cretheus, namely, Æson, Pheres, and Amythaon, who was a mighty warrior and charioteer.

[260] "Next to her I saw Antiope, daughter to Asopus, who could boast of having slept in the arms of even Jove himself, and who bore him two sons Amphion and Zethus. These founded Thebes with its seven gates, and built a wall all round it; for strong though they were they could not hold Thebes till they had walled it.

[266] "Then I saw Alcmena, the wife of Amphitryon, who also bore to Jove indomitable Hercules; and Megara who was daughter to great King Creon, and married the redoubtable son of Amphitryon.

[271] "I also saw fair Epicaste mother of king Œdipodes whose awful lot it was to marry her own son without suspecting it. He married her after having killed his father, but the gods proclaimed the whole story to the world; whereon he remained king of Thebes, in great grief for the spite the gods had borne him; but Epicaste went to the house of the mighty jailor Hades, having hanged herself for grief, and the avenging spirits haunted him as for an outraged mother—to his ruing bitterly thereafter.

[281] "Then I saw Chloris, whom Neleus married for her beauty, having given priceless presents for her. She was youngest daughter to Amphion son of Iasus and king of Minyan Orchomenus, and was Queen in Pylos. She

bore Nestor, Chromius, and Periclymenus, and she also bore that marvellously lovely woman Pero, who was wooed by all the country round; but Neleus would only give her to him who should raid the cattle of Iphicles from the grazing grounds of Phylace, and this was a hard task. The only man who would undertake to raid them was a certain excellent seer, but the will of heaven was against him, for the rangers of the cattle caught him and put him in prison; nevertheless when a full year had passed and the same season came round again, Iphicles set him at liberty, after he had expounded all the oracles of heaven. Thus, then, was the will of Jove accomplished.

[298] "And I saw Leda the wife of Tyndarus, who bore him two famous sons, Castor breaker of horses, and Pollux the mighty boxer. Both these heroes are lying under the earth, though they are still alive, for by a special dispensation of Jove, they die and come to life again, each one of them every other day throughout all time, and they have the rank of gods.

[305] "After her I saw Iphimedeia wife of Alœus who boasted the embrace of Neptune. She bore two sons Otus and Ephialtes, but both were short lived. They were the finest children that were ever born in this world, and the best looking, Orion only excepted; for at nine years old they were nine fathoms high, and measured nine cubits round the chest. They threatened to make war with the gods in Olympus, and tried to set Mount Ossa on the top of Mount Olympus, and Mount Pelion on the top of Ossa, that they might scale heaven itself, and they would have done it too if they had been grown up, but Apollo, son of Leto, killed both of them, before they had got so much as a sign of hair upon their cheeks or chin.

[321] "Then I saw Phædra, and Procris, and fair Ariadne daughter of the magician Minos, whom Theseus was carrying off from Crete to Athens, but he did not enjoy her, for before he could do so Diana killed her in the island of Dia on account of what Bacchus had said against her.

[326] "I also saw Mæra and Clymene and hateful Eriphyle, who sold her own husband for gold. But it would take me all night if I were to name every single one of the wives and daughters of heroes whom I saw, and it is time for me to go to bed, either on board ship with my crew, or here. As for my escort, heaven and yourselves will see to it."

[333] Here he ended, and the guests sat all of them enthralled and speechless throughout the covered cloister. Then Arete said to them:

[336] "What do you think of this man, O Phæacians? Is he not tall and good looking, and is he not clever? True, he is my own guest, but you all of you share in the distinction. Do not be in a hurry to send him away, nor niggardly in the presents you make to one who is in such great need, for heaven has blessed all of you with great abundance."

[342] Then spoke the aged hero Echeneus who was one of the oldest men among them, "My friends," said he, "what our august queen has just said to us is both reasonable and to the purpose, therefore be persuaded by it; but the decision whether in word or deed rests ultimately with King Alcinous."

[347] "The thing shall be done," exclaimed Alcinous, "as surely as I still live and reign over the Phæacians. Our guest is indeed very anxious to get home, still we must persuade him to remain with us until to-morrow, by which time I shall be able to get together the whole sum that I mean to give him. As regards his escort it will be a matter for you all, and mine above all others as the chief person among you."

[354] And Ulysses answered, "King Alcinous, if you were to bid me to stay here for a whole twelve months, and then speed me on my way, loaded with your noble gifts, I should obey you gladly and it would redound greatly to my advantage, for I should return fuller-handed to my own people, and should thus be more respected and beloved by all who see me when I get back to Ithaca."

[362] "Ulysses," replied Alcinous, "not one of us who sees you has any idea that you are a charlatan or a swindler. I know there are many people going about who tell such plausible stories that it is very hard to see through them, but there is a style about your language which assures me of your good disposition. Moreover you have told the story of your own misfortunes, and those of the Argives, as though you were a practised bard; but tell me, and tell me true, whether you saw any of the mighty heroes who went to Troy at the same time with yourself, and perished there. The evenings are still at their longest, and it is not yet bed time—go on, therefore, with your divine story, for I could stay here listening till to-morrow morning, so long as you will continue to tell us of your adventures."

[377] "Alcinous," answered Ulysses, "there

is a time for making speeches, and a time for going to bed; nevertheless, since you so desire, I will not refrain from telling you the still sadder tale of those of my comrades who did not fall fighting with the Trojans, but perished on their return, through the treachery of a wicked woman.

[385] "When Proserpine had dismissed the female ghosts in all directions, the ghost of Agamemnon son of Atreus came sadly up to me, surrounded by those who had perished with him in the house of Ægisthus. As soon as he had tasted the blood he knew me, and weeping bitterly stretched out his arms towards me to embrace me; but he had no strength nor substance any more, and I too wept and pitied him as I beheld him. 'How did you come by your death,' said I, 'King Agamemnon? Did Neptune raise his winds and waves against you when you were at sea, or did your enemies make an end of you on the mainland when you were cattle-lifting or sheep-stealing, or while they were fighting in defence of their wives and city?'

[404] " 'Ulysses,' he answered, 'noble son of Lærtes, I was not lost at sea in any storm of Neptune's raising, nor did my foes despatch me upon the mainland, but Ægisthus and my wicked wife were the death of me between them. He asked me to his house, feasted me, and then butchered me most miserably as though I were a fat beast in a slaughter house, while all around me my comrades were slain like sheep or pigs for the wedding breakfast, or picnic, or gorgeous banquet of some great nobleman. You must have seen numbers of men killed either in a general engagement, or in single combat, but you never saw anything so truly pitiable as the way in which we fell in that cloister, with the mixing-bowl and the loaded tables lying all about, and the ground reeking with our blood. I heard Priam's daughter Cassandra scream as Clytemnestra killed her close beside me. I lay dying upon the earth with the sword in my body, and raised my hands to kill the slut of a murderess, but she slipped away from me; she would not even close my lips nor my eyes when I was dying, for there is nothing in this world so cruel and so shameless as a woman when she has fallen into such guilt as hers was. Fancy murdering her own husband! I thought I was going to be welcomed home by my children and my servants, but her abominable crime has brought disgrace on herself and all women who shall come after—even on the good ones.'

[435] "And I said, 'In truth Jove has hated the house of Atreus from first to last in the matter of their women's counsels. See how many of us fell for Helen's sake, and now it seems that Clytemnestra hatched mischief against you too during your absence.'

[441] " 'Be sure, therefore,' continued Agamemnon, 'and not be too friendly even with your own wife. Do not tell her all that you know perfectly well yourself. Tell her a part only, and keep your own counsel about the rest. Not that your wife, Ulysses, is likely to murder you, for Penelope is a very admirable woman, and has an excellent nature. We left her a young bride with an infant at her breast when we set out for Troy. This child no doubt is now grown up happily to man's estate, and he and his father will have a joyful meeting and embrace one another as it is right they should do, whereas my wicked wife did not even allow me the happiness of looking upon my son, but killed me ere I could do so. Furthermore I say—and lay my saying to your heart —do not tell people when you are bringing your ship to Ithaca, but steal a march upon them, for after all this there is no trusting women. But now tell me, and tell me true, can you give me any news of my son Orestes? Is he in Orchomenus, or at Pylos, or is he at Sparta with Menelaus—for I presume that he is still living.'

[462] "And I said, 'Agamemnon, why do you ask me? I do not know whether your son is alive or dead, and it is not right to talk when one does not know.'

[465] "As we two sat weeping and talking thus sadly with one another the ghost of Achilles came up to us with Patroclus, Antilochus, and Ajax who was the finest and goodliest man of all the Danaans after the son of Peleus. The fleet descendant of Æacus knew me and spoke piteously, saying, 'Ulysses, noble son of Lærtes, what deed of daring will you undertake next, that you venture down to the house of Hades among us silly dead, who are but the ghosts of them that can labour no more?'

[477] "And I said, 'Achilles, son of Peleus, foremost champion of the Achæans, I came to consult Teiresias, and see if he could advise me about my return home to Ithaca, for I have never yet been able to get near the Achæan land, nor to set foot in my own country, but have been in trouble all the time. As for you, Achilles, no one was ever yet so fortunate as you have been, nor ever will be, for you were adored by all us Argives as long as you were alive, and now that you are here you are a great prince among the dead. Do not, therefore, take it so much to heart even if you are dead.'

[487] "'Say not a word,' he answered, 'in death's favour; I would rather be a paid servant in a poor man's house and be above ground than king of kings among the dead. But give me news about my son; is he gone to the wars and will he be a great soldier, or is this not so? Tell me also if you have heard anything about my father Peleus—does he still rule among the Myrmidons, or do they show him no respect throughout Hellas and Phthia now that he is old and his limbs fail him? Could I but stand by his side, in the light of day, with the same strength that I had when I killed the bravest of our foes upon the plain of Troy—could I but be as I then was and go even for a short time to my father's house, any one who tried to do him violence or supersede him would soon rue it.'

[504] "'I have heard nothing,' I answered, 'of Peleus, but I can tell you all about your son Neoptolemus, for I took him in my own ship from Scyros with the Achæans. In our councils of war before Troy he was always first to speak, and his judgement was unerring. Nestor and I were the only two who could surpass him; and when it came to fighting on the plain of Troy, he would never remain with the body of his men, but would dash on far in front, foremost of them all in valour. Many a man did he kill in battle—I cannot name every single one of those whom he slew while fighting on the side of the Argives, but will only say how he killed that valiant hero Eurypylus son of Telephus, who was the handsomest man I ever saw except Memnon; many others also of the Ceteians fell around him by reason of a woman's bribes. Moreover, when all the bravest of the Argives went inside the horse that Epeus had made, and it was left to me to settle when we should either open the door of our ambuscade, or close it, though all the other leaders and chief men among the Danaans were drying their eyes and quaking in every limb, I never once saw him turn pale nor wipe a tear from his cheek; he was all the time urging me to break out from the horse—grasping the handle of his sword and his bronze-shod spear, and breathing fury against the foe. Yet when we had sacked the city of Priam he got his handsome share of the prize money and went on board (such is the fortune of war) without a wound upon him, neither from a thrown spear nor in close combat, for the rage of Mars is a matter of great chance.'

[538] "When I had told him this, the ghost of Achilles strode off across a meadow full of asphodel, exulting over what I had said concerning the prowess of his son.

[541] "The ghosts of other dead men stood near me and told me each his own melancholy tale; but that of Ajax son of Telamon alone held aloof—still angry with me for having won the cause in our dispute about the armour of Achilles. Thetis had offered it as a prize, but the Trojan prisoners and Minerva were the judges. Would that I had never gained the day in such a contest, for it cost the life of Ajax, who was foremost of all the Danaans after the son of Peleus, alike in stature and prowess.

[552] "When I saw him I tried to pacify him and said, 'Ajax, will you not forget and forgive even in death, but must the judgement about that hateful armour still rankle with you? It cost us Argives dear enough to lose such a tower of strength as you were to us. We mourned you as much as we mourned Achilles son of Peleus himself, nor can the blame be laid on anything but on the spite which Jove bore against the Danaans, for it was this that made him counsel your destruction—come hither, therefore, bring your proud spirit into subjection, and hear what I can tell you.'

[563] "He would not answer, but turned away to Erebus and to the other ghosts; nevertheless, I should have made him talk to me in spite of his being so angry, or I should have gone on talking to him, only that there were still others among the dead whom I desired to see.

[568] "Then I saw Minos son of Jove with his golden sceptre in his hand sitting in judgement on the dead, and the ghosts were gathered sitting and standing round him in the spacious house of Hades, to learn his sentences upon them.

[572] "After him I saw huge Orion in a meadow full of asphodel driving the ghosts of the wild beasts that he had killed upon the mountains, and he had a great bronze club in his hand, unbreakable for ever and ever.

[576] "And I saw Tityus son of Gaia stretched upon the plain and covering some nine acres of ground. Two vultures on either side of him were digging their beaks into his liver, and he kept on trying to beat them off with his hands, but could not; for he had violated Jove's mistress Leto as she was going through Panopeus on her way to Pytho.

[582] "I saw also the dreadful fate of Tantalus, who stood in a lake that reached his chin; he was dying to quench his thirst, but could never reach the water, for whenever the poor

creature stooped to drink, it dried up and vanished, so that there was nothing but dry ground —parched by the spite of heaven. There were tall trees, moreover, that shed their fruit over his head—pears, pomegranates, apples, sweet figs and juicy olives, but whenever the poor creature stretched out his hand to take some, the wind tossed the branches back again to the clouds.

[593] "And I saw Sisyphus at his endless task raising his prodigious stone with both his hands. With hands and feet he tried to roll it up to the top of the hill, but always, just before he could roll it over on to the other side, its weight would be too much for him, and the pitiless stone would come thundering down again on to the plain. Then he would begin trying to push it up hill again, and the sweat ran off him and the steam rose after him.

[601] "After him I saw mighty Hercules, but it was his phantom only, for he is feasting ever with the immortal gods, and has lovely Hebe to wife, who is daughter of Jove and Juno. The ghosts were screaming round him like scared birds flying all whithers. He looked black as night with his bare bow in his hands and his arrow on the string, glaring around as though ever on the point of taking aim. About his breast there was a wondrous golden belt adorned in the most marvellous fashion with bears, wild boars, and lions with gleaming eyes; there was also war, battle, and death. The man who made that belt, do what he might, would never be able to make another like it. Hercules knew me at once when he saw me, and spoke piteously, saying, 'My poor Ulysses, noble son of Lærtes, are you too leading the same sorry kind of life that I did when I was above ground? I was son of Jove, but I went through an infinity of suffering, for I became bondsman to one who was far beneath me—a low fellow who set me all manner of labours. He once sent me here to fetch the hell-hound —for he did not think he could find anything harder for me than this, but I got the hound out of Hades and brought him to him, for Mercury and Minerva helped me.'

[627] "On this Hercules went down again into the house of Hades, but I stayed where I was in case some other of the mighty dead should come to me. And I should have seen still other of them that are gone before, whom I would fain have seen—Theseus and Pirithous —glorious children of the gods, but so many thousands of ghosts came round me and uttered such appalling cries, that I was panic stricken lest Proserpine should send up from the house of Hades the head of that awful monster Gorgon. On this I hastened back to my ship and ordered my men to go on board at once and loose the hawsers; so they embarked and took their places, whereon the ship went down the stream of the river Oceanus. We had to row at first, but presently a fair wind sprang up.

. . . .

Hesiod

Hesiod, born sometime between 750 and 700 B.C., is often referred to as the Father of didactic poetry, so called because of its characteristic moral and instructive tone. Hesiod's best known poem *Works and Days,* the oldest surviving example of didactic poetry, especially appealed to the middle and lower classes in Greece. *Works and Days* presents the reader with a picture of the Greek farmer as well as some of his more important characteristics—shrewdness, superstition and pessimism. When Hesiod's father died, his farm was divided between Hesiod and his brother Perses. However, Perses bribed the magistrates and received more of the farm, and better land, than he deserved. Later, "Perses squandered much of his ill-gotten gains in strife and dissipation." Hesiod wrote this poem mainly to teach Perses how to be a better farmer. *Works and Days* is full of sayings and witticisms which were common at that time. Also it relates the story of the creation of the first woman, Pandora, and how she released all the misfortunes which have plagued mankind from that day to this. All that was left, according to Hesiod, was Hope, still trapped within the jar. In addition, Hesiod shows his own pessimism by detailing the various ages of mankind, each one worse than the last. He then brings the poem to a conclusion by telling the farmers which days were lucky and which were unlucky for planting and harvesting, for getting married and for being born.

Hesiod, the first great poet to lay down the rules of conduct, contributed the concepts of temperance and justice to the Greek ideal.

WORKS AND DAYS

... Zeus bade Hephaestus (Vulcan) ... with all speed mix earth and water, and endue it with man's voice and strength, and to liken in countenance to immortal goddesses the fair, lovely beauty of a maiden: then he bade Athena (Minerva) teach her work, to weave the highly wrought web; and golden Aphrodite (Venus) to shed around her head grace, and painful desire ... and endue her with a shameless mind and tricksy manners.

... they obeyed Zeus the sovereign son of Kronus; and forthwith out of the earth the famous crippled god fashioned one like unto a modest maiden, and the goddess, gleaming-eyed Athena girdled and arrayed her. ... But in her breast, Mercury wrought falsehoods and wily speeches and tricksy manners and the herald of the gods placed within her a winning voice, and the woman he called Pandora.

But when he had perfected the dire inextricable snare, father Zeus proceeded to send to Epimetheus, the famous slayer of Argus, a swift messenger of the gods, carrying her as a gift. Nor did Epimetheus consider how Prometheus had told him never to accept a gift from Olympian Zeus but to send it back, lest haply any ill should arise to mortals. But he, after receiving it, felt the evil, when now he possessed it.

Now before this time the races of men lived on the earth apart and free from ills, and without harsh labor, and painful diseases which have brought death on mortals; for in misery men grow old quickly. But the woman, with her hands removed the great lid from the jar and dispersed the evils to mankind and her thought caused sorrow and mischief to men. And Hope alone remained, kept within, beneath the edge of the jar and did not go forth abroad. ... But myriad other ills roamed forth among men. For full indeed is the earth of woes, and full is the sea and by day as well as at night unhidden diseases haunt mankind, silently bearing ills to men; for wise Zeus took away speech from them. Thus not in any way is it possible to escape the will of Zeus. [Hesiod then describes the various ages of the world]

First of all the gods who dwell in Olympus made a golden race of speaking men. And as gods they lived, and with a life devoid of care, apart from and without labors and trouble nor was wretched old age at all impending, but ever the same in hands and feet, did they delight themselves in festivals out of the reach of all ills; and they died as if overcome by sleep....

Afterwards again the gods who dwell in Olympus formed a second race of silver, far inferior, like unto the golden ones neither in shape nor mind.... Them indeed Zeus buried in his wrath, because they gave not due honors to the blessed gods who occupy Olympus....

And yet a third race of speech gifted men formed by Zeus from brass, not at all like unto the silver, formidable and mighty by reason of their ashen spears; who loved the mournful deeds of Ares (Mars) and violence....

But when the earth covered this race also, again Zeus, brought yet another, a fourth, upon the fruitful earth, more just and more worthy, a godlike race of hero-men, who are called demi-gods, the race before our own....

Would that I had not mingled with the fifth race of men, but had either died before, or been born afterward. For now in truth is the iron race and men never rest from labor and sorrow by day and from perishing by night and the gods will give them severe cards. And Zeus will destroy this race also as soon as they become white haired. Nor will father be like minded to sons, nor sons at all agree with their father nor quest to host nor comrade to comrade, nor will brother be dear to brother.... [Hesiod then continues with much advice to his dissolute brother Perses]

This man, indeed, is far best, who shall have understood everything for himself . . . and good again is he who shall have listened well to one advising him; but whosoever when he listens to another hath no understanding nor kept it to heart, he on the other hand is a worthless man. Do thou then, high-born Perses, be ever mindful of my precept, work on so famine may hate you; fill your barn with substance. For mind you, famine is ever the sluggard's companion.... Now work is no disgrace but sloth is a disgrace. And if you should work, quickly will the sluggard envy you growing rich, for esteem and glory accompany wealth.... A bad neighbor is as great a misfortune as a good one is a great blessing. He who gains a worthy neighbor, has truly gained something of honor.... Duly measure when you borrow from a neighbor and duly repay, in the very measure and better, if you can, that so when in want you may find that which may be relied on in the future.... Do not let a woman with sweeping train beguile your mind, with winning and coaxing ways. It's your barn she is seeking; for whoever trusts a woman, that man, I believe, trusts knaves.... [Hesiod then continues with advice to all farmers]

Bring home a wife to your house when you are not very far short of thirty years nor have added very much to it, for such a marriage is reasonable. Let the woman be in her bloom four years (14) and married in her fifth (19). Marry a maiden that you may teach her chaste morals. Most of all marry her who lives near you, but only after you have looked around, so that your marriage will not be a joke to your neighbors. For nothing better does a man gain than the good wife and nothing worse than a bad one.... Mind well, too and teach your servants fittingly the days which come from Zeus; that the thirtieth day of the month is best for inspecting work done and distributing supplies.... In the first place, the first, the fourth and the seventh is a holy (good) day. The eighth and ninth are two days of the month for the works of man and the eleventh and twelfth are both good; the one for shearing sheep the other for reaping fruits.... Avoid the thirteenth for beginning your sowing, though it is the best day to set plants. The sixteenth is very unprofitable to plants but auspicious for the birth of men, though for a girl it is not good, either to be born or to be joined in wedlock. Nor is the sixth day suitable for the birth of girls . . . but is favorable for the birth of boys, but they will be fond of uttering lies and cunning words.... But on the twentieth day, in broad day, is best for a wise man to be born, for he will be very cautious of mind. Lucky for raising sons is the tenth day, and the fourteenth for girls.... On the fourth of the month lead home a bride, after having examined the omens . . . but avoid the fifth days, since they are both mischievous and destructive.... And the ninth day in a month is wholly harmless to mortals since lucky indeed is this day for planting and for birth, to man as well as woman and never is it a day altogether bad. Again few know that the twenty-ninth of the month is best for both opening a wine jar and putting yoke on the neck of oxen and mules and fleet footed steeds . . . and few know that the twenty-fourth of the month is best at the break of day but toward evening it is worse. These days indeed are a great benefit to men on the earth. But the others falling between are harmless, bringing nothing of value.... Blessed and fortunate is he who knowingly does all these things with reference to these days, without offending the gods, discerning omens and avoiding transgressions.

Sappho

Sappho was a prominent poetess in the first half of the 6th century B.C. who lived on the island of Lesbos, a rather luxury loving area where the women of the upper class enjoyed free and unconstrained lives and were not considered inferior to the men. Sappho, a woman of culture and of noble birth, had a tremendous literary reputation in her own day. The parts of her work which have survived seem to confirm the judgment of the ancient Greeks.

Sappho, like Homer, discussed many topics which can be seen as helping form a part of the Greek ideal. Love was often prominent in her poems and this concept of love was to become one of the basic subjects of Greek art and literature. With Plato's writing, love became idealized in Greek philosophy. Sappho was also a keen and sympathetic observer of nature, as is seen in many of her poems. Furthermore she drew amazingly individualized portraits in her poetry and could on occasion indulge in biting satire. Perhaps the most important point to remember about Sappho is that she contributed to the formation of the Greek ideal inasmuch as her work was dedicated to the reflection and creation of beauty. This resulted from her concepts of love and nature.

In the following selections of Sappho's works, the *Ode to Aphrodite* and *An Hymn to Venus* are different translations of the same poem. They have both been included in order to show the difference between a 20th century translation *(Ode)* and an 18th century translation *(Hymn)*.

One other poet who contributed to the Greek ideal was Pindar, who lived from 518 to 438 B.C. Although no selection from his writings is included, it should be noted that the keynote of his poetry is *splendor*. The best preserved of his poems are The Odes which celebrate victories in athletic contests. Pindar admired the Greek athletes and wrote in order to glorify the human body. Rejoicing in health, beauty and athletic aptitude, he was a champion of the old Greek aristocracy and spoke for the outstanding individual. Pindar added the concept of inborn excellence to the Greek ideal.

ODE TO ANACTORIA

Peer of Gods to me is the man thy presence
Crowns with joy; who hears, as he sits beside thee,
Accents sweet of thy lips the silence breaking,
    With lovely laughter;

Tones that make the heart in my bosom flutter,
For if I, the space of a moment even,
Near to thee come, any word I would utter
    Instantly fails me;

Vain my stricken tongue would a whisper fashion,
Subtly under my skin runs fire ecstatic;
Straightway mists surge dim to my eyes and leave them
    Reft of their vision;

Echoes ring in my ears; a trembling seizes
All my body bathed in soft perspiration;
Pale as grass I grow in my passion's madness,
    Like one insensate:

But must I dare all, since to me unworthy,
Bliss thy beauty brings that a God might envy;
Never yet was fervid woman a fairer
    Image of Kypris.

Ah! undying Daughter of God, befriend me!
Calm my blood that thrills with impending transport;
Feed my lips the murmur of words to stir her
    Bosom to pity;

Overcome with kisses her faintest protest,
Melt her mood to mine with amorous touches,
Till her low assent and her sigh's abandon
    Lure me to rapture.

CLËIS

Daughter of mine, so fair,
  With a form like a golden flower,
Wherefore thy pensive air
  And the dreams in the myrtle bower

Clëis, beloved, thy eyes
  That are turned from my gaze, thy hand
That trembles so, I prize
  More than all the Lydian land;

More than the lovely hills
  With the Lesbian olive crowned; —
Tell me, darling, what ills
  In the gloom of thy thought are found?

Daughter of mine, come near
  Any they head on my knees recline;
Whisper and never fear,
  For the beat of thy heart is mine.

Sweet mother, I can turn
  With content to my loom no more;
My bosom throbs, I yearn
  For a youth that my eyes adore;

Lykas of Eresus,
  Whom I knew when a little child;
My heart by Love is thus
  With the sweetest of pain beguiled.

THE DUST OF TIMAS

This is the dust of Timas! Here inurned
Rest the dear ashes where so late had burned
Her spirit's flame. She perished, gentle maid,
Before her bridal day and now a shade,
Silent and sad, she evermore must be
In the dark chamber of Persephone.
When life had faded with the flower and leaf,
Each girl friend sweet, in token of her grief,
Resigned her severed locks with bended head,
Beauty's fair tribute to the lovely dead.

ODE TO APHRODITE

NEWER

Aphrodite, subtle of soul and deathless,
Daughter of God, weaver of wiles, I pray thee
Neither with care, dread Mistress, nor with anguish,
    Slay thou my spirit!

But in pity hasten, come now if ever
From afar of old when my voice implored thee,
Thou hast deigned to listen, leaving the golden
    House of thy father

With the chariot yoked; and with doves that drew thee,
Fair and fleet around the dark earth from heaven,
Dipping vibrant wings down and the azure distance,
    Through the mid-ether;

Very swift they came; and thou, gracious Vision,
Leaned with face that smiled in immortal beauty,
Leaned to me and asked, "What misfortune threatened?
    Why I had called thee?"

"What my frenzied heart craved in utter yearning,
Whom its wild desire would persuade to passion?
What disdainful charms, madly worshipped, slight thee?
    Who wrongs thee, Sappho?"

"She that fain would fly, she shall quickly follow,
She that now rejects, yet with gifts shall woo thee,
She that heeds thee not, soon shall love to madness,
    Love thee, the loth one!'

Come to me now thus, Goddess, and release me
From distress and pain; and all my distracted
Heart would seek, do thou, once again fulfilling,
    Still be my ally!

AN HYMN TO VENUS[2]

OLDER

I.
Venus, bright Goddess of Skies,
To whom unnumber'd Temples rise
Jove's Daughter fair, whose wily Arts
Delude fond Lovers of their Hearts;
O! listen gracious to my Prayer,
And free my Mind from anxious Care.

II.
If e'er you heard my ardent Vow,
Propitious Goddess, hear me now!
And oft my ardent Vow you've heard,
By Cupid's friendly Aid preferr'd,
Oft left the golden Courts of Jove,
To listen to my Tales of Love.

III.
The radiant Car your Sparrows drew;
You give the Word, and swift they flew,
Through liquid Air they wing'd their Way,
I saw their quivering Pinions play;
To my plain Roof they bore their Queen,
Of Aspect mild, and Look serene.

IV.
Soon as you came, by your Command,
Back flew the wanton feather'd Band,
Then, with a sweet enchanting Look,

From *The Poems of Sappho*, an Interpretative Rendition into English, by John Myers O'Hara. Portland; Smith and Sale, Publishers, 1910.

[2]From *The Works of Anacreon, Sappho, Bion, Moschus and Musaeus*. Translated into English by a Gentleman of Cambridge, London; Printed for J. Newberry in St. Paul's Church yard; and L. Davis and C. Reymers in Holborn, 1760.

Divinely smiling, thus you spoke:
"Why didst thou call me to thy Cell?
"Tell me, my gentle Sappho, tell.

V.

"What healing Medicine shall I find
"To cure thy love-distemper'd Mind?
"Say, shall I lend thee all my Charms,
"To win young Phaon to thy Arms?
"Or does some other Swain subdue
"Thy Heart? my Sappho, tell me Who?

VI.

"Though now, averse, thy Charms he slight,
"He soon shall view thee with Delight;
"Though now he scorns thy Gifts to take,
"He soon to thee shall Offerings make;
"Though now thy Beauties fail to move,
"He soon shall melt with equal Love."

VII.

Once more, O Venus, hear my Prayer,
And ease my Mind of anxious Care;
Again vouchsafe to be my Guest,
And calm this Tempest in my Breast!
To thee, bright Queen, my Vows aspire;
O grant me all my Heart's Desire!

FRAGMENTS OF SAPPHO

Fragment I.

The Pleiads now no more are seen,
Nor shines the silver Moon serene,
In dark and dismal Clouds o'ercast;
The love appointed Hour is past:
Midnight usurps her sable Throne,
And yet, alas! I lie alone.

Fragment II.

Whene'er the Fates resume thy Breath,
No bright Reversion shalt thou gain,
Unnotic'd thou shalt sink in Death,
Nor ev'n thy Memory remain:
For thy rude Hand ne'er pluck'd the lovely Rose,
Which on the Mountain of Pieria blows.

To Pluto's Mansions shalt thou go,
The stern inexorable King,
Among th'ignoble Shades below
A vain, ignoble Thing;
While honour'd Sappho's muse-embellish'd Name
Shall flourish in Eternity of Fame.

Fragment III.

Venus, Queen of Smiles and Love,
Quit, O! quit the Skies above;
To my lowly Roof descend,
At the mirthful Feast attend;

Hand the golden Goblet round,
With delicious Nectar crown'd:
None but joyous Friends you'll see,
Friends of Venus, and of Me.

Fragment IV.

Cease, gentle Mother, cease your sharp Reproof,
My Hands no more can ply the Curious Woof,
While on my Mind the Flames of Cupid prey,
And lovely Phaon steals my Soul away.

Sophocles

There were three great playwrights in the period of classical Greece. The first of these was Aeschylus (525–456 B.C.), best known for *Prometheus Bound*. The second, Euripides (480–406 B.C.), wrote 92 complete plays, although only nineteen have survived. The third great playwright was Sophocles (496–406 B.C.). His first tragic tetralogy won first prize when it was performed at the festival of Dionysus in 468 B.C. From then on his name was one of the most dominant in Athenian drama. He wrote more than 120 plays but only seven complete tragedies survive. The play *Oedipus Rex* is hailed by most critics as the masterpiece of Sophocles and perhaps the greatest of all Greek tragedies. You will note that the entire play is dominated by the figure of Oedipus. He was proud, had a tempestuous temper and was a man of excessive passions. He also had a certain lack of humility. Despite his faults, however, he was basically a good man and it is sometimes hard for the reader to feel that Oedipus deserved the terrible punishment which was his fate. Sophocles, however, felt that there was harmonious purpose guiding the universe, even though mortals could not comprehend it. Therefore, man must accept the responsibility for his acts and their consequences-thus the final scene. Sophocles believed in the freedom of the human will, but felt that his freedom was limited. Man may be free to choose, but each choice would limit the following choice. Still, the chain of circumstances could be broken at many points; Oedipus, however, did not break this chain. Oedipus was guilty, but killing his father or marrying his mother was not his real sin. It was his attempt to raise himself to the level of the gods by not listening to their will, as revealed by Apollo's oracle. He was punished for his pride and disobedience.

In reading the play note the role of the chorus, how it responds as if it were a spectator and how it clarifies for the reader the experiences and feelings of the characters in the play. It is also important to pay attention to the character of both Creon and Jocasta—Creon since he often serves as a standard by which we judge Oedipus, and Jocasta, who although a loving wife, often shows a maternal attitude toward Oedipus.

When you finish reading the play think a little about whether Oedipus could have changed the terrible fate which befell him. Could he have broken this chain of circumstances? Should he have asked questions before assuming the kingship of Thebes or marrying Jocasta? In your own mind did Oedipus have redeeming qualities or do you feel he deserved the fate he received?

OEDIPUS REX

Characters in the Play

OEDIPUS, *King of Thebes*

JOCASTA, *Queen of Thebes, wife and mother of* OEDIPUS

CREON, *brother of* JOCASTA

TIRESIAS, *a prophet*

BOY, *attendant of* TIRESIAS

PRIEST OF ZEUS

SHEPHERD

FIRST MESSENGER, *from Corinth*

SECOND MESSENGER

CHORUS *of Theban elders*

ATTENDANTS

SCENE: *Before the doors of the palace of* OEDIPUS *at Thebes. A crowd of citizens are seated next to the two altars at the sides. In front of one of the altars stands the* PRIEST OF ZEUS.

THE GREEKS

Enter OEDIPUS

OEDIPUS:
Why are you here as suppliants, my children,
You in whose veins the blood of Cadmus flows?
What is the reason for your boughs of olive,
The fumes of incense, the laments and prayers
That fill the city? Because I thought it wrong,
My children, to depend on what was told me,
I have come to you myself, I, Oedipus,
Renowned in the sight of all. (*to* PRIEST) Tell me—you are
Their natural spokesman—what desire or fear
Brings you before me? I will gladly give you   10
Such help as is in my power. It would be heartless
Not to take pity on a plea like this.

PRIEST:
King Oedipus, you see us, young and old,
Gathered about your altars: some, mere fledglings
Not able yet to fly; some, bowed with age;
Some, priests, and I the priest of Zeus among them;
And these, who are the flower of our young manhood.
The rest of us are seated—the whole city—
With our wreathed branches in the market places,
Before the shrines of Pallas, before the fire   20
By which we read the auguries of Apollo.
Thebes, as you see yourself, is overwhelmed
By the waves of death that break upon her head.
No fruit comes from her blighted buds; her cattle
Die in the fields; her wives bring forth dead children.
A hideous pestilence consumes the city,
Striking us down like a god armed with fire,
Emptying the house of Cadmus, filling full
The dark of Hades with loud lamentation.
I and these children have not thronged your altars   30
Because we hold you equal to the immortals,
But because we hold you foremost among men,
Both in the happenings of daily life
And when some visitation of the gods
Confronts us. For we know that when you came here,
You freed us from our bondage, the bitter tribute
The Sphinx wrung from us by her sorceries.
And we know too that you accomplished this
Without foreknowledge, or clue that we could furnish.
We think, indeed, some god befriended you,   40
When you renewed our lives. Therefore, great king,
Glorious in all men's eyes, we now beseech you
To find some way of helping us, your suppliants,
Some way the gods themselves have told you of,
Or one that lies within our mortal power;
For the words of men experienced in evil
Are mighty and effectual. Oedipus!
Rescue our city and preserve your honor,
Since the land hails you as her savior now
For your past service. Never let us say   50
That when you ruled us, we were lifted up
Only to be thrown down. Restore the state
And keep it forever steadfast. Bring again
The happiness and good fortune you once brought us.
If you are still to reign as you reign now,
Then it is better to have men for subjects
Than to be king of a mere wilderness,
Since neither ship nor town has any value
Without companions or inhabitants.

OEDIPUS:
I pity you, my children. Well I know   60
What hopes have brought you here, and well I know
That all of you are suffering. Yet your grief,
However great, is not so great as mine.
Each of you suffers for himself alone,
But my heart feels the heaviness of my sorrow,
Your sorrow, and the sorrow of all the others.
You have not roused me, I have not been sleeping.
No. I have wept, wept long and bitterly,
Treading the devious paths of anxious thought;
And I have taken the only hopeful course   70
That I could find. I have sent my kinsman, Creon,
Son of Menoeceus, to the Pythian home[1]
Of Phoebus Apollo to find what word or deed
Of mine might save the city. He has delayed
Too long already, his absence troubles me;
But when he comes, I pledge myself to do
My utmost to obey the god's command.

PRIEST:
Your words are timely, for even as you speak
They sign to me that Creon is drawing near.

OEDIPUS:
O Lord Apollo! Grant he may bring to us   80
Fortune as smiling as his smiling face.

PRIEST:
Surely he brings good fortune. Look! The crown
Of bay leaves that he wears is full of berries.

OEDIPUS:
We shall know soon, for he is close enough
To hear us. Brother, son of Menoeceus, speak!
What news? What news do you bring us from the god?

Enter CREON

CREON:
Good news. If we can find the fitting way
To end this heavy scourge, all will be well.

OEDIPUS:
That neither gives me courage nor alarms me.
What does the god say? What is the oracle?   90

CREON:
If you wish me to speak in public, I will do so.
Otherwise let us go in and speak alone.

OEDIPUS:
Speak here before everyone. I feel more sorrow
For their sakes than I feel for my own life.

CREON:
Then I will give the message of Lord Phoebus:
A plain command to drive out the pollution
Here in our midst, and not to nourish it
Till our disease has grown incurable.

OEDIPUS:
What rite will purge us? How are we corrupted?

CREON:
We must banish a man, or have him put to death   100
To atone for the blood he shed, for it is blood
That has brought this tempest down upon the city.

OEDIPUS:
Who is the victim whose murder is revealed?

CREON:
King Laius, who was our lord before you came
To steer the city on its proper course.

OEDIPUS:
I know his name well, but I never saw him.

---

[1]That is the oracle at Delphi.

CREON:
> Laius was killed, and now we are commanded
> To punish his killers, whoever they may be.

OEDIPUS:
> How can they be discovered? Where shall we look
> For the faint traces of this ancient crime?   110

CREON:
> In Thebes, the god said. Truth can be always found:
> Only what is neglected ever escapes.

OEDIPUS:
> Where was King Laius murdered? In his home,
> Out in the fields, or in some foreign land?

CREON:
> He told us he was journeying to Delphi.
> After he left, he was never seen again.

OEDIPUS:
> Was no one with King Laius who saw what happened?
> You could have put his story to good use.

CREON:
> The sole survivor fled from the scene in terror,
> And there was only one thing he was sure of.   120

OEDIPUS:
> What was it? A clue might lead us far
> Which gave us even the faintest glimmer of hope.

CREON:
> He said that they were violently attacked
> Not by one man but by a band of robbers.

OEDIPUS:
> Robbers are not so daring. Were they bribed
> To commit this crime by some one here in Thebes?

CREON:
> That was suspected. But in our time of trouble
> No one appeared to avenge the death of Laius.

OEDIPUS:
> But your King was killed! What troubles could you have had
> To keep you from searching closely for his killers?   130

CREON:
> We had the Sphinx. Her riddle made us turn
> From mysteries to what lay before our doors.

OEDIPUS:
> Then I will start fresh and again make clear
> Things that are dark. All honor to Apollo
> And to you, Creon, for acting as you have done
> On the dead King's behalf. So I will take
> My rightful place beside you as your ally,
> Avenging Thebes and bowing to the god.
> Not for a stranger will I dispel this taint,
> But for my own sake, since the murderer,   140
> Whoever he is, may strike at me as well.
> Therefore in helping Laius I help myself.
> Come, children, come! Rise from the altar steps,
> And carry away those branches. Summon here
> The people of Cadmus. Tell them I mean to leave
> Nothing undone. So with Apollo's aid
> We may at last be saved—or meet destruction.

Exit OEDIPUS

PRIEST:
> My children, let us go. The King has promised
> The favor that we sought. And may Lord Phoebus
> Come to us with his oracles, assuage   150
> Our misery, and deliver us from death.

Exeunt. Enter CHORUS

CHORUS:
> The god's great word, in whose sweetness we ever rejoice,
>   To our glorious city is drawing nigh,
> Now, even now, from the gold of the Delphic shrine.
>   What next decree will be thine,
> Apollo, thou healer, to whom in our dread we cry?
>   We are anguished, racked, and beset by fears!
> What fate will be ours? One fashioned for us alone,
>   Or one that in ancient time was known
>   That returns once more with the circling years?   160
> Child of our golden hope, O speak, thou immortal voice!
>
> Divine Athene, daughter of Zeus, O hear![2]
>   Hear thou, Artemis! Thee we hail,
> Our guardian goddess throned in the market place.
>   Apollo, we ask thy grace.
> Shine forth, all three, and the menace of death will fail.
>   Answer our call! Shall we call in vain?
> If ever ye came in the years that have gone before,
>   Return, and save us from plague once more,
>   Rescue our city from fiery pain!   170
> Be your threefold strength our shield. Draw near to us now, draw near!
>
>   Death is upon us. We bear a burden of bitter grief.
> There is nothing can save us now, no device that our thought can frame.
>   No blossom, no fruit, no harvest sheaf
>   Springs from the blighted and barren earth.
> Women cry out in travail and bring no children to birth;
>   But swift as a bird, swift as the sweep of flame,
>   Life after life takes sudden flight
> To the western god, to the last, dark shore of night.
>   Ruin has fallen on Thebes. Without number her children are dead;   180
> Unmourned, unattended, unpitied, they lie polluting the ground.
>   Grey-haired mothers and wives new-wed
>   Wail at the altars everywhere,
> With entreaty, with loud lament, with clamor filling the air.
>   And songs of praise to Apollo, the healer, resound.
>   Athene, thou knowest our desperate need.
> Lend us thy strength. Give heed to our prayer, give heed!
>
>   Fierce Ares has fallen upon us. He comes unarrayed for war,
> Yet he fills our ears with shrieking, he folds us in fiery death.
>   Grant that he soon may turn in headlong flight from our land,   190
> Swept to the western deep by the fair wind's favoring breath,
>   Or swept to the savage sea that washes the Thracian shore.
> We few who escape the night are stricken down in the day.
> O Zeus, whose bolts of thunder are balanced within thy hand,
> Hurl down thy lightning upon him! Father, be swift to slay!
>
>   Save us, light-bringing Phoebus! The shower of thine arrows let fly;
> Loose them, triumphant and swift, from the golden string of thy bow!
>   O goddess, his radiant sister, roaming the Lycian glade,
> Come with the flash of thy fire! Artemis, conquer our foe!
>   And thou, O wine-flushed god to whom the Bacchantes cry,   200
> With thy brilliant torch ablaze amid shouts of thy maenad train,
>   With thy hair enwreathed with gold, O Bacchus, we beg thine aid
> Against our destroyer Ares, the god whom the gods disdain!

Enter OEDIPUS

OEDIPUS:
> You have been praying. If you heed my words
> And seek the remedy for your own disease,

---

[2]These appeals to the gods are understandable, chiefly as cries of despair. Ares, referred to in line 188, is the God of War and here chiefly suggests destruction. Bacchus or Dionysus (line 200) was the patron god of Thebes, and his devotees, the bacchantes, held wild revels in the streets of the city.

The gods will hear your prayers, and you will find
Relief and comfort. I myself know nothing
About this story, nothing about the murder,
So that unaided and without a clue
I could not have tracked it down for any distance. 210
And because I have only recently been received
Among you as a citizen, to you all,
And to all the rest, I make this proclamation:
Whoever knows the man who killed King Laius,
Let him declare his knowledge openly.
If he himself is guilty, let him confess
And go unpunished, except for banishment.
Or if he knows the murderer was an alien,
Let him by speaking earn his due reward,
And thanks as well. But if he holds his tongue, 220
Hoping to save himself or save a friend,
Then let him hear what I, the King, decree
For all who live in Thebes, the land I rule.
No one shall give this murderer shelter. No one
Shall speak to him. No one shall let him share
In sacrifice or prayer or lustral rites.
The door of every house is barred against him.
The god has shown me that he is polluted.
So by this edict I ally myself
With Phoebus and the slain. As for the slayer, 230
Whether he had accomplices or not,
This is my solemn prayer concerning him:
May evil come of evil; may he live
A wretched life and meet a wretched end.
And as for me, if I should knowingly
Admit him as a member of my household,
May the same fate which I invoked for others
Fall upon me. Make my words good, I charge you,
For love of me, Apollo, and our country
Blasted by the displeasure of the gods. 240
You should not have left this guilt unpurified,
Even without an oracle to urge you,
When a man so noble, a man who was your King,
Had met his death. Rather, it was your duty
To seek the truth. But now, since it is I
Who hold the sovereignty that once was his,
I who have wed his wife, who would have been
Bound to him by the tie of having children
Born of one mother, if he had had a child
To be a blessing, if fate had not struck him down— 250
Since this is so, I intend to fight his battle
As though he were my father. I will leave
Nothing undone to find his murderer,
Avenging him and all his ancestors.
And I pray the gods that those who disobey
May suffer. May their fields bring forth no harvest,
Their wives no children; may the present plague,
Or one yet worse, consume them. But as for you,
All of you citizens who are loyal to me,
May Justice, our champion, and all the gods 260
Show you their favor in the days to come.

CHORUS:
King Oedipus, I will speak to avoid your curse.
I am no slayer, nor can I point him out.
The question came to us from Phoebus Apollo;
It is for him to tell us who is guilty.
OEDIPUS:
Yes. But no man on earth is strong enough
To force the gods to act against their will.
CHORUS:
There is, I think, a second course to follow.

OEDIPUS:
If there is yet a third, let me know that.
CHORUS:
Tiresias, the prophet, has the clearest vision 270
Next to our Lord Apollo. He is the man
Who can do most to help us in our search.
OEDIPUS:
I have not forgotten. Creon suggested it,
And I have summoned him, summoned him twice.
I am astonished he is not here already.
CHORUS:
The only rumors are old and half-forgotten.
OEDIPUS:
What are they? I must find out all I can.
CHORUS:
It is said the King was killed by travelers.
OEDIPUS:
So I have heard, but there is no eye-witness.
CHORUS:
If fear can touch them, they will reveal themselves 280
Once they have heard so dreadful a curse as yours.
OEDIPUS:
Murderers are not terrified by words.
CHORUS:
But they can be convicted by the man
Being brought here now, Tiresias. He alone
Is godlike in his knowledge of the truth.

Enter TIRESIAS,[4] *led by a* BOY
OEDIPUS:
You know all things in heaven and earth, Tiresias:
Things you may speak of openly, and secrets
Holy and not to be revealed. You know,
Blind though you are, the plague that ruins Thebes.
And you, great prophet, you alone can save us. 290
Phoebus has sent an answer to our question,
An answer that the messengers may have told you,
Saying there was no cure for our condition
Until we found the killers of King Laius
And banished them or had them put to death.
Therefore, Tiresias, do not begrudge your skill
In the voice of birds or other prophecy,
But save yourself, save me, save the whole city,
Save everything that the pestilence defiles.
We are at your mercy, and man's noblest task 300
Is to use all his powers in helping others.
TIRESIAS:
How dreadful a thing, how dreadful a thing is wisdom,
When to be wise is useless! This I knew
But I forgot, or else I would never have come.
OEDIPUS:
What is the matter? Why are you so troubled?
TIRESIAS:
Oedipus, let me go home. Then you will bear
Your burden, and I mine, more easily.
OEDIPUS:
Custom entitles us to hear your message.
By being silent you harm your native land.

---

[3]This whole passage is filled with dramatic irony: that is, the audience understands the words in another sense than the speaker means them.

[4]Tiresias is a blind prophet, a priest of Apollo. He seems to have been almost infinitely old, and was both masculine and feminine. Consequently his wisdom was almost without bounds. Priests often made their prophecies after observing flights of birds, listening to the cries of birds, observing the entrails of sacrificial animals, etc.

TIRESIAS:
    You do not know when, and when not to speak.
    Silence will save me from the same misfortune.
OEDIPUS:
    If you can be of help, then all of us
    Kneel and implore you not to turn away.
TIRESIAS: None of you know the truth, but I will never
    Reveal my sorrow—not to call it yours.
OEDIPUS: What are you saying? You know and will not speak?
    You mean to betray us and destroy the city?
TIRESIAS: I refuse to pain you. I refuse to pain myself.
    It is useless to ask me. I will tell you nothing.
OEDIPUS: You utter scoundrel! You would enrage a stone!
    Is there no limit to your stubbornness?
TIRESIAS: You blame my anger and forget your own.
OEDIPUS: No one could help being angry when he heard
    How you dishonor and ignore the state.
TIRESIAS: What is to come will come, though I keep silent.
OEDIPUS: If it must come, your duty is to speak.
TIRESIAS: I will say no more. Rage to your heart's content.
OEDIPUS:
    Rage? Yes, I will rage! I will spare you nothing.
    In the plot against King Laius, I have no doubt
    That you were an accomplice, yes, almost
    The actual killer. If you had not been blind,
    I would have said that you alone were guilty.
TIRESIAS:
    Then listen to my command! Obey the edict
    That you yourself proclaimed and never speak,
    From this day on, to me or any Theban.
    You are the sinner who pollutes our land.
OEDIPUS:
    Have you no shame? How do you hope to escape
    The consequence of such an accusation?
TIRESIAS:
    I have escaped. My strength is the living truth.
OEDIPUS: This is no prophecy. Who taught you this?
TIRESIAS: You did. You forced me to speak against my will.
OEDIPUS: Repeat your slander. Let me learn it better.
TIRESIAS:
    Are you trying to tempt me into saying more?
    I have spoken already. Have you not understood?
OEDIPUS: No, not entirely. Give your speech again.
TIRESIAS: I say you are the killer, you yourself.
OEDIPUS: Twice the same insult! You will pay for it.
TIRESIAS: Shall I say more to make you still more angry?
OEDIPUS: Say what you want to. It will make no sense.
TIRESIAS:
    You are living in shame with those most dear to you,
    As yet in ignorance of your dreadful fate.
OEDIPUS:
    Do you suppose that you can always use
    Language like that and not be punished for it?
TIRESIAS: Yes. I am safe, if truth has any strength.
OEDIPUS:
    Truth can save anyone excepting you,
    You with no eyes, no hearing, and no brains!
TIRESIAS:
    Poor fool! You taunt me, but you soon will hear
    The self-same insults heaped upon your head.
OEDIPUS:
    You live in endless night. What can you do
    To me or anyone else who sees the day?
TIRESIAS:
    Nothing. I have no hand in your destruction.
    For that, Apollo needs no help from me.
OEDIPUS: Apollo! Is this your trick, or is it Creon's?
TIRESIAS: Creon is guiltless. The evil is in you.
OEDIPUS:
    How great is the envy roused by wealth, by kingship,
    By the subtle skill that triumphs over others
    In life's hard struggle! Creon, who has been
    For years my trusted friend, has stealthily
    Crept in upon me anxious to seize my power,
    The unsought gift the city freely gave me.
    Anxious to overthrow me, he has bribed
    This scheming mountebank, this fraud, this trickster,
    Blind in his art and in everything but money!
    Your art of prophecy! When have you shown it?
    Not when the watch-dog of the gods was here,
    Chanting her riddle. Why did you say nothing,
    When you might have saved the city? Yet her puzzle
    Could not be solved by the first passer-by.
    A prophet's skill was needed, and you proved
    That you had no such skill, either in birds
    Or any other means the gods have given.
    But I came, I, the ignorant Oedipus,
    And silenced her. I had no birds to help me.
    I used my brains. And it is I you now
    Are trying to destroy in the hope of standing
    Close beside Creon's throne. You will regret
    This zeal of yours to purify the land,
    You and your fellow-plotter. You seem old;
    Otherwise you would pay for your presumption.
CHORUS:
    Sir, it appears to us that both of you
    Have spoken in anger. Anger serves no purpose.
    Rather we should consider in what way
    We best can carry out the god's command.
TIRESIAS:
    King though you are, I have a right to answer
    Equal to yours. In that I too am king.
    I serve Apollo. I do not acknowledge
    You as my lord or Creon as my patron.
    You have seen fit to taunt me with my blindness.
    Therefore I tell you this: you have your eyesight
    And cannot see the sin of your existence,
    Cannot see where you live or whom you live with,
    Are ignorant of your parents, bring disgrace
    Upon your kindred in the world below
    And here on earth. And soon the double lash
    Of your mother's and father's curse will drive you headlong

Out of the country, blinded, with your cries
　　　Heard everywhere, echoed by every hill
　　　In all Cithaeron. Then you will have learned
　　　The meaning of your marriage, learned in what harbor,
　　　After so fair a voyage, you were shipwrecked.
　　　And other horrors you could never dream of
　　　Will teach you who you are, will drag you down
　　　To the level of your children. Heap your insults
　　　On Creon and my message if you choose to.　　　410
　　　Still no one ever will endure the weight
　　　Of greater misery than will fall on you.

OEDIPUS:
　　　Am I supposed to endure such talk as this,
　　　Such talk from him? Go, curse you, go! Be quick!

TIRESIAS:
　　　Except for your summons I would never have come.

OEDIPUS:
　　　And I would never have sent for you so soon
　　　If I had known you would prove to be a fool.

TIRESIAS:
　　　Yes. I have proved a fool—in your opinion,
　　　And yet your parents thought that I was wise.

OEDIPUS:
　　　What parents? Wait! Who was my father? Tell me!　　　420

TIRESIAS:
　　　Today will see your birth and your destruction.

OEDIPUS:
　　　You cannot speak unless you speak in riddles!

TIRESIAS:
　　　And yet how brilliant you are in solving them!

OEDIPUS:
　　　You sneer at me for what has made me great.

TIRESIAS:
　　　The same good fortune that has ruined you.

OEDIPUS:
　　　If I have saved the city, nothing else matters.

TIRESIAS:
　　　In that case I will go. Boy, take me home.

OEDIPUS:
　　　Yes, let him take you. Here, you are in the way.
　　　Once you are gone, you will give no further trouble.

TIRESIAS:
　　　I will not go before I have said my say,　　　430
　　　Indifferent to your black looks. You cannot harm me.
　　　And I say this: the man whom you have sought,
　　　Whom you have threatened, whom you have proclaimed
　　　The killer of King Laius—he is here.
　　　Now thought an alien, he shall prove to be
　　　A native Theban, to his deep dismay.
　　　Now he has eyesight, now his wealth is great;
　　　But he shall make his way to foreign soil
　　　Blinded, in beggary, groping with a stick.
　　　In his own household he shall be shown to be　　　440
　　　The father of his children—and their brother,
　　　Son to the woman who bore him—and her husband,
　　　The killer and the bedfellow of his father.
　　　Go and consider this; and if you find
　　　That I have been mistaken, you can say
　　　That I have lost my skill in prophecy.

　　　　　　　　　　Exeunt OEDIPUS *and* TIRESIAS

CHORUS:
　What man is this the god from the Delphic rock denounces,
　　Whose deeds are too shameful to tell, whose murderous hands
　　　　are red?
　Let his feet be swifter now than hooves of horses racing
　　The storm-clouds overhead.　　　450
　For Zeus's son, Apollo, leaps in anger upon him,
　　Armed with lightning to strike and slay;
　And the terrible Fates, unflagging, relentless,
　　Follow the track of their prey.

　The words of the god have flashed from the peaks of snowy Parnassus,
　　Commanding us all to seek this killer as yet unknown.
　Deep in the tangled woods, through rocks and caves he is roaming
　　Like a savage bull, alone.
　On his lonely path he journeys, wretched, broken by sorrow,
　　Seeking to flee from the fate he fears;　　　460
　　But the voice from the center of earth that doomed him
　　　　Inescapably rings in his ears.

　Dreadful, dreadful those words! We can neither approve nor
　　　　deny them.
　　Shaken, confounded with fears, we know not what to say.
　Nothing is clear to us, nothing—what is to come tomorrow,
　　Or what is upon us today.
　If the prophet seeks revenge for the unsolved murder of Laius,
　　Why is Oedipus charged with crime?
　　Because some deep-rooted hate divides their royal houses?
　　The houses of Laius and Oedipus, son of the King of Corinth?　　　470
　　　There is none that we know of, now, or in ancient time.

　From Zeus's eyes and Apollo's no human secret is hidden;
　　But man has no test for truth, no measure his wit can devise.
　Tiresias, indeed, excels in every art of his office,
　　And yet we too may be wise.
　Though Oedipus stands accused, until he is proven guilty
　　We cannot blacken his name;
　For he showed his wisdom the day the wingéd maiden faced him.
　He triumphed in that ordeal, saved us, and won our affection.
　　We can never believe he stooped to an act of shame.　　　480

　　　　　　　　　　　　　　　　　　　Enter CREON

CREON:
　　　Thebans, I come here outraged and indignant,
　　　For I have learned that Oedipus has accused me
　　　Of dreadful crimes. If, in the present crisis,
　　　He thinks that I have wronged him in any way,
　　　Wronged him in word or deed, then let my life
　　　Come to a speedy close. I cannot bear
　　　The burden of such scandal. The attack
　　　Ruins me utterly, if my friends, and you,
　　　And the whole city are to call me traitor.

CHORUS:
　　　Perhaps his words were only a burst of anger,　　　490
　　　And were not meant as a deliberate insult.

CREON:
　　　He *did* say that I plotted with Tiresias?
　　　And that the prophet lied at my suggestion?

CHORUS:
　　　Those were his words. I cannot guess his motive.

CREON:
　　　Were his eyes clear and steady? Was his mind
　　　Unclouded, when he brought this charge against me?

CHORUS:
　　　I cannot say. To see what princes do
　　　Is not our province. Here comes the King himself.

Enter OEDIPUS

OEDIPUS:
So you are here! What brought you to my door?
Impudence? Insolence? You, my murderer! 500
You, the notorious stealer of my crown!
Why did you hatch this plot? What kind of man,
By heaven, what kind of man, could you have thought me?
A coward or a fool? Did you suppose
I would not see your trickery take shape,
Or when I saw it, would not counter it?
How stupid you were to reach for royal power
Without a troop of followers or rich friends!
Only a mob and money win a kingdom.

CREON:
Sir, let me speak. When you have heard my answer, 510
You will have grounds on which to base your judgment.

OEDIPUS:
I cannot follow all your clever talk.
I only know that you are dangerous.

CREON:
That is the issue. Let me explain that first.

OEDIPUS:
Do not explain that you are true to me.

CREON:
If you imagine that a blind self-will
Is strength of character, you are mistaken.

OEDIPUS:
As you are, if you strike at your own house,
And then expect to escape all punishment.

CREON:
Yes, you are right. That would be foolishness. 520
But tell me, what have I done? How have I harmed you?

OEDIPUS:
Did you, or did you not, urge me to summon
Tiresias, that revered, that holy prophet?

CREON:
Yes. And I still think my advice was good.

OEDIPUS:
Then answer this: how long ago was Laius—

CREON:
Laius! Why how am I concerned with him?

OEDIPUS:
How many years ago was Laius murdered?

CREON:
So many they cannot easily be counted.

OEDIPUS:
And was Tiresias just as cunning then?

CREON:
As wise and honored as he is today. 530

OEDIPUS:
At that time did he ever mention me?

CREON:
Not in my hearing. I am sure of that.

OEDIPUS:
And the murderer—a thorough search was made?

CREON:
Yes, certainly, but we discovered nothing.

OEDIPUS:
Then why did the man of wisdom hold his tongue?

CREON:
I cannot say. Guessing is not my habit.

OEDIPUS:
One thing at least you need not guess about.

CREON:
What is it? If I know it, I will tell you.

OEDIPUS:
Tiresias would not have said I murdered Laius,
If you two had not put your heads together. 540

CREON:
You best know what he said. But now I claim
The right to take my turn in asking questions.

OEDIPUS:
Very well, ask. You never can find me guilty.

CREON:
Then answer this: my sister is your wife?

OEDIPUS:
I cannot deny that fact. She is my wife.

CREON:
And in your rule she has an equal share?

OEDIPUS:
She has no wish that goes unsatisfied.

CREON:
And as the third I stand beside you both?

OEDIPUS:
True. That position proves your treachery.

CREON:
No. You would see, if you thought the matter through 550
As I have done. Consider. Who would choose
Kingship and all the terrors that go with it,
If, with the same power, he could sleep in peace?
I have no longing for a royal title
Rather than royal freedom. No, not I,
Nor any moderate man. Now I fear nothing.
Every request I make of you is granted,
And yet as king I should have many duties
That went against the grain. Then how could rule
Be sweeter than untroubled influence? 560
I have not lost my mind. I want no honors
Except the ones that bring me solid good.
Now all men welcome me and wish me joy.
Now all your suitors ask to speak with me,
Knowing they cannot otherwise succeed.
Why should I throw away a life like this
For a king's life? No one is treacherous
Who knows his own best interests. To conspire
With other men, or to be false myself,
Is not my nature. Put me to the test. 570
First, go to Delphi. Ask if I told the truth
About the oracle. Then if you find
I have had dealings with Tiresias, kill me.
My voice will echo yours in passing sentence.
But base your verdict upon something more
Than mere suspicion. Great injustice comes
From random judgments that bad men are good
And good men bad. To throw away a friend
Is, in effect, to throw away your life,
The prize you treasure most. All this, in time, 580
Will become clear to you, for time alone
Proves a man's honesty, but wickedness
Can be discovered in a single day.

CHORUS:
Sir, that is good advice, if one is prudent.
Hasty decisions always lead to danger.

OEDIPUS:
When a conspiracy is quick in forming,
I must move quickly to retaliate.
If I sat still and let my enemy act,
I would lose everything that he would gain.

CREON:
So then, my banishment is what you want? 590

OEDIPUS:
>No, not your banishment. Your execution.

CREON:
>I think you are mad. OE.: I can protect myself.

CREON:
>You should protect me also. OE.: You? A traitor?

CREON:
>Suppose you are wrong? OE.: I am the King. I rule.

CREON:
>Not if you rule unjustly. OE.: Thebes! Hear that!

CREON:
>Thebes is my city too, as well as yours.

CHORUS:
>No more, no more, sirs! Here is Queen Jocasta.
>She comes in time to help make peace between you.

Enter JOCASTA

JOCASTA:
>Oedipus! Creon! How can you be so foolish?
>What! Quarrel now about a private matter 600
>When the land is dying? You should be ashamed.
>Come, Oedipus, come in. Creon, go home.
>You make a trivial problem too important.

CREON:
>Sister, your husband has made dreadful threats.
>He claims the right to have me put to death
>Or have me exiled. He need only choose.

OEDIPUS:
>Yes. I have caught him at his treachery,
>Plotting against the person of the King.

CREON:
>If I am guilty, may it be my fate
>To live in misery and to die accursed. 610

JOCASTA:
>Believe him, Oedipus, believe him, spare him—
>I beg you by the gods—for his oath's sake,
>For my sake, for the sake of all men here.

CHORUS:
>Consent, O King. Be gracious. Hear us, we beg you.

OEDIPUS:
>What shall I hear? To what shall I consent?

CHORUS:
>Respect the evidence of Creon's wisdom,
>Respect the oath of innocence he has taken.

OE.:
>You know what this means? CH.: Yes. OE.: Tell me again what you ask for.

CHORUS:
>To yield, to relent.
>He is your friend and swears he is not guilty. 620
>Do not act in haste, convicting him out of hand.

OEDIPUS:
>When you ask for this, you ask for my destruction;
>You sentence me to death or to banishment.
>Be sure that you understand.

CHORUS:
>No, by Apollo, no!
>If such a thought has ever crossed my mind,
>Then may I never find
>A friend to love me or a god to save;
>And may dark doom pursue me to the grave.
>My country perishes, and now new woe 630
>Springs from your quarrel, one affliction more
>Has come upon us, and my heart is sore.

OEDIPUS:
>Let him go free, even though that destroys me.
>I shall be killed, or exiled in disgrace.
>Not his appeal but yours aroused my pity.
>I shall hate him always, no matter where he is.

CREON:
>You go beyond all bounds when you are angry,
>And are sullen when you yield. Natures like yours
>Inflict their heaviest torments on themselves.

OEDIPUS:
>Go! Go! Leave me in peace! CR.: Yes, I will go. 640
>You have not understood, but in the sight
>Of all these men here I am innocent.

Exit CREON

CHORUS: Take the King with you, Madam, to the palace.

JOCASTA: When I have learned what happened, we will go.

CHORUS: The King was filled with fear and blind suspicion.
>Creon resented what he thought injustice.

JOC.: Both were at fault? CH.: Both. JOC.: Why was the King suspicious?

CHORUS:
>Do not seek to know.
>We have said enough. In a time of pain and trouble
>Inquire no further. Let the matter rest. 650

OEDIPUS:
>Your well meant pleading turned me from my purpose,
>And now you come to this. You fall so low
>As to think silence best.

CHORUS:
>I say again, O King,
>No one except a madman or a fool
>Would throw aside your rule.
>For you delivered us; your single hand
>Lifted the load from our belovéd land.
>When we were mad with grief and suffering,
>In our extremity you found a way 660
>To save the city, as you will today.

JOCASTA:
>But tell *me*, Oedipus, tell *me*, I beg you,
>Why you were so unyielding in your anger.

OEDIPUS:
>I will, Jocasta, for I honor you
>More than I do the elders. It was Creon's plotting.

JOCASTA:
>What do you mean? What was your accusation?

OEDIPUS:
>He says I am the murderer of King Laius.

JOCASTA:
>Did he speak from first-hand knowledge or from hearsay?

OEDIPUS:
>He did not speak at all. His lips are pure.
>He bribed Tiresias, and that scoundrel spoke. 670

JOCASTA:
>Then you can rid your mind of any fear
>That you are guilty. Listen to me. No mortal
>Shares in the gods' foreknowledge. I can give you
>Clear proof of that. There came once to King Laius
>An oracle—I will not say from Phoebus,
>But from his priest—saying it was his fate
>That he should be struck down by his own child,
>His child and mine. But Laius, as we know,
>Was killed by foreign robbers at a place
>Where three roads came together. As for the child, 680
>When it was only three days old, its father
>Pierced both its ankles, pinned its feet together,
>And then gave orders that it be abandoned

On a wild mountainside. So in this case
Phoebus did not fulfill his oracle. The child
Was not its father's murderer, and Laius
Was not the victim of the fate he feared,
Death at his son's hands, although just that fate
Was what the seer predicted. Pay no heed
To prophecies. Whatever may be needful 690
The god himself can show us easily.

OEDIPUS: What have you said, Jocasta? What have you said? [REALIZATION]
The past comes back to me. How terrible!

JOCASTA: Why do you start so? What has happened to you?

OEDIPUS: It seemed to me—I thought you said that Laius
Was struck down where three roads came together.

JOCASTA: I did. That was the story, and still is.

OEDIPUS: Where was it that this murder was committed?

JOCASTA: In Phocis, where the road from Thebes divides,
Meeting the roads from Daulia and Delphi.

OEDIPUS: How many years ago did this occur?

JOCASTA: The news of it was published here in Thebes
Not long before you came to be our king.

OEDIPUS: Is this my fate? Is this what the gods decreed?

JOCASTA: What have I said that has so shaken you?

OEDIPUS: Do not ask me yet. Tell me about King Laius.
What did he look like? Was he young or old?

JOCASTA: His build was not unlike yours. He was tall.
His hair was just beginning to turn grey.

OEDIPUS: I cannot bear the thought that I called down
A curse on my own head unknowingly.

JOCASTA: What is it, Oedipus? You terrify me!

OEDIPUS: I dread to think Tiresias had clear eyesight; 710
But tell me one thing more, and I will know.

JOCASTA: And I too shrink, yet I will answer you.

OEDIPUS: How did he travel? With a few men only,
Or with his guards and servants, like a prince?

JOCASTA: There were five of them in all, with one a herald.
They had one carriage in which King Laius rode.

OEDIPUS: It is too clear, too clear! Who told you this?

JOCASTA: The only servant who escaped alive.

OEDIPUS: And is he still here now, still in the palace?

JOCASTA: No. When he came home and found Laius dead 720
And you the reigning king, he pleaded with me
To send him where the sheep were pasturing,
As far as possible away from Thebes.
And so I sent him. He was a worthy fellow
And, if a slave can, deserved a greater favor.

OEDIPUS: I hope it is possible to get him quickly.

JOCASTA: Yes, that is easy. Why do you want to see him?

OEDIPUS: Because I am afraid, deadly afraid
That I have spoken more than I should have done.

JOCASTA: He shall come. But Oedipus, have I no right 730
To learn what weighs so heavily on your heart?

OEDIPUS: You shall learn everything, now that my fears
Have grown so great, for who is dearer to me
Than you, Jocasta? Whom should I speak to sooner,
When I am in such straits? King Polybus
Of Corinth was my father. Meropé,
A Dorian, was my mother. I myself
Was foremost among all the citizens,
Till something happened, strange, but hardly worth
My feeling such resentment. As we sat 740
One day at dinner, a man who had drunk too much
Insulted me by saying I was not
My father's son. In spite of being angry,
I managed to control myself. Next day
I asked my parents, who were both indignant
That he had leveled such a charge against me.
This was a satisfaction, yet the thing
Still rankled, for the rumor grew widespread.
At last I went to Delphi secretly.
Apollo gave no answer to my question 750
But sent me off, anguished and terrified,
With fearful prophecies that I was fated
To be my mother's husband, to bring forth
Children whom men could not endure to see,
And to take my father's life. When I heard this
I turned and fled, hoping to find at length
Some place where I would know of Corinth only
As a far distant land beneath the stars,
Some place where I would never have to see
The infamies of this oracle fulfilled. 760
And as I went on, I approached the spot
At which you tell me Laius met his end.
Now this, Jocasta, is the absolute truth.
When I had come to where the three roads fork,
A herald met me, walking before a carriage,
Drawn by two colts, in which a man was seated,
Just as you said. The old man and the herald
Ordered me off the road with threatening gestures.
Then as the driver pushed me to one side,
I struck him angrily. And seeing this, 770
The old man, as I drew abreast, leaned out
And brought his driver's two-pronged goad down hard
Upon my head. He paid a heavy price
For doing that. With one blow of my staff
I knocked him headlong from his chariot
Flat on his back. Then every man of them
I killed. Now if the blood of Laius flowed
In that old stranger's veins, what mortal man
Could be more wretched, more accursed than I?
I whom no citizen or foreigner 780
May entertain or shelter, I to whom
No one may speak, I, I who must be driven
From every door. No other man has cursed me,
I have brought down this curse upon myself.
The hands that killed him now pollute his bed!
Am I not vile, foul, utterly unclean?
For I must fly and never see again
My people or set foot in my own land,
Or else become the husband of my mother

And put to death my father Polybus,
To whom I owe my life and my upbringing.
Men would be right in thinking that such things
Have been inflicted by some cruel fate.
May the gods' high and holy majesty
Forbid that I should see that day. No! No!
Rather than be dishonored by a doom
So dreadful may I vanish from the earth.

CHORUS:
Sir, these are terrible things, but there is hope
Until you have heard what the one witness says.

OEDIPUS:
That is the one remaining hope I have,
To wait for the arrival of the shepherd.

JOCASTA:
And when he *has* arrived, what can he do?

OEDIPUS:
He can do this. If his account agrees
With yours, I stand acquitted of this crime.

JOCASTA:
Was what I said of any consequence?

OEDIPUS:
You said his story was that robbers killed
King Laius. If he speaks of the same number,
Then I am not the murderer. One man
Cannot be several men. But if he says
One traveler, single-handed, did the deed,
Beyond all doubt the evidence points to me.

JOCASTA:
I am quite certain that was what he said.
He cannot change now, for the whole of Thebes
Heard it, not I alone. In any case,
Even supposing that his story *should*
Be somewhat different, he can never make
Laius's death fulfill the oracle.
Phoebus said plainly Laius was to die
At my son's hands. However, that poor child
Certainly did not kill him, for it died
Before its father. I would not waste my time
In giving any thought to prophecy.

OEDIPUS:
Yes, you are right. And yet have someone sent
To bring the shepherd here. Make sure of this.

JOCASTA:
I will, at once. Come, Oedipus, come in.
I will do nothing that you disapprove of.

Exeunt OEDIPUS *and* JOCASTA

CHORUS:
May piety and reverence mark my actions;
    May every thought be pure through all my days.
May those great laws whose dwelling is in heaven
    Approve my conduct with their crown of praise:
Offspring of skies that overarch Olympus,
    Laws from the loins of no mere mortal sprung,
Unslumbering, unfailing, unforgetting,
    Filled with a godhead that is ever young.

Pride breeds the tyrant. Insolent presumption,
    Big with delusive wealth and false renown,
Once it has mounted to the highest rampart
    Is headlong hurled in utter ruin down.
But pour out all thy blessings, Lord Apollo,
    Thou who alone hast made and kept us great,
On all whose sole ambition is unselfish,
    Who spend themselves in service to the state.
Let that man be accursèd who is proud,
    In act unscrupulous, in thinking base,
Whose knees in reverence have never bowed,
    In whose hard heart justice can find no place,
Whose hands profane life's holiest mysteries,
    How can he hope to shield himself for long
From the gods' arrows that will pierce him through?
If evil triumphs in such ways as these,
    Why should we seek, in choric dance and song,
To give the gods the praise that is their due?

I cannot go in full faith as of old,
To sacred Delphi or Olympian vale,
    Unless men see that what has been foretold
Has come to pass, that omens never fail.
    All-ruling Zeus, if thou art King indeed,
Put forth thy majesty, make good thy word,
    Faith in these fading oracles restore!
To priest and prophet men pay little heed;
    Hymns to Apollo are no longer heard;
And all religion soon will be no more.

Enter JOCASTA

JOCASTA:
Elders of Thebes, I thought that I should visit
The altars of the gods to offer up
These wreaths I carry and these gifts of incense.
The King is overanxious, overtroubled.
He is no longer calm enough to judge
The present by the lessons of the past,
But trembles before anyone who brings
An evil prophecy. I cannot help him.
Therefore, since thou art nearest, bright Apollo,
I bring these offerings to thee. O, hear me!
Deliver us from this defiling curse.
His fear infects us all, as if we were
Sailors who saw their pilot terrified.

Enter MESSENGER

MESSENGER:
Sirs, I have come to find King Oedipus.
Where is his palace, can you tell me that?
Or better yet, where is the King himself?

CHORUS:
Stranger, the King is there, within his palace.
This is the Queen, the mother of his children.

MESSENGER:
May all the gods be good to you and yours!
Madam, you are a lady richly blessed.

JOCASTA:
And may the gods requite your courtesy.
But what request or message do you bring us?

MESSENGER:
Good tidings for your husband and your household.

JOCASTA:
What is your news? What country do you come from?

MESSENGER:
From Corinth. And the news I bring will surely
Give you great pleasure—and perhaps some pain.

JOCASTA:
What message can be good and bad at once?

MESSENGER:
    The citizens of Corinth, it is said, 890
    Have chosen Oedipus to be their King.
JOCASTA:
    What do you mean? Their King is Polybus.
MESSENGER:
    No, madam. Polybus is dead and buried.
JOCASTA:
    What! Dead! The father of King Oedipus?
MESSENGER:
    If I speak falsely, let me die myself.
JOCASTA (to ATTENDANT):
    Go find the King and tell him this. Be quick!
    What does an oracle amount to now?
    This is the man whom Oedipus all these years
    Has feared and shunned to keep from killing him,
    And now we find he dies a natural death! 900

Enter OEDIPUS

OEDIPUS:
    My dear Jocasta, why have you sent for me?
JOCASTA:
    Listen to this man's message, and then tell me
    What faith you have in sacred oracles.
OEDIPUS:
    Where does he come from? What has he to say?
JOCASTA:
    He comes from Corinth and has this to say:
    The King, your father, Polybus is dead.
OEDIPUS (to MESSENGER):
    My father! Tell me that again yourself.
MESSENGER:
    I will say first what you first want to know.
    You may be certain he is dead and gone.
OEDIPUS:
    How did he die? By violence or sickness? 910
MESSENGER:
    The scales of life tip easily for the old.
OEDIPUS:
    That is to say he died of some disease.
MESSENGER:
    Yes, of disease, and merely of old age.
OEDIPUS:
    Hear that, Jocasta! Why should anyone
    Give heed to oracles from the Pythian shrine,
    Or to the birds that shriek above our heads?
    They prophesied that I must kill my father.
    But he is dead; the earth has covered him.
    And I am here, I who have never raised
    My hand against him—unless he died of grief, 920
    Longing to see me. Then I might be said
    To have caused his death. But as they stand, at least,
    The oracles have been swept away like rubbish.
    They are with Polybus in Hades, dead.
JOCASTA:
    Long ago, Oedipus, I told you that.
OEDIPUS:
    You did, but I was blinded by my terror.
JOCASTA:
    Now you need take these things to heart no longer.
OEDIPUS:
    But there is still my mother's bed to fear.
JOCASTA:
    Why should you be afraid? Chance rules our lives,
    And no one can foresee the future, no one. 930
    We live best when we live without a purpose
    From one day to the next. Forget your fear
    Of marrying your mother. That has happened
    To many men before this in their dreams.
    We find existence most endurable
    When such things are neglected and forgotten.
OEDIPUS:
    That would be true, Jocasta, if my mother
    Were not alive; but now your eloquence
    Is not enough to give me reassurance.
JOCASTA:
    And yet your father's death is a great comfort. 940
OEDIPUS:
    Yes, but I cannot rest while she is living.
MESSENGER:
    Sir, will you tell me who it is you fear?
OEDIPUS:
    Queen Meropé, the wife of Polybus.
MESSENGER:
    What is so terrible about the Queen?
OEDIPUS:
    A dreadful prophecy the gods have sent us.
MESSENGER:
    Are you forbidden to speak of it, or not?
OEDIPUS:
    It may be told. The Lord Apollo said
    That I was doomed to marry my own mother,
    And shed my father's blood with my own hands.
    And so for years I have stayed away from Corinth, 950
    My native land—a fortunate thing for me,
    Though it is very sweet to see one's parents.
MESSENGER:
    Was that the reason you have lived in exile?
OEDIPUS:
    Yes, for I feared my mother and my father.
MESSENGER:
    Then since my journey was to wish you well,
    Let me release you from your fear at once.
OEDIPUS:
    That would deserve my deepest gratitude.
MESSENGER:
    Sir, I *did* come here with the hope of earning
    Some recompense when you had gotten home.
OEDIPUS:
    No. I will never again go near my home. 960
MESSENGER:
    O son, son! You know nothing. That is clear—
OEDIPUS:
    What do you mean, old friend? Tell me, I beg you.
MESSENGER:
    If that is why you dare not come to Corinth.
OEDIPUS:
    I fear Apollo's word would be fulfilled.
MESSENGER:
    That you would be polluted through your parents?
OEDIPUS:
    Yes, yes! My life is haunted by that horror.
MESSENGER:
    You have no reason to be horrified.
OEDIPUS:
    I have no reason! Why? They are my parents.
MESSENGER:
    No. You are not the son of Polybus.
OEDIPUS:
    What did you say? Polybus not my father? 970

MESSENGER:
    He was as much your father as I am.
OEDIPUS:
    How can that be—my father like a stranger?
MESSENGER:
    But he was *not* your father, nor am I.
OEDIPUS:
    If that is so, why was I called his son?
MESSENGER:
    Because he took you as a gift, from me.
OEDIPUS:
    Yet even so, he loved me like a father?
MESSENGER:
    Yes, for he had no children of his own.
OEDIPUS:
    And when you gave me, had you bought or found me?
MESSENGER:
    I found you in the glens of Mount Cithaeron.
OEDIPUS:
    What could have brought you to a place like that?   980
MESSENGER:
    The flocks of sheep that I was tending there.
OEDIPUS:
    You went from place to place, hunting for work?
MESSENGER:
    I did, my son. And yet I saved your life.
OEDIPUS:
    How? Was I suffering when you took me up?
MESSENGER:
    Your ankles are the proof of what you suffered.
OEDIPUS:
    That misery! Why do you speak of that?
MESSENGER:
    Your feet were pinned together, and I freed them.
OEDIPUS:
    Yes. From my cradle I have borne those scars.
MESSENGER:
    They are the reason for your present name.[5]
OEDIPUS:
    Who did it? Speak! My mother, or my father?   990
MESSENGER:
    Only the man who gave you to me knows.
OEDIPUS:
    Then you yourself did not discover me.
MESSENGER:
    No. A man put you in my arms, some shepherd.
OEDIPUS:
    Do you know who he was? Can you describe him?
MESSENGER:
    He was, I think, one of the slaves of Laius.
OEDIPUS:
    The Laius who was once the King of Thebes?
MESSENGER:
    Yes, that is right. King Laius was his master.
OEDIPUS:
    How could I see him? Is he still alive?
MESSENGER:
    One of his fellow Thebans would know that.
OEDIPUS:
    Does anyone here know who this shepherd is?   1000
    Has anyone ever seen him in the city
    Or in the fields? Tell me. Now is the time
    To solve this mystery once and for all.
CHORUS:
    Sir, I believe the shepherd whom he means
    Is the same man you have already sent for.
    The Queen, perhaps, knows most about the matter.
OEDIPUS:
    Do you, Jocasta? You know the man we summoned.
    Is he the man this messenger spoke about?
JOCASTA:
    Why do you care? What difference can it make?
    To ask is a waste of time, a waste of time!   1010
OEDIPUS:
    I cannot let these clues slip from my hands.
    I must track down the secret of my birth.
JOCASTA:
    Oedipus, Oedipus! By all the gods,
    If you set any value on your life,
    Give up this search! I have endured enough.
OEDIPUS:
    Do not be frightened. Even if my mother
    Should prove to be a slave, and born of slaves,
    This would not touch the honor of your name.
JOCASTA:
    Listen, I beg you! Listen! Do not do this!
OEDIPUS:
    I cannot fail to bring the truth to light.   1020
JOCASTA:
    I know my way is best for you, I know it!
OEDIPUS:
    I know your best way is unbearable.
JOCASTA:
    May you be saved from learning who you are!
OEDIPUS:
    Go, someone. Bring the shepherd. As for her,
    Let her take comfort in her noble birth.
JOCASTA:
    You are lost! Lost! That is all I can call you now!
    That is all I will ever call you, ever again!

                                    Exit JOCASTA

CHORUS:
    What wild grief, sir, has driven the Queen away?
    Evil, I fear, will follow from her silence,
    A storm of sorrow that will break upon us.   1030
OEDIPUS:
    Then let it break upon us I must learn
    My parentage, whatever it may be.
    The Queen is proud, far prouder than most women,
    And feels herself dishonored by my baseness.
    But I shall not be shamed. I hold myself
    The child of Fortune, giver of all good.
    She brought me forth. And as I lived my life,
    The months, my brothers, watched the ebb and flow
    Of my well-being. Never could I prove
    False to a lineage like that, or fail   1040
    To bring to light the secret of my birth.
CHORUS:
    May Phoebus grant that I prove a true prophet!
      My heart foreknows what the future will bring:
    At tomorrow's full moon we shall gather, in chorus
      To hail Cithaeron, to dance and sing
    In praise of the mountain by Oedipus honored,
      Theban nurse of our Theban King.

    What long-lived nymph was the mother who bore you?
      What god whom the joys of the hills invite

---

[5]The name *Oedipus* means "swollen foot."

Was the god who begot you? Pan? or Apollo?
Or Hermes, Lord of Cylené's height?
Or on Helicon's slope did an oread place you
In Bacchus's arms for his new delight?

OEDIPUS:
Elders, I think I see the shepherd coming
Whom we have sent for. Since I never met him,
I am not sure, yet he seems old enough,
And my own slaves are the men bringing him.
But you, perhaps, know more of this than I,
If any of you have seen the man before.

CHORUS:
Yes, it is he. I know him, the King's shepherd,
As true a slave as Laius ever had.

Enter SHEPHERD

OEDIPUS:
I start with you, Corinthian. Is this man
The one you spoke of?   MESS.: Sir, he stands before you.

OEDIPUS:
Now you, old man. Come, look me in the face.
Answer my questions. You were the slave of Laius?

SHEPHERD:
Yes, but not bought. I grew up in his household.

OEDIPUS:
What was the work that you were given to do?

SHEPHERD:
Sheep-herding. I have always been a shepherd.

OEDIPUS:
Where was it that you took your sheep to pasture?

SHEPHERD:
On Mount Cithaeron, or the fields near by.

OEDIPUS:
Do you remember seeing this man there?

SHEPHERD:
What was he doing? What man do you mean?

OEDIPUS:
That man beside you. Have you ever met him?

SHEPHERD:
No, I think not. I cannot recollect him.

MESSENGER:
Sir, I am not surprised, but I am sure
That I can make the past come back to him.
He cannot have forgotten the long summers
We grazed our sheep together by Cithaeron,
He with two flocks, and I with one—three years,
From spring to autumn. Then, for the winter months,
I used to drive my sheep to their own fold,
And he drove his back to the fold of Laius.
Is that right? Did it happen as I said?

SHEPHERD:
Yes, you are right, but it was long ago.

MESSENGER:
Well then, do you remember you once gave me
An infant boy to bring up as my own?

SHEPHERD:
What do you mean? Why do you ask me that?

MESSENGER:
Because the child you gave me stands before you.

SHEPHERD:
Will you be quiet? Curse you! Will you be quiet?

OEDIPUS (*to* SHEPHERD):
You there! You have no reason to be angry.
You are far more to blame in this than he.

SHEPHERD:
What have I done, my Lord? What have I done?

OEDIPUS:
You have not answered. He asked about the boy.

SHEPHERD:
Sir, he knows nothing, nothing at all about it.

OEDIPUS:
And you say nothing. We must make you speak.

SHEPHERD:
My Lord, I am an old man! Do not hurt me!

OEDIPUS (*to* GUARDS):
One of you tie his hands behind his back.

SHEPHERD:
Why do you want to know these fearful things?

OEDIPUS:
Did you, or did you not, give him that child?

SHEPHERD:
I did. I wish that I had died instead.

OEDIPUS:
You will die now, unless you tell the truth.

SHEPHERD:
And if I speak, I will be worse than dead.

OEDIPUS:
You seem to be determined to delay.

SHEPHERD:
No. No! I told you that I had the child.

OEDIPUS:
Where did it come from? Was it yours or not?

SHEPHERD:
No, it was not mine. Someone gave it to me.

OEDIPUS:
Some citizen of Thebes? Who was it? Who?

SHEPHERD:
Oh! Do not ask me that! Not that, my Lord!

OEDIPUS:
If I must ask once more, you are a dead man.

SHEPHERD:
The child came from the household of King Laius.

OEDIPUS:
Was it a slave's child? Or of royal blood?

SHEPHERD:
I stand on the very brink of speaking horrors.

OEDIPUS:
And I of hearing horrors—but I must.

SHEPHERD:
Then hear. The child was said to be the King's.
You can best learn about this from the Queen.

OEDIPUS:
The Queen! She gave it to you?   SHEP.: Yes, my Lord.

OEDIPUS:
Why did she do that?   SHEP.: So that I should kill it.

OEDIPUS:
Her own child?   SHEP.: Yes, she feared the oracles.

OEDIPUS:
What oracles?   SHEP.: That it must kill its father.

OEDIPUS:
Then why did you give it up to this old man?

SHEPHERD:
I pitied the poor child. I thought the man
Would take it with him back to his own country.
He saved its life only to have it come
At last to this. If you should be the man
He says you are, you were born miserable.

OEDIPUS:
>All true! All, all made clear! Let me no longer
>Look on the light of day. I am known now
>For what I am—I, cursed in being born,
>Cursed in my marriage, cursed in the blood I shed.
>>*Exeunt* OEDIPUS AND SHEPHERD

CHORUS:
>Men are of little worth. Their brief lives last
>>A single day.
>They cannot hold elusive pleasure fast;
>>It melts away.
>All laurels wither; all illusions fade;
>Hopes have been phantoms, shade on air-built shade,
>>Since time began.
>Your fate, O King, your fate makes manifest
>Life's wretchedness. We can call no one blessed,
>>No, not one man.
>
>Victorious, unerring, to their mark
>>Your arrows flew.
>The Sphinx with her curved claws, her riddle dark,
>>Your wisdom slew.
>By this encounter you preserved us all,
>Guarding the land from death's approach, our tall,
>>Unshaken tower.
>From that time, Oedipus, we held you dear,
>Great King of our great Thebes, without a peer
>>In place and power.
>
>But now what sadder story could be told?
>>A life of triumph utterly undone!
>What fate could be more grievous to behold?
>>Father and son
>Both found a sheltering port, a place of rest,
>>On the same breast.
>Father and son both harvested the yield
>>Of the same bounteous field.
>How could that earth endure such dreadful wrong
>>And hold its peace so long?
>All-seeing time condemned your marriage lot;
>>In ways you least expected bared its shame—
>Union wherein begetter and begot
>>Were both the same.
>This loud lament, these tears that well and flow,
>>This bitter woe
>Are for the day you rescued us, O King,
>>From our great suffering;
>For the new life and happiness you gave
>>You drag down to the grave.

Enter SECOND MESSENGER

SECOND MESSENGER:
>Most honored elders, princes of the land,
>If you are true-born Thebans and still love
>The house of Labdacus,[6] then what a burden
>Of sorrow you must bear, what fearful things
>You must now hear and see! There is no river—
>No, not the stream of Ister or of Phasis—
>That could wash clean this house from the pollution
>It hides within it or will soon bring forth:
>Horrible deeds not done in ignorance,
>But done deliberately. The cruelest evils
>Are those that we embrace with open eyes.

CHORUS:
>Those we already know of are enough
>To claim our tears. What more have you to tell?

SECOND MESSENGER:
>It may be briefly told. The Queen is dead.

CHORUS:
>Poor woman! oh, poor woman! How? What happened?

SECOND MESSENGER:
>She killed herself. You have been spared the worst,
>Not being witnesses. Yet you shall learn
>What her fate was, so far as I remember.
>When she came in, almost beside herself,
>Clutching her hair with both her hands, she rushed
>Straight to her bedroom and slammed shut the doors
>Behind her, screaming the name of Laius—
>Laius long dead, but not her memory
>Of their own child, the son who killed his father,
>The son by whom his mother had more children.
>She cursed the bed in which she had conceived
>Husband by husband, children by her child,
>A dreadful double bond. Beyond this much
>I do not know the manner of her death,
>For with a great cry Oedipus burst in,
>Preventing us from following her fate
>To its dark end. On him our gaze was fixed,
>As in a frenzy he ran to and fro,
>Calling: 'Give me a sword! Give me a sword!
>Where is that wife who is no wife, that mother,
>That soil where I was sower and was sown?'
>And as he raved, those of us there did nothing,
>Some more than mortal power directed him.
>With a wild shriek, as though he had some sign,
>He hurled himself against the double doors,
>Forcing the bars out of their loosened sockets,
>And broke into his room. There was the Queen,
>Hanged in a noose, still swinging back and forth.
>When he saw this, the King cried out in anguish,
>Untied the knotted cord in which she swung,
>And laid the wretched woman on the ground.
>What happened then was terrible to see.
>He tore the golden brooches from her robe,
>Lifted them up as high as he could reach,
>And drove them with all his strength into his eyes,
>Shrieking, 'No more, no more shall my eyes see
>The horrors of my life—what I have done,
>What I have suffered. They have looked too long
>On those whom they ought never to have seen.
>They never knew those whom I longed to see.
>Blind, blind! Let them be blind!' With these wild words
>He stabbed and stabbed his eyes. At every blow,
>The dark blood dyed his beard, not sluggish drops,
>But a great torrent like a shower of hail.
>A two-fold punishment of two-fold sin
>Broke on the heads of husband and of wife.
>Their happiness was once true happiness,
>But now disgrace has come upon them, death,
>Sorrow, and ruin, every earthly ill
>That can be named. Not one have they escaped.

CHORUS:
>Is he still suffering? Has he found relief?

SECOND MESSENGER:
>He calls for someone to unbar the doors
>And show him to all Thebes, his father's killer,
>His mother's—no, I cannot say the word;
>It is unholy, horrible. He intends
>To leave the country, for his staying here

---

[6] Labdacus was a grandson of Cadmus and the father of Laius.

Would bring down his own curse upon his house. 1240
He has no guide and no strength of his own.
His pain is unendurable. This too
You will see. They are drawing back the bars.
The sight is loathsome and yet pitiful.

Enter OEDIPUS

CHORUS: Hideous, hideous! I have seen nothing so dreadful,
    Ever before!
      I can look no more.
  Oedipus, Oedipus! What madness has come upon you?
    What malignant fate
      Has leaped with its full weight, 1250
  Has struck you down with an irresistible fury,
    And born you off as its prey?
      Poor wretch! There is much that I yearn
      To ask of you, much I would learn;
  But I cannot. The sight of you fills me with horror!
    I shudder and turn away.

OEDIPUS: Oh, Oh! What pain! I cannot rest in my anguish!
    Where am I? Where?
  Where are my words? They die away as I speak them,
    Into thin air. 1260
      What is my fate to be?

CHORUS: A fate too fearful for men to hear of, for men to see.

OEDIPUS: Lost! Overwhelmed by the rush of unspeakable darkness!
    It smothers me in its cloud.
      The pain of my eyes is piercing.
  The thought of my sins, the horrors that I have committed,
    Racks me without relief.

CHORUS: No wonder you suffer, Oedipus, no wonder you cry aloud
    Under your double burden of pain and grief.

OEDIPUS: My friend, my friend! How steadfast you are, how ready 1270
    To help me in my great need!
      I feel your presence beside me.
  Blind as I am, I know your voice in the blackness
    Of my long-lasting night.

CHORUS: How could you put out your eyes, still another infamous deed?
    What god, what demon, induced you to quench their light?

OEDIPUS: It was Apollo, my friends, who brought me low,
  Apollo who crushed me beneath this unbearable burden;
    But it was my hand, mine, that struck the blow.
    Why should I see? What sight could have given me pleasure?

CHORUS: These things are as you say.

OEDIPUS: What is there now to love? What greeting can cheer me?
    Lead me away,
      Quickly, quickly! O lead me out of the country
      To a distant land! I am beyond redemption
      Accursed, beyond hope lost, the one man living
      Whom all the gods most hate.

CHORUS: Would we had never heard of your existence,
    Your fruitless wisdom and your wretched fate.

OEDIPUS: My curses be upon him, whoever freed 1290
    My feet from the cruel fetters, there on the mountain,
      Who restored me from death to life, a thankless deed.
    My death would have saved my friends and me from anguish.

CHORUS: I too would have had it so.

OEDIPUS: Then would I never have been my father's killer.
    Now all men know
  That I am the infamous son who defiled his mother,
    That I shared the bed of the father who gave me being.
  And if there is sorrow beyond any mortal sorrow,
    I have brought it upon my head. 1300

CHORUS: I cannot say that you have acted wisely.
    Alive and blind? You would be better dead.

OEDIPUS: Give me no more advice, and do not tell me
That I was wrong. What I have done is best.
For if I still had eyesight when I went
Down to the underworld, how could I bear
To see my father and my wretched mother?
After the terrible wrong I did them both,
It would not have been punishment enough
If I had hanged myself. Or do you think 1310
That I could find enjoyment in the sight
Of children born as mine were born? No! No!
Nor in the sight of Thebes with its towered walls
And sacred statues of the gods. For I—
Who is so wretched?—I, the foremost Theban,
Cut myself off from this by my own edict
That ordered everyone to shun the man
Polluting us, the man the gods have shown
To be accursed, and of the house of Laius.
Once I laid bare my shame, could I endure 1320
To look my fellow-citizens in the face?
Never! Never! If I had found some way
Of choking off the fountain of my hearing,
I would have made a prison of my body,
Sightless and soundless. It would be sweet to live
Beyond the reach of sorrow. Oh, Cithaeron!
Why did you give me shelter rather than slay me
As soon as I was given to you? Then
No one would ever have heard of my begetting.
Polybus, Corinth, and the ancient house 1330
I thought my forebears'! You reared me as a child.
My fair appearance covered foul corruption,
I am impure, born of impurity.
Oh, narrow crossroad where the three paths meet!
Secluded valley hidden in the forest,
You that drank up my blood, my father's blood
Shed by my hands, do you remember all
I did for you to see? Do you remember
What else I did when I came here to Thebes?
Oh marriage rites! By which I was begotten, 1340
You then brought forth children by your own child,
Creating foulest blood-relationship:
An interchange of fathers, brothers, sons,
Brides, wives, and mothers—the most monstrous shame
Man can be guilty of. I should not speak
Of what should not be done. By all the gods,
Hide me, I beg you, hide me quickly somewhere
Far, far away. Put me to death or throw me
Into the sea, out of your sight forever.
Come to me, friends, pity my wretchedness. 1350
Let your hands touch me. Hear me. Do not fear,
My curse can rest on no one but myself.

CHORUS: Creon is coming. He is the one to act
On your requests, or to help you with advice.
He takes your place as our sole guardian.

OEDIPUS: Creon! What shall I say? I cannot hope
That he will trust me now, when my past hatred
Has proved to be so utterly mistaken.

Enter CREON

CREON:
    I have not come to mock you, Oedipus,
    Or to reproach you for any evil-doing.   1360
    (*to* ATTENDANTS) You there. If you have lost all your respect
    For men, revere at least the Lord Apollo,
    Whose flame supports all life. Do not display
    So nakedly pollution such as this,
    Evil that neither earth nor holy rain
    Nor light of day can welcome. Take him in,
    Take him in, quickly. Piety demands
    That only kinsmen share a kinsman's woe.

OEDIPUS:
    Creon, since you have proved my fears were groundless,
    Since you have shown such magnanimity   1370
    To one so vile as I, grant my petition.
    I ask you not for my sake but your own.

CREON:
    What is it that you beg so urgently?

OEDIPUS:
    Drive me away at once. Drive me far off.
    Let me not hear a human voice again.

CREON:
    I have delayed only because I wished
    To have the god reveal to me my duty.

OEDIPUS:
    But his command was certain: put to death
    The unholy parricide. And I am he.

CREON:
    True. But as things are now, it would be better   1380
    To find out clearly what we ought to do.

OEDIPUS:
    An oracle for a man so miserable?

CREON:
    Yes. Even you will now believe the god.

OEDIPUS:
    I will. Creon, I charge you with this duty.
    Accept it, I entreat you. Give to her
    Who lies within such burial as you wish,
    For she belongs to you. You will perform
    The proper obsequies. But as for me,
    Let not my presence doom my father's city,
    But send me to the hills, to Mount Cithaeron,   1390
    My mountain, which my mother and my father
    Chose for my grave. So will I die at last
    By the decree of those who sought to slay me.
    And yet I know I will not die from sickness
    Or anything else. I was preserved from death
    To meet some awful, some mysterious end.
    My own fate does not matter, only my children's.
    Creon, my sons need give you no concern,
    For they are men, and can find anywhere
    A livelihood. But Creon, my two girls!   1400
    How lost, how pitiable! They always ate
    Their daily bread with me, at my own table,
    And had their share of everything I touched.
    Take care of them! O Creon, take care of them!
    And one thing more—if I could only touch them
    And with them weep. O prince, prince, grant me this!
    Grant it, O noble Creon! If I touched them,
    I could believe I saw them once again.

Enter ISMENE *and* ANTIGONE

    What! Do I hear my daughters? Hear them sobbing?
    Has Creon had pity on me? Has he sent them,   1410
    My children, my two darlings? Is it true?

CREON:
    Yes. I have had them brought. I knew how much
    You used to love them, how you love them still.

OEDIPUS:
    May the gods bless you, Creon, for this kindness;
    And may they guard you better on your journey
    Than they have guarded me. Children, where are you?
    Come to your brother's hands, the hands that made
    Your father's clear eyes into what these are—
    Your father, who saw nothing and knew nothing,
    Begetting you where he had been conceived.   1420
    I cannot see you, but I weep for you,
    Weep for the bitter lives that you must lead
    Henceforward. Never, never will you go
    To an assembly with the citizens,
    Or to a festival, and take your part.
    You will turn back in tears. And when you come
    To the full bloom of womanhood, what man
    Will run the risk of bringing on himself
    Your shame, my daughters, and your children's shame?
    Is there one evil, one, that is not ours?   1430
    'Your father killed his father; he begot
    Children of his own mother; she who bore you
    Bore him as well.' These are the taunts, the insults
    That you will hear. Who, then, will marry you?
    No one, my children. Clearly it is your fate
    To waste away in barren maidenhood.
    Creon, Creon, their blood flows in your veins.
    You are the only father left to them;
    They have lost both their parents. Do not let them
    Wander away, unmarried, destitute,   1440
    As miserable as I. Have pity on them,
    So young, so utterly forlorn, so helpless
    Except for you. You are kind-hearted. Touch me
    To tell me that I have your promise. Children,
    There is so much, so much that I would say,
    If you were old enough to understand it,
    But now I only teach you this one prayer:
    May I be given a place in which to live,
    And may my life be happier than my father's.

CREON:
    Come, come with us. Have done with further woe.   1450

OE.: Obedience is hard.   CR.: No good in life endures beyond
    its season.

OE.: Do you know why I yield?   CR.: When I have heard your
    reason I will know.

OE.: You are to banish me.   CR.: The gods alone can grant you
    that entreaty.

OE.: I am hated by the gods.   CR.: Then their response to you
    will not be slow.

OE.: So you consent to this?   CR.: I say no more than I have
    said already.

OE.: Come, then, lead me away.   CR.: Not with your children.
    You must let them go.

OE.: Creon, not that, not that!   CR.: You must be patient.
    Nothing can restore
    Your old dominion. You are King no more.

Exeunt CREON, OEDIPUS, ISMENE, *and* ANTIGONE

CHORUS:
    Behold him, Thebans: Oedipus, great and wise,
    Who solved the famous riddle. This is he   1460
      Whom all men gazed upon with envious eyes,
    Who now is struggling in a stormy sea,
      Crushed by the billows of his bitter woes.
    Look to the end of mortal life. In vain
      We say a man is happy, till he goes
    Beyond life's final border, free from pain.

Thucydides

This oration is one given by the great Athenian leader Pericles as reported by Thucydides in his work *The History of the Peloponnesian War*.

Thucydides, considered to be one of the world's greatest historians, was interested in wars and thought that the Peloponnesian war was a major event in world history. Therefore, he carefully recorded its history. Actually the war, fought between Sparta and Athens, was very much a civil war among the Greek city states, and this oration was delivered during the war. Pericles was the leader of Athens for fourteen years from 445 B.C. to about 431 B.C. During this period, known as the Age of Pericles, Athens reached a high point in both political and cultural development. One notable achievement of the period was the erection of the Parthenon.

Pericles, in this oration, spoke to the relatives of those who had been killed in a particular battle. The bones of the warriors had been collected and piled next to the tent where the relatives and friends were gathered.

Note in particular the description of Athenian democracy and the ideals of the Athenian way of life. Also of importance is the attitude which Pericles has toward the supreme sacrifice which these men made for Athens.

FUNERAL ORATION

"Most of those who have spoken here before me have commended the lawgiver who added this oration to our other funeral customs; it seemed to them a worthy thing that such an honor should be given at their burial to the dead who have fallen on the field of battle. But I should have preferred that, when men's deeds have been brave, they should be honored in deed only, and with such an honor as this public funeral, which you are now witnessing. Then the reputation of many would not have been imperilled on the eloquence or want of eloquence of one, and their virtues believed or not as he spoke well or ill. For it is difficult to say neither too little nor too much; and even moderation is apt not to give the impression of truthfulness. The friend of the dead who knows the facts is likely to think that the words of the speaker fall short of his knowledge and of his wishes; another who is not so well informed, when he hears of anything which surpasses his own powers, will be envious and will suspect exaggeration. Mankind are tolerant of the praises of others so long as each hearer thinks that he can do as well or nearly as well himself, but, when the speaker rises above him, jealousy is aroused and he begins to be incredulous. However, since our ancestors have set the seal of their approval upon the practice, I must obey, and to the utmost of my power shall endeavor to satisfy the wishes and beliefs of all who hear me.

"I will speak first of our ancestors, for it is right and becoming that now, when we are lamenting the dead, a tribute should be paid to their memory. There has never been a time when they did not inhabit this land, which by their valor they have handed down from generation to generation, and we have received from them a free state. But if they were worthy of praise, still more were our fathers, who added to their inheritance, and after many a struggle transmitted to us their sons this great empire. And we ourselves assembled here to-day, who are still most of us in the vigor of life, have chiefly done the work of improvement, and have richly endowed our city with all things, so that she is sufficient for herself both in peace and war. Of the military exploits by which our various possessions were acquired, or of the energy with which we or our fathers drove back the tide of war, Hellenic or Barbarian, I will not speak; for the tale would be long and is familiar to you. But before I praise the dead, I should like to point out by what principles of action we rose to power, and under what institutions and through what manner of life our empire became great. For I conceive that such thoughts are not unsuited to the occasion, and that this numerous assembly of citizens and strangers may profitably listen to them.

From Thucydides, *History of the Peloponnesian War*, translated by Benjamin Jowett (Boston: Lothrop, 1883).

"Our form of government does not enter into rivalry with the institutions of others. We do not copy our neighbors, but are an example to them. It is true that we are called a democracy, for the administration is in the hands of the many and not of the few. But while the law secures equal justice to all alike in their private disputes, the claim of excellence is also recognized; and when a citizen is in any way distinguished, he is preferred to the public service, not as a matter of privilege, but as the reward of merit. Neither is poverty a bar, but a man may benefit his country whatever be the obscurity of his condition. There is no exclusiveness in our public life, and in our private intercourse we are not suspicious of one another, nor angry with our neighbor if he does what he likes; we do not put on sour looks at him which, though harmless, are not pleasant. While we are thus unconstrained in our private intercourse, a spirit of reverence pervades our public acts; we are prevented from doing wrong by respect for authority and for the laws, having an especial regard to those which are ordained for the protection of the injured as well as to those unwritten laws which bring upon the transgressor of them the reprobation of the general sentiment.

"And we have not forgotten to provide for our weary spirits many relaxations from toil; we have regular games and sacrifices throughout the year; at home the style of our life is refined; and the delight which we daily feel in all these things helps to banish melancholy. Because of the greatness of our city the fruits of the whole earth flow in upon us; so that we enjoy the goods of other countries as freely as of our own.

"Then, again, our military training is in many respects superior to that of our adversaries. Our city is thrown open to the world, and we never expel a foreigner or prevent him from seeing or learning anything of which the secret if revealed to an enemy might profit him. We rely not upon management or trickery, but upon our own hearts and hands. And in the matter of education, whereas they from early youth are always undergoing laborious exercises which are to make them brave, we live at ease, and yet are equally ready to face the perils which they face. And here is the proof. The Lacedaemonians come into Attica not by themselves, but with their whole confederacy following; we go alone into a neighbor's country; and although our opponents are fighting for their homes and we on a foreign soil, we have seldom any difficulty in overcoming them. Our enemies have never yet felt our united strength; the care of a navy divides our attention, and on land we are obliged to send our own citizens everywhere. But they, if they meet and defeat a part of our army, are as proud as if they had routed us all, and when defeated they pretend to have been vanquished by us all.

"If then we prefer to meet danger with a light heart but without laborious training, and with a courage which is gained by habit and not enforced by law, are we not greatly the gainers? Since we do not anticipate the pain, although, when the hour comes, we can be as brave as those who never allow themselves to rest; and thus too our city is equally admirable in peace and in war. For we are lovers of the beautiful, yet simple in our tastes, and we cultivate the mind without loss of manliness. Wealth we employ, not for talk and ostentation, but when there is a real use for it. To avow poverty with us is no disgrace: the true disgrace is in doing nothing to avoid it. An Athenian citizen does not neglect the state because he takes care of his own household; and even those of us who are engaged in business have a very fair idea of politics. We alone regard a man who takes no interest in public affairs, not as a harmless, but as a useless character; and if few of us are originators, we are all sound judges of a policy. The great impediment to action is, in our opinion, not discussion, but the want of that knowledge which is gained by discussion preparatory to action. For we have a peculiar power of thinking before we act and of acting too, whereas other men are courageous from ignorance but hesitate upon reflection. And they are surely to be esteemed the bravest spirits who, having the clearest sense both of the pains and pleasures of life, do not on that account shrink from danger. In doing good, again, we are unlike others; we make our friends by conferring, not by receiving favors. Now he who confers a favor is the firmer friend, because he would fain by kindness keep alive the memory of an obligation; but the recipient is colder in his feelings, because he knows that in requiting another's generosity he will not be winning gratitude, but only paying a debt. We alone do good to our neighbors not upon a calculation of interest, but in the confidence of freedom and in a frank and fearless spirit. To sum up: I say that Athens is the school of Hellas, and that the individual Athenian in his own person seems to have the power of adapting himself to the most varied forms of action with the utmost versatility and grace. This is no passing and idle word, but truth and fact; and the assertion is verified by the position to which these qualities have raised the state. For in the hour of trial Athens alone among her contemporaries is superior to the report of her. No enemy who comes against her is indignant at the reverses which he sustains at the hands of such a city; no subject complains that his masters are unworthy of him. And we shall assuredly not be without witnesses; there are mighty monuments of our power which will make us the wonder of this and of succeeding ages; we shall not need the praises of Homer or of any other panegyrist whose poetry may please for the moment, although his representation of the facts will not bear the light of day. For we have compelled every land and every sea to open a path for our valor, and have everywhere planted eternal memorials of our friendship and of our enmity. Such is the city for whose sake these men nobly fought and died; they could not bear the thought that she might be taken from them; and every one of us who survive should gladly toil on her behalf.

"I have dwelt upon the greatness of Athens because I want to show you that we are contending for a higher prize than those who enjoy none of these privileges, and to establish by manifest proof the merit of these men whom I am now commemorating. Their loftiest praise has been already spoken. For in magnifying the city I have magnified them, and men like them whose virtues made her glorious. And of how few Hellenes can it be said as of them, that their deeds when weighed in the balance have been found equal to their fame! Methinks that a death such as theirs has been gives the true measure of a man's worth; it may be the first revelation of his virtues, but is at any rate their final seal. For even those who come short in other ways may justly plead the valor with which they have fought for their country; they have blotted out the evil with the good, and have benefited the state more by their public services than they have injured her by their private actions. None of these men were enervated by wealth or hesitated to resign the pleasures of life; none of them put off the evil day in the hope, natural to poverty, that a man, though poor, may one day become rich. But, deeming that the punishment of their enemies was sweeter than any of these things, and that they could fall in no nobler cause, they determined at the hazard of their lives to be honorably avenged, and to leave the rest. They resigned to hope their unknown chance of happiness; but in the face of death they resolved to rely upon themselves alone. And when the moment came they were minded to resist and suffer, rather than to fly and save their lives; they ran away from the word of dishonor, but on the battle-field their feet stood fast, and in an instant, at the height of their fortune, they passed away from the scene, not of their fear, but of their glory.

"Such was the end of these men; they were worthy of Athens, and the living need not desire to have a more heroic spirit although they may pray for a less fatal issue. The value of such a spirit is not to be expressed in words. Any one can discourse to you for ever about the advantages of a brave defence which you know already. But instead of listening to him I would have you day by day fix your eyes upon the greatness of Athens, until you become filled with the love of her; and when you are impressed by the spectacle of her glory, reflect that this empire has been acquired by men who knew their duty and had the courage to do it, who in the hour of conflict had the fear of dishonor always present to them, and who, if ever they failed in an enterprise, would not allow their virtues to be lost to their country, but freely gave their lives to her as the fairest offering which they could present at her feast. The sacrifice which they collectively made was individually repaid to them; for they received again each one for himself a praise which grows not old, and the noblest of all sepulchres—I speak not of that in which their remains are laid, but of that in which their glory survives, and is proclaimed always and on every fitting occasion both in word and deed. For the whole earth is the sepulchre of famous men; not only are they commemorated by columns and inscriptions in their own country, but in foreign lands there dwells also an unwritten memorial of them, graven not on stone but in the hearts of men. Make them your examples, and, esteeming courage to be freedom and freedom to be happiness, do not weigh too nicely the perils of war. The unfortunate who has no hope of a change for the better has less reason to throw away his life than the prosperous who, if he survive, is always liable to a change for the worse, and to whom any accidental fall makes the most serious difference. To a man of spirit, cowardice and disaster coming together are far more bitter than death, striking him unperceived at a time when he is full of courage and animated by the general hope.

"Wherefore I do not now commiserate the parents of the dead who stand here; I would rather comfort them. You know that your life has been passed amid manifold vicissitudes; and that they may be deemed fortunate who have gained most honor, whether an honorable death like theirs, or an honorable sorrow like yours, and whose days have been so ordered that the term of their happiness is likewise the term of their life. I know how hard it is to make you feel this, when the good fortune of others will too often remind you of the gladness which once lightened your hearts. And sorrow is felt at the want of those blessings, not which a man never knew, but which were a part of his life before they were taken from him. Some of you are of an age at which they may hope to have other children, and they ought to bear their sorrow better; not only will the children who may hereafter be born make them forget their own lost ones, but the city will be doubly a gainer. She will not be left desolate, and she will be safer. For a Man's counsel cannot have equal weight or worth, when he alone has no children to risk in the general danger. To those of you who have passed their prime, I say; 'Congratulate yourselves that you have been happy during the greater part of your days; remember that your life of sorrow will not last long, and be comforted by the glory of those who are gone. For the love of honor alone is ever young, and not riches, as some say, but honor is the delight of men when they are old and useless.'

"To you who are the sons and brothers of the departed, I see that the struggle to emulate them will be an arduous one. For all men praise the dead, and, however pre-eminent your virtue may be, hardly will you be thought, I do not say to equal, but even to approach them. The living have their rivals and detractors, but when a man is out of the way, the honor and good-will which he receives is unalloyed. And, If I am to speak of womanly virtues to those of you who will henceforth be widows, let me sum them up in one short admonition: To a woman not to show more weakness than is natural to her sex is a great glory, and not to be talked about for good or for evil among men.

"I have paid the required tribute, in obedience to the law, making use of such fitting words as I had. The tribute of deeds has been paid in part; for the dead have been honorably interred, and it remains only that their children should be maintained at the public charge until they are grown up; this is the solid prize with which, as with a garland, Athens crowns her sons living and dead, after a struggle like theirs. For where the rewards of virtue are greatest, there the noblest citizens are enlisted in the service of the state. And now, when you have duly lamented, every one his own dead, you may depart."

Such was the order of the funeral celebrated in this winter, with the end of which ended the first year of the Peloponnesian War.

Plato

Plato (427-347 B.C.) was a younger friend and the greatest disciple of Socrates. Many believe that he was the greatest thinker who ever lived; certainly it is safe to say he was one of the two or three most influential thinkers in history. A member of the aristocracy, he received a well-rounded education. After the death of Socrates he left Athens and traveled widely. About the year 387 he established the Academy in Athens and there he became a celebrated teacher. You will note from the selections you read that he did not write in cold academic form but dramatized his philosophy in dialogue. Reputedly he is one of the great literary stylists of all time.

Although his writings ranged over a wide variety of concepts and ideas, it is possible to arrange his thought under three major headings: (1) the universe and how man knows it; (2) ethics; and (3) the community. You will note in the selections which follow how these areas are covered by Plato.

Included in these readings are selections from the *Apology*, the *Crito*, *Phaedo* and *The Republic*.

In the *Apology* we read of the defense delivered by Socrates before the law court. It is almost certain that this was not the actual speech but it does represent the ideas of a man who refused to abandon his convictions even at the risk of his own life.

In the next selection, the *Crito*, we are told of certain events which took place while Socrates was in prison awaiting his death. Note as you read this selection how Socrates was urged to escape and how everything had been arranged. Socrates, however, refused to do so, stating what he considered to be his responsibility toward himself, toward the philosophy which he had preached throughout his life and toward the city state. In this selection also note Socrates' thoughts about democracy and the principal characteristics of a good man.

In the third selection, the *Phaedo*, we have a description of the death of Socrates. Here Socrates engaged in a discussion of suicide, immortality and the goal of the true philosopher. Note also his ideas concerning the soul. Finally, at the close of the selection comes the very moving description of the death of Socrates.

The final selection is from *The Republic*, which is a long discussion by Socrates of the ideal state in which every person was placed in the position for which he was designed by nature. The population was divided into two general classes, those who would work and those who would fight, govern and philosophize. This division was made on the basis of fitness, determined by rigid state-conducted tests. It is basically the description of a totalitarian state which bears an obvious resemblance to Sparta.

In this state the upper classes did not have private property, homes or families of their own. The purpose of this was to free the ruling classes from personal greed and narrow family loyalty, which so often had been the ruin of other aristocracies. The views expressed on the education of children and the position of women within the republic are of particular interest. Also note the great emphasis which Plato placed upon knowledge.

The selection closes with a segment from Book VII, usually known as the "Allegory of the Cave." Here we are confronted with one of Plato's major philosophical theories, his belief that the world revealed by our senses is not the real world but only a poor copy of it, and that the real world can be apprehended only intellectually. We also see the implication that education consists not of transferring knowledge from teacher to student but rather of directing the student's mind toward what is real and important and allowing him to apprehend it for himself. Finally, we see his faith that the universe is ultimately good and his conviction that enlightened men have an obligation to the rest of society.

SELECTIONS FROM THE APOLOGY[1]

How you, O Athenians, have been affected by my accusers, I cannot tell; but I know that they almost made me forget who I was — so persuasively did they speak; and yet they have hardly uttered a word of truth. But of the many falsehoods told by them, there was one which quite amazed me; — I mean when they said that you should be upon your guard and not allow yourselves to be deceived by the force of my eloquence. To say this, when they were certain to be detected as soon as I opened my lips and proved myself to be anything but a great speaker, did indeed appear to me most shameless — unless by the force of eloquence they mean the force of truth; for if such is their meaning, I admit that I am eloquent. But in how different a way from theirs! Well, as I was saying, they have scarcely spoken the truth at all; but from me you shall hear the whole truth: not, however, delivered after their manner in a set oration duly ornamented with words and phrases. No, by heaven! but I shall use the words and arguments which occur to me at the moment; for I am confident in the justice of my cause: at my time of life I ought not to be appearing before you, O men of Athens, in the character of a juvenile orator — let no one expect it of me. And I must beg of you to grant me a favour: — If I defend myself in my accustomed manner, and you hear me using the words which I have been in the habit of using in the agora, at the tables of the money-changers, or anywhere else, I would ask you not to be surprised, and not to interrupt me on this account. For I am more than seventy years of age, and appearing now for the first time in a court of law, I am quite a stranger to the language of the place; and therefore I would have you regard me as if I were really a stranger, whom you would excuse if he spoke in his native tongue, and after the fashion of his country. — Am I making an unfair request of you? Never mind the manner, which may or may not be good; but think only of the truth of my words, and give heed to that: let the speaker speak truly and the judge decide justly.

And first, I have to reply to the older charges and to my first accusers, and then I will go on to the later ones. For of old I have had many accusers, who have accused me falsely to you during many years; and I am more afraid of them than of Anytus and his associates, who are dangerous, too, in their own way. But far more dangerous are the others, who began when you were children, and took possession of your minds with their falsehoods, telling of one Socrates, a wise man, who speculated about the heaven above, and searched into the earth beneath, and made the worse appear the better cause. The disseminators of this tale are the accusers whom I dread; for their hearers are apt to fancy that such enquirers do not believe in the existence of the gods. And they are many, and their charges against me are of ancient date, and they were made by them in the days when you were more impressible than you are now — in childhood, or it may have been in youth — and the cause when heard went by default, for there was none to answer. And hardest of all, I do not know and cannot tell the names of my accusers; unless in the chance case of a comic poet. All who from envy and malice have persuaded you — some of them having first convinced themselves — all this class of men are most difficult to deal with; for I cannot have them up here, and cross-examine them, and therefore I must simply fight with shadows in my own defence, and argue when there is no one who answers. I will ask you then to assume with me, as I was saying, that my opponents are of two kinds; one recent, the other ancient: and I hope that you will see the propriety of my answering the latter first, for these accusations you heard long before the others, and much oftener.

Well, then, I must make my defence, and endeavour to clear away in a short time, a slander which has lasted a long time. May I succeed, if to succeed be for my good and yours, or likely to avail me in my cause! The task is not an easy one; I quite understand the nature of it. And so leaving the event with God, in obedience to the law I will now make my defence.

I will begin at the beginning, and ask what is the accusation which has given rise to the slander of me, and in fact has encouraged Meletus to prefer this charge against me. Well, what do the slanderers say? They shall be my prosecutors, and I will sum up their words in an affidavit: "Socrates is an evil-doer, and a curious person, who searches into things under the earth and in heaven, and he makes the worse appear the better cause; and he teaches the aforesaid doctrines to others." Such is the nature of the accusation: It is just what you have yourselves seen in the comedy of Aristophanes, who has introduced a man whom he calls Socrates, going about and saying that he walks in air, and talking a deal of nonsense concerning matters of which I do not pretend to know either much or little — not that I mean to speak disparagingly of any one who is a student of natural philosophy. I should be very sorry if Meletus could bring so grave a charge against me. But the simple truth is, O Athenians, that I have nothing to do with physical speculations. Very many of those here present are witnesses to the truth of this, and to them I appeal. Speak then, you who have

---
[1] Translated by Benjamin Jowett. Published by The Clarendon Press, Oxford. Plato's version of Socrates' speech of defense at his trial in 399 B.C. is much idealized.

heard me. and tell your neighbors whether any of you have ever known me hold forth in a few words or in many upon such matters . . . You hear their answer. And from what they say of this part of the charge you will be able to judge of the truth of the rest.

. . . .

I may say, Athenians, that some one among you will reply, "Yes, Socrates, but what is the origin of these accusations which are brought against you; there must have been something strange which you have been doing? All these rumours and this talk about you would never have arisen if you had been like other men: tell us, then, what is the cause of them, for we should be sorry to judge hastily of you." Now, I regard this as a fair challenge, and I will endeavour to explain to you the reason why I am called wise and have such an evil fame. Please to attend then. And although some of you may think that I am joking, I declare that I will tell you the entire truth. Men of Athens, this reputation of mine has come of a certain sort of wisdom which I possess. If you ask me what kind of wisdom, I reply, wisdom such as may perhaps be attained by man, for to that extent I am inclined to believe that I am wise; whereas the persons of whom I was speaking have a superhuman wisdom, which I may fail to describe, because I have it not myself; and he who says that I have, speaks falsely, and is taking away my character. And here, O men of Athens, I must beg you not to interrupt me, even if I seem to say something extravagant. For the word which I will speak is not mine. I will refer you to a witness who is worthy of credit; that witness shall be the god of Delphi — he will tell you about my wisdom, if I have any, and of what sort it is. You must have known Chaerephon; he was early a friend of mine, and also a friend of yours, for he shared in the recent exile of the people, and returned with you. Well, Chaerephon, as you know, was very impetuous in all his doings, and he went to Delphi and boldly asked the oracle to tell him whether — as I was saying, I must beg you not to interrupt — he asked the oracle to tell him whether any one was wiser than I was, and the Pythian prophetess answered, that there was no man wiser. Chaerephon is dead himself; but his brother, who is in court, will confirm the truth of what I am saying.

Why do I mention this? Because I am going to explain to you why I have such an evil name. When I heard the answer, I said to myself, What can the god mean? and what is the interpretation of his riddle? for I know that I have no wisdom, small or great. What then can he mean when he says that I am the wisest of men? And yet he is a god, and cannot lie; that would be against his nature. After long consideration, I thought of a method of trying the question. I reflected that if I could only find a man wiser than myself, then I might go to the god with a refutation in my hand. I should say to him, "Here is a man who is wiser than I am; but you said that I was the wisest." Accordingly I went to one who had the reputation of wisdom, and observed him — his name I need not mention; he was a politician whom I selected for examination — and the result was as follows: When I began to talk with him, I could not help thinking that he was not really wise, although he was thought wise by many, and still wiser by himself; and thereupon I tried to explain to him that he thought himself wise, but was not really wise, and the consequence was that he hated me, and his enmity was shared by several who were present and heard me. So I left him, saying to myself, as I went away: Well, although I do not suppose that either of us knows anything really beautiful and good, I am better off than he is, — for he knows nothing, and thinks that he knows; I neither know nor think that I know. In this latter particular, then, I seem to have slightly the advantage of him. Then I went to another who had still higher pretensions to wisdom, and my conclusion was exactly the same. Whereupon I made another enemy of him, and of many others besides him.

. . . .

This inquisition has led to my having many enemies of the worst and most dangerous kind, and has given occasion also to many calumnies. And I am called wise, for my hearers always imagine that I myself possess the wisdom which I find wanting in others: but the truth is, O men of Athens, that God only is wise; and by his answer he intends to show that the wisdom of men is worth little or nothing; he is not speaking of Socrates, he is only using my name by way of illustration, as if he said, He, O men, is the wisest, who, like Socrates, knows that his wisdom is in truth worth nothing. And so I go about the world obedient to the god, and search and make enquiry into the wisdom of any one, whether citizen or stranger, who appears to be wise; and if he is not wise, then in vindication of the oracle I show him that he is not wise; and my occupation quite absorbs me, and I have no time to give either to any public matter of interest or to any concern of my own, but I am in utter poverty by reason of my devotion to the god.

. . . .

I have said enough in my defence against the first class of my accusers; I turn to the second class. They are headed by Meletus, that good man and true lover of his country as he calls himself. Against these, too, I must try to make a defence: — Let their affidavit be read: it contains something of this kind: It says that Socrates is a doer of evil, who corrupts the youth; and who does not believe in the gods of the State, but has other new divinities of his own. Such is the charge; and now let us examine the particular counts. He says that I am a doer of evil, and corrupt the youth; but I say, O men of Athens, that Meletus is a doer of evil, in that he pretends to be in earnest when he is only in jest, and is so eager to bring men to trial from a pretended zeal and interest about matters in which he really never had the smallest interest. And the truth of this I will endeavour to prove to you.

. . . .

And now, Meletus, I will ask you another question — by Zeus I will: Which is better, to live among bad citizens, or among good ones? Answer, friend, I say; the question is one which may be easily answered. Do not the good do their neighbours good, and the bad do them evil?

Certainly.

And is there any one who would rather be injured than benefited by those who live with him? Answer, my good friend, the law requires you to answer — does any one like to be injured?

Certainly not.

And when you accuse me of corrupting and deteriorating the youth, do you allege that I corrupt them intentionally or unintentionally?

Intentionally, I say.

But you have just admitted that the good do their neighbours good, and the evil do them evil. Now, is that a truth which your superior wisdom has recognized thus early in life, and am I, at my age, in such darkness and ignorance as not to know that if a man with whom I have to live is corrupted by me, I am very likely to be harmed by him; and yet I corrupt him, and intentionally, too — so you say, although neither I nor any other human being is ever likely to be convinced by you. But either I do not corrupt them, or I corrupt them unintentionally; and on either view of the case you lie. If my offence is unintentional, the law has no cognizance of unintentional offences: you ought to have taken me privately, and warned and admonished me; for if I had been better advised, I should have left off doing what I only did unintentionally — no doubt I should, but you would have nothing to say to me and refused to teach me. And now you bring me up in this court, which is a place not of instruction, but of punishment.

It will be very clear to you, Athenians, as I was saying, that Meletus has no care at all, great or small, about the matter. But still I should like to know, Meletus, in what I am affirmed to corrupt the young. I suppose you mean, as I infer from your indictment, that I teach them not to acknowledge the gods which the State acknowledges, but some other new divinities or spiritual agencies in their stead. These are the lessons by which I corrupt the youth, as you say.

Yes, that I say emphatically.

Then, by the gods, Meletus, of whom we are speaking, tell me and the court, in somewhat plainer terms, what you mean! For I do not as yet understand whether you affirm that I teach other men to acknowledge some gods, and therefore that I do believe in gods, and am not an entire atheist — this you do not lay to my charge, — but only you say that they are not the same gods which the city recognizes — the charge is that they are different gods. Or, do you mean that I am an atheist simply, and a teacher of atheism?

I mean the latter — that you are a complete atheist.

What an extraordinary statement! Why do you think so, Meletus? Do you mean that I do not believe in the godhead of the sun, or moon, like other men?

I assure you, judges, that he does not: for he says that the sun is stone, and the moon earth.

Friend Meletus, you think that you are accusing Anaxagoras: and you have but a bad opinion of the judges, if you fancy them illiterate to such a degree as not to know that these doctrines are found in the books of Anaxagoras the Clazomenian, which are full of them. And so, forsooth, the youth are said to be taught them by Socrates, when there are not infrequently exhibitions of them at the theatre (price of admission one drachma at the most); and they might pay their money, and laugh at Socrates if he pretends to father these extraordinary views. And so, Meletus, you really think that I do not believe in any god?

I swear by Zeus that you believe absolutely in none at all.

Nobody will believe you, Meletus, and I am pretty sure that you do not believe yourself. I cannot help thinking, men of Athens, that Meletus is reckless and impudent, and that he has written this indictment in a spirit of mere wantonness and youthful bravado. Has he not compounded a riddle, thinking to try me? He said to himself: — I shall see whether the wise Socrates will discover my facetious contradiction, or whether I shall be able to deceive him and the rest of them. For he certainly does appear to me to contradict himself in the indictment as much as if he said that Socrates is guilty of not believing in the gods, and yet of believing in them — but this is not like a person who is in earnest.

I should like you, O men of Athens, to join me in examining what I conceive to be his inconsistency; and do you, Meletus, answer. And I must remind the audience of my request that they would not make a disturbance if I speak in my accustomed manner:

Did ever man, Meletus, believe in the existence of human things, and not of human beings? . . . I wish, men of Athens, that he would answer, and not be always trying to get up an interruption. Did ever any man believe in horsemanship, and not in horses? or in flute-playing, and not in flute-players? No, my friend; I will answer to you and to the court, as you refuse to answer for yourself. There is no man who ever did. But now please to answer the next question: Can a man believe in spiritual and divine agencies, and not in spirits or demigods?

He cannot.

How lucky I am to have extracted that answer, by the assistance of the court! But then you swear in the indictment that I teach and believe in divine or spiritual agencies (new or old, no matter for that); at any rate, I believe in spiritual agencies, — so you say and swear in the affidavit; and yet if I believe in divine beings, how can I help believing in spirits or demigods; — must I not? To be sure I must; and therefore I may assume that your silence gives consent. Now what are spirits or demigods? are they not either gods or the sons of gods?

Certainly they are.

But this is what I call the facetious riddle invented by you: the demigods or spirits are gods, and you say first that I do not believe in gods, and then again that I do believe in gods; that is, if I believe in demigods. For if the demigods are the illegitimate sons of gods, whether by the nymphs or by any other mothers, of whom they are said to be the sons — what human being will ever believe that there are no gods if they are the sons of gods? You might as well affirm the existence of mules, and deny that of horses and asses. Such nonsense, Meletus, could only have been intended by you to make trial of me. You have put this into the indictment because you had nothing real of which to accuse me. But no one who has a particle of understanding will ever be convinced by you that the same men can believe in divine and superhuman things, and yet not believe that there are gods and demigods and heroes.

I have said enough in answer to the charge of Meletus: any elaborate defence is unnecessary; but I know only too well how many are the enmities which I have incurred, and this is what will be my destruction if I am destroyed; — not Meletus, nor yet Anytus, but the envy and detraction of the world, which has been the death of many good men, and will probably be the death of many more; there is no danger of my being the last of them.

. . . .

I do know that injustice and disobedience to a better, whether God or man, is evil and dishonourable, and I will never fear or avoid a possible good rather than a certain evil. And therefore if you let me go now, and are not convinced by Anytus, who said that since I had been prosecuted I must be put to death; (or if not that I ought never to have been prosecuted at all); and that if I escape now, your sons will all be utterly ruined by listening to my words — if you say to me, Socrates, this time we will not mind Anytus, and you shall be let off, but upon one condition, that you are not to enquire and speculate in this way any more, and that if you are caught doing so again you shall die; — if this was the condition on which you let me go, I should reply: Men of Athens, I honour and love you; but I shall obey God rather than you, and while I have life and strength I shall never cease from the practice and teaching of philosophy, exhorting any one whom I meet and saying to him after my manner: You, my friend, — a citizen of the great and mighty and wise city of Athens, — are you not ashamed of heaping up the greatest amount of money and honour and reputation, and caring so little about wisdom and truth and the greatest improvement of the soul, which you never regard or heed at all? And if the person with whom I am arguing, says: Yes, but I do care; then I do not leave him or let him go at once; but I proceed to interrogate and examine and cross-examine him, and if I think that he has no virtue in him, but only says that he has, I reproach him with undervaluing the greater, and overvaluing the less. And I shall repeat the same words to every one whom I meet, young and old, citizen and alien, but especially to the citizens, inasmuch as they are my brethren. For know that this is the command of God; and I believe that no greater good has ever happened in the State than my service to the Good. For I do nothing but go about persuading you all, old and young alike, not to take thought for your persons or your properties, but first and chiefly to care about the greatest improvement of the soul. I tell you that virtue is not given by money, but that from virtue comes money and every other good of man, public as well as private. This is my teaching, and if this is the doctrine which corrupts the youth, I am a mischievous person. But if any one says that this is not my teaching, he is speaking an untruth. Wherefore, O men of Athens, I say to you, do as Anytus bids or not as Anytus bids, and either acquit me or not; but whichever you do, understand that I shall never alter my ways, not even if I have to die many times.

Men of Athens, do not interrupt, but hear me; there was an understanding between us that you should hear me to the end: I have something more to say, at which you may be inclined to cry out; but I believe that to hear me will be good for you, and therefore I beg that you will not cry out. I would have you know, that if you kill such a one as I am, you will injure yourselves more than you will injure me. Nothing will injure me, not Meletus nor yet Anytus — they cannot, for a bad man is not permitted to injure a better than himself. I do not deny that Anytus, may, perhaps, kill him, or drive him into exile, or deprive him of civil rights; and he may imagine, and others may imagine, that he is inflicting a great injury upon him: but there I do not agree. For the evil of doing as he is doing — the evil of unjustly taking away the life of another — is greater far.

And now, Athenians, I am not going to argue for my own sake, as you may think, but for yours, that you may not sin against the God by condemning me, who am his gift to you. For if you kill me you will not easily find a successor to me, who, if I may use such a ludicrous figure of speech, am a sort of gadfly, given to the State of God; and the State is a great and noble steed who is tardy in his motions owing to his very size, and requires to be stirred into life. I am that gadfly which God has attached to the State, and all day long and in all places am always fastening upon you, arousing and persuading and reproaching you. You will not easily find another like me, and therefore I would advise you to spare me. I dare say that you may feel out of temper (like a person who is suddenly awakened from sleep), and you think that you might easily strike me dead as Anytus advises, and then you would sleep on for the remainder of your lives, unless God in his care of you sent you another gadfly. When I say that I am given to you by God, the proof of my mission is this: — if I had been like other men, I should not have neglected all my own concerns or patiently seen the neglect of them during all these years, and have been doing yours, coming to you individually like a father or elder brother, exhorting you to regard virtue; such conduct, I say, would be unlike human nature. If I had gained anything, or if my exhortations had been paid, there would have been some sense in my doing so; but now, as you will perceive, not even the impudence of my accusers dares to say that I have ever exacted or sought pay of any one; of that they have no witness. And I have sufficient witness to the truth of what I say — my poverty.

. . . .

Well, Athenians, this and the like of this is all the defence which I have to offer. Yet a word more. Perhaps there may be some one who is offended at me, when he calls to mind how he himself on a similar, or even a less serious occasion, prayed and entreated the judges with many tears, and how he produced his children in court, which was a moving spectacle, together with a host of relations and friends; whereas I, who am probably in danger of my life, will do none of these things. The contrast may occur to his mind, and he may be set against me, and vote in anger because he is displeased at me on this account. Now, if there be such a person among you, — mind, I do not say that there is, — to him I may fairly reply: My friend, I am a man, and like other men, a creature of flesh and blood, and not "of wood or stone" as Homer says; and I have a family, yes, and sons, O Athenians, three in number, one almost a man, and two others who are still young; and yet I will not bring any of them hither in order to petition you for an acquittal. And why not? Not from any self-assertion or want of respect for you. Whether I am or am not afraid of death is another question, of which I will not now speak. But, having regard to public opinion, I feel that such conduct would be discreditable to myself, and to you, and to the whole State. One who has reached my years, and who has a name for wisdom, ought not to demean himself. Whether this opinion of me be deserved or not, at any rate the world has decided that Socrates is in some way superior to other men. And if those among you who are said to be superior in wisdom and courage, and any other virtue, demean themselves in this way, how shameful is their conduct! I have seen men of reputation, when they have been condemned, behaving in the strangest manner: they seemed to fancy that they were going to suffer something dreadful if they died, and that they could be immortal if you only allowed them to live; and I think that such are a dishonour to the State, and that any stranger coming in would have said of them that the most eminent men of Athens, to whom the Athenians themselves give honour and command, are not better than women. And I say that these things ought not to be done by those of us who have a reputation; and if they are done, you ought not to permit them; you ought rather to show that you are far more disposed to condemn the man who gets up a doleful scene and makes the city ridiculous, than him who holds his peace.

But, setting aside the question of public opinion, there seems to be something wrong in asking a favour of a judge, and thus procuring an acquittal, instead of informing and convincing him. For his duty is, not to make a present of justice, but to give judgment; and he has sworn that he will judge according to the laws, and not according to his own good pleasure; and we ought not to encourage you, nor should you allow yourselves to be encouraged, in this habit of perjury—there can be no piety in that. Do not then require me to do what I consider dishonourable and impious and wrong, especially now, when I am being tried for impiety on the indictment of Meletus. For if, O Men of Athens, by force of persuasion and entreaty I could overpower your oaths, then I should be teaching you to believe that there are no gods, and in defending should simply convict myself of the charge of not believing in them. But that is not so — far otherwise. For I do believe that there are gods, and in a sense higher than that in which any of my accusers believe in them. And to you and to God I commit my cause, to be determined by you as is best for you and me.

. . . .

There are many reasons why I am not grieved, O men of Athens, at the vote of condemnation. I expected it, and am only surprised that the votes are so nearly equal; for I had thought that the majority against me would have been far larger; but now, had thirty votes gone over to the other side, I should have been acquitted. And I may say, I think that I have escaped Meletus. I may say more; for without the assistance of Anytus and Lycon, any one may see that he would not have had a fifth part of the votes, as the law requires, in which case he would have incurred a fine of a thousand drachmae.

And so he proposes death as the penalty. And what shall I propose on my part, O men of Athens: Clearly that which is my due, And what is my due? What returns shall be made to the man who has never had the wit to be idle during his whole life; but has been careless of what the many care for — wealth, and family interests and military offices, and speaking in the assembly, and magistracies, and plots, and parties. Reflecting that I was really too honest a man to be a politician and live, I did not go where I could do no good to you or to myself; but where I could do the greatest good privately to every one of you, thither I went, and sought to persuade every man among you that he must look to himself and seek virtue and wisdom before he looks to his private interests, and look to the State before he looks to the interests of the State; and that this should be the order which he observes in all his actions. What shall be done to such an one? Doubtless some good thing, O men of Athens, if he has his reward; and the good should be of a kind suitable to him. What would be a reward suitable to a poor man who is your benefactor, and who desires leisure that he may instruct you? There can be no reward so fitting as maintenance in the Prytaneum, O men of Athens, a reward which he deserves far more than the citizen who has won the prize at Olympia in the horse or chariot race, whether the chariots were drawn by two horses or by many. For I am in want, and he has enough; and he only gives you the appearance of happiness, and I give you the reality. And if I am to estimate the penalty fairly, I should say that maintenance in the Prytaneum is the just return.

Perhaps you think that I am braving you in what I am saying now, as in what I said before about the tears and prayers. But this is not so. I speak rather because I am convinced that I never intentionally wronged any one, although I cannot convince you — the time has been too short; if there were a law at Athens, as there is in other cities, that a capital cause should not be decided in one day, then I believe that I should have convinced you. But I cannot in a moment refute great slanders; and, as I am convinced that I never wronged another, I will assuredly not wrong myself. I will not say of myself that I deserve any evil, or propose any penalty. Why should I? Because I am afraid of the penalty of death which Meletus proposes? When I do not know whether death is a good or an evil, why should I propose a penalty which would certainly be an evil? Shall I say imprisonment? And why should I live in prison, and be the slave of the magistrate of the year — of the Eleven? Or shall the penalty be a fine, and imprisonment until the fine is paid? There is the same objection. I should have to lie in prison, for money I have none, and cannot pay. And if I say exile (and this may possibly be the penalty which you will affix), I must indeed be blinded by the love of life if I am so irrational as to expect that when you, who are my own citizens, cannot endure my discourses and words, and have found them so grievous and odious that you will have no more of them, others are likely to endure me. No indeed, men of Athens, that is not very likely. And what a life should I lead, at my age, wandering from city to city, ever changing my place of exile, and always being driven out! For I am quite sure that wherever I go, there, as here, the young men will flock to me; and if I drive them away, their elders will drive me out at their request; and if I let them come, their fathers and friends will drive me out for their sakes.

Some one will say: Yes, Socrates, but cannot you hold your tongue, and then you may go into a foreign city, and no one will interfere with you? No, I have great difficulty in making you understand my answer to this. For if I tell you that to do as you say would be a disobedience to the God, and therefore that I cannot hold my tongue, you will not believe that I am serious; and if I say again that daily to discourse about virtue, and of those other things about which you hear me examining myself and others, is the greatest good of man, and that the unexamined life is not worth living, you are still less likely to believe me. Yet I say what is true, although a thing of which it is hard for me to persuade you. Also, I have never been accustomed to think that I deserve to suffer any harm. Had I money I might have estimated the offence at what I was able to pay, and not have been much the worse. But I have none, and therefore I must ask you to proportion the fine to my means. Well, perhaps I could afford a mina, and therefore I propose that penalty: Plato, Crito, Critobulus, and Apollodorus, my friends here, bid me say thirty minae, and they will be the sureties. Let thirty minae be the penalty; for which sum they will be ample security to you.

Not much time will be gained, O Athenians, in return for the evil name which you will get from the detractors of the city, who will say that you killed Socrates, a wise man; for they will call me wise, even although I am not wise, when they want to reproach you. If you had waited a little while, your desire would have been fulfilled in the course of nature. For I am far advanced in years, as you may perceive, and not far from death. I am speaking now not to all of you, but only to those who have condemned me to death. And I have another thing to say to them: You think that I was convicted because I had no words of the sort which would have procured my acquittal — I mean, if I had thought fit to leave nothing undone or unsaid. Not so; the deficiency which led to my conviction was not of words — certainly not. But I had not the boldness or impudence or inclination to address you as you would have liked me to do, weeping and wailing and lamenting, and saying and doing many things which you have been accustomed to hear from others, and which, as I maintain, are unworthy of me. I thought at the time that I ought not to do anything common or mean when in danger: nor do I now repent of the style of my defence; I would rather die having spoken after my manner, than speak in your manner and live. For neither in war nor yet at law ought I or any man to use every way of escaping death. Often in battle there can be no doubt that if a man will throw away his arms, and fall on his knees before his pursuers, he may escape death; and in other dangers there are other ways of escaping death, if a man is willing to say and do anything. The difficulty, my friends, is not to avoid death, but to avoid unrighteousness; for that runs faster than death. I am old and move slowly, and the slower runner has overtaken me, and my accusers are keen and quick, and the faster runner, who is unrighteousness, has overtaken them. And now I depart hence condemned by you to suffer the penalty of death. — they too go their ways condemned by the truth to suffer the penalty of villainy and wrong; and I must abide by my award — let them abide by theirs. I suppose that these things may be regarded as fated, — and I think that they are well.

And now, O men who have condemned me, I would fain prophesy to you; for I am about to die, and in the hours of death men are gifted with prophetic power. And I prophesy to you who are my murderers, that immediately after my departure punishment far heavier than you have inflicted on me will surely await you. Me you have killed because you wanted to escape the accuser, and not to give an account of your lives. But that will not be as you suppose: far otherwise, For I say that there will be more accusers of you than there are now; accusers whom hitherto I have restrained: and as they are younger they will be more inconsiderate with you, and you will be more offended at them. If you think that by killing men you can prevent some one from censuring your evil lives, you are mistaken; that is not a way of escape which is either possible or honourable; the easiest and the noblest way is not to be disabling others, but to be improving yourselves. This is the prophecy which I utter before my departure to the judges who have condemned me.

Friends, who would have acquitted me, I would like also to talk with you about the thing which has come to pass, while the magistrates are busy, and before I go to the place at which I must die. Stay then a little, for we may as well talk with one another while there is time. You are my friends, and I should like to show you the meaning of this event which has happened to me. O my judges — for you I may truly call judges — I should like to tell you of a wonderful circumstance. Hitherto the divine faculty of which the internal oracle is the source has constantly been in the habit of opposing me even about trifles, if I was going to make a slip or error in any matter; and now as you see there has come upon me that which may be thought, and is generally believed to be, the last and worst evil. But the oracle made no sign of opposition, either when I was leaving my house in the morning, or when I was on my way to the court, or while I was speaking, at anything which I was going to say; and yet I have often been stopped in the middle of a speech, but now in nothing I either said or did touching the matter in hand has the oracle opposed me. What do I take to be the explanation of this silence? I will tell you. It is an intimation that what has happened to me is a good, and that those of us who think that death is an evil are in error. For the customary sign would surely have opposed me had I been going to evil and not to good.

Let us reflect in another way, and we shall see that there is great reason to hope that death is a good; for one of two things — either death is a state of nothingness and utter unconsciousness, or, as men say, there is a change and migration of the soul from this world to another. Now, if you suppose that there is no consciousness, but a sleep like the sleep of him who is undisturbed even by dreams, death will be an unspeakable gain. For if a person were to select the night in which his sleep was undisturbed even by dreams, and were to compare with this the other days and nights of his life, and then were to tell us how many days and nights he had passed in the course of his life better and more pleasantly than this one, I think that any man, I will not say a private man, but even the great king, will not find many such days or nights, when compared with the others. Now, if death be of such a nature, I say that to die is gain; for eternity is then only a single night. But if death is the journey to another place, and there, as men say, all the dead abide, what good, O my friends and judges, can be greater than this? If, indeed, when the pilgrim arrives in the world below, he is delivered from the professors of justice in this world, and finds the true judges who are said to give judgment there, Minos and Rhadamanthus and Aeacus and Triptolemus, and other sons of God who were righteous in their own life, that pilgrimage will be worth making. What would not a man give if he might converse with Orpheus and Musaeus and Hesiod and Homer? Nay, if this be true, let me die again and again. I myself, too, shall have a wonderful interest in there meeting and conversing with Palamedes, and Ajax the son of Telamon, and any other ancient hero who has suffered death through an unjust judgment; and there will be not small pleasure, as I think, in comparing my own sufferings with theirs. Above all, I shall then be able to continue my search into true and false knowledge; as in this world, so also in the next; and I shall find out who is wise, and who pretends to be wise, and is not. What would not a man give, O judges, to be able to examine the leader of the great Trojan expedition; or Odysseus or Sisyphus, or numberless others, men and women too! What infinite delight would there be in conversing with them and asking them questions! In another world they do not put a man to death for asking questions: assuredly not. For besides being happier than we are, they will be immortal, if what is said is true.

Wherefore, O judges, be of good cheer about death, and know of a certainty, that no evil can happen to a good man, either in life or after death. He and his are not neglected by the gods; nor has my own approaching end happened by mere chance. But I see clearly that the time had arrived when it was better for me to die and be released from trouble: wherefore the oracle gave no sign. For which reason, also, I am not angry with my condemners, or with my accusers; they have done me no harm, although they did not mean to do me any good; and for this I may gently blame them.

Still, I have a favour to ask of them. When my sons are grown up, I would ask you, O my friends, to punish them; and I would have you trouble them, as I have troubled you, if they seem to care about riches, or anything, more than about virtue; or if they pretend to be something when they are really nothing, — then reprove them, as I have reproved you, for not caring about that for which they ought to care, and thinking that they are something when they are really nothing. And if you do this, both I and my sons will have received justice at your hands.

The hour of departure has arrived, and we go our ways — I to die, and you to live. Which is better God only knows.

THE CRITO[1]

Persons of the Dialogue: Socrates, Crito.

Scene: The Prison of Socrates.

SOCRATES: Why have you come at this hour, Crito? It must be quite early?

CRITO: Yes, certainly.

SOC: What is the exact time?

CR: The dawn is breaking.

SOC: I wonder that the keeper of the prison would let you in.

CR: He knows me, because I often come, Socrates; moreover, I have done him a kindness.

SOC: And are you only just arrived?

CR: No, I came some time ago.

SOC: Then why did you sit and say nothing, instead of at once awakening me?

CR: I should not have liked myself, Socrates, to be in such great trouble and unrest as you are — indeed I should not: I have been watching with amazement your peaceful slumbers; and for that reason I did not awake you, because I wished to minimize the pain. I have always thought you to be of a happy disposition; but never did I see anything like the easy, tranquil manner in which you bear this calamity.

---

[1] *Dialogues of Plato*, Benjamin Jowett (trans.). Oxford, 1875.

SOC: Why, Crito, when a man has reached my age he ought not to be repining at the approach of death.

CR: And yet other old men find themselves in similar misfortunes, and age does not prevent them from repining.

SOC: That is true. But you have not told me why you come at this early hour.

CR: I come to bring you a message which is sad and painful; not, as I believe, to yourself, but to all of us who are your friends, and saddest of all to me.

SOC: What? Has the ship come from Delos, on the arrival of which I am to die?

CR: No, the ship has not actually arrived, but she will probably be here today, as persons who have come from Sunium tell me that they left her there; and therefore tomorrow, Socrates, will be the last day of your life.

SOC: Very well, Crito; if such is the will of God, I am willing; but my belief is that there will be a delay of a day.

CR: Why do you think so?

SOC: I will tell you. I am to die on the day after the arrival of the ship.

CR: Yes; that is what the authorities say.

SOC: But I do not think that the ship will be here until tomorrow; this I infer from a vision which I had last night, or rather only just now, when you fortunately allowed me to sleep.

CR: And what was the nature of the vision?

SOC: There appeared to me the likeness of a woman, fair and comely, clothed in bright raiment, who called to me and said: O Socrates, "The third day hence to fertile Phthia shalt thou go."

CR: What a singular dream, Socrates!

SOC: There can be no doubt about the meaning, Crito, I think.

CR: Yes; the meaning is only too clear. But, oh! my beloved Socrates, let me entreat you once more to take my advice and escape. For if you die I shall not only lose a friend who can never be replaced, but there is another evil: people who do not know you and me will believe that I might have saved you if I had been willing to give money, but that I did not care. Now, can there be a worse disgrace than this — that I should be thought to value money more than the life of friend? For the many will not be persuaded that I wanted you to escape, and that you refused.

SOC: But why, my dear Crito, should we care about the opinion of the many? Good men, and they are the only persons who are worth considering, will think of these things truly as they occurred.

CR: But you see, Socrates, that the opinion of the many must be regarded, for what is now happening shows that they can do the greatest evil to any one who has lost their good opinion.

SOC: I only wish it were so, Crito; and that the many could do the greatest evil; for then they would also be able to do the greatest good — and what a fine thing this would be! But in reality they can do neither; for they cannot make a man either wise or foolish; and whatever they do is the result of chance.

CR: Well, I will not dispute with you; but please to tell me, Socrates, whether you are not acting out of regard to me and your other friends: are you not afraid that if you escape from prison we may get into trouble with the informers for having stolen you away, and lose either the whole or a great part of our property; or that even a worse evil may happen to us? Now, if you fear on our account, be at ease; for in order to save you, we ought surely to run this, or even a greater risk; be persuaded, then, and do as I say.

SOC: Yes, Crito, that is one fear which you mention, but by no means the only one.

CR: Fear not — there are persons who are willing to get you out of prison at no great cost; and as for the informers, they are far from being exorbitant in their demands — a little money will satisfy them. My means, which are certainly ample, are at your service, and if you have a scruple about spending all mine, here are strangers who will give you the use of theirs; and one of them, Simmias the Theban, has brought a large sum of money for this very purpose; and Cebes and many others are prepared to spend their money in helping you to escape. I say, therefore, do not hesitate on our account, and do not say, as you did in the court, that you will have a difficulty in knowing what to do with yourself anywhere else. For men will love you in other places to which you may go, and not in Athens only; there are friends of mine in Thessaly, if you like to go to them, who will value and protect you, and no Thessalian will give you any trouble. Nor can I think that you are at all justified, Socrates, in betraying your own life when you might be saved; in acting thus you are playing into the hands of your enemies, who are hurrying on your destruction. And further I should say that you are deserting your own children; for you might bring them up and educate them; instead of which you go away and leave them, and they will be small thanks to you. No man should bring children into the world who is unwilling to persevere to the end in their nurture and education. But you appear to be choosing the easier part, not the better and manlier, which would have been more becoming in one who professes to care for virtue in all his actions, like yourself. And, indeed, I am ashamed not only of you, but of us who are your friends, when I reflect that the whole business will be attributed entirely to our want of courage. The trial need never have come on, or might have been managed differently; and this last act, or crowning folly, will seem to have occurred through our negligence and cowardice, who might have saved you, if we had been good for anything; and you might have saved yourself, for there was no difficulty at all. See now, Socrates, how sad and discreditable are the consequences, both to us and you. Make up your mind, then, or rather have your mind already made up, for the time of deliberation is over, and there is only one thing to be done, which must be done this very night, and if we delay at all will be no longer practicable or possible; I beseech you therefore, Socrates, be persuaded by me, and do as I say.

SOC: Dear Crito, your zeal is invaluable, if a right one; but if wrong, the greater the zeal the greater the danger; and therefore we ought to consider whether I shall or shall not do as you say. For I am and always have been one of those natures who must be guided by reason, whatever the reason may be which upon reflection appears to me to be the best; and now that this chance has befallen me, I cannot repudiate my own words: the principles which I have hitherto honoured and revered I still honour, and unless we can at once find other and better principles, I am certain not to agree with you; no, not even if the power of the multitude could inflict many more imprisonments, confiscations, deaths, frightening us like children with hobgoblin terrors. What will be the fairest way of considering the question? Shall I return to your old argument about the opinions of men? — we were saying that some of them are to be regarded, and others not. Now, were we right in maintaining this before I was condemned? And has the argument which was once good now proved to be talk for the sake of talking — mere childish nonsense? That is what I want to consider with your help, Crito: — whether, under my present circumstances, the argument appears to be in any way different or not; and is to be allowed by me or disallowed. That argument, which, as I believe, is maintained by many persons of authority, was to the effect, as I was saying, that the opinions of some men are to be regarded, and of other men not to be regarded. Now you, Crito, are not going to die tomorrow — at least, there is no human probability of this — and therefore you are disinterested and not liable to be deceived by the circumstances in which you are placed. Tell me, then, whether I am right in saying that some opinions, and the opinions of some men only, are to be valued, and that other opinions, and the opinions of other men, are not to be valued. I ask you whether I was right in maintaining this?

CR: Certainly.

SOC: The good are to be regarded, and not the bad?

CR: Yes.

SOC: And the opinions of the wise are good, and the opinions of the unwise are evil?

CR: Certainly.

SOC: And what was said about another matter? Is the pupil who devotes himself to the practice of gymnastics supposed to attend to the praise and blame and opinion of every man, or of one man only — his physician or trainer, whoever he may be?

CR: Of one man only.

SOC: And he ought to fear the censure and welcome the praise of that one only, and not of the many?

CR: Clearly so.

SOC: And he ought to act and train, and eat and drink in the way which seems good to his single master who has understanding, rather than according to the opinion of all other men put together?

CR: True.

SOC: And if he disobeys and disregards the opinion and approval of the one, and regards the opinion of the many who have no understanding, will he not suffer?

CR: Certainly he will.

SOC: And what will the evil be, whither tending and what affecting, in the disobedient person?

CR: Clearly, affecting the body; that is what is destroyed by the evil.

SOC: Very good; and is not this true, Crito, of other things which we need not separately enumerate? In questions of just and unjust, fair and foul, good and evil, which are the subjects of our present consultation, ought we to follow the opinion of the many and to fear them: or the opinion of the one man who had understanding? Ought we not to fear and reverence him more than all the rest of the world: and if we desert him shall we not destroy and injure that principle in us which may be assumed to be improved by justice and deteriorated by injustice; — there is such a principle?

CR: Certainly there is Socrates.

SOC: Take a parallel instance: — if, acting under the advice of those who have no understanding, we destroy that which is improved by health and is deteriorated by disease, would life be worth having? And that which has been destroyed is — the body?

CR: Yes.

SOC: Could we live, having an evil and corrupted body?

CR: Certainly not.

SOC: And will life be worth having, if that higher part of man be destroyed, which is improved by justice and depraved by injustice? Do we suppose that principle, whatever it may be in man, which has to do with justice and injustice, to be inferior to the body?

CR: Certainly not.

SOC: More honourable than the body?

CR: Far more.

SOC: Then, my friend, we must not regard what the many say of us: but what he, the one man who has understanding of just and unjust, will say, and what the truth will say. And therefore you begin in error when you advise that we should regard the opinion of the many about just and unjust, good and evil, honourable and dishonourable. — "Well," Some one will say, "but the many can kill us."

CR: Yes, Socrates; that will clearly be the answer.

SOC: And it is true; but still I find with surprise that the old argument is unshaken as ever. And I should like to know whether I may say the same of another proposition — that not life, but a good life, is to be chiefly valued?

CR: Yes.

SOC: From these premises I proceed to argue the question whether I ought not to try to escape without the consent of the Athenians: and if I am clearly right in escaping, then I will make the attempt; but if not, I will abstain. The other considerations which you mention, of money and loss of character and the duty of educating one's children, are, I fear, only the doctrines of the multitude, who would be as ready to restore people to life, if they were able, as they are to put them to death — and with as little reason. But now, since the argument has thus far prevailed, the only question which remains to be considered is, whether we shall do rightly either in escaping or in suffering others to aid in our escape and paying them in money and thanks, or whether in reality we shall not do rightly; and if the latter, then death or any other calamity which may ensue on my remaining here must not be allowed to enter into the calculation.

CR: I think that you are right, Socrates; how then shall we proceed?

SOC: Let us consider the matter together, and do you either refute me if you can, and I will be convinced; or else cease, my dear friend, from repeating to me that I ought to escape against the wishes of the Athenians: for I highly value your attempts to persuade me to do so, but I may not be persuaded against my own better judgment. And now please to consider my first position, and try how you can best answer me.

CR: I will.

SOC: Are we to say that we are never intentionally to do wrong, or that in one way we ought and in another way we ought not to do wrong, or is doing wrong always evil and dishonourable, as I was just now saying, and as has been already acknowledged by us? Are all our former admissions which were made within a few days to be thrown away? And have we, at our age, been earnestly discoursing with one another all our life long only to discover that we are no better than children? Or, in spite of the opinion of the many, and in spite of consequences whether better or worse, shall we insist on the truth of what was then said, that injustice is always an evil and dishonour to him who acts unjustly? Shall we say so or not?

CR: Yes.

SOC: Then we must do no wrong?

CR: Certainly not.

SOC: Nor when injured injure in return, as the many imagine; for we must injure no one at all?

CR: Clearly not.

SOC: Again, Crito, may we do evil?

CR: Surely not, Socrates.

SOC: And what of doing evil in return for evil, which is the morality of the many — is that just or not?

CR: Not just.

SOC: For doing evil to another is the same as injuring him?

CR: Very true.

SOC: Then we ought not to retaliate or render evil for evil to any one, whatever evil we may have suffered from him. But I would have you consider, Crito, whether you really mean what you are saying. For this opinion has never been held, and never will be held, by any considerable number of persons; and those who are agreed and those who are not agreed upon this point have no common ground, and can only despise one another when they see how widely they differ. Tell me, then, whether you agree with and assent to my first principle, that neither injury nor retaliation nor warding off evil by evil is ever right. And shall that be the premise of our argument? Or do you decline and dissent from this? For so I have ever thought, and continue to think; but, if you are of another opinion, let me hear what you have to say. If, however, you remain of the same mind as formerly, I will proceed to the next step.

CR: You may proceed, for I have not changed my mind.

SOC: Then I will go on to the next point, which may be put in the form of a question: — Ought a man to do what he admits to be right, or ought he to betray the right?

CR: He ought to do what he thinks right.

SOC: But if this is true, what is the application? In leaving the prison against the will of the Athenians, do I wrong any? or rather do I not wrong those whom I ought least to wrong? Do I not desert the principles which were acknowledged by us to be just — what do you say?

CR: I cannot tell Socrates; for I do not know.

SOC: Then consider the matter in this way: — Imagine that I am about to play truant (you may call the proceeding by any name which you like), and the laws and the government come and interrogate me: "Tell us, Socrates," they say, "what are you about? Are you not going by an act of yours to overturn us — the laws, and the whole State, as far as in you lies? Do you imagine that a State can subsist and not be overthrown, in which the decisions of law have no power, but are set aside and trampled upon by individuals?" What will be our answer, Crito, to these and the like words? Any one, and especially a rhetorician, will have a good deal to say on behalf of the law which requires a sentence to be carried out. He will argue that this law should not be set aside; and shall we reply, "Yes, but the State has injured us and given an unjust sentence." Suppose I say that?

CR: Very good, Socrates.

SOC: "And was that our agreement with you?" the law would answer, "or were you to abide by the sentence of the State?" And if I were to express my astonishment at their words, the law would probably add: "Answer, Socrates, instead of opening your eyes — you are in the habit of asking and answering questions. Tell us, — What complaint have you to make against us which justifies you in attempting to destroy us and the State? In the first place did we not bring you into existence? Your father married your mother by our aid and begat you. Say whether you have any objection to urge against those of us who regulate marriage?" None, I should reply. "Or against those of us who after birth regulate the nurture and education of children, in which you also were trained? Were not the laws which have the charge of education, right in commanding your father to train you in music and gymnastic?" Right, I should reply. "Well, then, since you were brought into the world and nurtured and educated by us, can you deny in the first place that you are our child and slave, as your fathers were before you? And if this is true, you are not on equal terms with us; nor can you think that you have a right to do to us what we are doing to you. Would you have any right to strike or revile or do any other evil to your father or your master, if you had one, because you have been struck or reviled by him, or received some other evil at his hands? — you would not say this? And because we think right to destroy you, do you think that you have any right to destroy us in return, and your country as far as in you lies? Will you, O professor of true virtue, pretend that you are justified in this? Has a philosopher like you failed to discover that our country is more to be valued and higher and holier far than mother or father or any ancestor, and more to be regarded in the eyes of the gods and of men of understanding? Also to be soothed, and gently and reverently entreated when angry, even more than a father, and either to be persuaded, or if not persuaded, to be obeyed? And when we are punished by her, whether with imprisonment or stripes, the punishment is to be endured in silence; and if she lead us to wounds or death in battle, thither we follow as is right; neither may any one yield or retreat or leave his rank, but whether in battle or in a court of law, or in any other place, he must do what his city and his country order him; or he must change their view of what is just: and if he may do no violence to his father or mother, much less may he do violence to his country". What answer shall we make to this, Crito? Do the laws speak truly, or do they not?

CR: I think that they do.

SOC: Then the laws will say: "Consider, Socrates, if we are speaking truly that in your present attempt you are going to do us an injury. For, having brought you into the world, and nurtured and educated you, and given you and every other citizen a share in every good which we had to give, we further proclaim to any Athenian by the liberty which we allow him, that if he does not like us when he has become of age and has seen the ways of the city, and made our acquaintance, he may go where he pleases and take his goods with him. None of us laws will forbid him or interfere with him. Anyone who does not like us and the city, and who wants to emigrate to a colony or to any other city, may go where he likes, retaining his property. But he who has experience of the manner in which we order justice and administer the State, and still remains, has entered into an implied contract that he will do as we command him. And he who disobeys us is, as we maintain, thrice wrong; first, because in disobeying us he is disobeying his parents; secondly, because we are the authors of his education; thirdly, because he has made an agreement with us that he will duly obey our commands; and he neither obeys them nor convinces us that our commands are unjust; and we do not rudely impose them, but give him the alternative of obeying or convincing us; — that is what we offer, and he does neither.

"These are the sort of accusations to which, as we were saying, you, Socrates, will be exposed if you accomplish your intentions; you, above all other Athenians." Suppose now I ask, why I rather than anybody else? They will justly retort upon me that I above all other men have acknowledged the agreement. "There is clear proof," they will say, "Socrates, that we and the city were not displeasing to you. Of all Athenians you have been the most constant resident in the city, which, as you never leave, you may be supposed to love. For you never went out of the city either to see the games, except once when you went to the Isthmus, or to any other place unless when you were on military service; nor did you travel as other men do. Nor had you any curiosity to know other States or their laws: your affections did not go beyond us and our State: we were your special favourites, and you acquiesced in our government of you; and here in this city you begat your children, which is a proof of your satisfaction. Moreover, you might in the course of the trial, if you had liked, have fixed the penalty at banishment; the State which refuses to let you go now would have let you go then. But you pretended that you preferred death to exile, and that you were not unwilling to die. And now you have forgotten these fine sentiments, and pay no respect to us, the laws, of whom you are the destroyer; and are doing what only a miserable slave would do, running away and turning your back upon the compacts and agreements which you made as a citizen. And, first of all, answer this very question: Are we right in saying that you agreed to be governed according to us in deed, and not in word only? Is that true or not? How shall we answer, Crito? Must we not assent?

CR: We cannot help it, Socrates.

SOC: Then will they not say: "You, Socrates, are breaking the covenants and agreements which you made with us at your leisure, not in any haste or under any compulsion or deception, but after you have had seventy years to think of them, during which time you were at liberty to leave the city, if we were not to your mind, or if our covenants appeared to you to be unfair. You had your choice, and might have gone either to Lacedaemon or Crete, both of which States are often praised by you for their good government, or to some other Hellenic or foreign States. Whereas you, above all other Athenians, seemed to be so fond of the State, or, in other words, of us, her laws (and who would care about a State which has no laws?), that you never stirred out of her; the halt, the blind, the maimed were not more stationary in her than you were. And now you run away and forsake your agreements. Not so, Socrates, if you will take our advice; do not make yourself ridiculous by escaping out of the city. "For just consider, if you transgress and err in this sort of way, what good will you do either to yourself or to your friends? That your friends will be driven into exile and deprived of citizenship, or will lose their property, is tolerably certain; and you yourself, if you fly to one of the neighbouring cities, as, for example, Thebes or Megara, both of which are well governed, will come to them as an enemy, Socrates, and their government will be against you, and all patriotic citizens will cast an evil eye upon you as a subverter of the laws, and you will confirm in the minds of the judges the justice of their own condemnation of you. For he who is a corruptor of the laws is more than likely to be a corrupter of the young and foolish portion of mankind. Will you then flee from well-ordered cities and virtuous men? and is existence worth having on these terms? Or will you go to them without shame, and talk to them, Socrates? And what will you say to them? What you say here about virtue and justice and institutions and laws being the best things among men? Would that be decent of you? Surely not. But if you go away from well-governed States to Crito's friends in Thessaly, where there is great disorder and license, they will be charmed to hear the tale of your escape from prison, set off with ludicrous particulars of the manner in which you were wrapped in a goatskin or some other disguise, and metamorphosed as the manner is of runaways; but will there be no one to remind you that in your old age you were not ashamed to violate the most sacred laws from a miserable desire of a little more life? Perhaps not, if you keep them in a good temper; but if they are out of temper you will hear many degrading things; you will live, but how? — as the flatterer of all men, and the servant of all men; and doing what? — eating and drinking in Thessaly, having gone abroad in order that you may get a dinner. And where will be your fine sentiments about justice and virtue? Say that you wish to live for the sake of your children — you want to bring them up and educate them — will you take them into Thessaly and deprive them of Athenian citizenship? Is this the benefit which you will confer upon them? Or are you under the impression that they will be better cared for and educated here if you are still alive, although absent from them; for your friends will take care of them? Do you fancy that if you are an inhabitant of Thessaly they will take care of them, and if you are an inhabitant of the other world that they will not take care of them? Nay; but if they who call themselves friends are good for anything, they will — to be sure they will.

"Listen, then, Socrates, to us who have brought you up. Think not of life and children first, and of justice afterwards, but of justice first, that you may be justified before the princes of the world below. For neither will you nor any that belong to you be happier or holier or juster in this life, or happier in another, if you do as Crito bids. Now you depart in innocence, a sufferer and not a doer of evil; a victim, not of the laws but of men. But if you go forth, returning evil for evil, and injury for injury, breaking the covenants and agreements which you have made with us, and wronging those whom you ought least of all to wrong, that is to say, yourself, your friends, your country, and us, we shall be angry with you while you live, and our brethren, the laws in the world below, will receive you as an enemy; for they will know that you have done your best to destroy us. Listen, then, to us and not to Crito." This, dear Crito, is the voice which I seem to hear murmuring in my ears, like the sound of the flute in the ears of the mystic; that voice, I say, is humming in my ears, and prevents me from hearing any other. And I know that anything more which you may say will be vain. Yet speak, if you have anything to say.

CR: I have nothing to say, Socrates.

SOC: Leave me then, Crito, to fulfil the will of God, and to follow whither he leads.

PHAEDO (Phaidon)

The Death of Socrates, 399 B.C.

Echecrates, Phaidon.

Apollodoros, Socrates, Cebes, Simmias, Criton.

ECHECRATES: Were you there yourself, Phaidon, with Socrates, on the day when he took the poison in prison, or did you hear about it from someone?

PHAIDON: I was there myself, Echecrates.

ECHECRATES: Then what was it our friend said before his death? And how did he end? I should be glad to hear. You see no one at all from our part of the world[1] goes now to visit in Athens, and no visitor has come to us from there this long time who might be able to tell us properly what happened; all they could say was, he took the poison and died; no one could tell us anything about the other details.

PHAIDON: Then you never heard how things went at the trial?

ECHECRATES: Yes, somebody did bring news of that, and we were surprised how long it seemed between the sentence and his death. Why was that, Phaidon?

PHAIDON: It was just a piece of luck, Echecrates; for the day before the trial it so happened that the wreath was put on the poop of the ship which the Athenians send to Delos.

ECHECRATES: What ship is that?

PHAIDON: That is the ship, as the Athenians say, in which Theseus once went off to Crete with those "twice seven," you know, and saved them and saved himself.[2] The Athenians vowed to Apollo then, so it is said, that if the lives of these were saved, they would send a sacred mission every year to Delos; and they do send it still, every year ever since that, to honour the god. As soon as the mission has begun, then, it is their law to keep the city pure during that time, and to put no one to death before the ship arrives at Delos and comes back again here; this often takes some time, when the winds happen to delay them. The beginning of the mission is when the priest of Apollo lays a wreath on the poop of the ship, and this happened, as I say, the day before the trial. Accordingly Socrates had a long time in prison between the trial and his death.

ECHECRATES: Then what about the death itself, Phaidon? What was said or done, and which of his friends were with him? Or did the magistrates forbid their presence, and did he die alone with no friends there?

PHAIDON: Oh no, friends were with him, quite a number of them.

ECHECRATES: That's just what I want to know; please be so kind as to tell me all about it as clearly as possible, unless you happen to be busy.

PHAIDON: Oh, I have plenty of time, and I will try to tell you the whole story; indeed, to remember Socrates, and what he said himself, and what was said to him is always the most precious thing in the world to me.

ECHECRATES: Well, Phaidon, those who are going to hear you will feel the same; pray try to tell the whole story as exactly as you can.

PHAIDON: I must say I had the strangest feeling being there. I felt no pity, as one might, being present at the death of a dear friend; for the man seemed happy to me, Echecrates, in bearing and in speech. How fearlessly and nobly he met his end! I could not help thinking that divine providence was with that man as he passed from this world to the next, and on coming there also it would be well with him, if ever with anyone that ever was. For this reason I felt no pity at all, as one might at a scene of mourning; and yet not the pleasure we used to have in our philosophic discussions. The conversation was certainly of that sort, but I really had an extraordinary feeling, a strange mixture of pleasure and pain at once, when I remembered that then and there that man was to make his end. And all of us who were present were very much in the same state, sometimes laughing, sometimes shedding tears, and one of us particularly, Apollodoros —no doubt you know the man and his ways.

ECHECRATES: Oh yes, of course.

PHAIDON: Well, he behaved quite as usual, and I was broken down myself, and so were others.

ECHECRATES: But who were they, Phaidon?

PHAIDON: Of our countrymen[3] there was this Apollodoros I have mentioned, and Critobulos and his father, and, besides, Hermogenes and Epigenes and Aischines and Antisthenes; there was also Ctesippos the Paianian and Menexenos, and others of our countrymen; but Plato was ill, I think.

ECHECRATES: Were any foreigners present?

PHAIDON: Yes, Simmias the Theban and Cebes and Phaidondes; and from Megara, Eucleides and Terpsion.

ECHECRATES: Oh, were not Aristippos and Cleombrotos present?

PHAIDON: No, they were said to be in Aegina.

ECHECRATES: Was anyone else there?

PHAIDON: I think these are about all who were present.

ECHECRATES: Very well; tell me, what did you talk about?

PHAIDON: I will try to tell you the whole story from the beginning. You see we had been accustomed during all the former days to visit Socrates, myself and the rest. We used to gather early at the court where the trial had been, for that was near the prison. We always waited until the prison was opened, passing the time together, for it was not opened early; and when it was opened we went in to Socrates and generally spent the day with him. That day, however, we gathered earlier than usual; for the day before, after we left the prison in the evening, we learnt that the ship had come in from Delos; so we warned one another to come as early as possible to the usual place. We came early, then, and the porter who used to answer the door came out to us, and told us to wait and not to go in till he gave the word; for, he said, "The Eleven[4] are knocking off his fetters and informing him that he must die today."

---

[1] Phlius, a small town in the Peloponnesus (Morea) about sixty miles from Athens.

[2] In Athenian legend, Athens because of a past misdeed had to send seven youths and seven maidens every ninth year to King Minos in Crete to be devoured by the Minotaur. Theseus of Athens went to Crete and killed the monster.

[3] Athenians.

[4] In charge of the prison and of executions.

After a short while he came back and told us to go in. So we went in, and found Socrates just released, and Xanthippe,[5] you know her, with his little boy, sitting beside him. Then when Xanthippe saw us, she cried out in lamentation and said as women do, "O Socrates! Here is the last time your friends will speak to you and you to them!"

Socrates glanced at Criton and said quietly, "Please let someone take her home, Criton."

Then some of Criton's people led her away crying and beating her breast. Socrates sat up on his bed, and bent back his leg and rubbed it with his hand, and said while he rubbed it, "How strange a thing it seems, my friends, that which people call pleasure! And how wonderful is its relation to pain, which they suppose to be its opposite; both together they will not come to a man, yet if he pursues one of the pair, and catches it, he is almost compelled to catch the other, too; so they seem to be both hung together from one head. I think that Aesop would have made a fable, if he had noticed this; he would have said they were at war, and God wanted to make peace between them and could not, and accordingly hung them together by their heads to the same thing, and therefore whenever you get one, the other follows after. That's just what it seems like to me; first came the pain in my leg from the irons, and here seems to come following after it, pleasure."

Cebes took up here, and said, "Upon my word, Socrates, I am much obliged to you for reminding me. About your poems, I mean, when you put into verse Aesop's fables, and the prelude for Apollo; many people have asked me, for example Euenos, the other day, what on earth put it in your mind to make those poems after you came into prison, although you never made any before. Then if you care that I should be able to answer Euenos, next time he asks me, and I'm sure he will, tell me what to say."

"Tell him then, Cebes," he said, "just the truth: that I did not want to rival him or his creations when I did it, for I knew it would not be easy; but I was trying to find out the meaning of certain dreams, and getting it off my conscience, in case they meant to command me to attempt that sort of composition. The dreams went like this: In my past life, the same dream often used to come to me, in different shapes at different times, but saying the same thing, 'Socrates, get to work and compose music!'[6] Formerly I took this to mean what I was already doing; I thought the dream was urging and encouraging me, as people do in cheering on their own men when they are running a race, to compose—which, taking philosophy to be the highest form of composition, I was doing already; but now after the trial, while the festival was putting off my execution, I thought that, if the dream should really command me to work at this common kind of composition, I ought not to disobey the dream but to do so. For it seemed safer not to go away before getting it off my conscience by composing poetry, and so obeying the dream. So first of all I composed in honour of the god[7] whose festival this was; after the god, I considered that a poet must compose fiction if he was to be a poet, not true tales, and I was no fiction-monger, and therefore I took the fictions that I found to my hand and knew, namely Aesop's, and composed the first that came. Then tell Euenos that, Cebes, and bid him farewell, and tell him to follow me as soon as he can, if he is sensible. I am going away, as it seems, today; for so the Athenians command."

"What advice, Socrates," he said, "to give to Euenos! I have often met the man; from what I have seen of him so far he will be the last man to obey!"

"Why," said he, "is not Euenos a philosopher?"

"I think so," said Simmias.

"Then Euenos will be willing enough, and so will everyone who goes properly into the subject. But perhaps he will not do violence to himself; for they say that is not lawful."

As he spoke, he let down his legs on to the ground, and sat thus during the rest of the talk. Then Cebes asked him, "What do you mean, Socrates, by saying, that it is not lawful for a man to do violence to himself, but that the philosopher would be willing to follow the dying?"

"Why, Cebes," he said, "have not you and Simmias heard all about such things from Philolaos, when you were his pupils?"

"Nothing clear, Socrates."

"Well truly, all I say myself is only from hearsay; however, what I happen to have heard I don't mind telling you. Indeed, it is perhaps most proper that one who is going to depart and take up his abode in that world should think about the life over there and say what sort of life we imagine it to be: for what else could one do with the time till sunset?"

"Well then, why pray do they say it is not lawful for a man to take his own life, my dear Socrates? I have already heard Philolaos myself, as you asked me just now, when he was staying in our parts, and I have heard others too, and they all said we must not do that; but I never heard anything clear about it."

"Well, go on trying," said Socrates, "and perhaps you may hear something. It might perhaps seem surprising to you if in this one thing, of all that happens to a human being, there is never any exception—if it never chances to a man amongst the other chances of his life that sometimes for some people it is better to die than to live; but it does probably seem surprising to you if those people for whom it *is* better to die may not rightly do this good to themselves, but must wait for some other benefactor."

And Cebes answered, with a light laugh. "True for ye, by Zeus!" using his native Doric.

"Indeed, put like this," said Socrates, "it would seem unreasonable; but possibly there is a grain of reason in it. At least, the tale whispered in secret about these things is that we men are in a sort of custody, and a man must not release himself or run away, which appears a great mystery to me and not easy to see through. But I do think, Cebes, it is right to say the gods are those who take care of us, and that we men are one of the gods' possessions—don't you think so?"

"Yes, I do," said Cebes.

"Then," said he, "if one of your own possessions, your slave, should kill himself, without your indicating to him that you wanted him to die, you would be angry with him, and punish him if there were any punishment?"

"Certainly," said he.

"Possibly, then, it is not unreasonable in that sense, that a man must not kill himself before God sends on him some necessity, like that which is present here now."

"Yes indeed, that seems likely," said Cebes. "But you said just now, Socrates, that philosophers ought cheerfully to be willing to die; that does seem unreasonable, at least if there is reason in what we have just said, that God is he who cares for us and we are his possessions. That the wisest men should not object to depart out of this service in which we are overseen by the best overseers there are, gods, there is no reason in that. For I don't suppose a wise man thinks he will care better for himself when he is free. But a foolish man might well believe that he should run away from an owner; and he would not remember that from a good one he ought not to run away but

---

[5]Socrates' wife.
[6]"Music" included poetry.
[7]Apollo.

to stay as long as he could, and so he would thoughtlessly run away, while the man of sense would desire always to be with one better than himself. Indeed, in this case, Socrates, the opposite of what was said would be likely: It is proper that wise men should object to die, and foolish men should be glad."

Socrates, hearing this, was pleased, I thought, at the way Cebes dealt with the matter; and, glancing away at us, he said, "Cebes is always on the hunt for arguments, and won't believe straight off whatever one says."

And Simmias added, "But I tell you, Socrates, I think I now see something in what Cebes says, myself; for what could men want, if they are truly wise, in running away from owners better than themselves, and lightly shaking them off? And I really think Cebes is aiming his argument at you, because you take it so easily to leave both us and good masters, as you admit yourself, gods!"

"Quite right," said he. "I think I must answer this before you just as if you were a court!"

"Exactly," said Simmias.

"Very well," said he, "I will try to convince you better than I did my judges. I believe, my dear Simmias and Cebes, that I shall pass over first of all to other gods, both wise and good, secondly to dead men better than those in this world; and if I did not think so, I should do wrong in not objecting to death; but, believing this, be assured that I hope I shall find myself in the company of good men, although I would not maintain it for certain; but that I shall pass over to gods who are very good masters, be assured that if I would maintain for certain anything else of the kind, I would with certainty maintain this. Then for these reasons, so far from objecting, I have good hopes that something remains for the dead, as has been the belief from time immemorial, and something much better for the good than for the bad."

"Then," said Simmias, "do you mean to keep this idea to yourself and go away with it, or will you give us a share? This good find seems to be a case of findings is sharings[8] between us, and don't forget you are on your defence, to see if you can convince us."

"Well, I'll try," he said.

"But first I see Criton here has been wanting to say something ever so long; let's ask what it is."

"Only this," Criton said, "the man who is to give you the poison keeps telling me to advise you not to talk too much. He says people get hotter by talking, and nothing like that ought to accompany the poison; otherwise people who do that often have to take two or three potions."

And Socrates said, "Oh, let him be; he must just be ready to give me two, or three if necessary."

"I guessed as much," said Criton, "but he keeps bothering me."

"Oh, let him be," said he. "Now then, I want to give the proof at once, to you as my judges, why I think it likely that one who has spent his life in philosophy should be confident when he is going to die, and have good hopes that he will win the greatest blessings in the next world when he has ended: so Simmias and Cebes my judges, I will try to show how this could be true.

"The fact is, those who tackle philosophy aright are simply and solely practising dying, practising death, all the time, but nobody sees it. If this is true, then it would surely be unreasonable that they should earnestly do this and nothing else all their lives, yet when death comes they should object to what they had been so long earnestly practising."

Simmias laughed at this, and said, "I don't feel like laughing just now, Socrates, but you have made me laugh. I think the many if they heard that would say, 'That's a good one for the philosophers!' And other people in my city would heartily agree that philosophers are really suffering from a wish to die, and now they have found them out, that they richly deserve it!"

"That would be true, Simmias," said Socrates, "except the words 'found out.' For they have not found out in what sense the real philosophers wish to die and deserve to die, and what kind of death it is. Let us say good-bye to them," he went on, "and ask ourselves: Do we think there is such a thing as death?"

"Certainly," Simmias put in.

"Is it anything more than the separation of the soul from the body?" said Socrates. "Death is, that the body separates from the soul, and remains by itself apart from the soul, and the soul, separated from the body, exists by itself apart from the body. Is death anything but that?"

"No," he said, "that is what death is."

"Then consider, my good friend, if you agree with me here, for I think this is the best way to understand the question we are examining. Do you think it the part of a philosopher to be earnestly concerned with what are called pleasures, such as these—eating and drinking, for example?"

"Not at all," said Simmias.

"The pleasures of love, then?"

"Oh no."

"Well, do you suppose a man like that regards the other bodily indulgences as precious? Getting fine clothes and shoes and other bodily adornments—ought he to price them high or low, beyond whatever share of them it is absolutely necessary to have?"

"Low, I think," he said, "if he is a true philosopher."

"Then in general," he said, "do you think that such a man's concern is not for the body, but as far as he can he stands aloof from that and turns towards the soul?"

"I do."

"Then firstly, is it not clear that in such things the philosopher as much as possible sets free the soul from communion with the body, more than other men?"

"So it appears."

"And I suppose, Simmias, it must seem to most men that he who has no pleasure in such things and takes no share in them does not deserve to live, but he is getting pretty close to death if he does not care about pleasures which he has by means of the body."

"Quite true, indeed."

"Well then, what about the actual getting of wisdom? Is the body in the way or not, if a man takes it with him as companion in the search? I mean, for example, is there any truth for men in their sight and hearing? Or as poets are forever dinning into our ears, do we hear nothing and see nothing exactly? Yet if these of our bodily senses are not exact and clear, the others will hardly be, for they are all inferior to these, don't you think so?"

"Certainly," he said.

"Then," said he, "when does the soul get hold of the truth? For whenever the soul tries to examine anything in company with the body, it is plain that it is deceived by it."

"Quite true."

"Then is it not clear that in reasoning, if anywhere, something of the realities becomes visible to it?"

"Yes."

"And I suppose it reasons best when none of these senses disturbs it, hearing or sight, or pain, or pleasure indeed, but when it is completely by itself and says good-bye to the body,

---

[8] A proverb.

THE GREEKS

and so far as possible has no dealings with it, when it reaches out and grasps that which really is."

"That is true."

"And is it not then that the philosopher's soul chiefly holds the body cheap and escapes from it, while it seeks to be by itself?"

"So it seems."

"Let us pass on, Simmias. Do we say there is such a thing as justice by itself, or not?"

"We do say so, certainly!"

"Such a thing as the good and beautiful?"

"Of course!"

"And did you ever see one of them with your eyes?"

"Never," said he.

"By any other sense of those the body has did you ever grasp them? I mean all such things, greatness, health, strength, in short everything that really is the nature of things whatever they are: Is it through the body that the real truth is perceived? Or is this better—whoever of us prepares himself most completely and most exactly to comprehend each thing which he examines would come nearest to knowing each one?"

"Certainly."

"And would he do that most purely who should approach each with his intelligence alone, not adding sight to intelligence, or dragging in any other sense along with reasoning, but using the intelligence uncontaminated alone by itself, while he tries to hunt out each essence uncontaminated, keeping clear of eyes and ears and, one might say, of the whole body, because he thinks the body disturbs him and hinders the soul from getting possession of truth and wisdom when body and soul are companions—is not this the man, Simmias, if anyone, who will hit reality?"

"Nothing could be more true, Socrates," said Simmias.

"Then from all this," said Socrates, "genuine philosophers must come to some such opinion as follows, so as to make to one another statements such as these: 'A sort of direct path, so to speak, seems to take us to the conclusion that so long as we have the body with us in our enquiry, and our soul is mixed up with so great an evil, we shall never attain sufficiently what we desire, and that, we say, is the truth. For the body provides thousands of busy distractions because of its necessary food; besides, if diseases fall upon us, they hinder us from the pursuit of the real. With loves and desires and fears and all kinds of fancies and much rubbish, it infects us, and really and truly makes us, as they say, unable to think one little bit about anything at any time. Indeed, wars and factions and battles all come from the body and its desires, and from nothing else. For the desire of getting wealth causes all wars, and we are compelled to desire wealth by the body, being slaves to its culture; therefore we have no leisure for philosophy, from all these reasons. Chief of all is that if we do have some leisure, and turn away from the body to speculate on something, in our searches it is everywhere interfering, it causes confusion and disturbance, and dazzles us so that it will not let us see the truth; so in fact we see that if we are ever to know anything purely we must get rid of it, and examine the real things by the soul alone; and then, it seems, after we are dead, as the reasoning shows, not while we live, we shall possess that which we desire, lovers of which we say we are, namely wisdom. For if it is impossible in company with the body to know anything purely, one thing of two follows: either knowledge is possible nowhere, or only after death; for then alone the soul will be quite by itself apart from the body, but not before. And while we are alive, we shall be nearest to knowing, as it seems, if as far as possible we have no commerce or communion with the body which is not absolutely necessary, and if we are not infected with its nature, but keep ourselves pure from it, until God himself shall set us free. And so, pure and rid of the body's foolishness, we shall probably be in the company of those like ourselves, and shall know through our own selves complete incontamination, and that is perhaps the truth. But for the impure to grasp the pure is not, it seems, allowed.' So we must think, Simmias, and so we must say to one another, all who are rightly lovers of learning; don't you agree?"

"Assuredly, Socrates."

"Then," said Socrates, "if this is true, my comrade, there is great hope that when I arrive where I am travelling, there if anywhere I shall sufficiently possess that for which all our study has been pursued in this past life. So the journey which has been commanded for me is made with good hope, and the same for any other man who believes he has got his mind purified, as I may call it."

"Certainly," replied Simmias.

"And is not purification really that which has been mentioned so often in our discussion, to separate as far as possible the soul from the body, and to accustom it to collect itself together out of the body in every part, and to dwell alone by itself as far as it can, both at this present and in the future, being freed from the body as if from a prison?"

"By all means," said he.

"Then is not this called death—a freeing and separation of soul from body?"

"Not a doubt of that," said he.

"But to set it free, as we say, is the chief endeavour of those who rightly love wisdom, nay of those alone, and the very care and practice of the philosophers is nothing but the freeing and separation of soul from body, don't you think so?"

"It appears to be so."

"Then, as I said at first, it would be absurd for a man preparing himself in his life to be as near as possible to death, so to live, and then when death came, to object?"

"Of course."

"Then in fact, Simmias," he said, "those who rightly love wisdom are practising dying, and death to them is the least terrible thing in the world. Look at it in this way: If they are everywhere at enmity with the body, and desire the soul to be alone by itself, and if, when this very thing happens, they shall fear and object—would not that be wholly unreasonable? Should they not willingly go to a place where there is good hope of finding what they were in love with all through life (and they loved wisdom), and of ridding themselves of the companion which they hated? When human favourites and wives and sons have died, many have been willing to go down to the grave, drawn by the hope of seeing there those they used to desire, and of being with them; but one who is really in love with wisdom and holds firm to this same hope, that he will find it in the grave, and nowhere else worth speaking of —will he then fret at dying and not go thither rejoicing? We must surely think, my comrade, that he will go rejoicing, if he is really a philosopher; he will surely believe that he will find wisdom in its purity there and there alone. If this is true, would it not be most unreasonable, as I said just now, if such a one feared death?"

"Unreasonable, I do declare," said he.

"Then this is proof enough," he said, "that if you see a man fretting because he is to die, he was not really a philosopher, but a philosoma—not a wisdom-lover but a body-lover. And no doubt the same man is money-lover and honours-lover, one or both."

"It certainly is so, as you say," he replied.

"Then, Simmias," he said, "does not what is called courage belong specially to persons so disposed as philosophers are?"

"I have no doubt of it," said he.

"And the same with temperance, what the many call temperance, not to be agitated about desires but to hold them lightly and decently; does not this belong to those alone who hold the body lightly and live in philosophy?"

"That must be so," he said.

"You see," said he, "if you will consider the courage and temperance of others, you will think it strange."

"How so, Socrates?"

"You know," said he, "that everyone else thinks death one of the greatest evils?"

"Indeed I do," he said.

"Then is it not fear of greater evils which makes the brave endure death, when they do?"

"That is true."

"Then fear, and fearing, makes all men brave, except philosophers. Yet it is unreasonable to become brave by fear and cowardice!"

"Certainly."

"And what of the decent men? Are they not in the same case? A sort of intemperance makes them temperate! Although we say such a thing is impossible, nevertheless with that self-complacent temperance they are in a similar case; because they fear to be deprived of other pleasures, and because they desire them, they abstain from some because they are mastered by others. They say, of course, intemperance is 'to be ruled by pleasures'; yet what happens to them is, to master some pleasures and to be mastered by others, and this is much the same as what was said just now, that in a way intemperance has made them temperate."

"So it seems."

"Bless you, Simmias! This is hardly an honest deal in virtue—to trade pleasure for pleasure, and pain for pain, and fear for fear, and even greater for less, as if they were current coin; no, the only honest currency, for which all these must be traded, is wisdom, and all things are in truth to be bought with this and sold for this.[9] And courage and temperance and justice and, in short, true virtue, depend on wisdom, whether pleasure and fear and all other such things are added or taken away. But when they are deprived of wisdom and exchanged one for another, virtue of that kind is no more than a make-believe,[10] a thing in reality slavish and having no health or truth in it; and truth is in reality a cleansing from all such things, and temperance and justice and courage, and wisdom itself, are a means of purification. Indeed, it seems those who established our mystic rites were no fools; they in truth spoke with a hidden meaning long ago when they said that whoever is uninitiated and unconsecrated when he comes to the house of Hades will lie in mud, but the purified and consecrated when he goes there will dwell with gods. Indeed, as they say in the rites, 'Many are called but few are chosen',[11] and these few are in my opinion no others than those who have loved wisdom in the right way. One of these I have tried to be by every effort in all my life, and I have left nothing undone according to my ability; if I have endeavoured in the right way, if we have succeeded at all, we shall know clearly when we get there; very soon, if God will, as I think. There is my defence before you gentlemen on the bench, Simmias and Cebes, showing that in leaving you and my masters here, I am reasonable in not fretting or being upset, because I believe that I shall find there good masters and good comrades. So if I am more convincing to you in my defence than I was to the Athenian judges, I should be satisfied."

When Socrates had thus finished, Cebes took up the word: "Socrates," he said, "on the whole I think you speak well; but that about the soul is a thing which people find very hard to believe. They fear that when it parts from the body it is nowhere any more; but on the day when a man dies, as it parts from the body, and goes out like a breath or a whiff of smoke, it is dispersed and flies away and is gone and is nowhere any more. If it existed anywhere, gathered together by itself, and rid of these evils which you have just described, there would be great and good hope, Socrates, that what you say is true; but this very thing needs no small reassurance and faith, that the soul exists when the man dies, and that it has some power and sense."

"Quite true," said Socrates, "quite true, Cebes; well, what are we to do? Shall we discuss this very question, whether such a thing is likely or not?"

"For my part," said Cebes, "I should very much like to know what your opinion is about it."

Then Socrates answered, "I think no one who heard us now could say, not even a composer of comedies, that I am babbling nonsense and talking about things I have nothing to do with! So if you like, we must make a full enquiry.

"Let us enquire whether the souls of dead men really exist in the house of Hades or not. Well, there is the very ancient legend which we remember, that they are continually arriving there from this world, and further that they come back here and are born again from the dead. If that is true, and the living are born again from the dead, must not our souls exist there? For they could not be born again if they did not exist; and this would be sufficient proof that it is true, if it should be really shown that the living are born from the dead and from nowhere else. But if this be not true, we must take some other line."

"Certainly," said Cebes.

"Then don't consider it as regards men only," he said; "if you wish to understand more easily, think of all animals and vegetables, and, in a word, everything that was birth, let us see if everything comes into being like that, always opposite from opposite and from nowhere else; whenever there happens to be a pair of opposites, such as beautiful and ugly, just and unjust, and thousands of others like these. So let us enquire whether everything that has an opposite must come from its opposite and from nowhere else. For example, when anything becomes bigger, it must, I suppose, become bigger from being smaller before."

"Yes."

"And if it becomes smaller, it was bigger before and became smaller after that?"

"True," he said.

"And again, weaker from stronger, and slower from quicker?"

"Certainly."

"Very well, if a thing becomes worse, is it from being better, and more just from more unjust?"

"Of course."

"Have we established that sufficiently, then, that everything comes into being in this way, opposite from opposite?"

"Certainly."

"Again, is there not the same sort of thing in them all, between the two opposites two becomings, from the first to the second, and back from the second to the first; between greater and lesser increase and diminution, and we call one increasing and the other diminishing?"

"Yes," he said.

---

[9] Plato's text is doubtful here, and in the next two sentences.
[10] σκιαγραφαί, literally, a shadow-drawing.
[11] The Greek means "Wand-bearers are many, inspired mystics are few."

"And being separated and being mingled, growing cold and growing hot, and so with all; even if we have sometimes no names for them, yet in fact at least it must be the same everywhere, that they come into being from each other, and that there is a becoming from one to the other?"

"Certainly," said he.

"Well then," he said, "is there something opposite to being alive, as sleeping is opposite to being awake?"

"There is," he said.

"What?"

"Being dead," he said.

"Well, all these things come into being from each other, if they are opposites, and there are two becomings between each two?"

"Of course."

"Then," said Socrates, "I will speak of one of the two pairs that I mentioned just now, and its becomings; you tell me about the other. My pair is sleeping and being awake, and I say that being awake comes into being from sleeping and sleeping from being awake, and that their becomings are falling asleep and waking up. Is that satisfactory?"

"Quite so."

"Then you tell me in the same way about life and death. Do you not say that to be alive is the opposite of to be dead?"

"I do."

"And that they come into being from each other?"

"Yes."

"From the living, then, what comes into being?"

"The dead," he said.

"And what from the dead?"

"The living, I must admit."

"Then from the dead, Cebes, come living things and living men?"

"So it appears," he said.

"Then," said he, "our souls exist in the house of Hades."

"It seems so."

"Well, of the two becomings between them, one is quite clear. For dying is clear, I suppose, don't you think so?"

"Oh yes," said he.

"Then what shall we do?" he said. "Shall we refuse to grant in return the opposite becoming; and shall nature be lame in this point? Is it not a necessity to grant some becoming opposite to dying?"

"Surely it is," he said.

"What is that?"

"Coming to life again."

"Then," said he, "if there is coming to life again, this coming to life would be a being born from the dead into the living."

"Certainly."

"It is agreed between us, then, in this way also that the living are born from the dead, no less than the dead from the living: and since this is true, there would seem to be sufficient proof that the souls of the dead must of necessity exist somewhere, whence we assume they are born again."

"It seems to me, Socrates," he answered, "from our admissions that must of necessity be true."

"Another way of looking at this, Cebes," he said, "shows, as I think, that we were right to make those admissions. If opposites did not return back continually to replace opposites, coming into being just as if going round in a circle, but if birth were something going direct from the opposite once only into the exact opposite and never bent back and returned back again to its original, be sure that in the end all things would get the same form and go through the same process, and becomings would cease."

"How do you mean?" he asked.

"What I mean is nothing difficult to understand," said he.

"For example, if there were falling asleep, but waking up did not return back in its place, coming into being from the sleeping, be sure that in the end Endymion[12] would be nowhere and this would show his story to be nonsense, because everything else would be in the same state as he, fast asleep. And if everything were combined and nothing split up, the result would be the Chaos of Anaxagoras, 'all things together.' In the same way, my dear Cebes, if everything died that had any life, and when it died, the dead things remained in that state and never came to life again, is it not absolutely necessary that in the end all things would be dead and nothing alive? For if the living things came into being from things other than the dead, and the living died, all things must be swallowed up in death, and what device could possibly prevent it?"

"Nothing could possibly prevent it, Socrates, and what you say I think perfectly true."

"Yes, Cebes," he said, "I think this is all perfectly true, and we are not deceived in admitting what we did; but in fact coming to life again is really true, and living persons are born from the dead, and the souls of the dead exist."[13]

"Another thing," said Cebes, putting in, "you know that favourite argument of yours, Socrates, which we so often heard from you, that our learning is simply recollection: that also makes it necessary, I suppose, if it is true, that we learnt at some former time what we now remember; but this is impossible unless our soul existed somewhere before it was born in this human shape. In this way also the soul seems to be something immortal."

Then Simmias put in, "But, Cebes, what are the proofs of this? Remind me, for I don't quite remember now."

"There is one very beautiful proof," said Cebes, "that people, when asked questions, if they are properly asked, say of themselves everything correctly; yet if there were not knowledge in them, and right reason, they would not be able to do this. You see, if you show someone a diagram or anything like that, he proves most clearly that this is true."

Socrates said, "If you don't believe this, Simmias, look at it in another way and see whether you agree. You disbelieve, I take it, how what is called learning can be recollection?"

"Disbelieve you," said Simmias, "not I! I just want to have an experience of what we are now discussing—recollection. I almost remember and believe already from what Cebes tried to say; yet none the less I should like to hear how *you* were going to put it."

"This is how," he answered. "We agree, I suppose, that if anyone remembers something he must have known it before at some time."

"Certainly," he said.

"Then do we agree on this also, that when knowledge comes to him in such a way, it is recollection? What I mean is something like this: If a man has seen or heard something or perceived it by some other sense, and he not only knows that, but thinks of something else of which the knowledge is not the same but different, is it not right for us to say he remembered that which he thought of?"

"How do you mean?"

"Here is an example: Knowledge of a man and knowledge of a lyre are different."

"Of course."

---

[12]The Moon fell in love with Endymion, most beautiful of men, and kept him in a perpetual sleep on Mt. Latmos, so that she could embrace him nightly.

[13]Socrates' theory of a conservation of life is somewhat like our familiar theory of the conservation of energy.

"Well, you know about lovers, that when they see a lyre or a dress or anything else which their beloved uses, this is what happens to them: they know the lyre, and they conceive in the mind the figure of the boy whose lyre it is? Now this is recollection; just as when one sees Simmias, one often remembers Cebes, and there would be thousands of things like that."

"Thousands, indeed!" said Simmias.

"Then is that sort of thing," said he, "a kind of recollection? Especially when one feels this about things which one had forgotten because of time and neglect?"

"Certainly," he said.

"Very well then," said Socrates. "When you see a horse in a picture, or a lyre in a picture, is it possible to remember a man? And when you see Simmias in a picture, to remember Cebes?"

"Yes indeed."

"Or when you see Simmias in a picture, to remember Simmias himself?"

"Oh yes," said he.

["These being either like or unlike?"

"Yes."

"It makes no difference," he said. "Whenever, seeing one thing, from sight of this you think of another thing whether like or unlike, it is necessary," he said, "that that was recollection."

"Certainly."][11]

"Does it not follow from all this that recollection is both from like and from unlike things?"

"It does."

"But when a man remembers something from like things, must this not necessarily occur to him also—to reflect whether anything is lacking or not from the likeness of what he remembers?"

"He must."

"Consider then," he said, "if this is true. We say, I suppose, there is such a thing as the equal, not a stick equal to a stick, or a stone to a stone, or anything like that, but something independent which is alongside all of them, the equal itself, equality; yes or no?"

"Yes indeed," said Simmias, "upon my word, no doubt about it."

"And do we understand what that is?"

"Certainly," he said. "Where did we get the knowledge of it? Was it not from such examples as we gave just now, by seeing equal sticks or stones and so forth, from these we conceived that, which was something distinct from them? Don't you think it is distinct? Look at it this way also: Do not the same stones or sticks appear equal to one person and unequal to another?"

"Certainly."

"Well, did the really-equals ever seem unequal to you, I mean did equality ever seem to be inequality?"

"Never, Socrates."

"Then those equal things," said he, "are not the same as the equal itself."

"Not at all, I think, Socrates."

"Yet from these equals," he said, "being distinct from that equal, you nevertheless conceived and received knowledge of that equal?"

"Very true," he said.

"Well," said he, "how do we feel about the sticks as compared with the real equals we spoke of just now; do the equal sticks seem to us to be as equal as equality itself, or do they fall somewhat short of the essential nature of equality; or nothing short?"

"They fall short," he said, "a great deal."

"Then we agree on this: When one sees a thing, and thinks, 'This which I now see wants to be like something else—like one of the things that are, but falls short and is unable to be such as that is, it is inferior,' it is necessary, I suppose, that he who thinks thus has previous knowledge of that which he thinks it resembles but falls short of?"

"That is necessary."

"Very well, do we feel like that or not about equal things and the equal?"

"Assuredly we do."

"It is necessary then that we knew the equal before that time when, first seeing the equal things, we thought that all these aim at being such as the equal, but fall short."

"That is true."

"Well, we go on to agree here also: we did not and we could not get a notion of the equal by any other means than by seeing or grasping, or perceiving by some other sense. I say the same of equal and all the rest."

"And they are the same, Socrates, for what the argument wants to prove."

"Look here, then; it is from the senses we must get the notion that all these things of sense aim at that which is the equal, and fall short of it; or how do we say?"

"Yes."

"Then before we began to see and hear and use our other senses, we must have got somewhere knowledge of what the equal is, if we were going to compare with it the things judged equal by the senses and see that all things are eager to be such as that equal is, but are inferior to it."

"This is necessary from what we agreed, Socrates."

"Well, as soon as we were born we saw and heard and had our other senses?"

"Certainly."

"Then, we say, we must have got knowledge of the equal before that?"

"Yes."

"Before we were born, then, it is necessary that we must have got it."

"So it seems."

"Then if we got it before we were born and we were born having it, we knew before we were born and as soon as we were born, not only the equal and the greater and the less but all the rest of such things? For our argument now is no more about the equal than about the beautiful itself, and the good itself, and the just and the pious, and I mean everything which we seal with the name of 'that which is,' the essence, when we ask our questions and respond with our answers in discussion. So we must have got the proper knowledge of each of these before we were born."

"That is true."

"And if having got the knowledge, in each case, we have not forgotten, we must continue knowing this and know it through life; for to know is, having got knowledge of something, to keep it and not to lose it; dropping knowledge, Simmias, is what we call forgetfulness, isn't it?"

"Just so, Socrates," he said.

"But, I think, if we got it before birth, and lost it at birth, and if afterwards, using our senses about these things, we recover the knowledge which once before we had, would not what we call learning be to recover our own knowledge? And this we should rightly call recollection?"

"Certainly."

"For, you see, it has been shown to be possible that a man perceiving something, by sight or hearing or some other sense, thinks, from this perception, of some other thing which

---

[14]The bracketed passage has been transposed from 74 C-D of the Greek text, where it would appear to be meaningless.

he has forgotten, to which he compares this as being like or unlike. So as I say, there is choice of two things: either we were all born knowing them and we all know them throughout life; or afterwards those who we say learn just remember, and nothing more, and learning would be recollection."

"That is certainly true, Socrates."

"Which do you choose then, Simmias? Were we born knowing, or do we remember afterwards what we had got knowledge of before?"

"I can't choose all at once, Socrates."

"Another question, then; you can choose, and have some opinion about this. When a man knows anything, could he give an account of what he knows or not?"

"He must be able to do that, Socrates."

"Do you think that all could give account of the matters we have been discussing?"

"I would that they could," said Simmias, "but so far from that, I fear that tomorrow at this time there may be no one left in the world able to do that properly."

"Then, Simmias, you don't think that all know them?"

"Oh, no!"

"Then are they trying to remember what they once learnt?"

"It must be so."

"When did our souls get the knowledge of these things? For surely it is not since we became human beings."

"Certainly not."

"Then before."

"Yes."

"So, Simmias, our souls existed long ago, before they were in human shape, apart from bodies, and then had wisdom."

"Unless, indeed, we get all these knowledges at birth, Socrates; for this time is still left."

"Very well, my comrade; at what other time do we lose them? For we are not born having them, as we admitted just now. Do we lose them at the very same time as we get them? Can you suggest any other time?"

"Oh no, Socrates, I did not see I was talking nonsense."

"Is this the case then, Simmias?" he asked. "If all these exist which we are always harping on, the beautiful and the good and every such essence; and if we refer to these essences all the things which our senses perceive, finding out that the essences existed before and are ours now, and compare our sensations with them, it necessarily follows that, just as these exist, so our soul must have existed before our birth; but if they do not exist, this argument will be worthless. Is this true, and is there equal necessity that these things exist and our souls did before our birth, or if they do not exist, neither did our souls?"

"I am quite convinced, Socrates," said Simmias, "that there is the same necessity; our argument has found an excellent refuge when it maintains equally that our soul exists before we are born, and the essences likewise which you speak of. Nothing is clearer to me than this, that all such things exist most assuredly, beauty and good and the others which you named; and I think it has been sufficiently proved."

"And what thinks Cebes?" said Socrates. "We must convince Cebes too."

"It is good enough for him," said Simmias, "as I believe; but he is the most obstinate man in the world at disbelieving what is said; however, I believe he really is convinced that our soul existed before our birth.

"Yet will it exist after death too?" he went on. "I don't think myself that has been proved yet, Socrates. We are confronted still with what Cebes said just now: Can it be that when the man dies his soul is scattered abroad and that is the end of it, as so many say? For supposing it is composed from somewhere or other, and comes into existence before it even enters a human body; what hinders it, when it has entered and finally got rid of that body, from ending at that moment also, and being itself destroyed?"

"Well said, Simmias," said Cebes. "It does seem that half of what ought to be proved has been proved, that our soul exists before our birth; it must also be proved that when we die it will exist no less than before our birth, if the proof is to be completed."

"It has been proved already, my dear Simmias and Cebes," said Socrates, "if you choose to combine this argument with what we agreed to before it, that all the living comes from the dead. For if the soul exists before, and if it is necessary that when coming into life and being born it comes from death and from nothing else at all, it must certainly be necessary that it exists even when one dies, since it must be born again. Well then, what you said has in fact been proved already. Still, I think you and Cebes would be glad to investigate this argument yet further, and you seem to me to have the fear which children have—that really, when it leaves the body, the wind blows it away and scatters it, especially if anyone dies not in calm weather but in a great tempest."

Cebes laughed, and said, "Then think we are afraid of that, Socrates," he said, "and try to convince us against it; or better, don't think *we* are afraid, but imagine there is a kind of child in us which has such fears; then let us try to persuade this child not to fear death as if it were a bogey."

"No," said Socrates, "you must sing incantations over it every day, until you charm it out."

"My dear Socrates," he said, "where shall we get a good charmer of such things, since you are leaving us?"

"Hellas is a big place, my dear Cebes," he replied, "and there are many good men in it, and there are many barbarian nations too; and you must search through them all looking for such a charmer; you must spare neither money nor pains, since you could not spend money on anything more important. And you must not forget to search among yourselves; for perhaps you could not easily find any better able than yourselves to do that."

"Oh, that shall be done, of course," said Cebes; "but let us go back to where we left off—if you would like to."

"But certainly I should like to," he said; "of course I should!"

"That's well said," said Cebes.

"Very well then," said Socrates, "we must ask ourselves what sorts of things properly undergo this; I mean, what sorts of things are dissolved and scattered, for what sorts we must fear such an end, and for what not; next we must consider which sort the soul belongs to. We shall know then whether to be confident or fearful for our own soul."

"True," he said.

"Isn't it to the composite, which is by nature compounded, that dissolution is proper—I mean it is dissolved just as it was composed? And, on the other hand, an uncompounded thing, if indeed such exists, is least of all things naturally liable to dissolution?"

"That seems to me correct," said Cebes.

"Then what is always the same and in the same state is likely to be the uncompounded, but what is always changing and never keeps in the same state is likely to be the compounded?"

"I think so."

"Let us turn to what we have discussed already," he said. "This essence which we describe in all our questions and answers as existing—is it always in the same state or does it change? I mean the equal itself, the beautiful itself, everything which exists by itself, that which is—does it admit of any changes whatever? Or is it true that each thing that so exists, being of one form and itself alone, is always in the same state, and never admits of any change whatever in any way or at any time or in any place?"

"It must necessarily be always in the same state," said Cebes.

"And what of the many particulars, men or horses or dresses or what you will, things equal or beautiful and so forth, all that have the same name as those essences? Are they always in the same state; or, quite opposite to the essences, are they not constantly changing in themselves and in relation to each other, and, one might say, never keep in the same state?"

"That again is right," said Cebes, "they never keep in the same state."

"These, then, you could touch or see or perceive by the other senses, but those which continue in the same state cannot be grasped by anything except intellectual reasoning, and such things are unseen[15] and not visible?"

"Certainly that is true," he said.

"Shall we lay down, then, that there are two kinds of existing things, one visible, one unseen?"

"Yes," he said.

"And the unseen is always in the same state, but the visible constantly changing?"

"Yes to that also," he said.

"Now come," said he, "in ourselves one part is body and one part soul?"

"Just so," he said.

"Then which kind do we say the body would be more like and akin to?"

"The visible," he said, "that is clear to anyone."

"And the soul—is it visible, or unseen?"

"Not visible to mankind at least, Socrates," he said.

"But when we say visible and not visible, we mean to human senses, don't we?"

"Yes, we do."

"Then what of the soul—do we say that is visible or invisible?"

"Not visible."

"Unseen, then?"

"Yes."

"Then soul is more like to the unseen, and body to the visible."

"It surely must be."

"Now you remember that we were saying some time ago that the soul, when it has the body to help in examining things, either through sight or hearing or any other sense—for to examine something through the body means through the senses—then it is dragged by the body towards what is always changing, and the soul goes astray and is confused and staggers about like one drunken because she is taking hold of such things."

"Certainly."

"But when she examines by herself, she goes away yonder to the pure and everlasting and immortal and unchanging; and being akin to that, she abides ever with it, whenever it becomes possible for her to abide by herself. And there she rests from her wanderings, and while she is amongst those things she is herself unchanging because what she takes hold of is unchanging: and this state of the soul has the name of wisdom?"

"Most excellent and true, Socrates."

"Then which of the two kinds is she more like and more akin to, judging from what we said before and what we are saying now?"

"Everyone, even the most ignorant, would admit, I think, Socrates," he said, "from that way of reasoning, that soul is wholly and altogether more like the unchanging than the changing."

"And the body?"

"More like the changing."

"Look at it in this way also: When soul and body are together, our nature assigns the body to be slave and to be ruled, and the soul to be ruler and master; now, then, further, which of the two seems to be like the divine, and which like the mortal? Don't you think the divine is naturally such as to rule and to guide, and the mortal such as to be ruled and to be a slave?"

"I do."

"Then which is the soul like?"

"It is clear, Socrates, that the soul is like the divine, and the body like the mortal."

"Consider now, Cebes, whether it follows from all that we have said, that the soul is most like the divine and immortal and intellectual and simple and indissoluble and self-unchangeable, but on the contrary, the body is most like the human and mortal and manifold and unintellectual and dissoluble and ever-changing. Can we say anything to contradict that, my dear Cebes, or is that correct?"

"We cannot contradict it."

"Very well. This being so, is it not proper to the body to be quickly dissolved, but on the contrary to the soul to be wholly indissoluble or very nearly so?"

"Of course."

"You understand, then," he said, "that when the man dies, the visible part of him, the body—that which lies in the visible world, and which we call the corpse, for which it is proper to dissolve and disappear—does not suffer any of this at once but instead remains a good long time, and if a man dies with his body in a nice condition and age, a very long time. For if the body is shrivelled up and mummified like the mummies in Egypt it lasts almost whole, for an incredibly long time. And some portions of the body, even when it decays, bones and sinews and so forth, may almost be called immortal."

"Yes."

"But the soul, the 'unseen' part of us, which goes to another place noble and pure and unseen like itself, a true unseen Hades, to the presence of the good and wise God, where, if God will, my own soul must go very soon—shall our soul, then, being such and of such nature, when released from the body be straightway scattered by the winds and perish, as most men say? Far from it, my dear Simmias! This is much more likely: If it is pure when it gets free, and drags nothing of the body with it, since it has no communion with the body in life if it can help it, but avoids the body and gathers itself into itself, since it is always practising this—here we have nothing else but a soul loving wisdom rightly, and in reality practising death—don't you think this would be a practice of death?"

"By all means."

"Then, being thus, it goes away into the unseen, which is like itself, the divine and immortal and wise, where on arrival it has the opportunity to be happy, freed from wandering and folly and fears and wild loves and all other human evils, and, as they say of the initiated, really and truly passing the rest of time with the gods. Is that what we are to say, Cebes?"

"Yes indeed," said Cebes.

"But if contrariwise, I think, if it leaves the body polluted and unpurified, as having been always with it and attending it and in love with it and bewitched by it through desires and pleasures, so that it thinks nothing to be true but the bodily

---

[15] The word used is ἀειδής, unseen or without form. Plato introduces it here because it sounds significantly like the word Ἀιδης, Hades, suggesting that the unchanging essences are immaterial and belong to the other world.

—what one could touch and see and drink and eat and use for carnal passion; if what is darksome to the eyes and 'unseen' but intellectual and to be caught by philosophy, if this, I say, it is accustomed to hate and fear and flee; do you think a soul in that state will get away pure and incorrupt in itself?"

"By no possible means whatever," he said.

"No, I think it is interpenetrated by the bodily, which the association and union with it of the body has by constant practice made ingrained."

"Exactly."

"A heavy load, my friend, we must believe that to be, heavy and earthy and visible; and such a soul with this on board is weighed down and dragged back into the visible world, by fear of the unseen, Hades so-called, and cruises[16] about restless among tombs and graves, where you know shadowy apparitions of souls have often been seen, phantoms such as are produced by souls like this, which have not been released purely, but keep something of the visible, and so they are seen."

"That is likely, Socrates."

"Indeed it is likely; and likely that these are not the souls of the good, but souls of the mean, which are compelled to wander about such places as a penalty for their former way of life, which was evil; and wander they must until by desire for the bodily which is always in their company they are imprisoned once more in a body. And they are imprisoned, as is likely, into the same habits which they had practised in life before."

"What sort of habits do you mean, Socrates?"

"It is likely, for example, that those who have practised gluttony and violence and drunkenness and have not taken heed to their ways enter the bodies of asses and suchlike beasts, don't you think so?"

"Very likely indeed."

"Those, again, who have preferred injustice and tyrannies and robberies, into the bodies of wolves and hawks and kites; or where else do we say they would go?"

"No doubt," said Cebes, "they pass into creatures like these."

"Then it is clear," said he, "that the rest go wherever they do go, to suit their own likenesses and habits?"

"Quite clear, of course," he said.

"Then of these the happiest people," he said, "and those who go to the best place, are those who have practised the public and political virtues which they call temperance and justice, got from habit and custom without philosophy and reason?"

"How are these happiest, pray?"

"Why, isn't it likely that they pass into another similar political and gentle race, perhaps bees or wasps or ants; or even into the same human race again, and that there are born from them decent men?"

"Yes, that is likely."

"But into the family of gods, unless one is a philosopher and departs wholly pure, it is not permitted for any to enter, except the lover of learning. Indeed, it is for the sake of this purity, Simmias and Cebes, my two good comrades, that those who truly seek wisdom steadfastly abstain from all bodily desires and refuse to give themselves over to them, not from having any fear of ruin of their home or of poverty, as the money-loving multitude has; and again, not from being afraid of dishonour, or a bad reputation for wickedness, as the honour-lovers and power-lovers are; that is why these abstain from them."

"No, Socrates," said Cebes, "that would not be proper."

"Not at all, by heaven," said he. "Therefore those who care at all for their own soul and do not live just serving[17] the body say good-bye to everyone of that kind and walk not after guides who know not where they are going; for they themselves believe they must not act contrary to philosophy, and its deliverance and purification, and so they turn to philosophy and follow by the way she leads them."

"How, Socrates?"

"I will tell you," he said.

"The lovers of learning understand," said he, "that philosophy found their soul simply imprisoned in the body and welded to it, and compelled to survey through this as if through prison bars the things that are, not by itself through itself, but wallowing in all ignorance; and she saw that the danger of this prison came through desire, so that the prisoner himself would be chief helper in his own imprisonment. As I say then, lovers of learning understand that philosophy, taking possession of their soul in this state, gently encourages it and tries to free it, by showing that surveying through the eyes is full of deceit, and so is perception through the ears and the other senses; she persuades the soul to withdraw from these, except so far as there is necessity to use them, and exhorts it to collect itself together and gather itself into itself, and to trust nothing at all but itself, and only whatever of the realities each in itself the soul itself by itself can understand; but that whatever of what varies with its environs the soul examines through other means, it must consider this to be no part of truth; such a thing, philosophy tells it, is a thing of the senses and of the visible, but what it sees itself is a thing of the intellect and of the 'unseen.' So the soul of the true philosopher believes that it must not oppose this deliverance, and therefore abstains from pleasures and desires and griefs and fears as much as possible, counting that when a man feels great pleasure or fear or pain or desire, he suffers not only the evil that one might think (for example, being ill or squandering money through his desires), but the greatest and worst of all evils, which he suffers and never counts."

"What is that, Socrates?" asked Cebes.

"That the soul of every man suffers this double compulsion: At the same time as it is compelled to feel great pleasure or pain about anything, it is compelled also to believe that the thing for which it specially feels this is most clearly real and true, when it is not. These are generally the visible things, aren't they?"

"Certainly."

"Then in this state especially the soul is imprisoned by the body?"

"Pray how?"

"Because each pleasure and pain seems to have a nail, and nails the soul to the body and pins it on and makes it bodily, and so it thinks the same things are true which the body says are true. For by having the same opinion as the body, and liking the same things, it is compelled, I believe, to adopt the same ways and the same nourishment, and to become such as never could come pure to the house of Hades, but would always go forth infected by the body; so it would fall again quickly into another body and there be sown and grown, and therefore would have neither part nor lot in communion with the divine and pure and simple."

"Most true, indeed," said Cebes.

"So then it is for these reasons, Cebes, that those who rightly love learning are decent and brave, not for the reasons which the many give; what do you think?"

"Certainly not."

---

[16] Literally "rolls about" (like a ship at sea).
[17] This word is doubtful in the Greek text.

"No indeed. Such would be the reasoning of the philosopher. His soul would not think it right that philosophy should set her free, and that while being set free she herself should surrender herself back again in bondage to pleasures and pains, and so perform the endless task of a Penelope unweaving the work of her loom.[18] No, she thinks she must calm these passions; and, following reason and keeping always in it, beholding the true and the divine and the certain, and nourishing herself on this, his soul believes that she ought to live thus, as long as she does live, and when she dies she will join what is akin and like herself, and be rid of human evils. After nurture of this kind there is nothing to fear, my dear Simmias and Cebes, and she need not expect in parting from the body to be scattered about and blown away by the winds, and to be gone like a bird and be nowhere any more."

* * * * * *

With these words, he got up and retired into another room for the bath, and Criton went after him, telling us to wait. So we waited discussing and talking together about what had been said, or sometimes speaking of the great misfortune which had befallen us, for we felt really as if we had lost a father and had to spend the rest of our lives as orphans. When he had bathed, and his children had been brought to see him—for he had two little sons, and one big—and when the women of his family had come, he talked to them before Criton and gave what instructions he wished. Then he asked the women and children to go, and came back to us. It was now near sunset, for he had spent a long time within. He came and sat down after his bath, and he had not talked long after this when the servant of the Eleven came in, and standing by him said, "O Socrates! I have not to complain of you as I do of others, that they are angry with me, and curse me, because I bring them word to drink their potion, which my officers make me do! But I have always found you in this time most generous and gentle, and the best man who ever came here. And now too, I know well you are not angry with me, for you know who are responsible, and you keep it for them. Now you know what I came to tell you, so farewell, and try to bear as well as you can what can't be helped."

Then he turned and was going out, with tears running down his cheeks. And Socrates looked up at him and said, "Farewell to you also, I will do so." Then, at the same time turning to us, "What a nice fellow!" he said. "All the time he has been coming and talking to me, a real good sort, and now how generously he sheds tears for me! Come along, Criton, let's obey him. Someone bring the potion, if the stuff has been ground; if not, let the fellow grind it."

Then Criton said, "But, Socrates, I think the sun is still over the hills, it has not set yet. Yes, and I know of others who, having been told to drink the poison, have done it very late; they had dinner first and a good one, and some enjoyed the company of any they wanted. Please don't be in a hurry, there is time to spare."

But Socrates said, "Those you speak of have very good reason for doing that, for they think they will gain by doing it; and I have good reasons why I won't do it. For I think I shall gain nothing by drinking a little later, only that I shall think myself a fool for clinging to life and sparing when the cask's empty.[19] Come along," he said, "do what I tell you, if you please."

And Criton, hearing this, nodded to the boy who stood near. The boy went out, and after spending a long time, came in with the man who was to give the poison[20] carrying it ground ready in a cup. Socrates caught sight of the man and said, "Here, my good man, you know about these things; what must I do?"

"Just drink it," he said, "and walk about till your legs get heavy, then lie down. In that way the drug will act of itself."

At the same time, he held out the cup to Socrates, and he took it quite cheerfully, Echecrates, not a tremble, not a change in colour or looks; but looking full at the man under his brows, as he used to do, he asked him. "What do you say about this drink? What of a libation to someone?[21] Is that allowed, or not?"

He said, "We only grind so much as we think enough for a moderate potion."

"I understand," he said, "but at least, I suppose, it is allowed to offer a prayer to the gods and that must be done, for good luck in the migration from here to there. Then that is my prayer, and so may it be!"

With these words he put the cup to his lips and, quite easy and contented, drank it up. So far most of us had been able to hold back our tears pretty well; but when we saw him begin drinking and end drinking, we could no longer. I burst into a flood of tears for all I could do, so I wrapped up my face and cried myself out; not for him indeed, but for my own misfortune in losing such a man and such a comrade. Criton had got up and gone out even before I did, for he could not hold the tears in. Apollodoros had never ceased weeping all this time, and now he burst out into loud sobs, and by his weeping and lamentations completely broke down every man there except Socrates himself. He only said, "What a scene! You amaze me. That's just why I sent the women away, to keep them from making a scene like this. I've heard that one ought to make an end in decent silence. Quiet yourselves and endure."

When we heard him we felt ashamed and restrained our tears. He walked about, and when he said that his legs were feeling heavy, he lay down on his back, as the man told him to do; at the same time the one who gave him the potion felt him, and after a while examined his feet and legs; then pinching a foot hard, he asked if he felt anything; he said no. After this, again, he pressed the shins; and, moving up like this, he showed us that he was growing cold and stiff. Again he felt him, and told us that when it came to his heart, he would be gone. Already the cold had come nearly as far as the abdomen, when Socrates threw off the covering from his face—for he had covered it over—and said, the last words he uttered, "Criton," he said, "we owe a cock to Asclepios;[22] pay it without fail."

"That indeed shall be done," said Criton. "Have you anything more to say?"

---

[18] Penelope prolonged her task for three years by unweaving at night what she wove by day. *Odyssey* xix. Bodily indulgence is unweaving and the soul would have to weave it up again.

[19] There's a proverb:
Cask full or failing, drink; but in between
Spare if you like; sparing at bottom's mean.
Hesiod, *Works and Days*, 368

[20] The poison was hemlock.

[21] The custom was for the butler to spill a drop into the cup which the drinker then spilt on the ground as a libation with a prayer; then the butler filled and the man drank.

[22] A thank-offering to the god of healing. The cock is the poor man's offering. The touching beauty and restraint of this account is heightened still more, if Plato, who was ill and unable to be present at the death of his dearest friend, took this last request to have been made for his sake.

When Criton had asked this, Socrates gave no further answer, but after a little time, he stirred, and the man uncovered him, and his eyes were still. Criton, seeing this, closed the mouth and eyelids.

This was the end of our comrade, Echecrates, a man, as we would say, of all then living we had ever met, the noblest and the wisest and most just.

THE REPUBLIC[1]

BOOK III

There can be no doubt that the elder must rule the younger.

Clearly.

And that the best of these must rule.

That is also clear.

Now, are not the best husbandmen those who are most devoted to husbandry?

Yes.

And as we are to have the best of guardians for our city, must they not be those who have most the character of guardians?

Yes.

And to this end they ought to be wise and efficient, and to have a special care of the State?

True.

And a man will be most likely to care about that which he loves?

To be sure.

And he will be most likely to love that which he regards as having the same interests with himself, and that of which the good or evil fortune is supposed by him at any time most to affect his own?

Very true, he replied.

Then there must be a selection. Let us note among the guardians those who in their whole life show the greatest eagerness to do what is for the good of their country, and the greatest repugnance to do what is against her interests.

Those are the right men.

And they will have to be watched at every age, in order that we may see whether they preserve their resolution, and never, under the influence either of force or enchantment, forget or cast off their sense of duty to the State.

How cast off? he said.

I will explain to you, I replied. A resolution may go out of a man's mind either with his will or against his will; with his will when he gets rid of a falsehood and learns better, against his will whenever he is deprived of a truth.

I understand, he said, the willing loss of a resolution; the meaning of the unwilling I have yet to learn.

Why, I said, do you not see that men are unwillingly deprived of good, and willingly of evil? Is not to have lost the truth an evil, and to possess the truth a good? and you would agree that to conceive things as they are is to possess the truth?

Yes, he replied; I agree with you in thinking that mankind are deprived of truth against their will.

And is not this involuntary deprivation caused either by theft, or force, or enchantment?

Still, he replied, I do not understand you.

I fear that I must have been talking darkly, like the tragedians. I only mean that some men are changed by persuasion and that others forget; argument steals away the hearts of one class, and time of the other; and this I call theft. Now you understand me?

Yes.

Those again who are forced, are those whom the violence of some pain or grief compels to change their opinion.

I understand, he said, and you are quite right.

And you would also acknowledge that the enchanted are those who change their minds either under the softer influence of pleasure, or the sterner influence of fear?

Yes, he said; everything that deceives may be said to enchant.

Therefore, as I was just now saying, we must enquire who are the best guardians of their own conviction that what they think the interest of the State is to be the rule of their lives. We must watch them from their youth upwards, and make them perform actions in which they are most likely to forget or to be deceived, and he who remembers and is not deceived is to be selected, and he who fails in the trial is to be rejected. That will be the way?

Yes.

And there should also be toils and pains and conflicts prescribed for them, in which they will be made to give further proof of the same qualities.

Very right, he replied.

And then, I said, we must try them with enchantments — that is the third sort of test — and see what will be their behaviour: like those who take colts amid noise and tumult to see if they are of a timid nature, so must we take our youth amid terrors of some kind, and again pass them into pleasures, and prove them more thoroughly

---
[1] As translated by Benjamin Jowett.

than gold is proved in the furnace, that we may discover whether they are armed against all enchantments, and of a noble bearing always, good guardians of themselves and of the music which they have learned, and retaining under all circumstances a rhythmical and harmonious nature, such as will be most serviceable to the individual and to the State. And he who at every age, as boy and youth and in mature life, has come out of the trial victorious and pure, shall be appointed a ruler and guardian of the State; he shall be honoured in life and death, and shall receive sepulture and other memorials of honour, the greatest that we have to give. But him who fails, we must reject. I am inclined to think that this is the sort of way in which our rulers and guardians should be chosen and appointed. I speak generally, and not with any pretension to exactness.

And, speaking generally, I agree with you, he said.

And perhaps the word 'guardian' in the fullest sense ought to be be applied to this higher class only who preserve us against foreign enemies and maintain peace among our citizens at home, that the one may not have the will, or the others the power, to harm us. The young men whom we before called guardians may be more properly designated auxiliaries and supporters of the principles of the rulers.

I agree with you, he said.

How then may we devise one of those needful falsehoods of which we lately spoke — just one royal lie which may deceive the rulers, if that be possible, and at any rate the rest of the city?

What sort of lie? he said.

Nothing new, I replied; only an old Phoenician tale of what has often occurred before now in other places, (as the poets say, and have made the world believe,) though not in our time, and I do not know whether such an event could ever happen again, or could now even be made probable, if it did.

How your words seem to hesitate on your lips!

You will not wonder, I replied, at my hesitation when you have heard.

Speak, he said, and fear not.

Well then, I will speak, although I really know not how to look you in the face, or in what words to utter the audacious fiction, which I propose to communicate gradually, first to the rulers, then to the soldiers, and lastly to the people. They are to be told that their youth was a dream, and the education and training which they received from us, an appearance only; in reality during all that time they were being formed and fed in the womb of the earth, where they themselves and their arms and appurtenances were manufactured, when they were completed, the earth, their mother, sent them up; and so, their country being their mother and also their nurse, they are bound to advise for her good, and to defend her against attacks, and her citizens they are to regard as children of the earth and their own brothers.

You had good reason, he said, to be ashamed of the lie which you were going to tell.

True, I replied, but there is more coming. I have only told you half. Citizens, we shall say to them in our tale, you are brothers, yet God has framed you differently. Some of you have the power of command, and in the composition of these he has mingled gold, wherefore also they have the greatest honour; others he has made of silver, to be auxiliaries; others again who are to be husbandmen and craftsmen he has composed of brass and iron; and the species will generally be preserved in the children. But as all are of the same original stock, a golden parent will sometimes have a silver son, or a silver parent a golden son. And God proclaims as a first principle to the rulers, and above all else, that there is nothing which they should so anxiously guard, or of which they are to be such good guardians, as of the purity of the race. They should observe what elements mingle in their offspring; for if the son of a golden or silver parent has an admixture of brass and iron, then nature orders a transposition of ranks, and the eye of the ruler must not be pitiful towards the child because he has to descend in the scale and become a husbandman or artisan, just as there may be sons of artisans who having an admixture of gold or silver in them are raised to honour, and become guardians or auxiliaries. For an oracle says that when a man of brass or iron guards the State, it will be destroyed. Such is the tale; is there any possibility of making our citizens believe in it?

Not in the present generation, he replied; there is no way of accomplishing this; but their sons may be made to believe in the tale, and their sons' sons, and posterity after them.

I see the difficulty, I replied; yet the fostering of such a belief will make them care more for the city and for one another. Enough, however, of the fiction, which may now fly abroad upon the wings of rumour, while we arm our earth-born heroes, and lead them forth under the command of their rulers. Let them look around and select a spot whence they can best suppress insurrection, if any prove refractory within, and also defend themselves against enemies, who like wolves may come down on the fold from without; there let them encamp, and when they have encamped, let them sacrifice to the proper Gods and prepare their dwellings.

Just so, he said.

And their dwellings must be such as will shield them against the cold of winter and the heat of summer.

I suppose that you mean houses, he replied.

Yes, I said; but they must be the houses of soldiers, and not of shop-keepers.

What is the difference? he said.

That I will endeavour to explain, I replied. To keep

watch-dogs, who, from want of discipline or hunger, or some evil habit or other, would turn upon the sheep and worry them, and behave not like dogs but wolves, would be a foul and monstrous thing in a shepherd?

Truly monstrous, he said.

And therefore every care must be taken that our auxiliaries, being stronger than our citizens, may not grow to be too much for them and become savage tyrants instead of friends and allies?

Yes, great care should be taken.

And would not a really good education furnish the best safeguard?

But they are well-educated already, he replied.

I cannot be so confident, my dear Glaucon, I said; I am much more certain that they ought to be, and that true education, whatever that may be, will have the greatest tendency to civilize and humanize them in their relations to one another, and to those who are under their protection.

Very true, he replied.

And not only their education, but their habitations, and all that belongs to them, should be such as will neither impair their virtue as guardians, nor tempt them to prey upon the other citizens. Any man of sense must acknowledge that.

He must.

Then now let us consider what will be their way of life, if they are to realize our idea of them. In the first place, none of them should have any property of his own beyond what is absolutely necessary; neither should they have a private house or store closed against any one who has a mind to enter; their provisions should be only such as are required by trained warriors, who are men of temperance and courage; they should agree to receive from the citizens a fixed rate of pay, enough to meet the expenses of the year and no more; and they will go to mess and live together like soldiers in a camp. Gold and silver we will tell them that they have from God; the diviner metal is within them, and they have therefore no need of the dross which is current among men, and ought not to pollute the divine by any such earthly admixture; for that commoner metal has been the source of many unholy deeds, but their own is undefiled. And they alone of all the citizens may not touch or handle silver or gold, or be under the same roof with them, or wear them, or drink from them. And this will be their salvation, and they will be the saviours of the State. But should they ever acquire homes or lands or moneys of their own, they will become housekeepers and husbandmen instead of guardians, enemies and tyrants instead of allies of the other citizens; hating and being hated, plotting and being plotted against, they will pass their whole life in much greater terror of internal than of external enemies, and the hour of ruin, both to themselves and to the rest of the State, will be at hand. For all which reasons may we not say that thus shall our State be ordered, and that these shall be the regulations appointed by us for our guardians concerning their houses and all other matters?

Yes, said Glaucon.

BOOK IV

Here Adeimantus interposed a question: How would you answer, Socrates, said he, if a person were to say that [for their own good] you are making these people miserable, and that they are the cause of their own unhappiness; the city in fact belongs to them, but they are none the better for it; whereas other men acquire lands, and build large and handsome houses, and have everything handsome about them, offering sacrifices to the gods on their own account, and practising hospitality; moreover, as you were saying just now, they have gold and silver, and all that is usual among the favourites of fortune; but our poor citizens are no better than mercenaries who are quartered in the city and are always mounting guard?

Yes, I said; and you may add that they are only fed, and not paid in addition to their food, like other men; and therefore they cannot, if they would, take a journey of pleasure; they have no money to spend on a mistress or any other luxurious fancy, which, as the world goes, is thought to be happiness; and many other accusations of the same nature might be added.

But, said he, let us suppose all this to be included in the charge.

You mean to ask, I said, what will be our answer?

Yes.

If we proceed along the old path, my belief, I said, is that we shall find the answer. And our answer will be that, even as they are, our guardians may very likely be the happiest of men; but that our aim in founding the State was not the disproportionate happiness of any one class, but the greatest happiness of the whole; we thought that in a State which is ordered with a view to the good of the whole we should be most likely to find justice, and in the ill-ordered State injustice: and, having found them, we might then decide which of the two is the happier. At present, I take it, we are fashioning the happy State, not piecemeal, or with a view of making a few happy citizens, but as a whole; and by-and-by we will proceed to view the opposite kind of State. Suppose that we were painting a statue, and some one came up to us and said, Why do you not put the most beautiful colours on the most beautiful parts of the body — the eyes ought to be purple, but you have made them black — to him we might fairly answer, Sir, you would not surely have us beautify the eyes to such a degree that they are no longer eyes; consider rather whether, by giving this and the other features their due proportion, we make the whole beautiful. And so I say to you, do not compel us to assign to the guardians a sort of happiness which will make them anything but guardians; for we too can clothe our husbandmen in royal apparel, and set crowns of gold on their heads, and bid them till the ground as much as they like, and no more. Our potters also might be allowed to repose on couches, and feast by the fireside, passing round the winecup, while their wheel is conveniently at hand, and working at pottery only as much as they like; in this way we might make every class happy — and then, as you imagine, the whole State would be happy. But do not put this idea into our heads; for, if we listen to you, the husbandman will be no longer a husbandman, the potter will cease to be a potter, and no one will have the character of any distinct class in the State. Now this is not of much consequence where the corruption of society, and pretension to be what you are not, is confined to cobblers; but when the guardians of the laws and of the government are only seeming and not real guardians, then see how they turn the State upside down; and on the other hand they alone have the power of giving order and happiness to the State. We mean our guardians to be true saviours and not the destroyers of the State, whereas our opponent is thinking of peasants at a festival, who are enjoying a life of revelry, not of citizens who are doing their duty to the State. But, if so, we mean different things, and he is speaking of something which is not a State. And therefore we must consider whether in appointing our guardians we would look to their greatest happiness individually, or whether this principle of happiness does not rather reside in the State as a whole. But if the latter be the truth, then the guardians and auxiliaries, and all others equally with them, must be compelled or induced to do their own work in the best way. And thus the whole State will grow up in a noble order, and the several classes will receive the proportion of happiness which nature assigns to them.

I think that you are quite right.

I wonder whether you will agree with another remark which occurs to me.

What may that be?

There seem to be two causes of the deterioration of the arts.

What are they?

Wealth, I said, and poverty.

How do they act?

The process is as follows: When a potter becomes rich, will he, think you, any longer take the same pains with his art?

Certainly not.

He will grow more and more indolent and careless?

Very true.

And the result will be that he becomes a worse potter?

Yes; he greatly deteriorates.

But, on the other hand, if he has no money, and cannot provide himself with tools or instruments, he will not work equally well himself, nor will he teach his sons or apprentices to work equally well.

Certainly not.

Then, under the influence either of poverty or of wealth, workmen and their work are equally liable to degenerate?

That is evident.

Here, then, is a discovery of new evils, I said, against which the guardians will have to watch, or they will creep into the city unobserved.

What evils?

Wealth, I said, and poverty; the one is the parent of luxury and indolence, and the other of meanness and viciousness, and both of discontent.

That is very true, he replied; but still I should like to know, Socrates, how our city will be able to go to war, especially against an enemy who is rich and powerful, if deprived of the sinews of war.

There would certainly be a difficulty, I replied, in going to war with one such enemy; but there is no difficulty where there are two of them.

How so? he asked.

In the first place, I said, if we have to fight, our side will be trained warriors fighting against an army of rich men.

That is true, he said.

And do you not suppose, Adeimantus, that a single boxer who was perfect in his art would easily be a match for two stout and well-to-do gentlemen who were not boxers?

Hardly, if they came upon him at once.

What, not, I said, if he were able to run away and then turn and strike at the one who first came up? And supposing he were to do this several times under the heat of a scorching sun, might he not, being an expert, overturn more than one stout personage?

Certainly, he said, there would be nothing wonderful in that.

And yet rich men probably have a greater superiority in the science and practise of boxing than they have in military qualities.

Likely enough.

Then we may assume that our athletes will be able to fight with two or three times their own number?

I agree with you, for I think you right.

And suppose that, before engaging, our citizens send an embassy to one of the two cities, telling them what is the truth: Silver and gold we neither have nor are permitted to have, but you may; do you therefore come and help us in war, and take the spoils of the other city: Who, on hearing these words, would choose to fight against lean wiry dogs, rather than, with the dogs on their side, against fat and tender sheep?

That is not likely; and yet there might be a danger to the poor State if the wealth of many States were to be gathered into one.

But how simple of you to use the term State at all of any but our own!

THE GREEKS

Why so?

You ought to speak of other States in the plural number; not one of them is a city, but many cities, as they say in the game. For indeed any city, however small, is in fact divided into two, one the city of the poor, the other of the rich; these are at war with one another; and in either there are many smaller divisions, and you would be altogether beside the mark if you treated them all as a single State. But if you deal with them as many, and give the wealth or power or persons of the one to the others, you will always have a great many friends and not many enemies. And your State, while the wise order which has now been prescribed continues to prevail in her, will be the greatest of States, I do not mean to say in reputation or appearance, but in deed and truth, though she number not more than a thousand defenders. A single State which is her equal you will hardly find, either among Hellenes or barbarians, though many that appear to be as great and many times greater.

That is most true, he said.

And what, I said, will be the best limit for our rulers to fix when they are considering the size of the State and the amount of territory which they are to include, and beyond which they will not go?

What limit would you propose?

I would allow the State to increase so far as is consistent with unity; that, I think, is the proper limit.

Very good, he said.

Here then, I said, is another order which will have to be conveyed to our guardians: Let our city be accounted neither large nor small, but one and self-sufficing.

And surely, said he, this is not a very severe order which we impose upon them.

And the other, said I, of which we were speaking before is lighter still, — I mean the duty of degrading the offspring of the guardians when inferior, and of elevating into the rank of guardians the offspring of the lower classes, when naturally superior. The intention was, that, in the case of the citizens generally, each individual should be put to the use for which nature intended him, one to one work, and then every man would do his own business, and be one and not many; and so the whole city would be one and not many.

Yes, he said; that is not so difficult.

The regulations which we are prescribing my good Adeimantus, are not, as might be supposed, a number of great principles, but trifles all, if care be taken, as the saying is, of the one great thing, — a thing, however, which I would rather call, not, great, but sufficient for our purpose.

What may that be? he asked.

Education, I said, and nurture: If our citizens are well educated, and grow into sensible men, they will easily see their way through all these, as well as other matters which I omit; such, for example, as marriage, the possession of women and the procreation of children, which will all follow the general principle that friends have all things in common, as the proverb says.

That will be the best way of settling them.

Also, I said, the State, if once started well moves with accumulating force like a wheel. For good nurture and education implant good constitutions, and these good constitutions taking root in a good education improve more and more, and this improvement affects the breed in man as in other animals. . . .

BOOK V

What sort of community of women and children is this which is to prevail among our guardians? And how shall we manage the period between birth and education, which seems to require the greatest care? Tell us how these things will be.

For men born and educated like our citizens, the only way, in my opinion, of arriving at a right conclusion about the possession and use of women and children is to follow the path on which we originally started, when we said that the men were to be the guardians and watchdogs of the herd.

True.

Let us further suppose the birth and education of our women to be subject to similar or nearly similar regulations; then we shall see whether the result accords with our design.

What do you mean?

What I mean may be put into the form of a question, I said: Are dogs divided into hes and shes, or do they share equally in hunting and in keeping watch and in the other duties of dogs? Or do we entrust to the males the entire and exclusive care of the flocks, while we leave the females at home, under the idea that the bearing and suckling their puppies is labour enough for them?

No, he said, they share alike; the only difference between them is that the males are stronger and the females weaker.

But can you use different animals for the same purpose, unless they are bred and fed in the same way?

You cannot.

Then, if women are to have the same duties as men, they must have the same nurture and education?

Yes.

The education which was assigned to the men was music and gymnastic.

Yes.

Then women must be taught music and gymnastic and also the art of war, which they must practise like the men?

That is the inference, I suppose. . . .

The law, I said, which is the sequel of this and of all that has preceded, is to the following effect, — 'that the wives of our guardians are to be common, and their children are to be common, and no parent is to know his own child, nor any child his parent.' . . .

I do not think, I said, that there can be any dispute about the very great utility of having wives and children in common; the possibility is quite another matter, and will be very much disputed. . . . If you have no objection, I will endeavour with your help to consider the advantages of the measure; and hereafter the question of possibility.

I have no objection; proceed.

First, I think that if our rulers and their auxiliaries are to be worthy of the name which they bear, there must be willingness to obey in the one and the power of command in the other; the guardians must themselves obey the laws, and they must also imitate the spirit of them in any details which are entrusted to their care.

That is right, he said.

You, I said, who are their legislator, having selected the men, will now select the women and give them to them; — they must be as far as possible of like natures with them; and they must live in common houses and meet at common meals. None of them will have anything specially his or her own; they will be together, and will be brought up together and will associate at gymnastic exercises. And so they will be drawn by a necessity of their natures to have intercourse with each other — necessity is not too strong a word, I think?

Yes, he said; — necessity, not geometrical, but another sort of necessity which lovers know, and which is far more convincing and constraining to the mass of mankind.

True, I said; and this, Glaucon, like all the rest, must proceed after an orderly fashion; in a city of the blessed, licentiousness is an unholy thing which the rulers will forbid.

Yes, he said, and it ought not to be permitted.

Then clearly the next thing will be to make matrimony sacred in the highest degree, and what is most beneficial will be deemed sacred?

Exactly.

And how can marriages be made most beneficial? — that is a question which I put to you, because I see in your house dogs for hunting, and of the nobler sort of birds not a few. Now, I beseech you, do tell me, have you ever attended to their pairing and breeding?

In what particulars?

Why, in the first place, although they are all of a good sort, are not some better than others?

True.

And do you breed from them all indifferently, or do you take care to breed from the best only?

From the best.

And do you take the oldest or the youngest, or only those of ripe age?

I choose only those of ripe age.

And if care was not taken in the breeding, your dogs and birds would greatly deteriorate?

Certainly.

And the same of horses and of animals in general?

Undoubtedly.

Good heavens! my dear friend, I said, what consummate skill will our rulers need if the same principle holds of the human species!

Certainly, the same principle holds; but why does this involve any particular skill?

Because, I said, our rulers will often have to practice upon the body corporate with medicines. Now you know that when patients do not require medicines, but have only to be put under a regimen, the inferior sort of practitioner is deemed to be good enough, but when medicine has to be given, then the doctor should be more of a man.

That is quite true, he said; but to what are you alluding?

I mean, I replied, that our rulers will find a considerable dose of falsehood and deceit necessary for the good of their subjects: we were saying that the use of all these things regarded as medicines might be of advantage.

And we were very right.

And this lawful use of them seems likely to be often needed in the regulations of marriages and births.

How so?

Why, I said, the principle has been already laid down that the best of either sex should be united with the best as often, and the inferior with the inferior, as seldom as possible; and that they should rear the offspring of the one sort of union, but not of the other, if the flock is to be maintained in first-rate condition. Now these goings on must be a secret which the rulers only know, or there will be a further danger of our herd, as the guardians may be termed, breaking out into rebellion.

Very true.

Had we not better appoint certain festivals at which we will bring together the brides and bridegrooms, and sacrifices will be offered and suitable hymeneal songs composed by our poets: the number of weddings is a matter which must be left to the discretion of the rulers, whose aim will be to preserve the average of population? There are many other things which they will have to consider, such as the effects of wars and diseases and any similar agencies, in order as far as this is possible to prevent the State from becoming either too large or too small.

Certainly, he replied.

We shall have to invent some ingenious kind of lots which the less worthy may draw on each occasion of our bringing them together, and then they will accuse their own ill-luck and not the rulers.

To be sure, he said.

And I think that our braver and better youth, besides their other honours and rewards, might have greater facilities of intercourse with women given them; their bravery will be a reason, and such fathers ought to have as many sons as possible.

True.

And the proper officers, whether male or female or both, for offices are to be held by women as well as by men —

Yes —

The proper officers will take the offspring of the good parents to the pen or fold, and there they will deposit them with certain nurses who dwell in a separate quarter; but the offspring of the inferior, or of the better when they chance to be deformed, will be put away in some mysterious, unknown place, as they should be.

Yes, he said, that must be done if the breed of the guardians is to be kept pure.

They will provide for their nurture, and will bring the mothers to the fold when they are full of milk, taking the greatest possible care that no mother recognises her own child; and other wet-nurses may be engaged if more are required. Care will also be taken that the process of suckling shall not be protracted too long, and the mothers will have no getting up at night or other trouble, but will hand over all this sort of thing to the nurses and attendants.

You suppose the wives of our guardians to have a fine easy time of it when they are having children.

Why, said I, and so they ought. Let us, however, proceed with our scheme. We were saying that the parents should be in the prime of life?

Very true.

And what is the prime of life? May it not be defined as a period of about twenty years in a woman's life, and thirty in a man's?

Which years do you mean to include?

A woman, I said, at twenty years of age may begin to bear children to the State, and continue to bear them until forty; a man may begin at five and twenty, when he has passed the point at which the pulse of life beats quickest, and continue to beget children until he be fifty-five.

Certainly, he said, both in men and women those years are the prime of physical as well as of intellectual vigour.

Any one above or below the prescribed ages who takes part in the public hymeneals shall be said to have done an unholy and unrighteous thing; the child of which he is the father, if it steals into life, will have been conceived under auspices very unlike the sacrifices and prayers, which at each hymeneal priestesses and priests and the whole city will offer, that the new generation may be better and more useful than their good and useful parents, whereas his child will be the offspring of darkness and strange lust.

Very true, he replied.

And the same law will apply to any one of those within the prescribed age who forms a connection with any woman in the prime of life without the sanction of the rulers; for we shall say that he is raising up a bastard to the State, uncertified and unconsecrated.

Very true, he replied.

This applies, however, only to those who are within the specified age: after that we allow them to range at will, except that a man may not marry his daughter or his daughter's daughter, or his mother or his mother's mother; and women, on the other hand, are prohibited from marrying their sons or fathers, or son's son or father's father, and so on in either direction. And we grant all this, accompanying the permission with strict orders to prevent any embryo which may come into being from seeing the light; and if any force a way to the birth, the parents must understand that the offspring of such an union cannot be maintained, and arrange accordingly.

That also, he said, is a reasonable proposition. But how will they know who are fathers and daughters, and so on?

They will never know. The way will be this: — dating from the day of the hymeneal, the bridegroom who was then married will call all the male children who are born in the seventh and the tenth month afterwards, his sons, and the female children his daughters, and they will call him father, and he will call their children his grandchildren, and they will call the elder generation grandfathers and grandmothers. All who were begotten at the time when their fathers and mothers came together will be called their brothers and sisters, and these, as I was saying, will be forbidden to intermarry. This, however, is not to be understood as an absolute prohibition of the marriage of brothers and sisters; if the lot favours them, and they receive the sanction of the Pythian oracle, the law will allow them.

Quite right, he replied.

Such is the scheme, Glaucon, according to which the guardians of our State are to have their wives and families in common. And now you would have the argument show that this community is consistent with the rest of our polity, and also that nothing can be better — would you not?

Yes, certainly.

Shall we try to find a common basis by asking of ourselves what ought to be the chief aim of the legislator in making laws and in the organization of a State, — what is the greatest good, and what is the greatest evil, and then consider whether our previous description has the stamp of the good or of the evil?

By all means.

Can there be any greater evil than discord and distraction and plurality where unity ought to reign? or any greater good than the bond of unity?

There cannot.

And there is unity where there is community of pleasures and pains — where all the citizens are glad or grieved on the same occasions of joy and sorrow?

No doubt.

Yes; and where there is no common but only private feeling a State is disorganized — when you have one half of the world triumphing and the other plunged in grief at the same events happening to the city or the citizens?

Certainly.

Such differences commonly originate in a disagreement about the use of the terms 'mine' and 'not mine,' 'his' and 'not his.'

Exactly so.

And is not that the best-ordered State in which the greatest number of persons apply the terms 'mine' and 'not mine' in the same way to the same thing?

Quite true.

Or that again which most nearly approaches to the condition of the individual — as in the body, when but a finger of one of us is hurt, the whole frame, drawn towards the soul as a centre and forming one kingdom under the ruling power therein, feels the hurt and sympathizes all together with the part affected, and we say that the man has a pain in his finger; and the same expression is used about any other part of the body, which has a sensation of pain at suffering or of pleasure at the alleviation of suffering.

Very true, he replied; and I agree with you that in the best-ordered State there is the nearest approach to this common feeling which you describe.

Then when any one of the citizens experiences any good or evil, the whole State will make his case their own, and will either rejoice or sorrow with him?

Yes, he said, that is what will happen in a well-ordered State.

It will now be time, I said, for us to return to our State and see whether this or some other form is most in accordance with these fundamental principles.

Very good.

Our State like every other has rulers and subjects?

True.

All of whom will call one another citizens?

Of course.

But is there not another name which people give to their rulers in other States?

Generally they call them masters, but in democratic States they simply call them rulers.

And in our State what other name besides that of citizens do the people give the rulers?

They are called saviours and helpers, he replied.

And what do the rulers call the people?

Their maintainers and foster-fathers.

And what do they call them in other States?

Slaves.

And what do the rulers call one another in other States?

Fellow-rulers.

And what in ours?

Fellow-guardians.

Did you ever know an example in any other State of a ruler who would speak of one of his colleagues as his friend and of another as not being his friend?

Yes, very often.

And the friend he regards and describes as one in whom he has an interest, and the other as a stranger in whom he has no interest?

Exactly.

But would any of your guardians think or speak of any other guardian as a stranger?

Certainly he would not; for every one whom they meet will be regarded by them either as a brother or sister, or father or mother, or son or daughter, or as the child or parent of those who are thus connected with him.

Capital, I said; but let me ask you once more: Shall they be a family in name only; or shall they in all their actions be true to the name? For example, in the use of the word 'father,' would the care of a father be implied and the filial reverence and duty and obedience to him which the law commands; and is the violator of these duties to be regarded as an impious and unrighteous person who is not likely to receive much good either at the hands of God or of man? Are these to be or not to be the strains which the children will hear repeated in their ears by all the citizens about those who are intimated to them to be their parents and the rest of their kinsfolk?

These, he said, and none other; for what can be more ridiculous than for them to utter the names of family ties with the lips only and not to act in the spirit of them?

Then in our city the language of harmony and concord will be more often heard than in any other. As I was describing before, when any one is well or ill, the universal word will be 'with me it is well' or 'it is ill.'

Most true.

And agreeably to this mode of thinking and speaking, were we not saying that they will have their pleasures and pains in common?

Yes, and so they will.

And they will have a common interest in the same thing which they will alike call 'my own,' and having this common interest they will have a common feeling of pleasure and pain?

THE GREEKS

Yes, far more so than in other States.

And the reason of this, over and above the general constitution of the State, will be that the guardians will have a community of women and children?

That will be the chief reason.

And this unity of feeling we admitted to be the greatest good, as was implied in our own comparison of a well-ordered State to the relation of the body and the members, when affected by pleasure or pain?

That we acknowledged, and very rightly.

Then the community of wives and children among our citizens is clearly the source of the greatest good to the State?

Certainly.

And this agrees with the other principle which we were affirming, — that the guardians were not to have houses or lands or any other property; their pay was to be their food, which they were to receive from the other citizens, and they were to have no private expenses; for we intended them to preserve their true character of guardians.

Right, he replied.

Both the community of property and the community of families, as I am saying, tend to make them more truly guardians; they will not tear the city in pieces by differing about 'mine' and 'not mine'; each man dragging any acquisition which he has made into a separate house of his own, where he has a separate wife and children and private pleasures and pains; but all will be affected as far as may be by the same pleasures and pains because they are all of one opinion about what is near and dear to them, and therefore they all tend towards a common end.

Certainly, he replied.

And as they have nothing but their persons which they can call their own, suits and complaints will have no existence among them; they will be delivered from all those quarrels of which money or children or relations are the occasion.

Of course they will.

Neither will trials for assault or insult ever be likely to occur among them. For that equals should defend themselves against equals we shall maintain to be honourable and right; we shall make the protection of the person a matter of necessity.

That is good, he said.

Yes; and there is a further good in the law; viz. that if a man has a quarrel with another he will satisfy his resentment then and there, and not proceed to more dangerous lengths.

Certainly.

To the elder shall be assigned the duty of ruling and chastising the younger.

Clearly.

Nor can there be a doubt that the younger will not strike or do any other violence to an elder, unless the magistrates command him; nor will he slight him in any way. For there are two guardians, shame and fear, mighty to prevent him: shame, which makes men refrain from laying hands on those who are to them in the relation of parents; fear, that the injured one will be succoured by the others who are his brothers, sons, fathers.

That is true, he replied.

Then in every way the laws will help the citizens to keep the peace with one another?

Yes, there will be no want of peace.

And as the guardians will never quarrel among themselves there will be no danger of the rest of the city being divided either against them or against one another. . . .

Until philosophers are kings, or the kings and princes of this world have the spirit and power of philosophy, and political greatness and wisdom meet in one, and those commoner natures who pursue either to the exclusion of the other are compelled to stand aside, cities will never have rest from their evils — no, nor the human race, as I believe — and then only will this our State have a possibility of life and behold the light of day. Such was the thought, my dear Glaucon, which I would fain have uttered if it had not seemed too extravagant; for to be convinced that in no other State can there be happiness private or public is indeed a hard thing.

Socrates, what do you mean? I would have you consider that the word which you have uttered is one at which numerous persons, and very respectable persons too, in a figure pulling off their coats all in a moment, and seizing any weapon that comes to hand, will run at you might and main, before you know where you are, intending to do heaven knows what; and if you don't prepare an answer, and put yourself in motion, you will be 'pared by their fine wits', and no mistake.

You got me into the scrape, I said.

And I was quite right; however, I will do all I can to get you out of it; but I can only give you good-will and good advice, and, perhaps, I may be able to fit answers to your questions better than another — that is all. And now, having such an auxiliary, you must do your best to show the unbelievers that you are right.

I ought to try, I said, once you offer me such invaluable assistance. And I think that, if there is to be a chance of our escaping, we must explain to them whom we mean when we say that philosophers are to rule in the State; then we shall be able to defend ourselves: There will be discovered to be some natures who ought to study philosophy and to be leaders in the State; and others who are not born to be philosophers, and are meant to be followers rather than leaders. . . .

BOOK VII

And now, I said, let me show in a figure how far our nature is enlightened or unenlightened;—Behold! human beings living in an underground den, which has a mouth open towards the light and reaching all along the den; here they have been from their childhood, and have their legs and necks chained so that they cannot move and can only see before them, being prevented by the chains from turning round their heads. Above and behind a fire is blazing at a distance, and between the fire and the prisoners there is a raised way, like the screen which marionette players have in front of them, over which they show the puppets.

I see.

And do you see, I said, men passing along the wall carrying all sorts of vessels, and statues and figures of animals made of wood and stone and various materials, which appear over the wall? Some of them are talking, others silent.

You have shown me a strange image, and they are strange prisoners.

Like ourselves, I replied; and they see only their own shadows, or the shadows of one another, which the fire throws on the opposite wall of the cave?

True, he said; how could they see anything but the shadows if they were never allowed to move their heads?

And of the objects which are being carried in like manner they would only see the shadows?

Yes, he said.

And if they were able to converse with one another, would they not suppose that they were naming what was actually before them?

Very true.

And suppose further that the prison had an echo which came from the other side, would they not be sure to fancy when one of the passers-by spoke that the voice which they heard came from the passing shadow?

No question, he replied.

To them, I said, the truth would be literally nothing but the shadows of the images.

That is certain.

And now look again, and see what will naturally follow if the prisoners are released and disabused of their error. At first, when any of them is liberated and compelled suddenly to stand up and turn his neck round and walk and look towards the light, he will suffer sharp pains; the glare will distress him, and he will be unable to see the realities of which in his former state he had seen the shadows; and then conceive someone saying to him, that what he saw before was an illusion, but that now, when he is approaching nearer to being and his eye is turned towards more real existence, he has a clearer vision,—what will be his reply? And you may further imagine that his instructor is pointing to the objects as they pass and requiring him to name them—will he not be perplexed? Will he not fancy that the shadows which he formerly saw are truer than the objects which are now shown to him?

Far truer.

And if he is compelled to look straight at the light, will he not have a pain in his eyes which will make him turn away to take refuge in the objects of vision which he can see, and which he will conceive to be in reality clearer than the things which are now being shown to him?

True, he said.

And suppose once more, that he is reluctantly dragged up a steep and rugged ascent, and held fast until he is forced into the presence of the sun himself, is he not likely to be pained and irritated? When he approaches the light his eyes will be dazzled, and he will not be able to see anything at all of what are now called realities.

Not all in a moment, he said.

He will require to grow accustomed to the sight of the upper world. And first he will see the shadows best, next the reflections of men and other objects in the water, and then the objects themselves; then he will gaze upon the light of the moon and the stars and the spangled heaven; and he will see the sky and the stars by night better than the sun or the light of the sun by day?

Certainly.

Last of all he will be able to see the sun,[1] and not mere reflections of it in the water, but he will see it in its own proper place, and not in another; and he will contemplate it as it is.

Certainly.

He will then proceed to argue that this is it which gives the season and the years, and is the guardian of all that is in the visible world, and in a certain way the cause of all things which he and his fellows have been accustomed to behold?

Clearly, he said, he would first see the sun and then reason about it.

_____

[1] Imagine that the sun is Plato's idea of The Good.

And when he remembered his old habitation, and the wisdom of the den and his fellow-prisoners, do you not suppose that he would congratulate himself on the change and pity them?

Certainly, he would.

And if they were in the habit of conferring honours among themselves on those who were quickest to observe the passing shadows and to remark which of them went before, and which followed after, and which were together; and who were therefore best able to draw conclusions as to the future, do you think that he would care for such honors and glories, or envy the possessors of them? Would he not say with Homer,

"Better to be the poor servant of a poor master," and to endure anything, rather than think as they do and live after their manner?

Yes, he said, I think that he would rather suffer anything than entertain these false notions and live in this miserable manner.

Imagine once more, I said, such an one coming suddenly out of the sun to be replaced in his old situation; would he not be certain to have his eyes full of darkness?

To be sure, he said.

And if there were a contest, and he had to compete in measuring the shadows with the prisoners who had never moved out of the den, while his sight was still weak, and before his eyes had become steady (and the time which would be needed to acquire this new habit of sight might be very considerable), would he not be ridiculous? Men would say of him that up he went and came back without his eyes; and that it was better not even to think of ascending; and if any one tried to loose another and lead him up to the light, let them only catch the offender, and they would put him to death.

No question, he said.

This entire allegory, I said, you may now append, dear Glaucon, to the previous argument; the prison-house is the world of sight, the light of the fire is the sun, and you will not misapprehend me if you interpret the journey upwards to be the ascent of the soul into the intellectual world according to my poor belief, which, at your desire, I have expressed—whether rightly or wrongly God knows. But whether true or false, my opinion is that in the world of knowledge the idea of good appears last of all, and is seen only with an effort; and when seen, is also inferred to be the universal author of all things beautiful and right, parent of light and of the lord of light in this visible world, and the immediate source of reason and truth in the intellectual; and that this is the power upon which he who would act rationally either in public or private life must have his eye fixed.

I agree, he said, as far as I am able to understand you.

Moreover, I said, you must not wonder that those who attain to this beatific vision are unwilling to descend to human affairs; for their souls are ever hastening into the upper world where they desire to dwell; which desire of theirs is very natural, if our allegory may be trusted.

Yes, very natural.

And is there anything surprising in one who passes from divine contemplations to the evil state of man, misbehaving himself in a ridiculous manner; if, while his eyes are blinking and before he has become accustomed to the surrounding darkness, he is compelled to fight in courts of law, or in other places, about the images or the shadows of images of justice, and is endeavoring to meet the conceptions of those who have never yet seen absolute justice?

Anything but surprising, he replied.

Anyone who has common sense will remember that the bewilderments of the eyes are of two kinds, and arise from two causes, either from coming out of the light or from going into the light, which is true of the mind's eye, quite as much as of the bodily eye; and he who remembers this when he sees anyone whose vision is perplexed and weak, will not be too ready to laugh; he will first ask whether that soul of man has come out of the brighter life, and is unable to see because unaccustomed to the dark, or having turned from darkness to the day is dazzled by excess of light.

The business of us who are the founders of the State will be to compel the best minds to attain that knowledge which we have already shown to be the greatest of all—they must continue to ascend until they arrive at the good; but when they have ascended and seen enough we must not allow them to do as they do now.

What do you mean?

I mean that they remain in the upper world; but this must not be allowed; they must be made to descend again among the prisoners in the den, and partake of their labors and honors, whether they are worth having or not.

A Question:

Why does Plato insist that the one who has gone through all of the difficulties involved in coming to see and know the true light *must* return to the cave, that he must even partake of the labors and honors of the people in the cave, even though he recognizes that these are foolish?

Aristotle

Aristotle (384-322 B.C.) was the third of the great Greek philosophers. Born in Stagira, at the age of seventeen he entered Plato's Academy, where he stayed as a student and teacher for twenty years. He then was invited to be the tutor of the future Alexander the Great, a position he held for several years. Returning to Athens, he founded his own school which became known as the Lyceum. Here Aristotle was extremely popular, gaining distinction as a teacher and a philosopher in his own right.

He was greatly influenced by Plato, but his philosophy differed from Plato's in several outstanding respects. For instance, Aristotle was much more down to earth and much more practical than Plato; his interests were more in the scientific areas, such as biology and medicine. In addition, Aristotle avoided the extreme dualism which is often found in Plato. For example, he rejected Plato's idealism and mysticism on the one hand and the extreme of materialism on the other. This is but one example of Aristotle's moderation or what he called following the "golden mean."

The two selections included here are good examples of this moderation on the part of Aristotle. The first selection is taken from Aristotle's *Politics*. Contrast the examples which Aristotle used in this selection with those which you have read in *The Republic* by Plato. Aristotle utilized concrete examples, set up specific types of government and then described the type of government which he preferred. He did not, however, push his choice and admitted that it might not be the best under certain circumstances. The second selection from Aristotle is an excerpt from *The Nichomachean Ethics*. Here Aristotle discussed ethics and what was involved in the good life. Again, moderation was the watch word and was presented as one of the Greek ideals. In this particular selection note what Aristotle thought was the greatest good in life, his definition of happiness, and his definition of virtue.

MORAL EXCELLENCE

POLITICS [1]

BOOK III

He who would enquire into the nature and various kinds of government must first of all determine 'What is a state?' At present this is a disputed question. Some say that the state has done a certain act; others, no, not the state, but the oligarchy or the tyrant. And the legislator or statesman is concerned entirely with the state; a constitution or government being an arrangement of the inhabitants of a state. But a state is composite, and, like any other whole, made up of many parts;—these are the citizens, who compose it. It is evident, therefore, that we must begin by asking, Who is the citizen, and what is the meaning of the term? For here again there may be a difference of opinion. He who is a citizen in a democracy will often not be a citizen in an oligarchy. Leaving out of consideration those who have been made citizens, or who have obtained the name of citizen in any other accidental manner, we may say, first, that a citizen is not a citizen because he lives in a certain place, for resident aliens and slaves share in the place; nor is he a citizen who has no legal right except that of suing and being sued; for this right may be enjoyed under the provisions of a treaty. Even resident aliens in many places possess such rights, although in an imperfect form; for they are obliged to have a patron. Hence they do but imperfectly participate in citizenship, and we call them citizens only in a qualified sense, as we might apply the term to children who are too young to be on the register, or to old men who have been relieved from state duties.

[1] Translated by Benjamin Jowett, Oxford at the Clarendon Press, 1916.

Of these we do not say simply that they are citizens, but add in the one case that they are not of age, and in the other, that they are past the age, or something of that sort; the precise expression is immaterial, for one meaning is clear. Similar difficulties to those which I have mentioned may be raised and answered about deprived citizens and about exiles. But the citizen, whom we are seeking to define, is a citizen in the strictest sense, against whom no such exception can be taken, and his special characteristic is that he shares in the administration of justice, and in offices. Now of offices some have a limit of time, and the same persons are not allowed to hold them twice, or can only hold them after a fixed interval; others have no limit of time—for example, the office of dicast or ecclesiast. It may, indeed, be argued that these are not magistrates at all, and that their functions give them no share in the government. But surely it is ridiculous to say that those who have the supreme power do not govern. Not to dwell further upon this, which is a purely verbal question, what we want is a common term including both dicast and ecclesiast. Let us, for the sake of distinction, call it 'indeterminate office,' and we will assume that those who share in such office are citizens. This is the most comprehensive definition of a citizen, and best suits all those who are generally so called.

But we must not forget that things of which the underlying notions differ in kind, one of them being first, another second, another third, have, when regarded in this relation, nothing, or hardly anything, worth mentioning in common. Now we see that governments differ in kind, and that some of them are prior and that others are posterior; those which are faulty or perverted are necessarily posterior to those which are perfect. (What we mean by perversion will be hereafter explained.) The citizen then of necessity differs under each form of government; and our definition is best adapted to the citizen of a democracy; but not necessarily to other states. For in some states the people are not acknowledged, nor have they any regular assembly, but only extraordinary ones; and suits are distributed in turn among the magistrates. At Lacedaemon, for instance, the Ephors determine suits about contracts, which they distribute among themselves, while the elders are judges of homicide, and other causes are decided by other magistrates. A similar principle prevails at Carthage; there certain magistrates decide all causes. We may, indeed, modify our definition of the citizen so as to include these states. [But strictly taken it only applies in democracies.] In other states it is the holder of a determinate, not of an indeterminate, office who legislates and judges, and to some or all such holders of determinate offices is reserved the right of deliberating or judging about some things or about all things. The conception of the citizen now begins to clear up.

He who has the power to take part in the deliberative or judicial administration of any state is said by us to be a citizen of that state; and speaking generally, a state is a body of citizens sufficing for the purposes of life.

But in practice a citizen is defined to be one of whom both the parents are citizens; others insist on going further back; say to two or three or more grandparents. This is a short and practical definition; but there are some who raise the further question: How this third or fourth ancestor came to be a citizen? Gorgias of Leontini, partly because he was in a difficulty, partly in irony, said—'Mortars are made by the mortar-makers, and the citizens of Larissa are also a manufactured article, made, like the kettles which bear their name [$\lambda\alpha\rho\iota\sigma\alpha\iota\omicron\iota$], by the magistrates.' Yet the question is really simple, for if, according to the definition just given, they shared in the government, they were citizens. [This is a better definition than the other.] For the words, 'born of a father or mother, who is a citizen,' cannot possibly apply to the first inhabitants or founders of a state.

There is a greater difficulty in the case of those who have been made citizens after a revolution, as by Cleisthenes at Athens after the expulsion of the tyrants, for he enrolled in tribes a number of strangers and slaves and resident aliens. The doubt in these cases is, not who is, but whether he, who is, ought to be a citizen; and there will still be a further doubt, whether he ought not to be a citizen is one in fact, for what ought not to be is what is false and is not. Now, there are some who hold office, and yet ought not to hold office, whom we call rulers, although they rule unjustly. And the citizen was defined by the fact of his holding some kind of rule or office—he who holds a judicial or legislative office fulfils our definition of a citizen. It is evident, therefore, that the citizens about whom the doubt has arisen must be called citizens; whether they ought to be so or not is a question which is bound up with the previous enquiry.

A parallel question is raised respecting the state whether a certain act is or is not an act of the state; for example, in the transition from an oligarchy or a tyranny to a democracy. In such cases persons refuse to fulfil their contracts or any other obligations on the ground that the tyrant, and not state, contracted them; they argue that some constitutions are established by force, and not for the sake of the common good. But this would apply equally to democracies, for they too may be founded on violence, and then the acts of the democracy will be neither more nor less legitimate than those of an oligarchy or of a tyranny. This question runs up into another—When shall we say that the state is the same, and when different? It would be a very superficial view which considered only the place and the inhabitants; for the soil and the population may be separated, and some of the inhabitants may live in one place and some in another. This, however, is not a very serious difficulty; we need only remark that the word 'state' is ambiguous, meaning both state and city.

It is further asked: When are men, living in the same place, to be regarded as a single city—what is the limit? Certainly not the wall of the city, for you might surround all Peloponnesus with a wall. But a city, having such vast circuit, would contain a nation rather than a state, like Babylon, which, as they say, had been taken for three days before some part of the inhabitants became aware of the fact. This difficulty may, however, with advantage be deferred to another occasion; the statesman has to consider the size of the state, and whether it should consist of more than one nation or not.

Again, shall we say that while the race of inhabitants, as well as their place of abode, remain the same, the city is also the same, although the citizens are always dying and being born, as we call rivers and fountains the same, although the water is always flowing away and coming again? Or shall we say that the generations of men, like the rivers, are the same, but that the state changes? For, since the state is a community of citizens united by sharing in one form of government, when the form of the government changes and becomes different, then it may be supposed that the state is no longer the same, just as a tragic differs from a comic chorus, although the members of both may be identical. And in this manner we speak of every union or composition of elements, when the form of their composition alters; for example, harmony of the same sounds is said to be different, accordingly as the Dorian or the Phrygian mode is employed. And if this is true it is evident that the sameness of the state consists chiefly in the sameness of the constitution, and may be called or not called by the same name, whether the inhabitants are the same or entirely different. It is quite another question, whether a state ought or ought not to fulfil engagements when the form of government changes.

There is a point nearly allied to the preceding: Whether the virtue of a good man and a good citizen is the same or not. But, before entering on this discussion, we must first obtain some general notion of the virtue of the citizen. Like the sailor, the citizen is a member of a community. Now, sailors have different functions, for one of them is a rower, another a pilot, a third a look-out man, and a fourth is described by some similar term; and while the precise definition of each individual's virtue applies exclusively to him, there is, at the same time, a common definition applicable to them all. For they have all of them a common object, which is safety in navigation. Similarly, one citizen differs from another, but the salvation of the community is the common business of them all. This community is the state; the virtue of the citizen must therefore be relative to the constitution of which he is a member. If, then, there are many forms of government, it is evident that the virtue of the good citizen cannot be the one perfect virtue. But we say that the good man is he who has perfect virtue. Hence it is evident that the good citizen need not of necessity possess the virtue which makes a good man.

The same question may also be approached by another road, from a consideration of the perfect state. If the state cannot be entirely composed of good men, and each citizen is expected to do his own business well, and must therefore have virtue, inasmuch as all the citizens cannot be alike, the virtue of the citizen and of the good man cannot coincide. All must have the virtue of the good citizen—thus, and thus only, can the state be perfect; but they will not have the virtue of a good man, unless we assume that in the good state all the citizens must be good.

Again, the state may be compared to the living being: as the first elements into which the living being is resolved are soul and body, as the soul is made up of reason and appetite, the family of husband and wife, property of master and slave, so out of all these, as well as other dissimilar elements, the state is composed; and, therefore, the virtue of all the citizens cannot possibly be the same, any more than the excellence of the leader of a chorus is the same as that of the performer who stands by his side. I have said enough to show why the two kinds of virtue cannot be absolutely and always the same.

But will there then be no case in which the virtue of the good citizen and the virtue of the good man coincide? To this we answer [not that the good citizen, but] that the good ruler is a good and wise man, and that he who would be a statesman must be a wise man. And some persons say that even the education of the ruler should be of a special kind; for are not the children of kings instructed in riding and military exercises? As Euripides says:

'No subtle arts for me, but what the state requires.'

As though there were a special education needed by a ruler. If then the virtue of a good ruler is the same as that of a good man, and we assume further that the subject is a citizen as well as the ruler, the virtue of the good citizen and the virtue of the good man cannot be always the same, although in some cases [i.e., in the perfect state] they may; for the virtue of a ruler differs from that of a citizen. It was the sense of this difference which made Jason say that 'he felt hungry when he was not a tyrant,' meaning that he could not endure to live in a private station. But, on the other hand, it may be argued that men are praised for knowing both how to rule and how to obey, and he is said to be a citizen of approved virtue who is able to do both. Now if we suppose the virtue of a good man to be that which rules, and the virtue of the citizen to include ruling and obeying, it cannot be said that they are equally worthy of praise. Since, then, it is occasionally held that the ruler and the ruled should learn different things and not the same things, and that the citizen must know and share in both; the inference is obvious. There is, indeed, the rule of a master which is concerned with menial offices,—the master need not know how to perform these, but may employ others in the execution of them: anything else would be degrading; and by anything else I mean the menial duties which vary much in character and are executed by various classes of slaves, such, for example, as handicraftsmen, who, as their name signifies, live by the labour of their hands:—under these the mechanic is included. Hence in ancient times, and among some nations, the working classes had no share in the government—a privilege which they only acquired under the extreme democracy. Certainly the good man and the statesman and the good citizen ought not to learn the crafts of inferiors except for their own occasional use; if they habitually practise them, there will cease to be a distinction between master and slave.

This is not the rule of which we are speaking; but there is a rule of another kind, which is exercised over freemen and equals by birth—a constitutional rule, which the ruler must learn by obeying, as he would learn the duties of a general of cavalry by being under the orders of a general of cavalry, or the duties of a general of infantry by being under the orders of a general of infantry, or by having had the command of a company or brigade. It has been well said that 'he who has never learned to obey cannot be a good commander.' The two are not the same, but the good citizen ought to be capable of both; he should know how to govern like a freeman, and how to obey like a freeman—these are the virtues of a citizen. And, although the temperance and justice of a ruler are distinct from those of a subject, the virtue of a good man will include both; for the good man, who is free and also a subject, will not have one virtue only, say justice, but he will have distinct kinds of virtue, the one qualifying him to rule, the other to obey, and differing as the temperance and courage of men and women differ. For a man would be thought a coward if he had no more courage than a courageous woman, and a woman would be thought loquacious if she imposed no more restraint on her conversation than the good man; and indeed their part in the management of the household is different, for the duty of the one is to acquire, and of the other to preserve. Practical wisdom only is characteristic of the ruler: it would seem that all other virtues must equally belong to ruler and subject. The virtue of the subject is certainly not wisdom, but only true opinion; he may be compared to the maker of the flute, while his master is like the flute-player or user of the flute.

From these considerations may be gathered the answer to the question, whether the virtue of the good man is the same as that of the good citizen, or different, and how far the same, and how far different.

There still remains one more question about the citizen: Is he only a true citizen who has a share of office, or is the mechanic to be included? If they who hold no office are to be deemed citizens, not every citizen can have this virtue of ruling and obeying which makes a citizen. And if none of the lower class are citizens, in which part of the state are they to be placed? For they are not resident aliens, and they are not foreigners. To this objection may we not reply, that there is no more absurdity in excluding them than in excluding slaves and freedmen from any of the above-mentioned classes? It must be admitted that we cannot consider all those to be citizens who are necessary to the existence of the state; for example, children are not citizens equally with grown up men, who are citizens absolutely, but children, not being grown up, are only citizens in a qualified sense. Doubtless in ancient times, and among some nations, the artisan class were slaves or foreigners, and therefore the majority of them are so now. The best form of state will not admit them to citizenship; but if they are admitted, then our definition of the virtue of a citizen will apply to some citizens and freemen only, and not to those who work for their living. The latter class, to whom toil is a necessity, are either slaves who minister to the wants of individuals, or mechanics and labourers who are the servants of the community. These reflections carried a little further will explain their position; and indeed what has been said already is of itself explanation enough.

Since there are many forms of government there must be many varieties of citizens, and especially of citizens who are subjects; so that under some governments the mechanic and the labourer will be citizens, but not in others, as, for example, in aristocracy or the so-called government of the best (if there be such a one), in which honours are given according to virtue and merit; for no man can practise who is living the life of a mechanic or labourer. In oligarchies the qualification for office is high, and therefore no labourer can ever be a citizen; but a mechanic may, for many of them are rich. At Thebes there was a law that no man could hold office who had not retired from business for ten years. In many states the law goes to the length of admitting aliens; for in some democracies a man is a citizen though his mother only be a citizen [and his father an alien]; and a similar principle is applied to illegitimate children; the law is relaxed when there is a dearth of population. But when the number of citizens increases, first the children of a male or a female slave are excluded; then those whose mothers only are citizens; and at last the right of citizenship is confined to those whose fathers and mothers are both citizens.

Hence, as is evident, there are different kinds of citizens; and he is a citizen in the highest sense who shares in the honours of the state. In the poems of Homer, Achilles complains of Agamemnon treating him 'like some dishonoured stranger;' for he who is excluded from the honours of the state is no better than an alien. But when this exclusion is concealed, then the object is to deceive one's fellow-countrymen.

As to the question whether the virtue of the good man is the same as that of the good citizen, the considerations already adduced prove that in some states the two are the same, and in others different. When they are the same it is not the virtue of every citizen which is the same as that of the good man, but only the virtue of the statesman and of those who have or may have, alone or in conjunction with others, the conduct of public affairs.

Having determined these questions, we have next to consider whether there is only one form of government or many, and if many, what they are, and how many, and what are the differences between them.

A constitution is the arrangement of magistracies in a state, especially of the highest of all. The government is everywhere sovereign in the state, and the constitution is in fact the government. For example, in democracies the people are supreme, but in oligarchies, the few; and, therefore, we say that these two forms of government are different: and so other cases.

First, let us consider what is the purpose of a state, and how many forms of government there are by which human society is regulated. We have already said, in the former part of this treatise, when drawing a distinction between household-management and the rule of a master, that man is by nature a political animal. And therefore, men, even when they do not require one another's help, desire to live together all the same, and are in fact brought together by their common interests in proportion as they severally attain to any measure of well-being. This is certainly the chief end, both of individuals and of states. And also for the sake of mere life (in which there is possibly some noble element) mankind meet together and maintain the political community, so long as the evils of existence do not greatly overbalance the good. And we all see that men cling to life even in the midst of misfortune, seeming to find it in a natural sweetness and happiness.

There is no difficulty in distinguishing the various kinds of authority; they have been often defined already in popular works. The rule of a master, although the slave by nature and the master by nature have in reality the same interests, is nevertheless exercised primarily with a view to the interest of the master, but accidentally considers the slave, since, if the slave perish, the rule of the master perishes with him. On the other hand, the government of a wife and children and of a household, which we have called household-management, is exercised in the first instance for the good of the governed or for the common good of both parties, but essentially for the good of the governed, as we see to be the case in medicine, gymnastics, and the arts in general, which are only accidentally concerned with the good of the artists themselves.

(For there is no reason why the trainer may not sometimes practise gymnastics, and the pilot is always one of the crew.) The trainer or the pilot considers the good of those committed to his care. But, when he is one of the persons taken care of, he accidentally participates in the advantage, for the pilot is also a sailor, and the trainer becomes one of those in training. And so in politics: when the state is framed upon the principle of equality and likeness, the citizens think that they ought to hold office by turns. In the order of nature every one would take his turn of service; and then again, somebody else would look after his interest, just as he, while in office, had looked after theirs. [That was originally the way.] But nowadays, for the sake of the advantage which is to be gained from the public revenues and from office, men want to be always in office. One might imagine that the rulers, being sickly, were only kept in health while they continued in office; in that case we may be sure that they would be hunting after places. The conclusion is evident: that governments, which have a regard to the common interest, are constituted in accordance with strict principles of justice, and are therefore true forms; but those which regard only the interest of the rulers are all defective and perverted forms, for they are despotic, whereas a state is a community of freemen.

Having determined these points, we have next to consider how many forms of government there are, and what they are; and in the first place what are the true forms, for when they are determined the perversions of them will at once be apparent. The words constitution and government have the same meaning, and the government, which is the supreme authority in states, must be in the hands of one, or of a few, or of many. The true forms of government, therefore, are those in which the one, or the few, or the many, govern with a view to the common interest; but governments which rule with a view to the private interest, whether of the one, or of the few, or of the many, are perversions. For citizens, if they are truly citizens, ought to participate in the advantages of a state. Of forms of government in which one rules, we call that which regards the common interests, kingship or royalty; that in which more than one, but not many, rule, aristocracy [the rule of the best]; and it is so called, either because the rulers are the best men, or because they have at heart the best interests of the state and of the citizens. But when the citizens at large administer the state for the common interest, the government is called by the generic name—a constitution. And there is a reason for this use of language. One man or a few may excel in virtue; but of virtue there are many kinds: and as the number increases it becomes more difficult for them to attain perfection in every kind, though they may in military virtue, for this is found in the masses. Hence, in a constitutional government the fighting-men have the supreme power, and those who possess arms are the citizens.

Of the above-mentioned forms, the perversions are as follows:—of royalty, tyranny; of aristocracy, oligarchy; of constitutional government, democracy. For tyranny is a kind of monarchy which has in view the interest of the monarch only; oligarchy has in view the interest of the wealthy; democracy, of the needy: none of them the common good of all.

But there are difficulties about these forms of government, and it will therefore be necessary to state a little more at length the nature of each of them. For he who would make a philosophical study of the various sciences, and does not regard practice only, ought not to overlook or omit anything, but to set forth the truth in every particular. Tyranny, as I was saying, is monarchy exercising the rule of a master over political society; oligarchy is when men of property have the government in their hands; democracy, the opposite, when the indigent, and not the men of property, are the rulers. And here arises the first of our difficulties, and it relates to the definition just given. For democracy is said to be the government of the many. But what if the many are men of property and have the power in their hands? In like manner oligarchy is said to be the government of the few; but what if the poor are fewer than the rich, and have the power in their hands because they are stronger? In these cases the distinction which we have drawn between these different forms of government would no longer hold good.

Suppose, once more, that we add wealth to the few and poverty to the many, and name the governments accordingly—an oligarchy is said to be that in which the many and the poor are the rulers—there will still be a difficulty. For, if the only forms of government are the ones already mentioned, how shall we describe those other governments also just mentioned by us, in which the rich are the more numerous and the poor are the fewer, and both govern in their respective states?

The argument seems to show that, whether in oligarchies or in democracies, the number of the governing body, whether the greater number, as in a democracy, or the smaller number, as in an oligarchy, is an accident due to the fact that the rich everywhere are few, and the poor numerous. But if so, there is a misapprehension of the causes of the difference between them. For the real difference between democracy and oligarchy is poverty and wealth. Wherever men rule by reason of their wealth, whether they be few or many, that is an oligarchy, and where the poor rule, that is a democracy. But as a fact the rich are few and the poor many: for few are well-to-do, whereas freedom is enjoyed by all, and wealth and freedom are the grounds on which the oligarchical and democratical parties respectively claim power in the state.

Let us begin by considering the common definitions of oligarchy and democracy, and what is justice oligarchical and democratical. For all men cling to justice of some kind, but their conceptions are imperfect and they do not express the whole idea. For example, justice is thought by them to be, and is, equality, not, however, for all, but only for equals. And inequality is thought to be, and is, justice; neither is this for all, but only for unequals. When the persons are omitted, then men judge erroneously. The reason is that they are passing judgment on themselves, and most people are bad judges in their own case. And whereas justice implies a relation to persons as well as to things, and a just distribution, as I have already said in the Ethics, embraces alike persons and things, they acknowledge the equality of the things, but dispute about the merit of the persons, chiefly for the reason which I have just given—because they are bad judges in their own affairs; and secondly, because both the parties to the argument are speaking of a limited and partial justice, but imagine themselves to be speaking of absolute justice. For those who are unequal in one respect, for example wealth, consider themselves to be unequal in all; and any who are equal in one respect, for example freedom, consider themselves to be equal in all. But they leave out the capital point. For if men met and associated out of regard to wealth only, their share in the state would be proportioned to their property, and the oligarchical doctrine would then seem to carry the day. It would not be just that he who paid one mina should have the same share of a hundred minae, whether of the principal or of the profits, as he who paid the remaining ninety-nine. But a state exists for the sake of a good life, and not for the sake of life only: if life only were the object, slaves and brute animals might form a state, but they cannot, for they have no share in happiness or in a life of free choice. Nor does a state exist for the sake of alliance and security from injustice, nor yet for the sake of exchange and mutual intercourse; for then the Tyrrhenians and the Carthaginians, and all who have commercial treaties with one another, would be the citizens of one state. True, they have agreements about imports, and engagements that they will do no wrong to one another, and written articles of alliance. But there are no magistracies common to the contracting parties who will enforce their engagements; different states have each their own magistracies. Nor does one state take care that the citizens of the other are such as they ought to be, nor see that those who come under the terms of the treaty do no wrong or wickedness at all, but only that they do no injustice to one another. Whereas, those who care for good government take into consideration [the larger question of] virtue and vice in states. Whence it may be further inferred that virtue must be the serious care of a state which truly deserves the name: for [without this ethical end] the community becomes a mere alliance which differs only in place from alliances of which the members live apart; and law is only a convention, 'a surety to one another of justice,' as the sophist Lycophron says, and has no real power to make the citizens good and just.

This is obvious; for suppose distinct places, such as Corinth and Megara, to be united by a wall, still they would not be one city, not even if the citizens had the right to intermarry, which is one of the rights peculiarly characteristic of states. Again, if men dwelt at a distance from one another, but not so far off as to have no intercourse, and there were laws among them that they should not wrong each other in their exchanges, neither would this be a state. Let us suppose that one man is a carpenter, another a husbandman, another a shoemaker, and so on, and that their number is ten thousand: nevertheless, if they have nothing in common but exchange, alliance, and the like, that would not constitute a state. Why is this? Surely not because they are at a distance from one another: for even supposing that such a community were to meet in one place, and that each man had a house of his own, which was in a manner his state, and that they made alliance with one another, but only against evil-doers; still an accurate thinker would not deem this to be a state, if their intercourse with one another was of the same character after as before their union. It is clear then that a state is not a mere society, having a common place, established for the prevention of crime and for the sake of exchange. These are conditions without which a state cannot exist; but all of them together do not constitute a state, which is a community of well-being in families and aggregations of families, for the sake of a perfect and self-sufficing life. Such a community can only be established among those who live in the same place and intermarry. Hence arise in cities family connexions, brotherhoods, common sacrifices, amusements which draw men together. They are created by friendship, for friendship is the motive of society. The end is the good life, and these are the means towards it. And the state is the union of families and villages having for an end a perfect and self-sufficing life, by which we mean a happy and honourable life.

Our conclusion, then, is that political society exists for the sake of noble actions, and not of mere companionship. And they who contribute most to such a society have a greater share in it than those who have the same or a greater freedom or nobility of birth but are inferior to them in political virtue; or than those who exceed them in wealth but are surpassed by them in virtue.

From what has been said it will be clearly seen that all the partisans of different forms of government speak of a part of justice only.

BOOK IV

... We have now to enquire what is the best constitution for most states, and the best life for most men, neither assuming a standard of virtue which is above ordinary persons, nor an education which is exceptionally favoured by nature and circumstances, nor yet an ideal state which is an aspiration only, but having regard to the life in which the majority are able to share, and to the form of government which states in general can attain. As to those aristocracies, as they are called, of which we were just now speaking, they either lie beyond the possibilities of the greater number of states, or they approximate to the so-called constitutional government, and therefore need no separate discussion. And in fact the conclusion at which we arrive respecting all these forms rests upon the same grounds. For if it has been truly said in the Ethics that the happy life is the life according to unimpeded virtue, and that virtue is a mean, then the life which is in a mean, and in a mean attainable by every one, must be the best. And the same criteria of virtue and vice apply both to critics and to constitutions; for the constitution is in a figure the life of the city.

Now in all states there are three elements; one class is very rich, another very poor, and a third in a mean. It is admitted that moderation and the mean are best, and therefore it will clearly be best to possess the gifts of fortune in moderation; for in that condition of life men are most ready to listen to reason. But he who greatly excels in beauty, strength, birth or wealth, or on the other hand who is very poor, or very weak, or very much disgraced, finds it difficult to follow reason. Of these two the one sort grow into violent and great criminals, the others into rogues and petty rascals. And two sorts of offences correspond to them, the one committed from violence, the other from roguery. The petty rogues are disinclined to hold office, whether military or civil, and their aversion to these two duties is as great an injury to the state as their tendency to crime. Again, those who have too much of the goods of fortune, strength, wealth, friends, and the like, are neither willing nor able to submit to authority. The evil begins at home: for when they are boys, by reason of the luxury in which they are brought up, they never learn, even at school, the habit of obedience. On the other hand, the very poor, who are in the opposite extreme, are too degraded. So that the one class cannot obey, and can only rule despotically; the other knows not how to command and must be ruled like slaves. Thus arises a city, not of freemen, but of masters and slaves, the one despising, the other envying; and nothing can be more fatal to friendship and good fellowship in states than this: for good fellowship tends to friendship; when men are at enmity with one another, they would rather not even share the same path. But a city ought to be composed, as far as possible, of equals and similars; and these are generally the middle classes. Wherefore the city which is composed of middle-class citizens is necessarily best governed; they are, as we say, the natural elements of a state. And this is the class of citizens which is most secure in a state, for they do not, like the poor, covet their neighbours' goods; nor do others covet theirs, as the poor covet the goods of the rich; and as they neither plot against others, nor are themselves plotted against, they pass through life safely. Wisely then did Phocylides pray—

'Many things are best in the mean; I desire to be of a middle condition in my city.'

Thus it is manifest that the best political community is formed by citizens of the middle class, and that those states are likely to be well-administered, in which the middle class is large, and larger if possible than both the other classes, or at any rate than either singly; for the addition of the middle class turns the scale, and prevents either of the extremes from being dominant. Great then is the good fortune of a state in which the citizens have a moderate and sufficient property; for where some possess much, and the others nothing, there may arise an extreme democracy, or a pure oligarchy; or a tyranny may grow out of either extreme—either out of the most rampant democracy, or out of an oligarchy; but it is not so likely to arise out of a middle and nearly equal condition. I will explain the reason of this hereafter, when I speak of the revolutions of states. The mean condition of states is clearly best, for no other is free from faction; and where the middle class is large, there are least likely to be factions and dissensions. For a similar reason large states are less liable to faction than small ones, because in them the middle class is large; whereas in small states it is easy to divide all the citizens into two classes who are either rich or poor, and to leave nothing in the middle. And democracies are safer and more permanent than oligarchies, because they have a middle class which is more numerous and has a greater share in the government; for when there is no middle class, and the poor greatly exceed in number, troubles arise, and the state soon comes to an end. A proof of the superiority of the middle class is that the best legislators have been of a middle condition; for example, Solon, as his own verses testify; and Lycurgus, for he was not a king; and Charondas, and almost all legislators.

These considerations will help us to understand why most governments are either democratical or oligarchical. The reason is that the middle class is seldom numerous in them, and whichever party, whether the rich or the common people, transgresses the mean and predominates, draws the government to itself, and thus arises either oligarchy or democracy. There is another reason—the poor and the rich quarrel with one another, and whichever side gets the better, instead of establishing a just or popular government, regards political supremacy as the prize of victory, and the one party sets up a democracy and the other an oligarchy. Both the parties which had the supremacy in Hellas looked only to the interest of their own form of government, and established in states, the one, democracies, and the other, oligarchies; they thought of their own advantage, of the public not at all. For these reasons the middle form of government has rarely, if ever, existed, and among a very few only. One man alone of all who ever ruled in Hellas was induced to give this middle constitution to states. But it has now become a habit among the citizens of states, not even to care about equality; all men are seeking for dominion, or, if conquered, are willing to submit.

What then is the best form of government, and what makes it the best, is evident; and of other states, since we say that there are many kinds of democracy and many of oligarchy, it is not difficult to see which has the first and which the second or any other place in the order of excellence, now that we have determined which is the best. For that which is nearest to the best must of necessity be better, and that which is furthest from it worse, if we are judging absolutely and not relatively to given conditions: I say 'relatively to given conditions,' since a particular government may be preferable for some, but another form may be better for others.

We have now to consider what and what kind of government is suitable to what and what kind of men. I may begin by assuming, as a general principle common to all governments, that the portion of the state which desires permanence ought to be stronger than that which desires the reverse. Now every city is composed of quality and quantity. By quality I mean freedom, wealth, education, good birth, and by quantity, superiority of numbers. Quality may exist in one of the classes which make up the state, and quantity in the other. For example, the meanly-born may be more in number than the well-born, or the poor than the rich, yet they may not so much exceed in quantity as they fall short in quality; and therefore there must be a comparison of quantity and quality. Where the number of the poor is more than proportioned to the wealth of the rich, there will naturally be a democracy, varying in form with the sort of people who compose it in each case. If, for example, the husbandmen exceed in number, the first form of democracy will then arise; if the artisans and labouring class, the last; and so with the intermediate forms. But where the rich and the notables exceed in quality more than they fall short in quantity, there oligarchy arises, similarly assuming various forms according to the kind of superiority possessed by the oligarchs.

The legislator should always include the middle class in his government; if he makes his laws oligarchical, to the middle class let him look; if he makes them democratical, he should equally by his laws try to attach this class to the state. There only can the government ever be stable where the middle class exceeds one or both of the others, and in that case there will be no fear that the rich will unite with the poor against the rulers. For neither of them will ever be willing to serve the other, and if they look for some form of government more suitable to both, they will find none better than this, for the rich and the poor will never consent to rule in turn, because they mistrust one another. The arbiter is always the one trusted, and he who is in the middle is an arbiter. The more perfect the admixture of the political elements, the more lasting will be the state. Many even of those who desire to form aristocratical governments make a mistake, not only in giving too much power to the rich, but in attempting to overreach the people. There comes a time when out of a false good there arises a true evil, since the encroachments of the rich are more destructive to the state than those of the people.

NICOMACHEAN ETHICS[1]

Every art and every kind of inquiry, and similarly every act and purpose, seems to aim at some good; and so it has been well said that the good is that at which everything aims. But a difference is observable among these aims or ends. What is aimed at is sometimes the exercise of a faculty, sometimes a certain result beyond that exercise. And where there is an end beyond the act, there the result is better than the exercise of the faculty. Now since there are many kinds of actions and many arts and sciences, it follows that there are many ends also; the end of medicine is health, of shipbuilding, ships, of war, victory, and of economy, wealth. But when several of these are subordinated to some one art or science — as bridle-making and other arts concerned with horsemanship, and this in turn, along with all else the soldier does, to the art of war, and so on — then the end of the master-art is always more desired than the ends of the subordinate arts, since these are pursued for its sake. And this is equally true whether the end in view be the mere exercise of a faculty or something beyond that, as in the case of the sciences just mentioned.

If then in what we do there be some end which we wish for on its own account, choosing all the other ends as means to this, but not every end without exception as a means to something else (for so we should go on indefinitely and desire would be left void and without object) this evidently will be the good or the best of all goods. And surely from a practical point of view it concerns us much to know this good; for then, like archers shooting at a target, we shall be more likely to get what we want. If this be so, we must try to indicate roughly what it is, and first of all to which of the arts or sciences it belongs. It would seem to belong to the highest art or science, that one which most of all deserves the name of master-art or master-science. Politics seems to answer this description. [Politics for Aristotle covers the whole field of human life; it must determine (a) what is the good and (b) what law can do to promote this good]. For politics prescribes which of the sciences a state needs, and which each man shall study, and how much; and to politics we see subordinated even the highest arts, such as economy [the management of a household], rhetoric, and war. Since then politics makes use of the other practical sciences, and since further it ordains what men are to do and from what to refrain, its end must include the ends or objectives of the others, and this end is the good of man. For though this good is the same for the individual as well as the state, yet the good of the state seems a larger and more perfect thing both to attain and to secure; and glad as one would be to do this service for a single individual, to do it for a people and for a number of city-states is nobler and more divine. This then is the aim of the present inquiry, which is political science.

We must be content if we can attain to so much precision in our statement as the subject will permit, for the same degree of accuracy is no more to be expected in all kinds of reasoning than in all kinds of manufacture. Now what is noble and just (with which political science deals) is so various and uncertain, that some think that these are merely conventional, and not natural, distinctions. There is a similar uncertainty also about what is good because good things often do people harm; men have before now been ruined by wealth or have lost their lives through courage. Our subject then and our data being of this nature, we must be content if we can indicate roughly and in outline the truth; and if, in dealing with matters not subject to immutable laws, and reasoning from premises that are but probable, we can arrive at probable conclusions. The reader, on his part, should take each of my statements in the same spirit; for it is the mark of an educated man to require, in each kind of study, just so much exactness as the subject permits; it is equally absurd to accept probable reasoning from a mathematician, and to demand scientific proof from an orator.

Now each man can form a judgment about what he knows, and is called a good judge of that — that is of any special matter in which he has received special training. And the man who has received an all-round education is a good judge in general. And hence a young man is not qualified to be a student of politics; for he lacks experience of the affairs of life which form the data and the subject matter of political science. Further, since he is apt to be swayed by his passions, he will derive no benefit from a study whose aim is practical and not speculative. And it makes no difference whether he is young in years or young in character, for the young man's disqualification is not a matter of time, but is due to the fact that feeling or passion rules his life and directs all his desires. Men of this character turn the knowledge they get to no practical account, as we see those we call incontinent; but those who direct their desires and ambitions by reason will gain much profit from a knowledge of these matters. So much, then by way of preface as to the student, and the spirit

---

[1] *Nicomachean Ethics of Aristotle,* translated by F. H. Peters, London, 1886.

in which he must accept what we say, and the object which we propose to ourselves.

Let us return once more to the question of what this good can be of which we are in search. It seems to be different in different kinds of action and in different arts; it is different in medicine, in war, and in the other arts. What then is the good in each of these? Surely that for the sake of which all else is done. And that in medicine is health, in war is victory, in building is a house —a different thing in each case, but always the end in whatever we do and in whatever we choose. For it is always for the sake of the end that all else is done. If then there be one end of all that man does, this end will be the good achievable in action, and if there be more than one, these will be the goods achievable by action. Our argument has thus come round by a different path to the same point; this we must try to explain more clearly. We see that there are many ends. But some of these are chosen only as means, as wealth, flutes, and the whole class of instruments. And so it is plain that not all ends are final. But the best of all things must be something final. If then there be only one final end, this will be what we are seeking; or if there be more than one, then the most final of them.

Now that which is pursued as an end in itself is more final that that which is pursued as a means to something else, and that which is never chosen as a means than that which is chosen both as an end in itself and as a means, and that is strictly final which is always chosen as an end in itself and never as a means. Happiness seems more than anything else to answer this description, for we always choose it for itself, and never for the sake of something else; while honor and pleasure and reason, and all virtue or excellence, we choose partly for themselves (for, apart from any result, we should choose each of them), but partly also for the sake of happiness, supposing that they will help to make us happy. But no one chooses happiness for the sake of those things, or as a means to anything else at all.

We seem to be led to the same conclusion when we start from the idea of self-sufficiency. The final good is thought to be self-sufficing or all-sufficing. In applying this term we do not regard a man as an individual leading a solitary life, but we take account also of parents, children, wife, and in short, friends and fellow-citizens generally since man is naturally a social being. Some limit must indeed be set for this; for if you go on to parents and descendants and friends of friends, you will never come to a stop. But this we will consider further on; for the present we will take self-sufficing to mean what by itself makes life desirable and in want of nothing. And happiness answers this description. And further, happiness is believed to be the most desirable thing in the world, and that not merely as one among other good things. If it were merely one among other good things [so that other things could be added to it] it is plain that the addition of the least of other goods must make it more desirable; for the addition becomes a surplus of good, and of two goods the greater is always more desirable. Thus it seems that happiness is something final and self-sufficing, and is the end of all that man does.

But perhaps the reader thinks that though no one will dispute the statement that happiness is the best thing in the world, yet a still more precise definition of it is needed. This will best be gained by asking, What is the function of man? For as the goodness and the excellence of the flute-player or the sculptor, or the practitioner of any art, and generally of those who have any business to do, lies in the function, so man's good would seem to lie in his function, if he possesses one. But can we suppose that, while a carpenter or a shoemaker has a function and a business of his own, man has no business and no function assigned to him as man by nature? Nay, surely as his several members, eye, hand, and foot, plainly have each its own function, so we must suppose that man also has some function over and above all of these. What then is it? Life evidently he has in common even with the plants, but we want that which is peculiar to man. We must exclude, therefore, the life of mere nutrition and growth. Next to this comes the life of sense; but this too he plainly shares with horses and cattle and all kinds of animals. There remains then the life whereby he acts — the life of his rational nature with its two aspects or divisions, one rational as obeying reason, the other rational as having and exercising reason. But as this expression is ambiguous, we must be understood to mean thereby the life that consists in the exercise of the faculties; for this seems to be more properly entitled to the name. The function of man, then, is the exercise of his soul on one side in obedience to reason, and on the other side with reason. But what is called the function of a man of any profession and the function of a man who is good in that profession are generically the same, that is to say, of a harper and of a good harper; and this holds in all cases without exception, only that in the case of the latter his superior excellence at his work is added; for we say a harper's function is to play the harp, and a good harper's function is to play the harp well. Man's function then being, as we say, a kind of life — that is, the exercise of his faculties and action of various kinds with reason — the good man's function is to do this well and nobly. But the function of anything is done well when it is done in accordance with the proper excellence of that thing. Putting all this together, then, we find that the good of man is the exercise of his faculties in accordance with excellence or virtue, or, if there be more than one, in accordance with the best and most complete virtue. But there must be a full term of years for this exercise; for one swallow or one fine day does not make a spring, nor does one day or any small space of time make a happy or virtuous man.

This, then, may be taken as a rough outline of the good; for this, I think, is the proper method: first to sketch the outline, and then to fill in the details. But it would seem that, the outline once fairly drawn, any one can carry on the work and fit in the several items which time reveals to us or aids us to discover. And this, indeed, is the way in which the arts and sciences have developed, for it requires no unusual genius to fill in the gaps. We must bear in mind, however, what was said earlier, and not demand the same degree of accuracy in all branches of inquiry, but in each case as much as the subject permits and as is proper to that kind of study. The carpenter and the geometer both look for the right angle, but in different ways; the former only wants such an approximation of it as his work requires, but the latter wants to know what constitutes a right angle, or what is its special quality — his aim is to find the truth. And so in other cases we must follow the same course, lest we spend more time on what is immaterial to our purpose than on the real business at hand. Nor must we in all cases alike demand the reason why. Sometimes it is sufficient if the undemonstrated fact be fairly pointed out, as in the case of the first principles of a science. Undemonstrated facts always form the first step or beginning of a science; and these first principles are arrived at some in one way and some in another way, some by induction, others by perception, others by some kind of training. But in each case we must attempt to apprehend them in the proper way, and do our best to define them clearly, for they have great influence upon the subsequent course of an inquiry. A good start is more than half the race, and our starting-point, once found, clears up a number of difficulties...

Excellence or virtue, then, being of two kinds, intellectual and moral, intellectual excellence owes its birth and growth mainly to teaching, and so requires time and experience, while moral excellence is the result of habit or custom (*ethike*), and has accordingly received in our language [Greek] a name formed by a slight change from the word *ethos* (habit). *From* this it is plain that none of the moral excellencies or virtues is implanted in us by nature; for that which is by nature implanted within us cannot be altered by training. For example, a stone naturally tends to fall downward, and you could not train it to rise upward, though you tried to do so by throwing it up ten thousand times, nor could you train fire to move downward, nor accustom anything which naturally behaves in one way to behave in any other way. The virtues, then, come neither by nature nor contrary to nature, but nature gives us the capacity for acquiring them, and this is developed by training.

Again, where we do things by nature we get the power first, and put this power forth in act afterwards (as we plainly see in the case of the senses); for it is not by constantly seeing and hearing that we acquire those faculties, but, on the contrary, we had the power first and then used it, instead of acquiring the power by use. But we acquire the virtues by doing the acts, as is the case with the arts. We learn an art by doing those things which we wish to do when we have learned the art; we become builders by building, and harpists by playing the harp. And so by doing just and virtuous acts we become just and virtuous, and by doing acts of temperance and courage we become temperate and courageous. This is confirmed by what happens in states; for the legislators make their citizens good by training, and this is the wish of all legislators. Those who do not succeed in this miss their aim, and it is this that distinguishes a good from a bad constitution.

Again, both virtues and vices result from and are formed by the same acts in which they manifest themselves, as is the case also with the arts. It is by playing the harp that good harpers and bad harpers alike are produced; and so it is with builders and the rest, by building well they will become good builders and bad builders by building badly. Indeed, if it were not so, they would not need anybody to teach them, but would all be born either good or bad at their trades. And it is just the same with the virtues also. It is by our conduct in our dealings with other men that we become just or unjust, and by acting in circumstances of danger, and training ourselves to feel fear or confidence, that we become courageous or cowardly. So too with our animal appetites and the passion of anger; for by behaving in this way or in that on occasions with which these passions are concerned, some become temperate and gentle, others profligate and ill-tempered. In a word, the several habits or characters are formed by the same kind of acts as those which they produce. Hence we ought to make certain that our acts be of a particular kind; for the resulting character varies as the acts vary. Instead of making a very small difference whether a man be trained from his youth up in this way or that, it makes a very great difference; indeed, it makes all the difference.

But our present study has not, like the rest, merely a theoretical aim. We are not inquiring simply to learn what excellence or virtue is, but in order to become good; for otherwise our study would be useless. We must ask therefore about these acts, and see of what kind they are to be; for, as we said, it is the acts that determine our habits or character. First of all, then, that they must be in accordance with right reason is a common characteristic of them, which we shall take for granted here, reserving for future discussion the question what this right reason is, and how it is related to the other excellencies or virtues. But let it be understood before we go on, that all reasoning on matters of practice must be in outline merely, and not scientifically exact; for as we said at the beginning the kind of reasoning demanded varies with the subject in hand, and in practical matters and questions of expediency there are no invariable laws, any more than in questions of health. And if our general conclusions are thus inexact, still more inexact is all reasoning about particular cases; for these fall under no system or scientifically established rules or traditional maxims, but the agent must always consider for himself what the special occasion requires, just as in medicine or navigation. In spite of this, however, we must try to give what help we can.

First of all then, we must observe that, in matters of this sort, to fall short and to go beyond are both fatal. To illustrate what we cannot see by what we can see: This is plain in the case of strength and health. Too much and too little exercise alike destroy strength, and to take too much meat and drink, or to take too little is equally ruinous to health; but the proper amount produces and increases strength and health. So it is with temperance also and courage and other virtues. The man who shuns and fears everything and never makes a stand becomes a coward; while the man who fears nothing at all, but will face anything, becomes foolhardy. So, too, the man who takes his fill of any kind of pleasure and abstains from none, is self-indulgent; but the man who avoids all pleasures (like a boor) lacks sensibility. For temperance and courage are destroyed both by excess and defect, but are preserved by moderation.

But habits or types of character are not only produced and preserved and destroyed by the same occasions and the same means, but they will also manifest themselves in the same circumstances. This is the case with obvious things like strength. Strength is produced by taking plenty of nourishment and doing plenty of hard work, and the strong man, in turn, has the greatest capacity for these. And the case is the same with the virtues. By abstaining from pleasure we become temperate, and when we have become temperate we are best able to abstain. And so with courage. By habituating ourselves to despise danger, and to face it, we become courageous; and when we have become courageous, we are best able to face danger.

The pleasure or pain that accompanies the acts must be taken as a test of the formed habit or character. He who abstains from the pleasures of the body and rejoices in the abstinence is temperate, while he who is vexed at having to abstain is self-indulgent. And, again, he who faces danger with pleasure, or at any rate, without pain is courageous, but he to whom this is painful is a coward. For moral virtue or excellence is closely concerned with pleasure and pain. It is pleasure that moves us to do what is base and pain that moves us to refrain from what is noble. And there, as Plato says, man needs to be so trained from his youth as to find pleasure and pain in the right objects. This is what sound education means. Another reason why virtue has to do with pleasure and pain is that it has to do with actions and passions or affections; but every affection and every act is accompanied by pleasure or pain. This is indicated also by the use of pleasure and pain in correction; they have a kind of curative property, and a cure is effected by administering the opposite of the disease.

Again, as we said before, every type of character or habit is essentially relative to, and concerned with, those things that form it for good or for ill; but it is through pleasure and pain that bad characters are formed — that is to say, through pursuing and avoiding them at the wrong time, or in the wrong manner, or in any other of the various ways of going wrong that may be distinguished. And hence some people go so far as to define the virtues as a kind of impassive or neutral state of mind. But they make a mistake in saying this absolutely, instead of qualifying it by the addition of the right and wrong manner, time, etc. We may lay down, therefore, that this kind of excellence [moral excellence or virtue] makes us do what is best in matters of pleasure and pain, while vice or badness has the contrary effect. The following considerations will throw additional light on the point. There are three kinds of things that move us to choose and three that move us to avoid them. On the one hand, the beautiful or noble, the advantageous, the pleasant. On the other hand, the ugly or base, the hurtful, the painful. Now the good man is apt to go right, and the bad man to go wrong about them all, but especially about pleasure; for pleasure is not only common to man and animals, but also accompanies all pursuit or objects of choice; for even the noble and advantageous appear pleasant.

Again, the feeling of pleasure has been fostered in us all from our infancy by our training, and has thus become so ingrained in our life that it can scarcely be washed out. And, indeed, we all more or less make pleasure our test in judging actions. For this reason too, then, our whole study must be concerned with these matters; since to be pleased and pained in the right or wrong way has great influence on our actions. And lastly, as Heraclitus says, it is harder to fight with pleasure than with wrath; and virtue, like art, is always more concerned with what is harder; for the harder the task, the better is success. For this reason also, then, both moral virtue or excellence and political science must always be concerned with pleasures and pains; for he that behaves rightly with regard to them will be good, and he that behaves badly will be bad. We will take it as established then, that moral virtue or excellence has to do with pleasures and pains; and that the acts which produce virtue develop it, and also, when done differently, destroy it; and that it manifests itself in the same acts which produced it.

But here we may be asked what we mean by saying that men can become just and temperate only by doing what is just and temperate. Surely, it may be said, if their acts are just and temperate, they themselves are already just and temperate, as they are grammarians and musicians if they do what is grammatical and musical. We may answer, I think firstly, that this is not quite the case even with the arts. A man may do something grammatical or write something correctly by chance, or at the prompting of another person. He will not be grammatical till he not only does something grammatical, but also does it like a grammatical person — because of his own knowledge of grammar. But secondly, the virtues are not in this point analogous to the arts. The products of art have their excellence in themselves, and so it is enough if when produced they are of a certain quality; but in the case of the virtues, a man is not said to act justly or temperately or like a just or temperate man if what he does merely be of a certain sort — he must also be in a certain state of mind when he does it. That is to say, first of all he must know what he is doing; secondly he must choose it, and choose it for himself; and thirdly his act must be the expression of a formed and stable character. Now, of these conditions, only one, the knowledge, is necessary for the possession of any art; but for the possession of the virtues, knowledge is of little or no value, while the other conditions that result from repeatedly doing what is just and temperate are not just slightly important, but all-important.

The thing that is done, therefore, is called just or temperate when it is such as the just or temperate man would do; but the man who does it is not just or temperate unless he also does it in the spirit of the just or temperate man. It is right then to say that by doing what is just a man becomes just, and temperate by doing what is temperate, while without doing thus he has no chance of ever becoming good. But most men, instead of doing thus, fly to theories and fancy that they are philosophizing and that this will make them good, like a sick man who listens attentively to what the doctor says and then disobeys all his orders. This sort of theorizing will no more produce a healthy habit of mind that this sort of treatment will produce a healthy habit of body.

Next we must consider what virtue is. Everything psychical is either (1) a passion or emotion, or (2) a power or faculty, or (3) a habit or a trained faculty; and so virtue must be one of these three. By (1) passion or emotion we mean appetite, anger, fear, confidence, envy, joy, love, hate, longing, emulation, pity or generally that which is accompanied by pleasure or pain; (2) a power or faculty is that in respect of which we are said to be capable of being affected in any of these ways as for instance, that in respect of which we are able to be angered or pained or to pity; and (3) a habit or trained faculty is that in respect of which we are well or ill regulated or disposed in the matter of our affections; as, for instance, in the matter of being angered, we are ill regulated if we are too violent or too slack, but if we are moderate in our anger we are well regulated. And so with the rest.

Now neither the virtues nor the vices are passions (1) because we are not called good or bad in respect of our emotions, but are called good or bad in respect of our virtues or vices; (2) because we are neither praised nor blamed in respect of our emotions (a man is not praised for being afraid or angry, nor blamed for being angry simply, but for being angry in a particular way), but we are praised or blamed in respect of our virtues or vices; (3) because we may be angered or frightened without deliberate choice, or at least are impossible without it; and (4) because in respect of our emotions we are said to be moved, but in respect of our virtues and vices we are not said to be moved, but to be regulated or disposed in this way or in that way. For these same reasons also they are not powers or faculties; for we are not called either good or bad for being merely capable of emotion, nor are we either praised or blamed for this. And further, while nature gives us our powers or faculties, she does not make us either good or bad. This point, however, we have already treated. If then, the virtues be neither emotions or faculties, it remains for them to be habits or trained faculties.

We have thus found the genus to which virtue belongs; but we want to know, not only that it is a trained faculty, but also what species of trained faculty it is. We may safely assert that the virtue or excellence of a thing causes that thing both to be itself in good condition and to perform its function well. The excellence of the eye, for example, makes both the eye and its work good; for it is by the excellence of the eye that we see well. Similarly the excellence of the horse makes a horse both good in itself and good at running and at carrying its rider and at awaiting the attack of the enemy. If this is true in every case, therefore, the virtue of man also will be the state of character which makes a man good and which makes him do his own work well.

How this is to be done we have already said, but we may exhibit the same conclusion in another way, by inquiring what the nature of this virtue is. Now, if we have any quantity, whether continuous or divisible, it is possible to take either a larger, or a smaller, or an equal amount, and that either absolutely or relatively to our own needs. By an equal or fair amount I understand a mean amount, or one that lies between excess and deficiency. By the absolute mean, or mean relatively to the thing itself, I understand that which is equidistant from both extremes, and this is one and the same for all. By the mean relatively to us I understand that which is neither too much nor too little for us; and this is not one and the same for all. For instance, if ten be larger and two be smaller, if we take six we take the mean relatively to the thing itself [or the arithmetical mean]; for it exceeds one extreme by the same amount by which it is exceeded by the other extreme. This is the mean in arithmetical proportion. But the mean relatively to us cannot be found in this way. If ten pounds of food is too much for a given man to eat, and two pounds too little, it does not follow that the trainer will order six pounds. For that also may perhaps be too much for the man in question or too little; too little for Milo [a famous Greek wrestler], too much for the beginner. The same holds true in running and wrestling. And so we say that generally a master in any art avoids what is too much and what is too little and seeks for the mean and chooses it — not the absolute but the relative mean.

Every art or science, then, perfects its work in this way, looking to the mean and bringing its work up to this standard; so that people are wont to say of a good work that nothing could be taken from it or added to it, implying that excellence is destroyed by excess or deficiency, but secured by observing the mean. And good artists do in fact keep their eyes fixed on this in all that they do. Virtue therefore, since like nature it is more exact and better than any art, must also aim at the mean — virtue of course meaning moral virtue or moral excellence; for it has to do with passions and actions, and it is these that admit of excess and deficiency and the mean. For example, it is possible to feel fear, confidence, desire, anger, pity, and generally to be affected pleasantly and painfully, either too much or too little, in either case wrongly; but to be thus affected at the right times, and on the right occasions, and toward the right persons, and with the right object, and in the right fashion, is the mean course and the best course, and these are characteristics of virtue. And in the same way our outward acts also admit of excess and deficiency, and the mean or intermediate. Virtue then is concerned with feelings or passions and with outward acts, in which excess is wrong and deficiency is also blamed, but the mean is praised and is right; and being praised and being successful are both characteristics of virtue. Virtue, therefore, is a kind of moderation or mean as it aims at the mean or moderate amount.

Again, there are many ways of going wrong (for evil is infinite in nature, to use a figure of the Pythagoreans, while good is finite or limited), but only one way of going right; so that the one is easy and the other hard — easy to miss the mark and hard to hit the mark. On this account also excess and deficiency are characteristics of vice; hitting the mean is characteristic of virtue:

"Goodness is simple, evil takes any shape."

Virtue, then, is a habit or trained faculty of choice, the characteristic of which lies in observing the mean relatively to the persons concerned, and which is guided by reason, that is, by the judgment of the prudent man. And it is a moderation, firstly, inasmuch as it comes in the middle or the mean between two vices, one on the side of excess, the other on the side of deficiency; and secondly, inasmuch as, while these vices fall short of or exceed the mean or intermediate measure in feeling and in action, it finds and chooses the mean, middling, or moderate amount. Regarded in essence, therefore, or according to the definition of its nature, virtue is a moderation or middle state, but viewed in its relation to what is best and right it is the extreme of perfection.

But it is not all actions nor all passions that admit of moderation; there are some whose very names imply badness, as malevolence, shamelessness, envy, and among acts, adultery, theft, murder. These and all other like things are blamed as being bad in themselves, and not merely in their excess or deficiency. It is impossible, therefore, to go right in them; they are always wrong. Rightness and wrongness in such things, adultery for example, does not depend upon whether it is the right woman, at the right time, and in the right way, but the mere doing of any one of them is wrong. It would be equally absurd to look for moderation or excess or deficiency in unjust, cowardly, or self-indulgent conduct; for then there would be moderation in excess or deficiency, and excess in excess, and deficiency in deficiency. The fact is that just as there can be no excess or deficiency in temperance or courage because the mean or moderate amount is, in a sense, an extreme, so in these kinds of conduct also there can be no moderation or excess or deficiency, but the acts are wrong however they be done.

It is not enough, however, to make these general statements about virtue and vice; we must go on and apply them to particulars — that is to the several virtues and vices. For in reasoning about matters of conduct general statements are too vague and do not convey as much truth as particular propositions. It is with particulars that conduct is concerned. Our statements, therefore, when applied to these particulars, should be found to hold good. These particulars then — the several virtues and vices and the several acts and affections with which they deal — we will take from the following [list].

Moderation in the feelings of fear and confidence is courage. Of those that exceed, he that exceeds in fearlessness has no name (as often happens), but he that exceeds in confidence is foolhardy, while he that exceeds in fear, but is deficient in confidence, is cowardly.

Moderation in respect of certain pleasures and also (though to a less extent) certain pains is temperance, while excess is self-indulgence or profligacy. But defectiveness in the matter of these pleasures is hardly ever found, and so this sort of people also have as yet received no name. Let us put them down as devoid of sensibility, or call them insensible.

In the matter of giving and taking money, moderation is liberality, excess and deficiency are prodigality and illiberality. But these two vices exceed and fall short in contrary ways. The prodigal exceeds in spending, but falls short in taking; while the illiberal man exceeds in taking, but falls short in spending. . . . But, besides these, there are other dispositions in the matter of money. There is a moderation which is called magnificence (for the magnificent is not the same as the liberal man; the former deals with large sums, the latter with small), and an excess which is called bad taste or vulgarity, and a deficiency which is called meanness; and these vices differ from those that are opposed to liberality. How they differ will be explained later.

With respect to honor and disgrace, there is a mean or moderation which is high-mindedness, and an excess which may be called vanity, and a deficiency which is little-mindedness. But just as we said that liberality is related to magnificence, differing only in that it deals with small sums, so here there is a virtue related to high-mindedness, and differing only in that it is concerned with small instead of great honors. A man may have a due desire for honor and also more or less than a moderate desire. He that carries this desire to excess is called ambitious, he that has a deficiency is called unambitious, while he that has the proper amount has no special name. There are also no abstract names for the characters, except "ambition" corresponding to ambitious. And on this account those who occupy the extremes lay claim to the middle place. And in common parlance too, the moderate man is sometimes called ambitious and sometimes unambitious, and sometimes the ambitious man is praised and sometimes the unambitious. Why this is so we will explain later. For the present we will continue the plan and enumerate the other types of character.

In the matter of anger also we find excess and deficiency and the mean or moderation. The characters themselves scarcely have recognized names, but as the moderate man is here called gentle, we will call his character gentleness; of those who go into extremes, we may use the term wrathful or irascible for him who exceeds, with wrathfulness or irascibility for the vice, and wrathless for him who is deficient, with wrathlessness for his character.

Besids these, there are three kinds of moderation, bearing some resemblance to one another, and yet different. They all have to do with intercourse in speech and action, but they differ in that one has to do with the truthfulness of this intercourse, while the other two have to do with its pleasantness — one of the two with pleasantness in matters of amusement, the other with pleasantness in all the relations of life. We must therefore speak of these qualities also in order that we may the more plainly see how, in all cases, moderation is praiseworthy, while the extreme courses are neither right nor praiseworthy, but blamable. In these cases also names are for the most part wanting, but we must try here as elsewhere to coin names in order to make our argument clear and easy to follow. In the matter of truth, then, let us call him who observes the mean a true or truthful person, and observance of the mean truth or truthfulness; pretence, when it exaggerates, may be called boasting and the person a boaster; when it understates, let the names be irony and ironical. With regard to pleasantness in amusement, he who observes the mean we may call witty, and his character wittiness; excess may be called buffoonery, and the man a buffoon; while we may call the deficient person boorish, and boorishness for his character. With regard to pleasantness in the other affairs of life, he who makes himself properly pleasant may be called friendly, and his moderation friendliness; he that exceeds may be called an obsequious person if he have no ulterior motive, but a flatterer if he is looking out for his own advantage; he that is deficient in this respect, and always makes himself disagreeable, may be called a quarrelsome and surly sort of person.

Moreover, in the emotions and passions and in our conduct with regard to them there are ways of observing the mean. For example, shame is not a virtue, but yet the modest man is praised. For in these matters also we speak of this man as observing the mean, of that man as going beyond it (as the shame-faced man whom the least things makes shy), while he who is deficient in the feeling, or lacks it altogether, is called shameless; but the term modest is applied to him who observes the mean.

Righteous indignation, again, hits the mean between envy and spite or malevolence. These have to do with feelings of pleasure and pain at what happens to our neighbors. A man is called righteously indignant when he feels pain at the sight of undeserved prosperity, but the envious man goes beyond and is pained by the sight of any one in prosperity, while the spiteful or malevolent man is so far from being pained that he actually exults in the sight of prosperous iniquity. . . .

THE ROMANS

Vergil

Publius Vergilius Maro (70 B.C.–19 B.C.) or Vergil as he is best known, was one of the great poets of Rome. One of his works entitled *Georgics* (Greek for *On Farming*) comprised four books concerned with farming and the pleasures of country life. His greatest work was *The Aeneid*, an epic poem dealing with the founding of Rome by the mythical Aeneas, a hero who had escaped from the burning ruins of Troy.

The many books of *The Aeneid* deal with the wanderings and adventures of Aeneas until he founded the city of Rome. Many are struck with the similarity between *The Odyssey* and *The Aeneid* since both deal with the wanderings of a mythical hero. As you have seen, the Greeks were most familiar with and proud of *The Odyssey*, and looked upon it as an account of their glorious past. Since Rome did not have a poem of this type, Vergil set out consciously to establish, in a somewhat retroactive fashion, a glorious Roman past. After working for many years on *The Aeneid*, Vergil became ill on a journey to Greece, and returned to Brundisium to die at the early age of 51. Since, according to his own standards, his great poem was still not ready for publication, he gave orders that it should be burned. Fortunately, the Emperor Augustus would not allow this. Many millions of later readers have been pleased with his decision.

In later years Vergil became a legendary figure and even something of a prophet. It was the custom as late as the 17th century for men to open the works of Vergil at random, to look at the first lines their eyes came upon, and to consider these lines prophetic of one's destiny or the answer to a crucial question or problem. The great Italian poet, Dante, spoke of Vergil as "my master and my author." He called him the poet who was the epitome of all humanity.

In Book VI, which is included here, Aeneas visited the underworld and found his father Anchises, who told him of the future of Rome and showed him the souls of the men who would contribute to its greatness. Note in this selection the character of Aeneas, the names of those great Romans who were yet to be born, and the efforts which Vergil took to give Rome a glorious past.

THE AENEID, BOOK VI

THE LOWER WORLD

Mourning for Palinurus, he drives the fleet
To Cumae's coast-line; the prows are turned, the anchor
Let down, the beach is covered by the vessels.
Young in their eagerness for the land in the west,
They flash ashore; some seek the seeds of flame
Hidden in veins of flint, and others spoil
The woods of tinder, and show where water runs.
Aeneas, in devotion, seeks the heights
Where stands Apollo's temple, and the cave
Where the dread Sibyl dwells, Apollo's priestess,
With the great mind and heart, inspired revealer
Of things to come. They enter Diana's grove,
Pass underneath the roof of gold.
　　　　　　　　　　　　　　　　The story
Has it that Daedalus fled from Minos' kingdom,[1]
Trusting himself to wings he made, and travelled
A course unknown to man, to the cold north,
Descending on this very summit; here,
Earth-bound again, he built a mighty temple,
Paying Apollo homage, the dedication
Of the oarage of his wings. On the temple doors
He carved, in bronze, Androgeos' death, and the payment

---
[1] Daedalus was a mythical artist and inventor. Imprisoned by King Minos of Crete, he constructed wings for himself and his son Icarus and flew away. Icarus flew too near the sun and melted the wax wings. The other pieces of sculpture mentioned here show other incidents in Daedalus' life.

Enforced on Cecrops' children, seven sons
For sacrifice each year: there stands the urn,
The lots are drawn—facing this, over the sea,
Rises the land of Crete: the scene portrays
Pasiphae in cruel love, the bull
She took to her by cunning, and their offspring,
The mongrel Minotaur, half man, half monster,
The proof of lust unspeakable; and the toil
Of the house is shown, the labyrinthine maze
Which no one could have solved, but Daedalus
Pitied a princess' love, loosened the tangle,
Gave her a skein to guide her way. His boy,
Icarus, might have been here, in the picture,
And almost was—his father had made the effort
Once, and once more, and dropped his hands; he could not
Master his grief that much. The story held them;
They would have studied it longer, but Achates[2]
Came from his mission; with him came the priestess,
Deiphobe, daughter of Glaucus, who tends the temple
For Phoebus and Diana; she warned Aeneas:
"It is no such sights the time demands; far better
To offer sacrifice, seven chosen bullocks,
Seven chosen ewes, a herd without corruption."
They were prompt in their obedience, and the priestess
Summoned the Trojans to the lofty temple.

   The rock's vast side is hollowed into a cavern,
With a hundred mouths, a hundred open portals,
Whence voices rush, the answers of the Sibyl.
They had reached the threshold, and the virgin cried:
"It is time to seek the fates; the god is here,
The god is here, behold him." And as she spoke
Before the entrance, her countenance and color
Changed, and her hair tossed loose, and her heart was heaving,
Her bosom swollen with frenzy; she seemed taller,
Her voice not human at all, as the god's presence
Drew nearer, and took hold on her. "Aeneas,"
She cried, "Aeneas, are you praying?
Are you being swift in prayer? Until you are,
The house of the gods will not be moved, nor open
Its mighty portals." More than her speech, her silence
Made the Trojans cold with terror, and Aeneas
Prayed from the depth of his heart: "Phoebus Apollo,
Compassionate ever, slayer of Achilles
Through aim of Paris' arrow, helper and guide
Over the seas, over the lands, the deserts,
The shoals and quicksands, now at last we have come
To Italy, we hold the lands which fled us:
Grant that thus far, no farther, a Trojan fortune
Attend our wandering. And spare us now,
All of you, gods and goddesses, who hated
Troy in the past, and Trojan glory. I beg you,
Most holy prophetess, in whose foreknowing
The future stands revealed, grant that the Trojans—
I ask with fate's permission—rest in Latium
Their wandering storm-tossed gods. I will build a temple,
In honor of Apollo and Diana,
Out of eternal marble, and ordain
Festivals in their honor, and for the Sibyl
A great shrine in our kingdom, and I will place there
The lots and mystic oracles for my people
With chosen priests to tend them. Only, priestess,
This once, I pray you, chant the sacred verses
With your own lips; do not trust them to the leaves,[3]
The mockery of the rushing wind's disorder."

   But the priestess, not yet subject to Apollo,
Went reeling through the cavern, wild, and storming
To throw the god, who presses, like a rider,
With bit and bridle and weight, tames her wild spirit,
Shapes her to his control. The doors fly open,
The hundred doors, of their own will, fly open,
And through the air the answer comes:—"O Trojans,
At last the dangers of the sea are over;
That course is run, but graver ones are waiting
On land. The sons of Dardanus[4] will reach
The kingdom of Lavinia[5]—be easy
On that account—the sons of Dardanus, also,
Will wish they had not come there. War, I see,
Terrible war, and the river Tiber foaming
With streams of blood. There will be another Xanthus,
Another Simois,[6] and Greek encampment,
Even another Achilles, born in Latium,
Himself a goddess' son. And Juno further
Will always be there: you will beg for mercy,
Be poor, turn everywhere for help. A woman
Will be the cause once more of so much evil,
A foreign bride, receptive to the Trojans,
A foreign marriage. Do not yield to evil,
Attack, attack, more boldly even than fortune
Seems to permit. An offering of safety,—
Incredible!—will come from a Greek city."

---

[2] The companion of Aeneas.

[3] The prophecies of this Cumaean Sibyl were usually written on leaves which the winds in the cave might scatter and confuse (v. Book III).

[4] The mythical founder of Troy.

[5] The daughter of the Italian King Latinus. Aeneas was later to marry her to establish his kingdom.

[6] Rivers near Troy that ran with blood during the Trojan War.

THE ROMANS

So, through the amplifiers of her cavern,
The hollow vaults, the Sibyl cast her warnings,
Riddles confused with truth; and Apollo rode her,
Reining her rage, and shaking her, and spurring
The fierceness of her heart. The frenzy dwindled,
A little, and her lips were still. Aeneas
Began:—"For me, no form of trouble, maiden,
Is new, or unexpected; all of this
I have known long since, lived in imagination.
One thing I ask: this is the gate of the kingdom,
So it is said, where Pluto reigns, the gloomy
Marsh where the water of Acheron[7] runs over.
Teach me the way from here, open the portals
That I may go to my belovèd father,
Stand in his presence, talk with him. I brought him,
Once, on these shoulders, through a thousand weapons
And following fire, and foemen. He shared with me
The road, the sea, the menaces of heaven,
Things that an old man should not bear; he bore them,
Tired as he was. And he it was who told me
To come to you in humbleness. I beg you
Pity the son, the father. You have power,
Great priestess, over all; it is not for nothing
Hecate[8] gave you this dominion over
Avernus' groves. If Orpheus could summon
Eurydice from the shadows with his music,
If Pollux could save his brother, coming, going,
Along this path,—why should I mention Theseus,
Why mention Hercules?[9] I, too, descended
From the line of Jupiter." He clasped the altar,
Making his prayer, and she made answer to him:
"Son of Anchises, born of godly lineage,
By night, by day, the portals of dark Dis[10]
Stand open: it is easy, the descending
Down to Avernus. But to climb again,
To trace the footsteps back to the air above,
There lies the task, the toil. A few, beloved
By Jupiter, descended from the gods,
A few, in whom exalting virtue burned,
Have been permitted. Around the central woods
The black Cocytus glides, a sullen river;
But if such love is in your heart, such longing
For double crossing of the Stygian lake,
For double sight of Tartarus, learn first
What must be done. In a dark tree there hides
A bough, all golden, leaf and pliant stem,
Sacred to Proserpine.[11] This all the grove
Protects, and shadows cover it with darkness.
Until this bough, this bloom of light, is found,
No one receives his passport to the darkness

Whose queen requires this tribute. In succession,
After the bough is plucked, another grows,
Gold-green with the same metal. Raise the eyes,
Look up, reach up the hand, and it will follow
With ease, if fate is calling; otherwise,
No power, no steel, can loose it. Furthermore,
(Alas, you do not know this!), one of your men
Lies on the shore, unburied, a pollution
To all the fleet, while you have come for counsel
Here to our threshold. Bury him with honor;
Black cattle slain in expiation for him
Must fall before you see the Stygian kingdoms,
The groves denied to living men."

                          Aeneas,
With sadness in his eyes, and downcast heart,
Turned from the cave, and at his side Achates
Accompanied his anxious meditations.
They talked together: who could be the comrade
Named by the priestess, lying there unburied?
And they found him on dry sand; it was Misenus,
Aeolus' son, none better with the trumpet
To make men burn for warfare. He had been
Great Hector's man-at-arms; he was good in battle
With spear as well as horn, and after Hector
Had fallen to Achilles, he had followed
Aeneas, entering no meaner service.
Some foolishness came over him; he made
The ocean echo to the blare of his trumpet
That day, and challenged the sea-gods to a contest
In martial music, and Triton, jealous, caught him,
However unbelievable the story,
And held him down between the rocks, and drowned him
Under the foaming waves. His comrades mourned him,
Aeneas most of all, and in their sorrow
They carry out, in haste, the Sibyl's orders,
Construct the funeral altar, high as heaven,
They go to an old wood, and the pine-trees fall
Where wild beasts have their dens, and holm-oak rings
To the stroke of the axe, and oak and ash are riven
By the splitting wedge, and rowan-trees come rolling

---

[7] This is the river that leads to Hades. Other rivers in the lower world are the Styx, which forms a boundary for the region, Cocytus, and Phlegethon, which serves as a barrier between the mild punishments and the more severe.

[8] Hecate is a very powerful goddess who, among many responsibilities, controlled the spirits of the dead. Avernus is a very deep pool surrounded by gloomy woods. Its depth and gloom inspired the idea that it led to the underworld.

[9] All of these are the names of mythical heroes who had descended into Hades and returned.

[10] Dis is another name for the underworld.

[11] Proserpine, as wife of Pluto, is queen of the underworld.

Down the steep mountain-side. Aeneas helps them,
And cheers them on; studies the endless forest,
Takes thought, and prays: "If only we might see it,
That golden bough, here in the depth of the forest,
Bright on some tree. She told the truth, our priestess,
Too much, too bitter truth, about Misenus."
No sooner had he spoken than twin doves
Came flying down before him, and alighted
On the green ground. He knew his mother's birds,[12]
And made his prayer, rejoicing,—"Oh, be leaders,
Wherever the way, and guide me to the grove
Where the rich bough makes rich the shaded ground.
Help me, O goddess-mother!" And he paused,
Watching what sign they gave, what course they set.
The birds flew on a little, just ahead
Of the pursuing vision; when they came
To the jaws of dank Avernus, evil-smelling,
They rose aloft, then swooped down the bright air,
Perched on the double tree, where the off-color
Of gold was gleaming golden through the branches.
As mistletoe, in the cold winter, blossoms
With its strange foliage on an alien tree,
The yellow berry gilding the smooth branches,
Such was the vision of the gold in leaf
On the dark holm-oak, so the foil was rustling,
Rattling, almost, the bract in the soft wind
Stirring like metal. Aeneas broke it off
With eager grasp, and bore it to the Sibyl.

    Meanwhile, along the shore, the Trojans mourned,
Paying Misenus' dust the final honors.
A mighty pyre was raised, of pine and oak,
The sides hung with dark leaves, and somber cypress
Along the front, and gleaming arms above.
Some made the water hot, and some made ready
Bronze caldrons, shimmering over fire, and others
Lave and anoint the body, and with weeping
Lay on the bier his limbs, and place above them
Familiar garments, crimson color; and some
Take up the heavy burden, a sad office,
And, as their fathers did, they kept their eyes
Averted, as they brought the torches nearer.
They burn gifts with him, bowls of oil, and viands,
And frankincense; and when the flame is quiet
And the ashes settle to earth, they wash the embers
With wine, and slake the thirsty dust. The bones
Are placed in a bronze urn by Corynaeus,
Who, with pure water, thrice around his comrades
Made lustral cleansing, shaking gentle dew
From the fruitful branch of olive; and they said
Hail and farewell! And over him Aeneas
Erects a mighty tomb, with the hero's arms,
His oar and trumpet, where the mountain rises
Memorial for ever, and named Misenus.

    These rites performed, he hastened to the Sibyl.
There was a cavern, yawning wide and deep,
Jagged, below the darkness of the trees,
Beside the darkness of the lake. No bird
Could fly above it safely, with the vapor
Pouring from the black gulf (the Greeks have named it
Avernus, or A-Ornos, meaning *birdless*),
And here the priestess for the slaughter set
Four bullocks, black ones, poured the holy wine
Between the horns, and plucked the topmost bristles
For the first offering to the sacred fire,
Calling on Hecate, a power in heaven,
A power in hell. Knives to the throat were driven,
The warm blood caught in bowls. Aeneas offered
A lamb, black-fleeced, to Night and her great sister,
A sterile heifer for the queen; for Dis
An altar in the night, and on the flames
The weight of heavy bulls, the fat oil pouring
Over the burning entrails. And at dawn,
Under their feet, earth seemed to shake and rumble,
The ridges move, and bitches bay in darkness,
As the presence neared. The Sibyl cried a warning,
"Keep off, keep off, whatever is unholy,
Depart from here! Courage, Aeneas; enter
The path, unsheathe the sword. The time is ready
For the brave heart." She strode out boldly, leading
Into the open cavern, and he followed.

    Gods of the world of spirit, silent shadows,
Chaos and Phlegethon, areas of silence,
Wide realms of dark, may it be right and proper
To tell what I have heard, this revelation
Of matters buried deep in earth and darkness!

    Vague forms in lonely darkness, they were going
Through void and shadow, through the empty realm
Like people in a forest, when the moonlight
Shifts with a baleful glimmer, and shadow covers
The sky, and all the colors turn to blackness.
At the first threshold, on the jaws of Orcus,
Grief and avenging Cares have set their couches,
And pale Diseases dwell, and sad Old Age,
Fear, evil-counselling Hunger, wretched Need,
Forms terrible to see, and Death, and Toil,
And Death's own brother, Sleep, and evil Joys,
Fantasies of the mind, and deadly War,
The Furies' iron chambers, Discord, raving,

---

[12] Aeneas' mother was Venus.

THE ROMANS

Her snaky hair entwined in bloody bands.
An elm-tree loomed there, shadowy and huge,
The aged boughs outspread, beneath whose leaves,
Men say, the false dreams cling, thousands on thousands.
And there are monsters in the dooryard, Centaurs,
Scyllas, of double shape, the beast of Lerna,
Hissing most horribly, Briareus,
The hundred-handed giant, a Chimaera
Whose armament is fire, Harpies, and Gorgons,
A triple-bodied giant. In sudden panic
Aeneas drew his sword, the edge held forward,
Ready to rush and flail, however blindly,
Save that his wise companion warned him, saying
They had no substance, they were only phantoms
Flitting about, illusions without body.

   From here, the road turns off to Acheron,
River of Hell; here, thick with muddy whirling,
Cocytus boils with sand. Charon is here,
The guardian of these mingling waters, Charon,
Uncouth and filthy, on whose chin the hair
Is a tangled mat, whose eyes protrude, are burning,
Whose dirty cloak is knotted at the shoulder.
He poles a boat, tends to the sail, unaided,
Ferrying bodies in his rust-hued vessel.
Old, but a god's senility is awful
In its raw greenness. To the bank come thronging
Mothers and men, bodies of great-souled heroes,
Their life-time over, boys, unwedded maidens,
Young men whose fathers saw their pyres burning,
Thick as the forest leaves that fall in autumn
With early frost, thick as the birds to landfall
From over the seas, when the chill of the year compels them
To sunlight. There they stand, a host, imploring
To be taken over first. Their hands, in longing,
Reach out for the farther shore. But the gloomy boatman
Makes choice among them, taking some, and keeping
Others far back from the stream's edge. Aeneas,
Wondering, asks the Sibyl, "Why the crowding?
What are the spirits seeking? What distinction
Brings some across the livid stream, while others
Stay on the farther bank?" She answers, briefly:
"Son of Anchises, this is the awful river,
The Styx, by which the gods take oath; the boatman
Charon; those he takes with him are the buried,
Those he rejects, whose luck is out, the graveless.
It is not permitted him to take them over
The dreadful banks and hoarse-resounding waters
Till earth is cast upon their bones. They haunt
These shores a hundred restless years of waiting
Before they end postponement of the crossing."
Aeneas paused, in thoughtful mood, with pity
Over their lot's unevenness; and saw there,
Wanting the honor given the dead, and grieving,
Leucaspis, and Orontes, the Lycian captain,
Who had sailed from Troy across the stormy waters,
And drowned off Africa, with crew and vessel,
And there was Palinurus, once his pilot,
Who, not so long ago, had been swept over,
Watching the stars on the journey north from Carthage.
The murk was thick; Aeneas hardly knew him,
Sorrowful in that darkness, but made question:
"What god, O Palinurus, took you from us?
Who drowned you in the deep? Tell me. Apollo
Never before was false, and yet he told me
You would be safe across the seas, and come
Unharmed to Italy; what kind of promise
Was this, to fool me with?" But Palinurus
Gave him assurance:—"It was no god who drowned me
No falsehood on Apollo's part, my captain,
But as I clung to the tiller, holding fast
To keep the course, as I should do, I felt it
Wrenched from the ship, and I fell with it, headlong.
By those rough seas I swear, I had less fear
On my account than for the ship, with rudder
And helmsman overboard, to drift at the mercy
Of rising seas. Three nights I rode the waters,
Three nights of storm, and from the crest of a wave,
On the fourth morning, sighted Italy,
I was swimming to land, I had almost reached it, heavy
In soaking garments; my cramped fingers struggled
To grasp the top of the rock, when barbarous people,
Ignorant men, mistaking me for booty,
Struck me with swords; waves hold me now, or winds
Roll me along the shore. By the light of heaven,
The lovely air, I beg you, by your father,
Your hope of young Iulus,[13] bring me rescue
Out of these evils, my unconquered leader!
Cast over my body earth—you have the power—
Return to Velia's harbor,—or there may be
Some other way—your mother is a goddess,
Else how would you be crossing this great river,
This Stygian swamp?—help a poor fellow, take me
Over the water with you, give a dead man
At least a place to rest in." But the Sibyl
Broke in upon him sternly:—"Palinurus,
Whence comes this mad desire? No man, unburied,
May see the Stygian waters, or Cocytus,

---

[13] This is Aeneas' son, also known as Ascanius.

The Furies' dreadful river; no man may come
Unbidden to this bank. Give up the hope
That fate is changed by praying, but hear this,
A little comfort in your harsh misfortune:
Those neighboring people will make expiation,
Driven by signs from heaven, through their cities
And through their countryside; they will build a tomb,
Thereto bring offerings yearly, and the place
Shall take its name from you, Cape Palinurus."
So he was comforted a little, finding
Some happiness in the promise.
                            And they went on,
Nearing the river, and from the stream the boatman
Beheld them cross the silent forest, nearer,
Turning their footsteps toward the bank. He challenged:—
"Whoever you are, O man in armor, coming
In this direction, halt where you are, and tell me
The reason why you come. This is the region
Of shadows, and of Sleep and drowsy Night;
I am not allowed to carry living bodies
In the Stygian boat; and I must say I was sorry
I ever accepted Hercules and Theseus
And Pirithous, and rowed them over the lake,
Though they were sons of gods and great in courage.
One of them dared to drag the guard of Hell,
Enchained, from Pluto's throne, shaking in terror,
The others to snatch our queen from Pluto's chamber."
The Sibyl answered briefly: "No such cunning
Is plotted here; our weapons bring no danger.
Be undisturbed: the hell-hound in his cavern
May bark forever, to keep the bloodless shadows
Frightened away from trespass; Proserpine,
Untouched, in pureness guard her uncle's threshold.
Trojan Aeneas, a man renowned for goodness,
Renowned for nerve in battle, is descending
To the lowest shades; he comes to find his father.
If such devotion has no meaning to you,
Look on this branch at least, and recognize it!"
And with the word she drew from under her mantle
The golden bough; his swollen wrath subsided.
No more was said; he saw the bough, and marvelled
At the holy gift, so long unseen; came sculling
The dark-blue boat to the shore, and drove the spirits,
Lining the thwarts, ashore, and cleared the gangway,
And took Aeneas aboard; as that big man
Stepped in, the leaky skiff groaned under the weight,
And the strained seams let in the muddy water,
But they made the crossing safely, seer and soldier,
To the far margin, colorless and shapeless,
Grey sedge and dark-brown ooze. They heard the baying

Of Cerberus, that great hound, in his cavern crouching,
Making the shore resound, as all three throats
Belled horribly; and serpents rose and bristled
Along the triple neck. The priestess threw him
A sop with honey and drugged meal; he opened
The ravenous throat, gulped, and subsided, filling
The den with his huge bulk. Aeneas, crossing,
Passed on beyond the bank of the dread river
Whence none return.
                      A wailing of thin voices[14]
Came to their ears, the souls of infants crying,
Those whom the day of darkness took from the breast
Before their share of living. And there were many
Whom some false sentence brought to death. Here Minos
Judges them once again; a silent jury
Reviews the evidence. And there are others,
Guilty of nothing, but who hated living,
The suicides. How gladly, now, they would suffer
Poverty, hardship, in the world of light!
But this is not permitted; they are bound
Nine times around by the black unlovely river;
Styx holds them fast.
                    They came to the Fields of
   Mourning,
So-called, where those whom cruel love had wasted
Hid in secluded pathways, under myrtle,
And even in death were anxious. Procris, Phaedra,
Eriphyle, displaying wounds her son
Had given her, Caeneus, Laodamia,
Caeneus, a young man once, and now again
A young man, after having been a woman.
And here, new come from her own wound, was Dido,[15]
Wandering in the wood. The Trojan hero,
Standing near by, saw her, or thought he saw her,
Dim in the shadows, like the slender crescent
Of moon when cloud drifts over. Weeping, he greets
   her:—
"Unhappy Dido, so they told me truly
That your own hand had brought you death. Was I—
Alas!—the cause? I swear by all the stars,
By the world above, by everything held sacred
Here under the earth, unwillingly, O queen,
I left your kingdom. But the gods' commands,
Driving me now through these forsaken places,
This utter night, compelled me on. I could not

---

[14]Here and about 190 lines later you might compare the sins and their punishments with the disposition Dante makes of the souls in Hell in Canto XI of the *Inferno*.

[15]Dido, Queen of Carthage, filled with rage and grief, had committed suicide when Aeneas sailed away from her city.

THE ROMANS

Believe my loss would cause so great a sorrow.
Linger a moment, do not leave me; whither,
Whom, are you fleeing? I am permitted only
This last word with you."
                          But the queen, unmoving
As flint or marble, turned away, her eyes
Fixed on the ground: the tears were vain, the words,
Meant to be soothing, foolish; she turned away,
His enemy forever, to the shadows
Where Sychaeus, her former husband, took her
With love for love, and sorrow for her sorrow.
And still Aeneas wept for her, being troubled
By the injustice of her doom; his pity
Followed her going.
                    They went on. They came
To the farthest fields, whose tenants are the warriors,
Illustrious throng. Here Tydeus came to meet him,
Parthenopaeus came, and pale Adrastus,
A fighter's ghost, and many, many others,
Mourned in the world above, and doomed in battle,
Leaders of Troy, in long array; Aeneas
Sighed as he saw them: Medon; Polyboetes,
The priest of Ceres; Glaucus; and Idaeus
Still keeping arms and chariot; three brothers,
Antenor's sons; Thersilochus; a host
To right and left of him, and when they see him,
One sight is not enough; they crowd around him,
Linger, and ask the reasons for his coming.
But Agamemnon's men, the Greek battalions,
Seeing him there, and his arms in shadow gleaming,
Tremble in panic, turn to flee for refuge,
As once they used to, toward their ships, but where
Are the ships now? They try to shout, in terror;
But only a thin and piping treble issues
To mock their mouths, wide-open.
                              One he knew
Was here, Deiphobus, a son of Priam,
With his whole body mangled, and his features
Cruelly slashed, and both hands cut, and ears
Torn from his temples, and his nostrils slit
By shameful wounds. Aeneas hardly knew him,
Shivering there, and doing his best to hide
His marks of punishment; unhailed, he hailed him:—
"Deiphobus, great warrior, son of Teucer,
Whose cruel punishment was this? Whose license
Abused you so? I heard, it seems, a story
Of that last night, how you had fallen, weary
With killing Greeks at last; I built a tomb,
Although no body lay there, in your honor,
Three times I cried, aloud, over your spirit,
Where now your name and arms keep guard. I could not,
Leaving my country, find my friend, to give him
Proper interment in the earth he came from."
And Priam's son replied:—"Nothing, dear comrade,
Was left undone; the dead man's shade was given
All ceremony due. It was my own fortune
And a Spartan woman's[16] deadliness that sunk me
Under these evils; she it was who left me
These souvenirs. You know how falsely happy
We were on that last night; I need not tell you.
When that dread horse came leaping over our walls,
Pregnant with soldiery, she led the dancing,
A solemn rite, she called it, with Trojan women
Screaming their bacchanals; she raised the torches
High on the citadel; she called the Greeks.
Then—I was worn with trouble, drugged in slumber,
Resting in our ill-omened bridal chamber,
With sleep as deep and sweet as death upon me—
Then she, that paragon of helpmates, deftly
Moved all the weapons from the house; my sword,
Even, she stole from underneath my pillow,
Opened the door, and called in Menelaus,
Hoping, no doubt, to please her loving husband,
To win forgetfulness of her old sinning.
It is quickly told: they broke into the chamber,
The two of them, and with them, as accomplice,
Ulysses came, the crime-contriving bastard.
O gods, pay back the Greeks; grant the petition
If goodness asks for vengeance! But you, Aeneas,
A living man—what chance has brought you here?
Vagrant of ocean, god-inspired,—which are you?
What chance has worn you down, to come, in sadness,
To these confusing sunless dwelling-places?"
    While they were talking, Aurora's rosy car
Had halfway crossed the heaven; all their time
Might have been spent in converse, but the Sibyl
Hurried them forward:—"Night comes on, Aeneas;
We waste the hours with tears. We are at the cross-road,
Now; here we turn to the right, where the pathway leads
On to Elysium, under Pluto's ramparts.
Leftward is Tartarus, and retribution,
The terminal of the wicked, and their dungeon."
Deiphobus left them, saying, "O great priestess,
Do not be angry with me; I am going;
I shall not fail the roll-call of the shadows.
Pride of our race, go on; may better fortune
Attend you!" and, upon the word, he vanished.

---

[16] This is Helen of Troy. Vergil believes that she was married to Deiphobus after Paris' death.

As he looked back, Aeneas saw, to his left,
Wide walls beneath a cliff, a triple rampart,
A river running fire, Phlegethon's torrent,
Rocks roaring in its course, a gate, tremendous,
Pillars of adamant, a tower of iron,
Too strong for men, too strong for even gods
To batter down in warfare, and behind them
A Fury, sentinel in bloody garments,
Always on watch, by day, by night. He heard
Sobbing and groaning there, the crack of the lash,
The clank of iron, the sound of dragging shackles.
The noise was terrible; Aeneas halted,
Asking, "What forms of crime are these, O maiden?
What harrying punishment, what horrible outcry?"
She answered:—"O great leader of the Trojans,
I have never crossed that threshold of the wicked;
No pure soul is permitted entrance thither,
But Hecate, by whose order I was given
Charge of Avernus' groves, my guide, my teacher,
Told me how gods exact the toll of vengeance.
The monarch here, merciless Rhadamanthus,
Punishes guilt, and hears confession; he forces
Acknowledgment of crime; no man in the world,
No matter how cleverly he hides his evil,
No matter how much he smiles at his own slyness,
Can fend atonement off; the hour of death
Begins his sentence. Tisiphone, the Fury,
Leaps at the guilty with her scourge; her serpents
Are whips of menace as she calls her sisters.
Imagine the gates, on jarring hinge, rasp open,
You would see her in the doorway, a shape, a sentry,
Savage, implacable. Beyond, still fiercer,
The monstrous Hydra dwells; her fifty throats
Are black, and open wide, and Tartarus
Is black, and open wide, and it goes down
To darkness, sheer deep down, and twice the distance
That earth is from Olympus. At the bottom
The Titans crawl, Earth's oldest breed, hurled under
By thunderbolts; here lie the giant twins,
Aloeus' sons, who laid their hands on heaven
And tried to pull down Jove; Salmoneus here
Atones for high presumption,—it was he
Who aped Jove's noise and fire, wheeling his horses
Triumphant through his city in Elis, cheering
And shaking the torch, and claiming divine homage,
The arrogant fool, to think his brass was lightning,
His horny-footed horses beat out thunder!
Jove showed him what real thunder was, what lightning
Spoke from immortal cloud, what whirlwind fury
Came sweeping from the heaven to overtake him.

Here Tityos, Earth's giant son, lies sprawling
Over nine acres, with a monstrous vulture
Gnawing, with crooked beak, vitals and liver
That grow as they are eaten; eternal anguish,
Eternal feast. Over another hangs
A rock, about to fall; and there are tables
Set for a banquet, gold with royal splendor,
But if a hand goes out to touch the viands,
The Fury drives it back with fire and yelling.
Why name them all, Pirithous, the Lapiths,
Ixion? The roll of crime would take forever.
Whoever, in his lifetime, hated his brother,
Or struck his father down; whoever cheated
A client, or was miserly—how many
Of these there seem to be!—whoever went
To treasonable war, or broke a promise
Made to his lord, whoever perished, slain
Over adultery, all these, walled in,
Wait here their punishment. Seek not to know
Too much about their doom. The stone is rolled,
The wheel keeps turning; Theseus forever
Sits in dejection; Phlegyas, accursed,
Cries through the halls forever: *Being warned,
Learn justice; reverence the gods!* The man
Who sold his country is here in hell; the man
Who altered laws for money; and a father
Who knew his daughter's bed. All of them dared,
And more than dared, achieved, unspeakable
Ambitions. If I had a hundred tongues,
A hundred iron throats, I could not tell
The fullness of their crime and punishment."
And then she added:—"Come: resume the journey,
Fulfill the mission; let us hurry onward.
I see the walls the Cyclops made, the portals
Under the archway, where, the orders tell us,
Our tribute must be set." They went together
Through the way's darkness, came to the doors, and halted,
And at the entrance Aeneas, having sprinkled
His body with fresh water, placed the bough
Golden before the threshold. The will of the goddess
Had been performed, the proper task completed.

   They came to happy places, the joyful dwelling,
The lovely greenery of the groves of the blessèd.
Here ampler air invests the fields with light,
Rose-colored, with familiar stars and sun.
Some grapple on the grassy wrestling-ground
In exercise and sport, and some are dancing,
And others singing; in his trailing robe
Orpheus strums the lyre; the seven clear notes

Accompany the dance, the song. And heroes
Are there, great-souled, born in the happier years,
Ilus,[17] Assaracus; the city's founder,
Prince Dardanus. Far off, Aeneas wonders,
Seeing the phantom arms, the chariots,
The spears fixed in the ground, the chargers browsing,
Unharnessed, over the plain. Whatever, living,
The men delighted in, whatever pleasure
Was theirs in horse and chariot, still holds them
Here under the world. To right and left, they banquet
In the green meadows, and a joyful chorus
Rises through groves of laurel, whence the river
Runs to the upper world. The band of heroes
Dwell here, all those whose mortal wounds were suffered
In fighting for the fatherland; and poets,
The good, the pure, the worthy of Apollo;
Those who discovered truth and made life nobler;
Those who served others—all, with snowy fillets
Binding their temples, throng the lovely valley.
And these the Sibyl questioned, most of all
Musaeus,[18] for he towered above the center
Of that great throng:—"O happy souls, O poet,
Where does Anchises dwell? For him we come here,
For him we have traversed Erebus' great rivers."
And he replied:—"It is all our home, the shady
Groves, and the streaming meadows, and the softness
Along the river-banks. No fixed abode
Is ours at all; but if it is your pleasure,
Cross over the ridge with me; I will guide you there
By easy going." And so Musaeus led them
And from the summit showed them fields, all shining,
And they went on over and down.

    Deep in a valley of green, father Anchises
Was watching, with deep earnestness, the spirits
Whose destiny was light, and counting them over,
All of his race to come, his dear descendants,
Their fates and fortunes and their works and ways,
And as he saw Aeneas coming toward him
Over the meadow, his hands reached out with yearning,
He was moved to tears, and called:—"At last, my son,—
Have you really come, at last? and the long road nothing
To a son who loves his father? Do I, truly,
See you, and hear your voice? I was thinking so,
I was hoping so, I was counting off the days,
And I was right about it. O my son!
What a long journey, over land and water,
Yours must have been! What buffeting of danger!
I feared, so much, the Libyan realm would hurt you."
And his son answered:—"It was your spirit, father,
Your sorrowful shade, so often met, that led me

To find these portals. The ships ride safe at anchor,
Safe in the Tuscan sea. Embrace me, father;
Let hand join hand in love; do not forsake me."
And as he spoke, the tears streamed down. Three times
He reached out toward him, and three times the image
Fled like the breath of the wind or a dream on wings.

    He saw, in a far valley, a separate grove
Where the woods stir and rustle, and a river,
The Lethe, gliding past the peaceful places,
And tribes of people thronging, hovering over,
Innumerable as the bees in summer
Working the bright-hued flowers, and the shining
Of the white lilies, murmuring and humming.
Aeneas, filled with wonder, asks the reason
For what he does not know, who are the people
In such a host, and to what river coming?
Anchises answers:—"These are spirits, ready
Once more for life; they drink of Lethe's water
The soothing potion of forgetfulness.
I have longed, for long, to show them to you, name them,
Our children's children; Italy discovered,
So much the greater happiness, my son."
"But, O my father, is it thinkable
That souls would leave this blessedness, be willing
A second time to bear the sluggish body,
Trade Paradise for earth? Alas, poor wretches,
Why such a mad desire for light?" Anchises
Gives detailed answer: "First, my son, a spirit
Sustains all matter, heaven and earth and ocean,
The moon, the stars; mind quickens mass, and moves it.
Hence comes the race of man, of beast, of wingèd
Creatures of air, of the strange shapes which ocean
Bears down below his mottled marble surface.
All these are blessed with energy from heaven;[19]
The seed of life is a spark of fire, but the body
A clod of earth, a clog, a mortal burden.
Hence humans fear, desire, grieve, and are joyful,
And even when life is over, all the evil
Ingrained so long, the adulterated mixture,
The plagues and pestilences of the body
Remain, persist. So there must be a cleansing,
By penalty, by punishment, by fire,
By sweep of wind, by water's absolution,
Before the guilt is gone. Each of us suffers
His own peculiar ghost. But the day comes

---

[17] These are all ancestors of Aeneas, all former kings of Troy.

[18] A mythical poet and singer.

[19] You might compare this with Dante's ideas on the same thing. See, for example, Purgatory, Cantos XVI and XVIII.

When we are sent through wide Elysium,
The Fields of the Blessed, a few of us, to linger
Until the turn of time, the wheel of ages,
Wears off the taint, and leaves the core of spirit
Pure sense, pure flame. A thousand years pass over
And the god calls the countless host to Lethe
Where memory is annulled, and souls are willing
Once more to enter into mortal bodies."

    The discourse ended; the father drew his son
And his companion toward the hum, the center
Of the full host; they came to rising ground
Where all the long array was visible,
Anchises watching, noting, every comer.
"Glory to come, my son, illustrious spirits
Of Dardan lineage, Italian offspring,
Heirs of our name, begetters of our future!
These I will name for you and tell our fortunes:
First, leaning on a headless spear, and standing
Nearest the light, that youth, the first to rise
To the world above, is Silvius; his name
Is Alban; in his veins Italian blood
Will run with Trojan; he will be the son
Of your late age; Lavinia will bear him,
A king and sire of kings; from him our race
Will rule in Alba Longa.[20] Near him, Procas,
A glory to the Trojan race; and Capys,
And Numitor, and Silvius Aeneas,
Resembling you in name, in arms, in goodness,
If ever he wins the Alban kingdom over.
What fine young men they are! What strength, what
    prowess!
The civic oak already shades their foreheads.
These will found cities, Gabii, Fidenae,
Nomentum; they will crown the hills with towers
Above Collatia, Inuus fortress, Bola,
Cora, all names to be, thus far ungiven.

    "And there will be a son of Mars; his mother
Is Ilia, and his name is Romulus,
Assaracus' descendant. On his helmet
See, even now, twin plumes; his father's honor
Confers distinction on him for the world.
Under his auspices Rome, that glorious city,
Will bound her power by earth, her pride by heaven,
Happy in hero sons, one wall surrounding
Her seven hills, even as Cybele, riding
Through Phrygian cities, wears her crown of towers,
Rejoicing in her offspring, and embracing
A hundred children of the gods, her children,
Celestials, all of them, at home in heaven.
Turn the eyes now this way; behold the Romans,
Your very own. These are Iulus' children,
The race to come. One promise you have heard
Over and over: here is its fulfillment,
The son of a god, Augustus Caesar, founder
Of a new age of gold, in lands where Saturn
Ruled long ago; he will extend his empire
Beyond the Indies, beyond the normal measure
Of years and constellations, where high Atlas
Turns on his shoulders the star-studded world.
Maeotia[21] and the Caspian seas are trembling
As heaven's oracles predict his coming,
And all the seven mouths of Nile are troubled.
Not even Hercules, in all his travels,
Covered so much of the world, from Erymanthus
To Lerna; nor did Bacchus, driving his tigers
From Nysa's summit. How can hesitation
Keep us from deeds to make our prowess greater?
What fear can block us from Ausonian land?

    "And who is that one yonder, wearing the olive,
Holding the sacrifice? I recognize him,
That white-haired king of Rome, who comes from Cures,
A poor land, to a mighty empire, giver
Of law to the young town. His name is Numa.
Near him is Tullus; he will rouse to arms
A race grown sluggish, little used to triumph.
Beyond him Ancus, even now too boastful,
Too fond of popular favor. And then the Tarquins,
And the avenger Brutus, proud of spirit,
Restorer of the balance. He shall be
First holder of the consular power; his children
Will stir up wars again, and he, for freedom
And her sweet sake, will call down judgment on them,
Unhappy, however future men may praise him,
In love of country and intense ambition.

    "There are the Decii,[22] and there the Drusi,
A little farther off, and stern Torquatus,
The man with the axe, and Camillus, the regainer
Of standards lost. And see those two, resplendent
In equal arms, harmonious friendly spirits
Now, in the shadow of night, but if they ever
Come to the world of light, alas, what warfare,
What battle-lines, what slaughter they will fashion,
Each for the other, one from Alpine ramparts
Descending, and the other ranged against him
With armies from the east, father and son

---

[20] One of the earliest of the Italian cities, near Rome. Supposedly founded by Ascanius.

[21] These names merely signify that the empire will extend from one end to the other of the known world.

[22] These are the names of families who produced famous men in Rome's history.

THE ROMANS

Through marriage, Pompey and Caesar. O my children,
Cast out the thoughts of war, and do not murder
The flower of our country. O my son,
Whose line descends from heaven, let the sword
Fall from the hand, be leader in forbearing!

"Yonder is one who, victor over Corinth,
Will ride in triumph home, famous for carnage
Inflicted on the Greeks; near him another,
Destroyer of old Argus and Mycenae
Where Agamemnon ruled; he will strike down
A king descended from Achilles; Pydna
Shall be revenge for Pallas' ruined temple,
For Trojan ancestors. Who would pass over,
Without a word, Cossus, or noble Cato,
The Gracchi, or those thunderbolts of warfare,
The Scipios, Libya's ruin, or Fabricius
Mighty with little, or Serranus, ploughing
The humble furrow? My tale must hurry on:
I see the Fabii next, and their great Quintus
Who brought us back an empire by delaying.
Others, no doubt, will better mould the bronze[23]
To the semblance of soft breathing, draw, from marble,
The living countenance; and others plead
With greater eloquence, or learn to measure,
Better than we, the pathways of the heaven,
The risings of the stars: remember, Roman,
To rule the people under law, to establish
The way of peace, to battle down the haughty,
To spare the meek. Our fine arts, these, forever."

Anchises paused a moment, and they marvelled,
And he went on:—"See, how Marcellus triumphs,
Glorious over all, with the great trophies
Won when he slew the captain of the Gauls,
Leader victorious over leading foeman.
When Rome is in great trouble and confusion
He will establish order, Gaul and Carthage
Go down before his sword, and triple trophies
Be given Romulus in dedication."

There was a young man going with Marcellus,
Brilliant in shining armor, bright in beauty,
But sorrowful, with downcast eyes. Aeneas
Broke in, to ask his father: "Who is this youth
Attendant on the hero? A son of his?
One of his children's children? How the crowd
Murmurs and hums around him! what distinction,
What presence, in his person! But dark night
Hovers around his head with mournful shadow.
Who is he, father?" And Anchises answered:—
"Great sorrow for our people! O my son,
Ask not to know it. This one fate will only
Show to the world; he will not be permitted
Any long sojourn. Rome would be too mighty,
Too great in the gods' sight, were this gift hers.
What lamentation will the field of Mars
Raise to the city! Tiber, gliding by
The new-built tomb, the funeral state, bear witness!
No youth from Trojan stock will ever raise
His ancestors so high in hope, no Roman
Be such a cause for pride. Alas for goodness,
Alas for old-time honor, and the arm
Invincible in war! Against him no one,
Whether on foot or foaming horse, would come
In battle and depart unscathed. Poor boy,
If you should break the cruel fates; if only—
You are to be Marcellus. Let me scatter
Lilies, or dark-red flowers, bringing honor
To my descendant's shade; let the gift be offered,
However vain the tribute."

So through the whole wide realm they went together,
Anchises and his son; from fields of air
Learning and teaching of the fame and glory,
The wars to come, the toils to face, or flee from,
Latinus' city and the Latin peoples,
The love of what would be.

There are two portals,
Twin gates of Sleep, one made of horn, where easy
Release is given true shades, the other gleaming
White ivory, whereby the false dreams issue
To the upper air. Aeneas and the Sibyl
Part from Anchises at the second portal.
He goes to the ships, again, rejoins his comrades,
Sails to Caieta's harbor, and the vessels
Rest on their mooring-lines.

---

[23] Probably these nine lines are a better expression of the best of the Roman spirit than can be found in any other place.

Cicero

Marcus Tullius Cicero (104-43 B.C.) was a prominent politician and orator during the last days of the Roman Republic. Too much of an idealist to be a great success in politics, Cicero was extremely eloquent as an orator, lending his name for all time to the particular style known as Ciceronian. During the turbulent days following Julius Caesar's assassination, Cicero gave a series of violent speeches (Philippics) against Marc Antony and sided with Octavian hoping that he would restore the power of the Senate. When Octavian and Antony combined forces the name of Cicero was placed on a proscription list of two hundred persons to be murdered. He was trapped in his house near Astura and murdered by Antony's men. In his hatred, Antony ordered Cicero's head and hands (those parts which had spoken and written the speeches) brought to Rome to be impaled in public view in the forum.

In this selection from the first book of *On The Laws* the dialogue is between Cicero, his brother Quintus and his good friend Atticus. Cicero promotes the concept of the natural law and elaborates on the idea he first covered in his *Republic* when he wrote: "Nor may any other law override it, nor may it be repealed as a whole or in part... Nor is it one thing at Rome and another at Athens, one thing today and another tomorrow, but one eternal and unalterable law, that binds all nations forever." Such ideas as expressed by Cicero, had much influence upon the thought of the middle ages and of the eighteenth century in regard to natural law.

SELECTIONS FROM THE LAWS[1]

MARCUS.—But the whole subject of universal law and jurisprudence must be comprehended in this discussion, in order that this which we call civil law, may be confined in some one small and narrow space of nature. For we shall have to explain the true nature of moral justice, which must be traced back from the nature of man. And laws will have to be considered by which all political states should be governed. And last of all, shall we have to speak of those laws and customs of nations, which are framed for the use and convenience of particular countries, (in which even our own people will not be omitted,) which are known by the title of civil laws.

QUINTUS.—You take a noble view of the subject, my brother, and go to the fountainhead, in order to throw light on the subject of our consideration; and those who treat civil law in any other manner, are not so much pointing out the paths of justice as those of litigation.

MARCUS.—That is not quite the case, my Quintus. It is not so much the science of law that produces litigation, as the ignorance of it. But more of this by-and-by. At present let us examine the first principles of Right.

Now, many learned men have maintained that it springs from law. I hardly know if their opinion be not correct, at least according to their own definition; for "law," say they, "is the highest reason implanted in nature, which prescribes those things which ought to be done, and forbids the contrary." And when this same reason is confirmed and established in men's minds, it is then law.

They therefore conceive that prudence is a law, whose operation is to urge us to good actions, and restrain us from evil ones. And they think, too, that the Greek name for law, [which is derived from a word meaning to distribute], implies the very nature of the thing, that is, to give every man his due. The Latin name, *lex*, conveys the idea of selection, *a legendo*. According to the Greeks, therefore, the name of law implies an equitable distribution: according to the Romans, an equitable selection. And, indeed, both characteristics belong peculiarly to law.

And if this be a correct statement, which it seems to me for the most part to be, then the origin of right is to be sought in the law. For this is the true energy of nature, —this is the very soul and reason of a wise man, and the test of virtue and vice. But since all this discussion of ours relates to a subject, the terms of which are of frequent occurrence in the popular language of the citizens, we shall be sometimes obliged to use the same terms as the vulgar, and to call that law, which in its written enactments sanctions what it thinks fit by special commands or prohibitions.

Let us begin, then, to establish the principles of justice on that supreme law, which has existed from all ages

---

[1] C. D. Yonge translation.

102

before any legislative enactments were drawn up in writing, or any political governments constituted. . . . Shall we, then, seek for the origin of justice at its fountainhead? When we have discovered which, we shall be in no doubt to what these questions which we are examining ought to be referred. . . . Since, then, we wish to maintain and preserve the constitution of that republic which Scipio . . . has proved to be the best, and since all our laws are to be accommodated to the kind of political government there described, we must also treat of the general principles of morals and manners, and not limit ourselves on all occasions to written laws; but I purpose to trace back the origin of right from nature itself, who will be our best guide in conducting the whole discussion.

ATTICUS. — You will do right, and when she is our guide it is absolutely impossible for us to err.

MARCUS.—Do you then grant, my Atticus (for I know my brother's opinion already), that the entire universe is regulated by the power of the immortal Gods, that by their nature, reason, energy, mind, divinity, or some other word of clearer signification, if there be such, all things are governed and directed? for if you will not grant me this, that is what I must begin by establishing.

ATTICUS.—I grant you all you can desire. But owing to this singing of birds and babbling of water, I fear my fellow-learners can scarcely hear me.

MARCUS.—You are quite right to be on your guard; for even the best men occasionally fall into a passion, and they will be very indignant if they hear you denying the first article of that notable book entitled "The Chief Doctrines of Epicurus," in which he says "that God takes care of nothing, neither of himself nor of any other being!"

ATTICUS.—Pray proceed, for I am waiting to know what advantage you mean to take of the concession I have made you.

MARCUS.—I will not detain you long. This is the bearing which they have on our subject. This animal — prescient, sagacious, complex, acute, full of memory, reason, and counsel, which we call man — has been generated by the supreme God in a most transcendent condition. For he is the only creature among all the races and descriptions of animated being who is endued with superior reason and thought, in which the rest are deficient. And what is there, I do not say in man alone, but in all heaven and earth, more divine than reason, which, when it becomes right and perfect is justly termed wisdom?

There exists, therefore, since nothing is better than reason, and since this is the common property of God and man, a certain aboriginal rational intercourse between divine and human natures. But where reason is common, there right reason must also be common to the same parties; and since this right reason is what we call law, God and men must be considered as associated by law. Again, there must also be a communion of right where there is a communion of law. And those who have law and right thus in common, must be considered members of the same commonwealth.

And if they are obedient to the same rule and the same authority, they are even much more so to this one celestial regency, this divine mind and omnipotent deity. So that the entire universe may be looked upon as forming one vast commonwealth of gods and men. And, as in earthly states certain ranks are distinguished with reference to the relationships of families, according to a certain principle which will be discussed in its proper place, that principle, in the nature of things, is far more magnificent and splendid by which men are connected with the Gods, as belonging to their kindred and nation.

For when we are reasoning on universal nature, we are accustomed to argue (and indeed the truth is just as it is stated in that argument) that in the long course of ages, and the uninterrupted succession of celestial revolutions, there arrived a certain ripe time for the sowing of the human race; and when it was sown and scattered over the earth, it was animated by the divine gift of souls. And as men retained from their terrestrial origin those other particulars by which they cohere together, which are frail and perishable, their immortal spirits were ingenerated by the Deity. From which circumstance it may be truly said, that we possess a certain consanguinity, and kindred, and fellowship with the heavenly powers. And among all the varieties of animals, there is not one except man which retains any idea of the Divinity. And among men, themselves, there is no nation so savage and ferocious as not to admit the necessity of believing in a God, however ignorant they may be what sort of God they ought to believe in. From whence we conclude that every man must recognize a Deity, who has any recollection and knowledge of his own origin.

Now, the law of virtue is the same in God and man, and in no other disposition besides them. This virtue is nothing else than a nature perfect in itself, and wrought up to the most consummate excellence. There exists, therefore, a similitude between God and man. And as this is the case, what connexion can there be which concerns us more nearly, and is more certain?

Therefore, nature has supplied such an abundance of supplies suited to the convenience and use of men, that the things which are thus produced appear to be designedly bestowed on us, and not fortuitous productions. Nor does this observation apply only to the fruits and vegetables which gush from the bosom of the earth, but likewise to cattle and the beasts of the field, some of which, it is clear, were intended for the use of mankind, others for propagation, and others for the food of man. Innumerable arts have likewise been discovered by the teaching of nature, whom reason has imitated, and thus skilfully discovered all things necessary to the happiness of life.

With respect to man, this same bountiful nature hath not merely allotted him a subtle and active spirit, but also physical senses, like so many servants and messengers. And she has laid bare before him the obscure but necessary explanation of many things, which are, as it were, the foundation of practical knowledge; and in all respects she has given him a convenient figure of body, suited to the bent of the human character. For while she has kept down the countenances of other animals, and fixed their eyes on their food, she has bestowed on man alone an erect stature, and prompted him to the contemplation of heaven, the ancient home of his kindred immortals. So exquisitely, too, has she fashioned the features of the human face, as to make them indicate the most recondite thoughts and sentiments. For our eloquent eyes speak forth every impulse and passion of our souls; and that which we call *expression,* which cannot exist in any other animal but man, betrays all our feelings, the power of which was well known to the Greeks, though they have no name for it.

I will not enlarge on the wonderful faculties and qualities of the rest of the body, the modulation of the voice, and the power of oratory, which is the greatest instrument of influence upon human society. For these matters do not all belong to the present occasion or the present subject, and I think that Scipio has already sufficiently explained them in those books of mine which you have read.

Since, then, the Deity has been pleased to create and adorn man to be the chief and president of all terrestrial creatures, so it is evident, without further argument, that human nature has also made very great advances by its own intrinsic energy; that nature, which without any other instruction than her own, has developed the first rude principles of the understanding, and strengthened and perfected reason to all the appliances of science and art.

ATTICUS.—Oh ye immortal Gods! to what a distance back are you tracing the principles of justice! However, you are discoursing in such a style that I will not show any impatience to hear what I expect you to say on the Civil Law. But I will listen patiently, even if you spend the whole day in this kind of discourse, for assuredly these, which perhaps you are embracing in your argument for the sake of others, are grander topics than even the subject for which they prepare the way.

MARCUS.—You may well describe these topics as grand, which we are now briefly discussing. But of all the questions which are ever the subject of discussion among learned men, there is none which it is more important thoroughly to understand than this, that man is born for justice, and that law and equity have not been established by opinion, but by nature. This truth will become still more apparent if we investigate the nature of human association and society.

For there is no one thing so like or so equal to another, as in every instance man is to man. And if the corruption of customs, and the variation of opinions, did not induce an imbecility of minds, and turn them aside from the course of nature, no one would more nearly resemble himself than all men would resemble all men. Therefore, whatever definition we give of man, will be applicable to the whole human race. And this is a good argument that there is no dissimilarity of kind among men; because if this were the case, one definition could not include all men.

In fact, reason, which alone gives us so many advantages over beasts, by means of which we conjecture, argue, refute, discourse, and accomplish and conclude our designs, is assuredly common to all men; for the faculty of acquiring knowledge is similar in all human minds, though the knowledge itself may be endlessly diversified. By the same senses we all perceive the same objects, and those things which move the senses at all, do move in the same way the senses of all men. And those first rude elements of intelligence which, as I before observed, are the earliest developments of thought, are similarly impressed upon all men; and that faculty of speech which is the intrepreter of the mind, agrees in the ideas which it conveys, though it may differ in the words by which it expresses them. And therefore there exists not a man in any nation, who, if he adopts nature for his guide, may not arrive at virtue.

Nor is this resemblance which all men bear to each other remarkable in those things only which are in accordance with right reason, but also in errors. For all men alike are captivated by pleasure, which, although it is a temptation to what is disgraceful, nevertheless bears some resemblance to natural good; for, as by its delicacy and sweetness it is delightful, it is through a mistake of the intellect adopted as something salutary.

And by an error scarcely less universal we shun death as if it were a dissolution of nature, and cling to life because it keeps us in that existence in which we were born. Thus, likewise, we consider pain as one of the greatest evils, not only on account of its present asperity, but also because it seems the precursor of mortality. Again, on account of the apparent resemblance between renown with honour, those men appear to us happy who are honoured, and miserable who happen to be inglorious. In like manner our minds are all similarly susceptible of inquietudes, joys, desires, and fears; nor if different men have different opinions, does it follow that those who deify dogs and cats, do not labour under superstition equally with other nations, though they may differ from them in the forms of its manifestation.

Again, what nation is there which has not a regard for kindness, benignity, gratitude, and mindfulness of benefits? What nation is there in which arrogance, malice, cruelty, and unthankfulness, are not reprobated and detested? And while this uniformity of opinions proves that the whole race of mankind is united together, the last point is that a system of living properly makes men better. If what I have said meets your approbation, I will proceed; or if any doubts occur to you, we had better clear them up first.

ATTICUS.—There is nothing which strikes us, if I may reply for both of us.

MARCUS.—It follows, then, that nature made us just that we might share our goods with each other, and supply each other's wants. You observe in this discussion, whenever I speak of nature, I mean nature in its genuine purity, but that there is, in fact, such corruption engendered by evil customs, that the sparks, as it were, of virtue which have been given by nature are extinguished, and that antagonist vices arise around it and become strengthened.

But if, as nature prompts them to, men would with deliberate judgment, in the words of the poet, "being men, think nothing that concerns mankind indifferent to them," then would justice be cultivated equally by all. For to those to whom nature has given reason, she has also given right reason, and therefore also law, which is nothing else than right reason enjoining what is good, and forbidding what is evil. And if nature has given us law, she hath also given us right. But she has bestowed reason on all, therefore right has been bestowed on all. And therefore did Socrates deservedly execrate the man who first drew a distinction between utility and nature, for he used to complain that this error was the source of all human vices, to which this sentence of Pythagoras refers — "The things belonging to friends are common" — and that other, "Friendly equality." From whence it appears, that when a wise man has displayed this benevolence which is so extensively and widely diffused towards one who is endowed with equal virtue, then that phenomenon takes place which is altogether incredible to some people, but which is a necessary consequence, that he loves himself not more dearly than he loves his friend. For how can a difference of interests arise where all interests are similar? If these could be ever so minute a difference of interests, then there would be an end of even the nature of friendship, the real meaning of which is such, that there is no friendship at all the moment that a person prefers anything happening to himself rather than to his friend. . . .

But in conformity with the method of philosophers (I do not mean the older sages of philosophy, but those modern ones, who have erected a magazine, as it were, of wisdom), those questions which were formerly discussed loosely and unconstrainedly, are now examined with strictness and distinctness. Nor will these men allow that we have done justice to the subject which we have now before us, unless we demonstrate in a distinct discussion that right is a part of nature. . . .

But were it the fear of punishment, and not the nature of the thing itself, that ought to restrain mankind from wickedness, what, I would ask, could give villains the least uneasiness, abstracting from all fears of this kind? And yet none of them was ever so audaciously impudent, but what he either denied that the action in question had been committed by him, or pretended some cause or other for his just indignation, or sought a defence of his deed in some right of nature. And if the wicked dare to appeal to this principle, with what respect ought not good men to treat them?

But if either direct punishment, or the fear of it, be what deters men from a vicious and criminal course of life, and not the turpitude of the thing itself, then none can be guilty of injustice, and the greatest offenders ought rather to be called imprudent than wicked.

On the other hand, those among us who are determined to the practice of goodness, not by its own intrinsic excellence, but for the sake of some private advantage, are cunning rather than good men. For what will not that man do in the dark who fears nothing but a witness and a judge? Should he meet a solitary individual in a desert place, whom he can rob of a large sum of money, and altogether unable to defend himself from being robbed, how will he behave? In such a case our man, who is just and honourable from principle and the nature of the thing itself, will converse with the stranger, assist him, and show him the way. But he who does nothing for the sake of another, and measures everything by the advantage it brings to itself, it is obvious, I suppose, how such a one will act; and should he deny that he would kill the man, or rob him of his treasure, his reason for this cannot be that he apprehends there is any moral turpitude in such actions, but only because he is afraid of a discovery, that is to say, that bad consequences will thence ensue — a sentiment this at which not only learned men but even clowns must blush.

It is therefore an absurd extravagance in some philosophers to assert, that all things are necessarily just which are established by the civil laws and the institutions of nations. Are then the laws of tyrants just, simply because they are laws? Suppose the thirty tyrants of Athens had imposed certain laws on the Athenians? Or, suppose again that these Athenians were delighted with these tyrannical laws, would these laws on that account have been considered just? For my own part, I do not think such laws deserve any greater estimation than that passed during our own interregnum, which ordained that the dictator should be empowered to put to death with impunity whatever citizens he pleased, without hearing them in their own defence.

For there is but one essential justice which cements society, and one law which establishes this justice. This law is right reason, which is the true rule of all commandments and prohibitions. Whoever neglects this law, whether written or unwritten, is necessarily unjust and wicked.

But if justice consists in submission to written laws and national customs, and if, as the same school affirms, everything must be measured by utility alone, he who thinks that such conduct will be advantageous to him will neglect the laws, and break them if it is in his power. And the consequence is, that real justice has really no existence if it have not one by nature, and if that which is established as such on account of utility is overturned by some other utility.

But if nature does not ratify law, then all the virtues may lose their sway. For what becomes of generosity, patriotism, or friendship? Where will the desire of benefiting our neighbors, or the gratitude that acknowledges kindness, be able to exist at all? For all these virtues proceed from our natural inclination to love mankind. And this is the true basis of justice, and without this not only the mutual charities of men, but the religious services of the Gods, would be at an end; for these are preserved, as I imagine, rather by the natural sympathy which subsists between divine and human beings, than by mere fear and timidity.

But if the will of the people, the decrees of the senate, the adjudications of magistrates, were sufficient to establish rights, then it might become right to rob, right to commit adultery, right to substitute forged wills, if such conduct were sanctioned by the votes or decrees of the multitude. But if the opinions and suffrages of foolish men had sufficient weight to outbalance the nature of things, then why should they not determine among them, that what is essentially bad and pernicious should henceforth pass for good and beneficial? Or why, since law can make right out of injustice, should it not also be able to change evil into good?

But we have no other rule by which we may be capable of distinguishing between a good or a bad law than that of nature. Nor is it only right and wrong which are discriminated by nature, but generally all that is honourable is by this means distinguished from all that is shameful; for common sense has impressed in our minds the first principles of things, and has given us a general acquaintance with them, but which we connect with virtue every honourable quality, and with vice all that is disgraceful.

But to think that these differences exist only in opinion, and not in nature, is the part of an idiot. For even the virtue of a tree or a horse, in which expression there is an abuse of terms, does not exist in our opinion only, but in nature; and if that is the case, then what is honourable and disgraceful, must also be discriminated by nature.

For if opinion could determine respecting the character of universal virtue, it might also decide respecting particular or partial virtues. But who will dare to determine that a man is prudent and cautious, not from his general conduct, but from some external appearances? For virtue evidently consists in perfect reason, and this certainly resides in nature. Therefore so does all honour and honesty in the same way. For as what is true and false, creditable and discreditable, is judged of rather by their essential qualities than their external relations; so the consistent and perpetual course of life, which is virtue, and the inconsistency of life, which is vice, are judged of according to their own nature, — and that inconstancy must necessarily be vicious.

We form an estimate of the opinions of youths, but not by their opinions. Those virtues and vices which reside in their moral natures must not be measured by opinions. And so of all moral qualities, we must discriminate between honourable and dishonourable by reference to the essential nature of the things themselves.

The good we commend, must needs contain in itself something commendable; for as I before stated, goodness is not a mode of opinion, but of nature. For if it were otherwise, opinion alone might constitute virtue and happiness, which is the most absurd of suppositions. And since we judge of good and evil by their nature, and since good and evil are the first principles of nature, certainly we should judge in the same manner of all honourable and all shameful things, referring them all to the law of nature.

But we are often too much disturbed by the dissensions of men and the variation of opinions. And because the same thing does not happen with reference to our senses, we look upon them as certain by nature. Those objects, indeed, which sometimes present to us one appearance, sometimes another, and which do not always appear to the same people in the same way, we term fictions of the senses; but it is far otherwise. For neither parent, nor nurse, nor master, nor poet, nor drama, deceive our senses; nor do popular prejudices seduce them from the truth. But all kinds of snares are laid for the mind, either by those errors which I have just enumerated, which taking possession of the young and uneducated, imbue them deeply, and bend them any way they please; or by that pleasure which is the imitator of goodness, being thoroughly and closely implicated with all our senses — the prolific mother of all evils. For she so corrupts us by her blandishments, that we no longer perceive some things which are essentially excellent, because they have none of this deliciousness and pruriency.

It follows that I may now sum up the whole of this argument by asserting, as is plain to every one from these positions which have been already laid down, that all right and all that is honourable is to be sought for its own sake. In truth, all virtuous men love justice and equity for what they are in themselves; nor is it like a good man to make a mistake, and love that which does not deserve their affection. Right, therefore, is desirable and deserving to be cultivated for its own sake; and if this be true of right, it must be true also of justice. What then shall we say of liberality? Is it exercised gratuitously, or does it covet some reward and recompense? If a man does good without expecting any recompense for his kindness, then it is gratuitous: if he does expect compensation, it is a mere matter of traffic. Nor is there any doubt that he who truly deserves the reputation of a generous and kind-hearted man, is thinking of his duty, not of his interest. In the same way the virtue of justice demands neither emolument nor salary, and therefore we desire it for its own sake. And the case of all the moral virtues in the same, and so is the opinion formed of them.

Besides this, if we weigh virtue by the mere utility and profit that attend it, and not by its own merit, the one virtue which results from such an estimate will be in fact a species of vice. For the more a man refers all his actions especially to his own advantage, the further he recedes from probity; so that they who measure virtue by profit, acknowledge no other virtue than this, which is a kind of vice. For who can be called benevolent, if no one ever acts kindly for the sake of another? And where are we to find a grateful person, if those who are disposed to be so can find no benefactor to whom they can show gratitude? What will become of sacred friendship, if we are not to love our friend for his own sake with all our heart and soul, as people say, if we are even to desert and discard him, as soon as we despair of deriving any further assistance or advantage from him? What can be imagined more inhuman than this conduct? But if friendship ought rather to be cultivated on its own account, so also for the same reason are society, equality, and justice desirable for their own sakes. If this be not so, then there can be no such thing as justice at all; for the most unjust thing of all is to seek a reward for one's just conduct.

What then shall we say of temperance, sobriety, continence, modesty, bashfulness, and chastity? Is it the fear of infamy, or the dread of judgments and penalties, which prevent men from being intemperate and dissolute? Do men then live in innocence and moderation, only to be well spoken of, and to acquire a certain fair reputation? Modest men blush even to speak of indelicacy. And I am greatly ashamed of those philosophers, who assert that there are no vices to be avoided but those which the laws have branded with infamy. For what shall I say? Can we call those persons truly chaste, who abstain from adultery merely from the fear of public exposure and that disgrace which is only one of its many evil consequences? For what can be either praised or blamed with reason, if you depart from that great law and rule of nature, which makes the difference between right and wrong? Shall corporal defects, if they are remarkable, shock our sensibilities, and shall those of the soul make no impression on us? — of the soul, I say, whose turpiture is so evidently proved by its vices. For what is there more hideous than avarice, more brutal than lust, more contemptible than cowardice, more base than stupidity and folly? Well, then, are we to call those persons unhappy, who are conspicuous for one or more of these, on account of some injuries, or disgraces, or suffering to which they are exposed, or on account of the moral baseness of their sins? And we may apply the same test in the opposite way to those who are distinguished for their virtue.

Lastly, if virtue be sought for on account of some other things, it necessarily follows that there is something better than virtue. Is it money, then? is it fame, or beauty, or health? all of which appear of little value to us when we possess them; nor can it be by any possibility certainly known how long they will last. Or is it (what it is shameful even to utter) that basest of all, pleasure? Surely not; for it is in the contempt and disdain of pleasure that virtue is most conspicuous. . . .

Let us, then, once more examine, before we come to the consideration of particular laws, what is the power and nature of law in general; lest, when we come to refer everything to it, we occasionally make mistakes from the employment of incorrect language, and show ourselves ignorant of the force of those terms which we ought to employ in the definition of laws.

QUINTUS.—This is a very necessary caution, and the proper method of seeking truth.

MARCUS.—This, then, as it appears to me, has been the decision of the wisest philosophers, — that law was neither a thing contrived by the genius of man, nor established by any decree of the people, but a certain eternal principle, which governs the entire universe, wisely commanding what is right and prohibiting what is wrong. Therefore they called that aboriginal and supreme law the mind of God, enjoining or forbidding each separate thing in accordance with reason. On which account it is, that this law, which the Gods have bestowed on the human race, is so justly applauded. For it is the reason and mind of a wise Being equally able to urge us to good and to deter us from evil.

QUINTUS.—You have, on more than one occasion, already touched on this topic. But before you come to treat of the laws of nations, I wish you would endeavour to explain the force and power of this divine and celestial law, lest the torrent of custom should overwhelm our understanding, and betray us into the vulgar method of expression.

MARCUS.—From our childhood we have learned, my Quintus, to call such phrases as this, "that a man appeals to justice, and goes to law," and many similar expressions, law, but, nevertheless, we should understand that these, and other similar commandments and prohibitions, have sufficient power to lead us on to virtuous actions and to call us away from vicious ones. Which power is not only far more ancient than any existence of states and peoples, but is coeval with God himself, who beholds and governs both heaven and earth. For it is impossible that the divine mind can exist in a state devoid of reason; and divine reason must necessarily be possessed of a power to determine what is virtuous and what is vicious. Nor, because it was nowhere written, that one man should maintain the pass of a bridge against the enemy's whole army, and that he should order the bridge behind him to be cut down, are we therefore to imagine that the valiant Cocles did not perform this great exploit agreeably to the laws of nature and the dictates of true bravery. Again, though in the reign of Tarquin there was no written law concerning adultery, it does not therefore follow that Sextus Tarquinius did not offend against the eternal law when he committed a rape on Lucretia, daughter of Tricipitinus. For, even then he had the light of reason deduced from the nature of things, that incites to good actions and dissuades from evil ones; and which does not begin for the first time to be a law when it is drawn up in writing, but from the first moment that it exists. And this existence of moral obligation is coeternal with that of the divine mind. Therefore, the true and supreme law, whose commands and prohibitions are equally authoritative, is the right reason of the Sovereign Jupiter.

QUINTUS.—I grant you, my brother, that whatever is just is also at all times the true law; nor can this true law either be originated or abrogated by the written forms in which decrees are drawn up.

MARCUS.—Therefore, as that Divine Mind, or reason, is the supreme law, so it exists in the mind of the sage, so far as it can be perfected in man. But with respect to civil laws, which are drawn up in various forms, and framed to meet the occasional requirements of the people, the name of law belongs to them not so much by right as by the favour of the people. For men prove by some such arguments as the following, that every law which deserves the name of a law, ought to be morally good and laudable. It is clear, say they, that laws were originally made for the security of the people, for the preservation of states, for the peace and happiness of society; and that they who first framed enactments of that kind, persuaded the people that they would write and publish such laws only as should conduce to the general morality and happiness, if they would receive and obey them. And then such regulations, being thus settled and sanctioned, they justly entitled *Laws*. From which we may reasonably conclude, that those who made unjustifiable and pernicious enactments for the people, acted in a manner contrary to their own promises and professions, and established anything rather than *laws*, properly so called, since it is evident that the very signification of the word *law*, comprehends the whole essence and energy of justice and equity.

I would, therefore, interrogate you on this point, my Quintus, as those philosophers are in the habit of doing. If a state wants something for the want of which it is reckoned no state at all, must not that something be something good?

QUINTUS.—A very great good.

MARCUS.—And if a state has no law, is it not for that reason to be reckoned no state at all?

QUINTUS.—We must needs say so.

MARCUS.—We must therefore reckon law among the very best things.

QUINTUS.—I entirely agree with you.

MARCUS.—If, then, in the majority of nations, many pernicious and mischievous enactments are made, which have no more right to the name of law than the mutual engagements of robbers, are we bound to call them laws? For as we cannot call the recipes of ignorant and unskilful empirics, who give poisons instead of medicines, the prescriptions of a physician, so likewise we cannot call that the true law of a people, of whatever kind it may be, if it enjoins what is injurious, let the people receive it as they will. For law is the just distinction between right and wrong, made conformable to that most ancient nature of all, the original and principal regulator of all things, by which the laws of men should be measured, whether they punish the guilty or protect and preserve the innocent. . . .

Let this, therefore, be a fundamental principle in all societies, that the Gods are the supreme lords and governors of all things, — that all events are directed by their influence, and wisdom, and Divine power; that they deserve very well of the race of mankind; and that they likewise know what sort of person every one really is; that they observe his actions, whether good or bad; that they take notice with what feelings and with what piety he attends to his religious duties, and that they are sure to make a difference between the good and the wicked.

For when once our minds are confirmed in these views, it will not be difficult to inspire them with true and useful sentiments. For what can be more true than that no man should be so madly presumptuous as to believe that he has either reason or intelligence, while he does not believe that the heaven and the world possess them likewise, or to think that those things which he can scarcely comprehend by the greatest possible exertion of his intellect, are put in motion without the agency of reason?

In truth, we can scarcely reckon him a man, whom neither the regular courses of the stars, nor the alternations of day and night, nor the temperature of the seasons, nor the productions that nature displays for his use and enjoyment, urge to gratitude towards heaven.

And as those beings which are furnished with reason are incomparably superior to those which want it, and as we cannot say, without impiety, that anything is superior to the universal Nature, we must therefore confess that divine reason is contained within her. And who will dispute the utility of these sentiments, when he reflects how many cases of the greatest importance are decided by oaths; how much the sacred rites performed in making treaties tend to assure peace and tranquility; and what numbers of people the fear of divine punishment has reclaimed from a vicious course of life; and how sacred the social rights must be in a society where a firm persuasion obtains the immediate intervention of the immortal Gods, both as witnesses and judges of our actions? Such is the "preamble of the law," to use the expression of Plato.

Ovid

Publius Ovidius Naso (43 B.C.–17 A.D.), better known as Ovid, was a member of a well-to-do family of Upper Italy and was trained to be a lawyer. Ovid, however, was much more interested in literature than in the law, and his success as a poet, reflecting the mores of his own day, was phenomenal. A born story teller, he was a master of melodious verse and soon became well known in Roman society. His best known work is the *Art of Love* from which the following selection is taken. Its primary purpose was to instruct his readers "on the means of winning the affections of the opposite sex," a goal which many feel he fulfilled admirably without resorting to coarse or vulgar language. Even so he prefaced his work by warning good women not to read it. His later works *Metamorphoses* and *Fasti,* depended upon Greek and Roman mythology for their themes.

Around the year 8 A.D., because of some as yet unexplained indiscretion or perhaps a plot against the government, Ovid was banished by Augustus to the small town of Tomi, on the shore of the Black Sea. In spite of his constant writing and pleading, his exile was never revoked and he died in 17 A.D. far removed from the Roman society of which he had once been such a prominent member.

ART OF LOVE

Young nobles, to my laws your attention lend;
And all you vulgar of my school, attend.
First then believe, all women may be won;
Attempt with confidence, the work is done.
The grasshopper will cease to sing
In summer season, or the birds in spring,
Before women can resist your flattering skill:
Even she will yield, who swears she never will.
To secret pleasure both the sexes move;
But women most, who most dissemble love.
It's best for us, if they would first declare,
Avow their passion, and submit to prayer.
. . . .
Man is more temperate in his lust than they,
and, more than women, can his passion sway.
. . . .
Ill omens in her frowns are understood;
When she's in humor, every day is good.
But when her birthday comes it's seldom worse;
When bribes and presents must be sent of course;
And that's a bloody day, that costs your purse
Be stanch; yet stinginess will be in vain
The craving sex will still her lover drain.
No skill can shift them off, nor art remove;
They will be begging, when they know we love.
The merchant comes upon the appointed day,
Who shall his wares before you display.
To choose for her she craves your kind advice;
Then begs again, to bargain for the price:
But when she has her purchase in her eye,
She hugs you close, and kisses you to buy:

"It's what I want, and it's just a penny's worth too,
In many years I will not trouble you."
If you complain you have no ready coin;
No matter, it's but writing of a line,
A little bill, not to be paid at sight;
(Now curse the time when you were taught to write.)
She keeps her birthday; you must send the cheer,
And she'll be born a hundred times a year.
. . . .
If to her heart you aim to find the way,
Extremely flatter her and extremely pray.
Priam by pryers did Hector's body gain'
Nor is an angry god invoked in vain.
With promised gifts her easy mind bewitch;
For even the poor in promise may be rich.
Vain hopes a while her appetite will stay;
For it's a deceitful but commodious way.
Who gives is mad, but make her still believe
It will come, and that's the cheapest way to give.
. . . .
Learn eloquence, you noble youth of Rome;
It will not only at the bar overcome;
Sweet words the people and the senate move;
But the chief end of eloquence is love.
But in your letter hide your moving arts;
Affect not to be thought a man of parts;
None but vain fools to simple women preach'
A learned letter often has made a breach.
In a familiar style your thoughts convey,
And write such things as if present you would say;
Such words as from the heart may seem to move;

It's wit enough to make her think you love.
If sealed she sends it back, and will not read,
Yet hope, in time the business may succeed.
. . . .
Water is soft, and marble hard; and yet
We see soft-water through hard marble eat.
. . . .
Dress not like a fop nor curl your hair,
Nor with a pumice make your body bare.
Leave those effeminate and useless toys
To eunuchs, who can give no solid joys.

Be not too finical; but yet be clean'
And wear well-fashioned clothes, like other men.
Let not your teeth be yellow, or be foul;
Nor in wide shoes your feet too loosely roll.
Of a black muzzle and long beard beward'
And let a skillful barber cut your hair;
Your nails be picked from filth, and even pared
Nor let your nasty nostrils bud with beard.
Cure your unsavory breath, gargle your throat
And free your armpits from the ram and goat.
Dress not, in short, too little or too much.
. . . .
Lay bashfulness, that rustic virtue, by;
To manly confidence your thoughts apply.
On fortune's foretop timely fix your hold;
Now speak and speed, for Venus loves the bold.
No rules of rhetoric here I need afford;
Only begin, and trust the following word;
It will be witty of its own accord.
Act well the lover; let your speech abound

In dying words, that represent your wound.
Distrust not her belief; she will be moved;
All women think they merit to be loved.
. . . .
By flatteries we prevail on womankind,
As hollow banks by streams are undermined.
Tell her, her face is fair, her eyes are sweet;
Praise her taper fingers and little feet.
Such praises even the chaste are pleased to hear.
Both maids and matrons hold their beauty dear.
. . . .
Thus justly women suffer by deceit;
Their practice authorizes us to cheat.
Beg her, with tears, your warm desires to grant;
For tears will pierce a heart of adamant.
If tears will not be squeezed, then rub your eye,
Or annoint the lids, and seem at least to cry.
Kiss, if you can; resistance if she make,
And will not give you kisses, let her take.
Fie, fie, you naughty man, are words of course;
She struggles, but to be subdued by force.
Kiss only soft, I charge you, and beware,
With your hard bristles not to brush the fair.
He who has gained a kiss and gains no more,
Deserves to lose the bliss he got before.
If once she kiss, her meaning is expressed;
There wants but little effort for the rest.
Which if you don't gain by strength or art,
The name of clown is your just desert;
It's downright dullness and a shameful part.

    Paraphrased by D.C. Riede

Martial

Marcus Valerius Martialis (40 A.D.–105), born in central Spain, came to Rome as a young man during the reign of Nero. Although Martial wrote twelve books of epigrams, his favorite form of verse, his income was quite small. Therefore he had to resort to a form of gentlemanly begging—depending upon the favors of wealthy men with literary tastes—which proved demeaning and unrewarding. Much bitterness and unhappiness is reflected in his writings. Many of his epigrams are biting and satirical, poking fun at various people and customs in Rome. Martial was not always popular with those who were the subjects of his brief verses, but he gives us an insight into Roman life. The following selections are only a small sample of his work, but they are typical of his thought and writing.

EPIGRAMS

Book I (CVI)

Rufus; you water your wine.
Even then, you drink little.
Has Naevia promised to sleep with you?
And you want to be sober enough to enjoy it?
Ah! you sigh, you are silent. She said "No."
So, drink up, Rufus,
You have nothing to look forward to but sleep.

> Anonymous translation 1877 paraphrased
> by N.W. Nolte

Book I (X)

Gemellus a rich widow courts?
Nor lovely she, nor made for sports.
'Tis to Gemellus charm enough
That she has got a grave-yard cough.

> Adaptation of a translation
> by Dr. Hoadley 1877

Book II (XXV)

Galla is always promising me favors,
But she never keeps her promises.
Since you're always a liar, Galla,
Next time I ask you, say "No."

> Anonymous translation 1877 paraphrased
> by N.W. Nolte

Book III (VIII)

Quintus is in love with one-eyed Thais.
   He must be blinder than she!

> Translated by N. W. Nolte

Book IV (XXIV)

Lycoris's friends are rarely of long life.
I wish she were acquainted with my wife.

> Anonymous translation, 1965

Book IV (XXXVIII)

Galla, say "No!" once in a while;
It makes my love grow strong.
But if you want to keep my love,
Don't say "No!" too long.

> Translated by N. W. Nolte

Book VI (XII)

The golden hair that Galla wears
Is hers; who would have thought it?
She swears 'tis hers, and true she swears,
For I know where she bought it.

> Translated by Sir John Harington (1561-1621)
> a godson of Queen Elizabeth

All of the above are from THE EPIGRAMS OF MARTIAL, Henry G. Bohn, ed. London: George Bell and Sons, 1877.

Juvenal

By the time of the reign of Augustus, Rome had become a great metropolis with a population of approximately one million people, and like any present-day city, Rome had its problems. The best picture of the crime, immorality, luxury and general urban blight in Rome is found in the biting satires of Decimus Junius Juvenalis.

Although little is known of the life of Juvenal, he apparently was born around 60 A.D. and died somewhere around the year 130. His birthplace was the town of Aquinum, but he spent most of his adult life in Rome, where he was a friend of Martial. Each of the sixteen satires attributed to Juvenal tends to be biting and full of hate toward life in his own day.

The third satire, from which the following selection is taken, has become most famous because his description of the problems of Roman city life could easily have been written about any large 20th century city.

THIRD SATIRE

Who fears in country towns, a houses' fall,
Or to be caught between a split wall?
But we inhabit a weak city, here;
Which buttresses and props scarcely bear:
And it's the village mason's daily calling,
To keep the world's metropolis from falling,
To cleanse the gutters, and the chinks to close,
And, for one night, secure his lord's repose.
At Cumae[1] we can sleep, quite round the year,
Not falls, nor fires, nor nightly dangers to fear;
While roaring flames from Roman turrets fly,
And the pale citizens for buckets cry.
. . . .
Poor Codrus[2] had but one bed, so short to boot,
That his short wife's short legs hung dangling out;
His cupboard only six earthen cups graced
Beneath them his trusty tankard was placed;. . .
His few Greek books a rotten chest contained
Whose covers much moldiness complained;
Where mice and rats devoured poetic bread,
And with heroic verse were luxuriously fed.
Its true, Codrus had nothing of which to boast,
And yet in flames poor Codrus his nothing lost;
He begged naked through the streets of wealthy
    Rome;
And found not one to feed, or take him home.
But if the palace of Arturius burn,
The nobles change their clothes, the matrons
    mourn;
The city praetor will no pleadings hear;
The very name of fire we hate and fear,
And look aghast, as if the Gauls were here.
While yet it burns, the officious nation flies,
Some to condole, and some to bring supplies

One sends him marble to rebuild; and one
White naked statues of the Parian stone,
The work of Polyclete, that seem to live;
While others images for altars give;
One books and screens, and Pallas to the breast;
Another bags of gold; and he gives best.
Childless Arturius, vastly rich before,
Thus by his losses multiplies his store;
Suspected for accomplice to the fire,
That burnt his palace but to build it higher.
. . . .
What house secure from noise the poor can keep
When even the rich can hardly afford to sleep?
So dear it costs to purchase rest in Rome'
And hence the sources of diseases come.
The cattle driver who is fellow driver meets
In narrow passages of winding streets'
The wagoners, that curse their standing teams
Would wake even drowsy Drusus from his dreams.
And yet the wealthy will not brook delay
But sweep above our heads; and make their way
Borne in high litters, and read and write,
Or sleep at ease: the shutters make it night. . . .
Unwieldy lumber in wagons borne,
Stretched full length, beyond their carriage lie,
And nod, and threaten ruin from on high;
For, should their axle break, its overthrow
Would crush, and pound to dust, the crowd below.
. . . .
And, first, behold our houses' dreadful height;
From whence come broken potsherds tumbling
    down;

1. A small town in Southern Italy
2. A poor, but intelligent man living in Rome

THE ROMANS

And leaky ware, from garret windows thrown;
Well may they break our heads, that mark the flinty stone.
It's bad sense to stay out too late,
Unless you've settled your estate.

. . . .

Poor me, who must by moonlight homeward wend,
Or lighted only with a candle's end,
Poor me the drunkard fights, if that be it, where
He only fights, and I only bear
He stands, and bids me stand; I must abide;
For he's the stronger, and is drunk beside.
"Where did you whet your knife tonight?" he cries,
"And cut the leeks that in your stomach rise?"
"What are you, dumb? Quick, with your answer, quick
Before my foot salutes you with a kick.

. . . .

Answer, or answer not, its all the same;
He lays me on and makes me bear the blame.
Before the bar, for beating him you come;
This is a poor man's liberty in Rome.
You beg his pardon; happy to retreat
With some remaining teeth, to chew your meat.
Nor is this all; for, when retired, you think
To sleep securely; when the candles wink,
When every door with iron chains is barred,
And the roaring from taverns is no longer heard;
The ruffian robbers, by no justice awed,
And unpaid cutthroat soldiers, are abroad,
Those venal souls, who hardened in each evil,
To save complaints and prosecution, kill.
Chased from their woods and bogs, the robbers come
To this vast city, as their native home;
To live at ease, and safely lurk in Rome.

. . . .

O happy ages of our ancestors,
Beneath the kings and tribunial powers,
One jail did all their criminals restrain,
Which, now, the walls of Rome can scarce contain.

Paraphrased by D.C. Riede

Marcus Aurelius

Originating in Hellenistic Greece, Stoicism became extremely popular in the Roman Empire, where many prominent citizens accepted its major ideas which stressed virtue, peace of mind, public service and the universal brotherhood of man. One of the most famous Stoics was the Emperor Marcus Aurelius (161–180), last of the "Five Good Emperors," who wrote his innermost thoughts at various intervals during his life. In this selection Marcus Aurelius ponders such things as good and evil, truth, how to proceed with ones daily tasks, man's relationship with the gods and his fellow man and finally the comparative insignificance of man upon the earth.

The *Meditations of Marcus Aurelius* demonstrates some of the loftiest ideals of pagan philosophy. Even more remarkably the Emperor did his best each day to live up to the high ideals of the Stoics.

MEDITATIONS

Begin the morning by saying to thyself, I shall meet with the busybody, the ungrateful, arrogant, deceitful, envious, unsocial. All these things happen to them by reason of their ignorance of what is good and evil. But I who have seen the nature of the good that it is beautiful and of the bad that it is ugly, and the nature of him who does wrong, that it is akin to me, not [only] of the same blood or seed, but that it participates in [the same] intelligence and [the same] portion of the divinity, I can neither be injured by any of them, for no one can fix on me what is ugly, nor can I be angry with my kinsman, nor hate him. For we are made for co-operation, like feet, like hands, like eyelids, like the rows of the upper and lower teeth. To act against one another then is contrary to nature; and it is acting against one another to be vexed and to turn away.

Whatever this is that I am, it is a little flesh and breath, and the ruling part. Throw away thy books; no longer distract thyself: it is not allowed; but as if thou wast now dying despise the flesh, it is blood and bones and a network, a contexture of nerves, veins and arteries. See the breath also, what kind of a thing it is; air, and not always the same, but every moment sent out and again sucked in. The third then is the ruling part: consider thus: Thou art an old man; no longer let this be a slave, no longer be pulled by the strings like a puppet to unsocial movements, no longer be either dissatisfied with thy present lot, or shrink from the future.

All that is from the gods is full of providence. That which is from fortune is not separated from nature or without an interweaving and involution with the things which are ordered by Providence. From thence all things flow; and there is besides necessity, and that which is for the advantage of the whole universe, of which thou art a part. But that is good for every part of nature which the nature of the whole brings, and what serves to maintain this nature. Now the universe is preserved, as by the changes of the elements so by the changes of things compounded of the elements. Let these principles be enough for thee; let them always be fixed opinions. But cast away the thirst after books, that thou mayest not die murmuring, but cheerfully, truly, and from thy heart thankful to the gods.

Remember how long thou hast been putting off these things, and how often thou hast received an opportunity from the gods, and yet dost not use it. Thou must now at last perceive of what universe thou art a part, and of what administrator of the universe thy existence is an efflux, and that a limit of time is fixed for thee, which if thou dost not use for clearing away the clouds from thy mind, it will go and thou wilt go, and it will never return.

Every moment think steadily as a Roman and a man to do what thou hast in hand with perfect and simple dignity, and feeling of affection, and freedom, and justice; and to give thyself relief from all other thoughts. And thou wilt give thyself relief, if thou doest every act of thy life as if it were the last, laying aside all carelessness and passionate aversion from the commands of reason, and all hypocrisy, and self-love, and discontent with the portion which has been given to thee. Thou seest how few the things are, the which if a man lays hold of, he is able to live a life which flows in quiet, and is like the existence of the gods; for the gods on their part will require nothing more from him who observes these things.

114

Do the things external which fall upon thee distract thee? Give thyself time to learn something new and good, and cease to be whirled around. But then thou must also avoid being carried about the other way. For those too are triflers who have wearied themselves in life by their activity, and yet have no object to which to direct every movement, and, in a word, all their thoughts.

Through not observing what is in the mind of another a man has seldom been seen to be unhappy; but those who do not observe the movements of their own minds must of necessity be unhappy....

Since it is possible that thou mayest depart from life this very moment, regulate every act and thought accordingly. But to go away from among men, if there are gods, is not a thing to be afraid of, for the gods will not involve thee in evil; but if indeed they do not exist, or if they have no concern about human affairs, what is it to me to live in a universe devoid of gods or devoid of providence? But in truth they do exist, and they do care for human things, and they have put all the means in man's power to enable him not to fall into real evils. And as to the rest, if there was anything evil, they would have provided for this also, that it should be altogether in a man's power not to fall into it. Now, that which does not make a man worse, how can it make a man's life worse? But neither through ignorance, nor having the knowledge, but not the power to guard against or correct these things, is it possible that the nature of the universe has overlooked them; nor is it possible that it has made so great a mistake either through want of power or want of skill, that good and evil should happen indiscriminately to the good and the bad. But death certainly, and life, honour and dishonour, pain and pleasure, all these things equally happen to good men and bad, being things which make us neither better nor worse. Therefore they are neither good nor evil....

To the aids which have been mentioned let this one still be added:—Make for thyself a definition or description of the thing which is presented to thee, so as to see distinctly what kind of a thing it is in its substance, in its nudity, in its complete entirety, and tell thyself its proper name and the names of the things of which it has been compounded, and into which it will be resolved. For nothing is so productive of elevation of mind as to be able to examine methodically and truly every object which is presented to thee in life, and always to look at things so as to see at the same time what kind of universe this is, and what kind of use everything performs in it, and what value everything has with reference to the whole and what with reference to man, who is a citizen of the highest city, of which all other cities are like families; what each thing is, and of what it is composed, and how long it is the nature of this thing to endure which now makes an impression on me, and what virtue I have need of with respect to it, such as gentleness, manliness, truth, fidelity, simplicity, contentment, and the rest. Wherefore, on every occasion of man should say: This comes from God; and this is according to the apportionment and spinning of the thread of destiny, and such-like coincidence and chance; and this is from one of the same stock and a kinsman and partner, one who knows not however what is according to his nature. But I know; for this reason I behave towards him according to the natural law of fellowship with benevolence and justice. At the same time however in things indifferent I attempt to ascertain the value of each.

If thou workest at that which is before thee, following right reason seriously, vigorously, calmly, without allowing anything else to distract thee, but keeping thy divine part pure, as if thou shouldst be bound to give it back immediately; if thou holdest to this, expecting nothing, fearing nothing but satisfied with thy present activity according to nature, and with heroic truth in every word and sound which thou utterest, thou wilt live happy. And there is no man who is able to prevent this....

If our intellectual part is common, the reason also, in respect of which we are rational beings, is common: if this is so, common also is the reason which commands us what to do, and what not to do; if this is so, there is a common law also; if this is so, we are fellow-citizens; if this is so, we are members of some political community; if this is so, the world is in a manner a state. For of what other common political community will any one say that the whole human race are members? And from thence, from this common political community comes also our very intellectual faculty and reasoning faculty and our capacity for law; or whence do they come? For as my earthly part is a portion given to me from certain earth, and that which is watery from another element, and that which is hot and fiery from some peculiar source (for nothing comes out of that which is nothing, as nothing also returns to non-existence), so also the intellectual part comes from some source...

Consider that everything which happens, happens justly, and if thou observest carefully, thou wilt find it to be so. I do not say only with respect to the continuity of the series of things, but with respect to what is just, and as if it were done by one who assigns to each thing its value. Observe then as thou hast begun; and whatever thou doest, do it in conjunction with this, the being good, and in the sense in which a man is properly understood to be good. Keep to this in every action.

Be not disgusted, nor discouraged, nor dissatisfied, if thou dost not succeed in doing everything according to right principles; but when thou hast failed, return back again, and be content if the greater part of what thou doest is consistent with man's nature, and love this to which thou returnest; and do not return to philosophy as if she were a master, but act like those who have sore eyes and apply a bit of sponge and egg, or as another applies a plaster, or drenching with water. For thus thou wilt not fail to obey reason and thou wilt repose in it. And remember that philosophy requires only the things which thy nature requires; but thou wouldst have something else which is not according to nature. It may be objected, Why, what is more agreeable than this [which I am doing]? But is not this the very reason why pleasure deceives us? And consider if magnanimity, freedom, simplicity, equanimity, piety are not more agreeable. For what is more agreeable than wisdon itself, when thou thinkest of the security and the happy course of all things which depend on the faculty of understanding and knowledge? . . .

If a thing is difficult to be accomplished by thyself, do not think that it is impossible for man; but if anything is possible for man and conformable to his nature, think that this can be attained by thyself too.

In the gymnastic exercises suppose that a man has torn thee with his nails, and by dashing against thy head has inflicted a wound. Well, we neither show any signs of vexation, nor are we offended, nor do we suspect him afterward as a treacherous fellow; and yet we are on our guard against him, not however as an enemy, nor yet with suspicion, but we quietly get out of his way. Something like this let thy behaviour be in all the other parts of life; let us overlook many things in those who are like antagonists in the gymnasium. For it is in our power, as I said, to get out of the way, and to have no suspicion nor hatred.

If any man is able to convince me and show me that I do not think or act right, I will gladly change; for I seek the truth by which no man was ever injured. But he is injured who abides in his error and ignorance.

I do my duty: other things trouble me not; for they are either things without life, or things without reason, or things that have rambled and know not the way. . . .

Take care that thou art not made into a Ceasar, that thou art not dyed with this dye; for such things happen. Keep thyself then simple, good, pure, serious, free from affectation, a friend of justice, a worshiper of the gods, kind, affectionate, strenuous in all proper acts. Strive to continue to be such as philosophy wished to make thee. Reverence the gods, and help men. Short is life. There is only one fruit of this terrene life, a pious disposition and social acts. Do everything as a disciple of Antoninus. Remember his constancy in every act which was conformable to reason, and his evenness in all things, and his piety, and the serenity of his countenance, and his sweetness, and his disregard of empty fame, and his efforts to understand things; and how he would never let anything pass without having first most carefully examined it and clearly understood it; and how he bore with those who blamed him unjustly without blaming them in return; how he did nothing in a hurry; and how he listened not to calumnies, and how exact an examiner of manners and actions he was; and not given to reproach people, nor timid, nor suspicious, nor a sophist; and with how little he was satisfied, such as lodging, bed, dress, food, servants; and how laborious and patient; and how he was able on account of his sparing diet to hold out to the evening, not even requiring to relieve himself by any evacuations except at the usual hour; and his firmness and uniformity in his friendships; and how he tolerated freedom of speech in those who opposed his opinions; and the pleasure that he had when any man showed him anything better; and how religious he was without superstition. Imitate all this that thou mayest have as good a conscience, when thy last hour comes, as he had.

I have often wondered how it is that every man loves himself more than all the rest of men, but yet sets less value on his own opinion of himself than on the opinion of others. If then a god or a wise teacher should present himself to a man and bid him to think of nothing and to design nothing which he would not express as soon as he conceived it, he could not endure it even for a single day. So much more respect have we to what our neighbours shall think of us than to what we shall think of ourselves. . . .

Practise thyself even in the things which thou despairest of accomplishing. For even the left hand, which is ineffectual for all other things for want of practice, holds the bridle more vigorously than the right hand; for it has been practised in this.

Consider in what condition, both in body and soul, a man should be when he is overtaken by death; and consider the shortness of life, the boundless abyss of time, past and future, the feebleness of all matter....

If it is not right, do not do it; if it is not true, do not say it.

In everything always observe what the thing is which produces for thee an appearance, and resolve it by dividing it into the formal, the material, the purpose, and the time within which it must end.

Perceive at last that thou hast in thee something better and more divine than the things which cause the various effects, and as it were pull thee by the strings. What is there now in my mind? is it fear, or suspicion, or desire, or anything of the kind?

First, do nothing inconsiderately, nor without a purpose. Second, make thy acts refer to nothing else than to a social end.

Consider that before long thou wilt be nobody and nowhere, nor will any of the things exist which thou now seest, nor any of those who are now living. For all things are formed by nature to change and be turned and to perish in order that other things in continuous succession may exist...

To those who ask, Where hast thou seen the gods, or how dost thou comprehend that they exist and so worshipest them, I answer, in the first place, they may be seen even with the eyes; in the second place neither have I seen even my own soul and yet I honour it. Thus then with respect to the gods, from what I constantly experience of their power, from this I comprehend that they exist and I venerate them.

The safety of life is this, to examine everything all through, what it is itself, what is its material, what the formal part; with all thy soul to do justice and to say the truth. What remains except to enjoy life by joining one good thing to another so as not to leave even the smallest intervals between....

What dost thou wish? to continue to exist? Well, dost thou wish to have sensation? movement? growth? and then again to cease to grow? to use thy speech? to think? What is there of all these things which seem to thee worth desiring? But if it is easy to set little value on all these things, turn to that which remains, which is to follow reason and god. But it is inconsistent with honouring reason and god to be troubled because by death a man will be deprived of the other things.

How small a part of the boundless and unfathomable time is assigned to every man? for it is very soon swallowed up in the eternal. And how small a part of the whole substance? and how small a part of the universal soul? and on what a small clod of the whole earth thou creepest? Reflecting on all this consider nothing to be great, except to act as thy nature leads thee, and to endure that which the common nature brings....

The man to whom that only is good which comes in due season, and to whom it is the same thing whether he has done more or fewer acts conformable to right reason, and to whom it makes no difference whether he contemplates the world for a longer or a shorter time—for this man neither is death a terrible thing.

Man, thou hast been a citizen in this great state [the world]: what difference does it make to thee whether for five years [or three]? for that which is conformable to the laws is just for all. Where is the hardship then, if no tyrant nor yet an unjust judge sends thee away from the state, but nature who brought thee into it; the same as if a praetor who has employed an actor dismisses him from the stage. "But I have not finished the five acts, but only three of them."—Thou sayest well, but in life the three acts are the whole drama; for what shall be a complete drama is determined by him who was once the cause of its composition, and now of its dissolution: but thou art the cause of neither. Depart then satisfied, for he also who releases thee is satisfied.

THE HEBREWS

The Old Testament

The following selections from the Old Testament* illustrate a few of the crucial periods in Hebrew history, from the time of Abraham until the sixth century B.C. According to Hebrew legend, Abraham came to the area of Palestine from the city of Ur in southern Sumeria, perhaps as early as 2000 B.C., at the command of the Lord (Genesis 12). After Abraham and his family had settled in Palestine, the Lord further revealed himself to Abraham in the form of a covenant. The following is the Genesis record of the covenant.

GENESIS 17:1-14

1 When Abram was ninety-nine years old the **Lord** appeared to Abram, and said to him, "I am God Almighty; walk before me, and be blameless. ² And I will make my covenant between me and you, and will multiply you exceedingly." ³ Then Abram fell on his face; and God said to him, ⁴ "Behold, my covenant is with you, and you shall be the father of a multitude of nations. ⁵ No longer shall your name be Abram, but your name shall be Abraham; for I have made you the father of a multitude of nations. ⁶ I will make you exceedingly fruitful; and I will make nations of you, and kings shall come forth from you. ⁷ And I will establish my covenant between me and you and your descendants after you throughout their generations for an everlasting covenant, to be God to you and to your descendants after you. ⁸ And I will give to you, and to your descendants after you, the land of your sojournings, all the land of Canaan, for an everlasting possession; and I will be their God."

9 And God said to Abraham, "As for you, you shall keep my covenant, you and your descendants after you throughout their generations. ¹⁰ This is my covenant, which you shall keep, between me and you and your descendants after you: Every male among you shall be circumcised. ¹¹ You shall be circumcised in the flesh of your foreskins, and it shall be a sign of the covenant between me and you. ¹² He that is eight days old among you shall be circumcised; every male throughout your generations, whether born in your house, or brought with your money from any foreigner who is not of your offspring, ¹³ both he that is born in your house and he that is bought with your money, shall be circumcised. So shall my covenant be in your flesh an everlasting covenant. ¹⁴ Any uncircumcised male who is not circumcised in the flesh of his foreskin shall be cut off from his people; he has broken my covenant."

The Hebrews descended from Abraham's son Isaac and his grandson Jacob. The Hebrew tribes descended from Jacob's twelve sons. About 1700 B.C., Jacob and his sons migrated to Egypt because of a famine. The Hebrews continued to live in Egypt until the early thirteenth century B.C., when Moses led them back to Palestine, the promised land of the covenant. The following selections from Exodus record the call of Moses, the renewal of the covenant, and the divine dictation of the Ten Commandments to Moses.

EXODUS 3:1-12

1 Now Moses was keeping the flock of his father-in-law, Jethro, the priest of Midian; and he led his flock to the west side of the wilderness, and came to Horeb, the mountain of God. ² And the angel of the **Lord** appeared to him in a flame of fire out of the midst of a bush; and he looked, and lo, the bush was burning, yet it was not consumed. ³ And Moses said, "I will turn aside and see this great sight, why the bush is not burnt." ⁴ When the **Lord** saw that he turned aside to see, God called to him out of the bush, "Moses, Moses!" And he said, "Here am I." ⁵ Then he said, "Do not come near; put off your shoes from your feet, for the place on which you are standing is holy ground." ⁶ And he said, "I am the God of your father, the God of Abraham, the God of Isaac, and the God of Jacob." And Moses hid his face, for he was afraid to look at God.

7 Then the **Lord** said, "I have seen the affliction of my people who are in Egypt, and have heard their cry because of their taskmasters; I know their sufferings, ⁸ and I have come down to deliver them

---

*The Scripture quotations in this publication are from the Revised Standard Version of the Bible, copyrighted 1946 and 1952 by the Division of Christian Education of the National Council of the Churches of Christ in the U.S.A., and used by permission.

out of the hand of the Egyptians, and to bring them up out of that land to a good and broad land, a land flowing with milk and honey, to the place of the Canaanites, the Hittites, the Amorites, the Per′iz·zites, the Hivites, and the Jebusites. ⁹ And now, behold, the cry of the people of Israel has come to me, and I have seen the oppression with which the Egyptians oppress them. ¹⁰ Come, I will send you to Pharaoh that you may bring forth my people, the sons of Israel, out of Egypt." ¹¹ But Moses said to God, "Who am I that I should go to Pharaoh, and bring the sons of Israel out of Egypt?" ¹² He said, "But I will be with you; and this shall be the sign for you, that I have sent you: when you have brought forth the people out of Egypt, you shall serve God upon this mountain."

EXODUS 6:1-8

1 But the **Lord** said to Moses, "Now you shall see what I will do to Pharaoh; for with a strong hand he will send them out, yea, with a strong hand he will drive them out of his land."

2 And God said to Moses, "I am the **Lord**. ³ I appeared to Abraham, to Isaac, and to Jacob, as God Almighty, but by my name the **Lord** I did not make myself known to them. ⁴ I also established my covenant with them, to give them the land of Canaan, the land in which they dwelt as sojourners. ⁵ Moreover I have heard the groaning of the people of Israel whom the Egyptians hold in bondage and I have remembered my covenant. ⁶ Say therefore to the people of Israel, 'I am the **Lord** and I will bring you out from under the burdens of the Egyptians, and I will deliver you from their bondange, and I will redeem you with an outstretched arm and with great acts of judgment, ⁷ and I will take you for my people, and I will be your God; and you shall know that I am the **Lord** your God, who has brought you out from under the burdens of the Egyptians. ⁸ And I will bring you into the land which I swore to give to Abraham, to Isaac, and to Jacob; I will give it to you for a possession. I am the **Lord**.'"

EXODUS 19:1-8

1 On the third new moon after the people of Israel had gone forth out of the land of Egypt, on that day they came into the wilderness of Sinai. ² And when they set out from Reph′i·dim and came into the wilderness of Sinai, they encamped in the wilderness; and there Israel encamped before the mountain. ³ And Moses went up to God, and the **Lord** called to him out of the mountain, saying, "Thus you shall say to the house of Jacob, and tell the people of Israel: ⁴ You have seen what I did to the Egyptians, and how I bore you on eagles' wings and brought you to myself. ⁵ Now therefore, if you will obey my voice and keep my covenant, you shall be my own possession among all peoples; for all the earth is mine, ⁶ and you shall be to me a kingdom of priests and a holy nation. These are the words which you shall speak to the children of Israel."

7 So Moses came and called the elders of the people, and set before them all these words which the **Lord** had commanded him. ⁸ And all the people answered together and said, "All that the **Lord** has spoken we will do." And Moses reported the words of the people to the **Lord**.

EXODUS 20:1-20

1 And God spoke all these words, saying,

2 "I am the **Lord** your God, who brought you out of the land of Egypt, out of the house of bondage.

3 "You shall have no other gods before me.

4 "You shall not make for yourself a graven image, or any likeness of anything that is in heaven above, or that is in the earth beneath, or that is in the water under the earth; ⁵ you shall not bow down to them or serve them; for I the **Lord** your God am a jealous God, visiting the iniquity of the fathers upon the children to the third and the fourth generation of those who hate me, ⁶ but showing steadfast love to thousands of those who love me and keep my commandments.

7 "You shall not take the name of the **Lord** your God in vain; for the **Lord** will not hold him guiltless who takes his name in vain.

8 "Remember the sabbath day, to keep it holy. ⁹ Six days you shall labor, and do all your work; ¹⁰ but the seventh day is a sabbath to the **Lord** your God; in it you shall not do any work, you, or your son, or your daughter, your manservant, or your maidservant, or your cattle, or the sojourner who is within your gates; ¹¹ for in six days the **Lord** made heaven and earth, the sea, and all that is in them, and rested the seventh day; therefore the **Lord** blessed the sabbath day and hallowed it.

12 "Honor your father and your mother, that your days may be long in the land which the **Lord** your God gives you.

13 "You shall not kill.

14 "You shall not commit adultery.

15 "You shall not steal.

THE HEBREWS

16 "You shall not bear false witness against your neighbor.

17 "You shall not covet your neighbor's house; you shall not covet your neighbor's wife, or his manservant, or his maidservant, or his ox, or his ass, or anything that is your neighbor's."

18 Now when all the people perceived the thunderings and the lightnings and the sound of the trumpet and the mountain smoking, the people were afraid and trembled; and they stood afar off, ¹⁹ and said to Moses, "You speak to us, and we will hear; but let not God speak to us, lest we die." ²⁰ And Moses said to the people, "Do not fear; for God has come to prove you, and that the fear of him may be before your eyes, that you may not sin."

First under Moses, then under the leadership of Joshua, the Hebrews conquered the promised land in the middle of the thirteenth century B.C. Then, after the death of Joshua, the Hebrews were ruled by Judges until the middle of the eleventh century, when Israel founded a centralized government under its first king, Saul (d. 1013). Israel continued to prosper under David (d. 970) and his son Solomon (d. 933). At Solomon's death, however, the ten northern tribes rebelled, and established a separate kingdom. The northern kingdom, with its capital at Samaria was called Israel; the southern kingdom, with its capital at Jerusalem, was called Judah. Israel was conquered by Assyria in the late eighth century. Many of the Hebrews were deported and Assyrians settled in their place. Thus the ten northern tribes eventually lost both their political and spiritual identity. The history of Judah was quite different. Although constantly threatened by the Assyrians, Judah was not subjected to conquest as was Israel, although Judah did become a political dependent of Assyria during the seventh century. With the Assyrian empire breaking up in the late seventh century, Judah made an abortive attempt to regain full political independence, only to fall to the armies of Nebuchadnezzar, the ruler of the new Babylonian empire which had replaced Assyria. As a result of this defeat in the 580's, much of the population of Judah was taken in captivity to Babylonia. During these two centuries of turmoil and defeat a number of Prophets arose, predicting Jehovah's punishment if the Hebrews did not return to the religion of their fathers. The Prophets were the national conscience. The first example is from Amos, a Prophet to Israel in the middle of the eighth century. His message was that Israel must return to a true worship of Jehovah, for Jehovah was not satisfied with their superficial religiousity. His was a prophesy of impending doom for Israel. Jeremiah, on the other hand, was the prophet of doom for Judah, in the late seventh century. His message to Judah was that the people had violated Jehovah's covenant and thus would be punished and disciplined by Jehovah.

AMOS 5:1-27

Hear this word which I take up over you in lamentation, O house of Israel:

2 "Fallen, no more to rise,
   is the virgin Israel;
forsaken on her land,
   with none to raise her up."

3 For thus says the Lord **God**:
"The city that went forth a thousand
   shall have a hundred left,
and that which went forth a hundred
   shall have ten left
to the house of Israel."

4 For thus says the **Lord** to the house of Israel:
"Seek me and live;
5 but do not seek Bethel,
and do not enter into Gilgal
   or cross over to Be·er-she′ba;
for Gilgal shall surely go into exile,
   and Bethel shall come to nought."

6 Seek the **Lord** and live,
   lest he break out like fire in the house of Joseph,
   and it devour, with none to quench it for Bethel,
7 O you who turn justice to wormwood,
   and cast down righteousness to the earth!

8 He who made the Ple′ia·des and Orion,
   and turns deep darkness into the morning,
   and darkens the day into night,
who calls for the waters of the sea,
   and pours them out upon the surface of the earth,
The **Lord** is his name,
9 who makes destruction flash forth

10 They hate him who reproves in the gate,
and they abhor him who speaks the truth.
11 Therefore because you trample upon the poor
and take from him exactions of wheat,
you have built houses of hewn stone,
but you shall not dwell in them;
you have planted pleasant vineyards,
but you shall not drink their wine.
12 For I know how many are your transgressions,
and how great are your sins—
you who afflict the righteous, who take a bribe,
and turn aside the needy in the gate.
13 Therefore he who is prudent will keep silent in such a time;
for it is an evil time.
14 Seek good, and not evil,
that you may live;
and so the **Lord**, the God of hosts, will be with you,
as you have said.
15 Hate evil, and love good,
and establish justice in the gate;
it may be that the **Lord**, the God of hosts,
will be gracious to the remnant of Joseph.
16 Therefore thus says the **Lord**, the God of hosts, the Lord:
"In all the squares there shall be wailing;
and in all the streets they shall say, 'Alas! alas!'
They shall call the farmers to mourning
and to wailing those who are skilled in lamentation,
17 and in all vineyards there shall be wailing,
for I will pass through the midst of you,"
says the **Lord**.

THE DAY OF THE LORD

18 Woe to you who desire the day of the **Lord**!
Why would you have the day of the **Lord**?
It is darkness, and not light;
19 as if a man fled from a lion,
and a bear met him;
or went into the house and leaned with his hand against the wall,
and a serpent bit him.
20 Is not the day of the **Lord** darkness, and not light,
and gloom with no brightness in it?
21 "I hate, I despise your feasts,
and I take no delight in your solemn assemblies.
22 Even though you offer me your burnt offerings and cereal offerings,
I will not accept them,
and the peace offerings of your fatted beasts
I will not look upon.
23 Take away from me the noise of your songs;
to the melody of your harps I will not listen.
24 But let justice roll down like waters,
and righteousness like an everflowing stream.

25 "Did you bring to me sacrifices and offerings the forty years in the wilderness, O house of Israel? 26 You shall take up Sakkuth your king, and Kaiwan your star-god, your images, which you made for yourselves; 27 therefore I will take you into exile beyond Damascus," says the **Lord**, whose name is the God of hosts.

JEREMIAH 11:1-13

1 The word that came to Jer·e·mi′ah from the **Lord**: 2 "Hear the words of this covenant, and speak to the men of Judah and the inhabitants of Jerusalem. 3 You shall say to them, Thus says the **Lord**, the God of Israel: Cursed be the man who does not heed the words of this covenant 4 which I commanded your fathers when I brought them out of the land of Egypt, from the iron furnace, saying, Listen to my voice, and do all that I command you. So shall you be my people, and I will be your

God, ⁵ that I may perform the oath which I swore to your fathers, to give them a land flowing with milk and honey, as at this day." Then I answered, "So be it, **Lord**."

6 And the **Lord** said to me, "Proclaim all these words in the cities of Judah, and in the streets of Jerusalem: Hear the words of this covenant and do them. ⁷ For I solemnly warned your fathers when I brought them up out of the land of Egypt, warning them persistently, even to this day, saying, Obey my voice. ⁸ Yet they did not obey or incline their ear, but every one walked in the stubbornness of his evil heart. Therefore I brought upon them all the words of this covenant, which I commanded them to do, but they did not."

9 Again the **Lord** said to me, "There is revolt among the men of Judah and the inhabitants of Jerusalem. ¹⁰ They have turned back to the iniquities of their forefathers, who refused to hear my words; they have gone after other gods to serve them; the house of Isreal and the house of Judah have broken my covenant which I made with their fathers. ¹¹ Therefore, thus says the **Lord**, Behold, I am bringing evil upon them which they cannot escape; though they cry to me, I will not listen to them. ¹² Then the cities of Judah and the inhabitants of Jerusalem will go and cry to the gods to whom they burn incense, but they cannot save them in the time of their trouble. ¹³ For your gods have become as many as your cities, O Judah; and as many as the streets of Jerusalem are the altars you have set up to shame, altars to burn incense to Baal.

The Old Testament also contains much beautiful poetry, such as the Psalms, Proverbs and The Song of Solomon. The Song of Solomon is a love poem.

THE SONG OF SOLOMON 7:1-12

How graceful are your feet in sandals,
   O queenly maiden!
Your rounded thighs are like jewels.
   the work of a master hand.

2 Your navel is a rounded bowl
   that never lacks mixed wine.
Your belly is a heap of wheat,
   encircled with lilies.

3 Your two breasts are like two fawns,
   twins of a gazelle.

4 Your neck is like an ivory tower.
Your eyes are pools in Heshbon,
   by the gate of Bath-rab′bim.

Your nose is like a tower of Lebanon,
   overlooking Damascus.

5 Your head crowns you like Carmel,
   and your flowing locks are like purple;
   a king is held captive in the tresses.

6 How fair and pleasant you are,
   O loved one, delectable maiden!

7 You are stately as a palm tree,
   and your breasts are like its clusters.

8 I say I will climb the palm tree
   and lay hold of its branches.
Oh, may your breasts be like clusters of the vine.
   and the scent of your breath like apples,

9 and your kisses like the best wine
   that goes down smoothly,
   gliding over lips and teeth.

10 I am my beloved's,
   and his desire is for me.

11 Come, my beloved,
   let us go forth into the fields,
   and lodge in the villages;

12 let us go out early to the vineyards,
   and see whether the vines have budded,
   whether the grape blossoms have opened
   and the pomegranates are in bloom.
There I will give you my love.

The book of Daniel is an example of Old Testament apocalyptic literature. Although the scene is Babylonia during the captivity of Judah in the sixth century, linguistic evidence seems to indicate that it was written during the age of Antiochus Epiphanes, about 168 B.C. Daniel's prophesies, particularly the portion reproduced here, have been important in both Jewish and Christian apocalyptic systems up to the present day.

DANIEL 2:1-49

1 In the second year of the reign of Neb·u·chad·nez′zar, Neb·u·chad·nez′zar had dreams; and his spirit was troubled and his sleep left him. ² Then the king commanded that the magicians, the enchanters, the sorcerers, and the Chal·de′ans be summoned, to tell the king his dreams. So they came in and stood before the king. ³ And the king said to them, "I had a dream, and my spirit is troubled to know the dream." ⁴ Then the Chal·de′ans said to the king, "O king, live for ever! Tell your servants the dream, and we will show the interpretation." ⁵ The king answered the Chal·de′ans,

"The word from me is sure: if you do not make known to me the dream and its interpretation, you shall be torn limb from limb, and your houses shall be laid in ruins. ⁶ But if you show the dream and its interpretation, you shall receive from me gifts and rewards and great honor. Therefore show me the dream and its interpretation." ⁷ They answered a second time, "Let the king tell his servants the dream, and we will show its interpretation." ⁸ The king answered, "I know with certainty that you are trying to gain time, because you see that the word from me is sure ⁹ that if you do not make the dream known to me, there is but one sentence for you. You have agreed to speak lying and corrupt words before me till the times change. Therefore tell me the dream, and I shall know that you can show me its interpretation." ¹⁰ The Chal·de'ans answered the king, "There is not a man on earth who can meet the king's demand; for no great and powerful king has asked such a thing of any magician or enchanter or Chal·de'an. ¹¹ The thing that the king asks is difficult, and none can show it to the king except the gods, whose dwelling is not with flesh."

12 Because of this the king was angry and very furious, and commanded that all the wise men of Babylon be destroyed. ¹³ So the decree went forth that the wise men were to be slain, and they sought Daniel and his companions, to slay them. ¹⁴ Then Daniel replied with prudence and discretion to Ar'i·och, the captain of the king's guard, who had gone out to slay the wise men of Babylon; ¹⁵ he said to Ar'i·och, the king's captain, "Why is the decree of the king so severe?" Then Ar'i·och made the matter known to Daniel. ¹⁶ And Daniel went in and besought the king to appoint him a time, that he might show to the king the interpretation.

17 Then Daniel went to his house and made the matter known to Han·a·ni'ah, Mish'a·el, and Az·a·ri'ah, his companions, ¹⁸ and told them to seek mercy of the God of heaven concerning this mystery, so that David and his companions might not perish with the rest of the wise men of Babylon. ¹⁹ Then the mystery was revealed to Daniel in a vision of the night. Then Daniel blessed the God of heaven. ²⁰ Daniel said:

"Blessed be the name of God for ever and ever,
to whom belong wisdom and might.
21 He changes times and seasons;
he removes kings and sets up kings;
he gives wisdom to the wise
and knowledge to those who have understanding;
22 he reveals deep and mysterious things;
he knows what is in the darkness,
and the light dwells with him.
23 To thee, O God of my fathers,
I give thanks and praise,
for thou has given me wisdom and strength,
and hast now made known to me what we asked of thee,
for thou hast now made known to us the king's matter."

24 Therefore Daniel went in to Ar'i·och, whom the king had appointed to destroy the wise men of Babylon; he went and said thus to him, "Do not destroy the wise men of Babylon; bring me in before the king, and I will show the king the interpretation.

25 Then Ar'i·och brought in Daniel before the king in haste, and said thus to him: "I have found among the exiles from Judah a man who can make known to the king the interpretation." ²⁶ The king said to Daniel, whose name was Bel·te·shaz'zar, "Are you able to make known to me the dream that I have seen and its interpretation?" ²⁷ Daniel answered the king, "No wise men, enchanters, magicians, or astrologers can show to the king the mystery which the king has asked, ²⁸ but there is a God in heaven who reveals mysteries, and he has made known to King Neb·u·chad·nez'zar what will be in the latter days. Your dream and the visions of your head as you lay in bed are these: ²⁹ To you, O king, as you lay in bed came thoughts of what would be hereafter, and he who reveals mysteries made known to you what is to be. ³⁰ But as for me, not because of any wisdom that I have more than all the living has this mystery been revealed to me, but in order that the interpretation may be made known to the king, and that you may know the thoughts of your mind.

31 "You saw, O king, and behold, a great image. This image, mighty and of exceeding brightness, stood before you, and its appearance was frightening. ³² The head of this image was of fine gold, its breast and arms of silver, its belly and thighs of bronze, ³³ its legs of iron, its feet partly of iron and partly of clay. ³⁴ As you looked, a stone was cut out by no human hand, and it smote the image on its feet of iron and clay, and broke them in pieces; ³⁵ then the iron, the clay, the bronze, the silver, and the gold, all together were broken in pieces, and became like the chaff of the summer threshing floors; and the wind carried them away, so that not a trace of them could be found. But the stone that

THE HEBREWS

struck the image became a great mountain and filled the whole earth.

36 "This was the dream; now we will tell the king its interpretation. ³⁷ You, O king, the king of kings, to whom the God of heaven has given the kingdom, the power, and the might, and the glory, ³⁸ and into whose hand he has given, wherever they dwell, the sons of men, the beasts of the field, and the birds of the air, making you rule over them all—you are the head of gold. ³⁹ After you shall arise another kingdom inferior to you, and yet a third kingdom of bronze, which shall rule over all the earth. ⁴⁰ And there shall be a fourth kingdom, strong as iron, because iron breaks to pieces and shatters all things; and like iron which crushes, it shall break and crush all these. ⁴¹ And as you saw the feet and toes partly of potter's clay and partly of iron, it shall be a divided kingdom; but some of the firmness of iron shall be in it, just as you saw iron mixed with the miry clay. ⁴² And as the toes of the feet were partly iron and partly clay, so the kingdom shall be partly strong and partly brittle. ⁴³ As you saw the iron mixed with miry clay, so they will mix with one another in marriage, but they will not hold together, just as iron does not mix with clay. ⁴⁴ And in the days of those things the God of heaven will set up a kingdom which shall never be destroyed, nor shall its sovereignty be left to another people. It shall break in pieces all these kingdoms and bring them to an end, and it shall stand for ever; ⁴⁵ just as you saw that a stone was cut from a mountain by no human hand, and that it broke in pieces the iron, the bronze, the clay, the silver, and the gold. A great God has made known to the king what shall be hereafter. The dream is certain, and its interpretation sure."

46 Then King Neb·u·chad·nez'zar fell upon his face, and did homage to Daniel, and commanded that an offering and incense be offered up to him. ⁴⁷ The king said to Daniel, "Truly, your God is God of gods and Lord of kings, and a revealer of mysteries, for you have been able to reveal this mystery." ⁴⁸ Then the king gave Daniel high honors and many great gifts, and made him ruler over the whole province of Babylon, and chief prefect over all the wise men of Babylon. ⁴⁹ Daniel made request of the king, and he appointed Shadrach, Meshach, and A·bed'ne·go over the affairs of the province of Babylon; but Daniel remained at the king's court.

During the late sixth century many of the exiles returned to Palestine from Babylon. Little is known about Jewish history in the fifth century. Palestine did, of course, become part of the empire of Alexander the Great in the fourth century, falling under the nominal rule of Egypt after the death of Alexander (323). Then, in the early second century, Antiochus the Great of Syria took Palestine from Egypt. Finding the Syrian rule oppressive, the Jews won their independence in 142 B.C., following more than twenty years of resistance under the leadership of a group of men called the Maccabees. Not quite a century later, in 63 B.C., the Romans took Palestine. Resentment of Roman rule smoldered for over a century, until open rebellion broke out in 66 A.D. In 70 A.D., the Romans took Jerusalem, burned the temple, and crushed the last vestiges of Jewish independence.

CHRISTIANITY

The Teachings of Christ and the Early Church: The New Testament

In 4 or 5 B.C. Jesus was born in Bethlehem. According to Jewish custom, Jesus began his public ministry as a rabbi when he was thirty years old. About three years later he was publicly crucified by the Romans. According to Christian teaching he was resurrected on the third day, thus assuring his followers that he was the Son of God. The following selections are from Matthew's account of the life and teachings of Jesus. Matthew's purpose was to demonstrate that Jesus was the Messiah prophesied in the Old Testament who would fulfill God's promises to his people. The first selection is the Sermon on the Mount, in which Jesus revealed his own ethic and related it to the Old Testament ethic. The second passage is the record of Peter's confession that Jesus was the Messiah, the Son of God.

MATTHEW 5:1-48

1 Seeing the crowds, he went up on the mountain, and when he sat down his disciples came to him. ² And he opened his mouth and taught them, saying:

3 "Blessed are the poor in spirit, for theirs is the kingdom of heaven.

4 "Blessed are those who mourn, for they shall be comforted.

5 "Blessed are the meek, for they shall inherit the earth.

6 "Blessed are those who hunger and thirst for righteousness, for they shall be satisfied.

7 "Blessed are the merciful, for they shall obtain mercy.

8 "Blessed are the pure in heart, for they shall see God.

9 "Blessed are the peacemakers, for they shall be called sons of God.

10 "Blessed are those who are persecuted for righteousness' sake, for theirs is the kingdom of heaven.

11 "Blessed are you when men revile you and persecute you and utter all kinds of evil against you falsely on my account. ¹² Rejoice and be glad, for your reward is great in heaven, for so men persecuted the prophets who were before you.

13 "You are the salt of the earth; but if salt has lost its taste, how shall its saltness be restored? It is no longer good for anything except to be thrown out and trodden under foot by men.

14 "You are the light of the world. A city set on a hill cannot be hid. ¹⁵ Nor do men light a lamp and put it under a bushel, but on a stand, and it gives light to all in the house. ¹⁶ Let your light so shine before men, that they may see your good works and give glory to your Father who is in heaven.

17 "Think not that I have come to abolish the law and the prophets; I have come not to abolish them but to fulfil them. ¹⁸ For truly, I say to you, till heaven and earth pass away, not an iota, not a dot, will pass from the law until all is accomplished. ¹⁹ Whoever then relaxes one of the least of these commandments and teaches men so, shall be called least in the kingdom of heaven; but he who does them and teaches them shall be called great in the kingdom of heaven. ²⁰ For I tell you, unless your righteousness exceeds that of the scribes and Pharisees, you will never enter the kingdom of heaven.

21 "You have heard that it was said to the men of old, 'You shall not kill; and whoever kills shall be liable to judgment.'" ²² But I say to you that every one who is angry with his brother shall be liable to judgment; whoever insults his brother shall be liable to the council, and whoever says, 'You fool!' shall be liable to the hell of fire. ²³ So if you are offering your gift at the altar, and there remember that your brother has something against you, ²⁴ leave your gift there before the altar and go; first be reconciled to your brother, and then come and offer your gift. ²⁵ Make friends quickly with your accuser, while you are going with him to court, lest your accuser hand you over to the judge, and the judge to the guard, and you be put in prison; ²⁶ truly, I say to you, you will never get out till you have paid the last penny.

27 "You have heard that it was said, 'You shall not commit adultery.' ²⁸ But I say to you that every one who looks at a woman lustfully has already committed adultery with her in his heart.

²⁹ If your right eye causes you to sin, pluck it out and throw it away; it is better that you lose one of your members than that your whole body be thrown into hell. ³⁰ And if your right hand causes you to sin, cut it off and throw it away; it is better that you lose one of your members than that your whole body go into hell.

31 "It was also said, 'Whoever divorces his wife, let him give her a certificate of divorce.' ³² But I say to you that every one who divorces his wife, except on the ground of unchastity, makes her an adulteress; and whoever marries a divorced woman commits adultery.

33 "Again you have heard that it was said to the men of old, 'You shall not swear falsely, but shall perform to the Lord what you have sworn.' ³⁴ But I say to you, Do not swear at all, either by heaven, for it is the throne of God, ³⁵ or by the earth, for it is his footstool, or by Jerusalem, for it is the city of the great King. ³⁶ And do not swear by your head, for you cannot make one hair white or black. ³⁷ Let what you say be simply 'Yes' or 'No'; anything more than this comes from evil.

38 "You have heard that it was said, 'An eye for an eye and a tooth for a tooth.' ³⁹ But I say to you, Do not resist one who is evil. But if any one strikes you on the right cheek, turn to him the other also; ⁴⁰ and if any one would sue you and take your coat, let him have your cloak as well; ⁴¹ and if any one forces you to go one mile, go with him two miles. ⁴² Give to him who begs from you, and do not refuse him who would borrow from you.

43 "You have heard that it was said, 'You shall love your neighbor and hate your enemy.' ⁴⁴ But I say to you, Love your enemies and pray for those who persecute you, ⁴⁵ so that you may be sons of your Father who is in heaven; for he makes his sun rise on the evil and on the good, and sends rain on the just and on the unjust. ⁴⁶ For if you love those who love you, what reward have you? Do not even the tax collectors do the same? ⁴⁷ And if you salute only your brethren, what more are you doing than others? Do not even the Gentiles do the same? ⁴⁸ You, therefore, must be perfect, as your heavenly Father is perfect.

MATTHEW 16:13-20

13 Now when Jesus came into the district of Caes·a·re′a Phi·lip′pi, he asked his disciples, "Who do men say that the Son of man is?" ¹⁴ And they said, "Some say John the Baptist, others say E·li′jah, and others Jer·e·mi′ah or one of the prophets." ¹⁵ He said to them, "But who do you say that I am?" ¹⁶ Simon Peter replied, "You are the Christ, the Son of the living God." ¹⁷ And Jesus answered him, "Blessed are you, Simon Bar-Jona! For the flesh and blood has not revealed this to you, but my Father who is in heaven. ¹⁸ And I tell you, you are Peter, and on this rock I will build my church, and the powers of death shall not prevail against it. ¹⁹ I will give you the keys of the kingdom of heaven, and whatever you bind on earth shall be bound in heaven, and whatever you loose on earth shall be loosed in heaven." ²⁰ Then he strictly charged the disciples to tell no one that he was the Christ.

The Gospel of John introduces Jesus as the eternal Word of God who became flesh. The second selection from John is one of the more famous salvational passages in the New Testament.

JOHN 1:1-14

1 In the beginning was the Word, and the Word was with God, and the Word was God. ² He was in the beginning with God; ³ all things were made through him, and without him was not anything made that was made. ⁴ In him was life, and the life was the light of men. ⁵ The light shines in the darkness, and the darkness has not overcome it.

6 There was a man sent from God, whose name was John. ⁷ He came for testimony, to bear witness to the light, that all might believe through him. ⁸ He was not the light, but came to bear witness to the light.

9 The true light that enlightens every man was coming into the world. ¹⁰ He was in the world, and the world was made through him, yet the world knew him not. ¹¹ He came to his own home, and his own people received him not. ¹² But to all who received him, who believed in his name, he gave power to become children of God; ¹³ who were born, not of blood nor of the will of the flesh nor of the will of man, but of God.

14 And the Word became flesh and dwelt among us, full of grace and truth; we have beheld his glory, glory as of the only Son from the Father.

JOHN 3:1-21

1 Now there was a man of the Pharisees, named Nicodemus, a ruler of the Jews. ² This man came to Jesus by night and said to him, "Rabbi, we know that you are a teacher come from God; for no one can do these signs that you do, unless God is with him." ³ Jesus answered him, "Truly, truly, I say to

you, unless one is born anew, he cannot see the kingdom of God." ⁴ Nicodemus said to him, "How can a man be born when he is old? Can he enter a second time into his mother's womb and be born?" ⁵ Jesus answered, "Truly, truly, I say to you, unless one is born of water and the Spirit, he cannot enter the kingdom of God. ⁶ That which is born of the flesh is flesh, and that which is born of the Spirit is spirit. ⁷ Do not marvel that I said to you, 'You must be born anew.' ⁸ The wind blows where it wills, and you hear the sound of it, but you do not know whence it comes or whither it goes; so it is with every one who is born of the Spirit." ⁹ Nicodemus said to him, "How can this be?" ¹⁰ Jesus answered him, "Are you a teacher of Israel, and yet you do not understand this? ¹¹ Truly, truly, I say to you, we speak of what we know, and bear witness to what we have seen; but you do not receive our testimony. ¹² If I have told you earthly things and you do not believe, how can you believe if I tell you heavenly things? ¹³ No one has ascended into heaven but he who descended from heaven, the Son of man. ¹⁴ And as Moses lifted up the serpent in the wilderness, so must the Son of man be lifted up, ¹⁵ that whoever believes in him may have eternal life."

16 For God so loved the world that he gave his only Son, that whoever believes in him should not perish but have eternal life. ¹⁷ For God sent the Son into the world, not to condemn the world, but that the world might be saved through him. ¹⁸ He who believes in him is not condemned; he who does not believe is condemned already, because he has not believed in the name of the only Son of God. ¹⁹ And this is the judgment, that the light has come into the world, and men loved darkness rather than light, because their deeds were evil. ²⁰ For every one who does evil hates the light, and does not come to the light, lest his deeds should be exposed. ²¹ But he who does what is true comes to the light, that it may be clearly seen that his deeds have been wrought in God.

The Acts of the Apostles is a history of the early Christian Church, the central theme of which is the expansion of Christianity to include Gentiles as well as Jews. The key figure in this expansion was Paul, also known as Saul. Before his conversion Saul was a zealous persecutor of the Christians. The following passage is the account of his conversion to Christianity and his call to be the apostle to the Gentiles.

ACTS 9:1-22

1 But Saul, still breathing threats and murder against the disciples of the Lord, went to the high priest ² and asked him for letters to the synagogues at Damascus, so that if he found any belonging to the Way, men or women, he might bring them bound to Jerusalem. ³ Now as he journeyed he approached Damascus, and suddenly a light from heaven flashed about him. ⁴ And he fell to the ground and heard a voice saying to him, "Saul, Saul, why do you persecute me?" ⁵ And he said, "Who are you, Lord?" And he said, "I am Jesus, whom you are persecuting; ⁶ but rise and enter the city, and you will be told what you are to do." ⁷ The men who were traveling with him stood speechless, hearing the voice but seeing no one. ⁸ Saul arose from the ground; and when his eyes were opened, he could see nothing; so they led him by the hand and brought him into Damascus. ⁹ And for three days he was without sight, and neither ate nor drank.

10 Now there was a disciple at Damascus named An·a·ni′as. The Lord said to him in a vision, "An·a·ni′as." And he said, "Here I am, Lord." ¹¹ And the Lord said to him, "Rise and go to the street called Straight, and inquire in the house of Judas for a man of Tarsus named Saul; for behold, he is praying, ¹² and he has seen a man named An·a·ni′as come in and lay his hands on him so that he might regain his sight." ¹³ But An·a·ni′as answered, "Lord, I have heard from many about this man, how much evil he has done to thy saints at Jerusalem; ¹⁴ and here he has authority from the chief priests to bind all who call upon thy name." ¹⁵ But the Lord said to him, "Go, for he is a chosen instrument of mine to carry my name before the Gentiles and kings and the sons of Israel; ¹⁶ for I will show him how much he must suffer for the sake of my name." ¹⁷ So An·a·ni′as departed and entered the house. And laying his hands on him he said, "Brother Saul, the Lord Jesus who appeared to you on the road by which you came, has sent me that you may regain your sight and be filled with the Holy Spirit." ¹⁸ And immediately something like scales fell from his eyes and he regained his sight. Then he rose and was baptized, ¹⁹ and took food and was strengthened.

For several days he was with the disciples at Damascus. ²⁰ And in the synagogues immediately he proclaimed Jesus, saying, "He is the Son of God." ²¹ And all who heard him were amazed, and said, "Is not this the man who made havoc in Jerusalem of those who called on this name? And he has come here for this purpose, to bring them bound before the chief priests." ²² But Saul increased all the more in strength, and confounded the Jews who lived in Damascus by proving that Jesus was the Christ.

Paul did become the apostle to the Gentiles, traveling throughout the eastern Mediterranean area preaching the Christian message and establishing churches. The following selection from his letter to the Romans shows what Paul thought was the relationship between the Christian message and the original covenant which the Lord made with Abraham.

ROMANS 4:1-25

1 What then shall we say about Abraham, our forefather according to the flesh? ² For if Abraham was justified by works, he has something to boast about, but not before God. ³ For what does the scripture say? "Abraham believed God, and it was reckoned to him as righteousness." ⁴ Now to one who works, his wages are not reckoned as a gift but as his due. ⁵ And to one who does not work but trusts him who justifies the ungodly, his faith is reckoned as righteousness. ⁶ So also David pronounces a blessing upon the man to whom God reckons righteousness apart from works:

7 "Blessed are those whose iniquities are forgiven, and whose sins are covered;
8 blessed is the man against whom the Lord will not reckon his sin."

9 Is this blessing pronounced only upon the circumcised, or also upon the uncircumcised? We say that faith was reckoned to Abraham as righteousness. ¹⁰ How then was it reckoned to him? Was it before or after he had been circumcised? It was not after, but before he was circumcised. ¹¹ He received circumcision as a sign or seal of the righteousness which he had by faith while he was still uncircumcised. The purpose was to make him the father of all who believe without being circumcised and who thus have righteousness reckoned to them, ¹² and likewise the father of the circumcised who are not merely circumcised but also follow the example of the faith which our father Abraham had before he was circumcised.

13 The promise to Abraham and his descendants, that they should inherit the world, did not come through the law but through the righteousness of faith. ¹⁴ If it is the adherents of the law who are to be the heirs, faith is null and the promise is void. ¹⁵ For the law brings wrath, but where there is no law there is no transgression.

16 That is why it depends on faith, in order that the promise may rest on grace and be guaranteed to all his descendants—not only to the adherents of the law but also to those who share the faith of Abraham, for he is the father of us all, ¹⁷ as it is written, "I have made you the father of many nations"—in the presence of the God in whom he believed, who gives life to the dead and calls into existence the things that do not exist. ¹⁸ In hope he believed against hope, that he should become the father of many nations; as he had been told, "So shall your descendants be." ¹⁹ He did not weaken in faith when he considered his own body, which was as good as dead because he was about a hundred years old, or when he considered the barrenness of Sarah's womb. ²⁰ No distrust made him waver concerning the promise of God, but he grew strong in his faith as he gave glory to God, ²¹ fully convinced that God was able to do what he had promised. ²² That is why his faith was "reckoned to him as righteousness." ²³ But the words, "it was reckoned to him," were written not for his sake alone, ²⁴ but for ours also. It will be reckoned to us who believe in him that raised from the dead Jesus our Lord, ²⁵ who was put to death for our trespasses and raised for our justification.

Paul's emphasis in his teachings was on faith in Christ as the Son of God for the forgiveness of sins. He did not, however, ignore Christ's ethical emphasis, as is evident in this selection from Paul's first letter to the Corinthians.

1 CORINTHIANS 13:1-13

1 If I speak in the tongues of men and of angels, but have not love, I am a noisy gong or a clanging cymbal. ² And if I have prophetic powers, and understand all mysteries and all knowledge, and if I have all faith, so as to remove mountains, but have not love, I am nothing. ³ If I give away all I have, and if I deliver my body to be burned, but have not love, I gain nothing.

4 Love is patient and kind; love is not jealous or boastful; ⁵ it is not arrogant or rude. Love does not insist on its own way; it is not irritable or resentful; ⁶ it does not rejoice at wrong, but rejoices in the right. ⁷ Love bears all things, believes all things, hopes all things, endures all things.

8 Love never ends; as for prophecies, they will

pass away; as for tongues, they will cease; as for knowledge, it will pass away. ⁹ For our knowledge is imperfect and our prophecy is imperfect; ¹⁰ but when the perfect comes, the imperfect will pass away. ¹¹ When I was a child, I spoke like a child, I thought like a child, I reasoned like a child; when I became a man, I gave up childish ways. ¹² For now we see in a mirror dimly, but then face to face. Now I know in part; then I shall understand fully, even as I have been fully understood. ¹³ So faith, hope, love abide, these three; but the greatest of these is love.

Christianity also has its apocalyptic literature. Christ and the early Christians expected the world to end soon. The first selection is the account in Matthew of Christ's teachings about the last days. Notice his reference to the prophecy of Daniel. The second passage, from Revelation, describes the millennial reign of Christ and the last judgment.

MATTHEW 24:1-51

1 Jesus left the temple and was going away, when his disciples came to point out to him the buildings of the temple. ² But he answered them, "You see all these, do you not? Truly, I say to you, there will not be left here one stone upon another, that will not be thrown down."

3 As he sat on the Mount of Olives, the disciples came to him privately, saying, "Tell us, when will this be, and what will be the sign of your coming and of the close of the age?" ⁴ And Jesus answered them, "Take heed that no one leads you astray. ⁵ For many will come in my name, saying, 'I am the Christ,' and they will lead many astray. ⁶ And you will hear of wars and rumors of wars; see that you are not alarmed; for this must take place, but the end is not yet. ⁷ For nation will rise against nation, and kingdom against kingdom, and there will be famines and earthquakes in various places: ⁸ all this is but the beginning of the sufferings.

9 "Then they will deliver you up to tribulation, and put you to death; and you will be hated by all nations for my name's sake. ¹⁰ And then many will fall away, and betray one another, and hate one another. ¹¹ And many false prophets will arise and lead many astray. ¹² And because wickedness is multiplied, most men's love will grow cold. ¹³ But he who endures to the end will be saved. ¹⁴ And this gospel of the kingdom will be preached throughout the whole world, as a testimony to all nations; and then the end will come.

15 "So when you see the desolating sacrilege spoken of by the prophet Daniel, standing in the holy place (let the reader understand), ¹⁶ then let those who are in Judea flee to the mountains; ¹⁷ let him who is on the housetop not go down to take what is in his house; ¹⁸ and let him who is in the field not turn back to take his mantle. ¹⁹ And alas for those who are with child and for those who give suck in those days! ²⁰ Pray that your flight may not be in winter or on a sabbath. ²¹ For then there will be great tribulation, such as has not been from the beginning of the world until now, no, and never will be. ²² And if those days had not been shortened, no human being would be saved; but for the sake of the elect those days will be shortened. ²³ Then if any one says to you, 'Lo, here is the Christ!' or 'There he is!' do not believe it. ²⁴ For false Christs and false prophets will arise and show great signs and wonders, so as to lead astray, if possible, even the elect. ²⁵ Lo, I have told you beforehand. ²⁶ So, if they say to you, 'Lo, he is in the wilderness,' do not go out; if they say, 'Lo, he is in the inner rooms,' do not believe it. ²⁷ For as the lightning comes from the east and shines as far as the west, so will the coming of the Son of man. ²⁸ Wherever the body is, there the eagles will be gathered together.

29 "Immediately after the tribulation of those days the sun will be darkened, and the moon will not give its light, and the stars will fall from heaven, and the powers of the heavens will be shaken; ³⁰ then will appear the sign of the Son of man in heaven, and then all the tribes of the earth will mourn, and they will see the Son of man coming on the clouds of heaven with power and great glory; ³¹ and he will send out his angels with a loud trumpet call, and they will gather his elect from the four winds, from one end of heaven to the other.

32 "From the fig tree learn its lesson: as soon as its branch becomes tender and puts forth its leaves, you know that summer is near. ³³ So also, when you see all these things, you know that he is near, at the very gates. ³⁴ Truly, I say to you, this generation will not pass away till all these things take place. ³⁵ Heaven and earth will pass away, but my words will not pass away.

36 "But of that day and hour no one knows, not even the angels of heaven, nor the Son, but the Father only. ³⁷ As were the days of Noah, so will be the coming of the Son of man. ³⁸ For as in those days before the flood they were eating and drinking, marrying and giving in marriage, until the day when Noah entered the ark, ³⁹ and they did not know until the flood came and swept them all

away, so will be the coming of the Son of man. ⁴⁰ Then two men will be in the field; one is taken and one is left. ⁴¹ Two women will be grinding at the mill; one is taken and one is left. ⁴² Watch therefore, for you do not know on what day your Lord is coming. ⁴³ But know this, that if the householder had known in what part of the night the thief was coming, he would have watched and would not have let his house be broken into. ⁴⁴ Therefore you also must be ready; for the Son of man is coming at an hour you do not expect.

45 "Who then is the faithful and wise servant, whom his master has set over his household, to give them their food at the proper time? ⁴⁶ Blessed is that servant whom his master when he comes will find so doing. ⁴⁷ Truly, I say to you, he will set him over all his possessions. ⁴⁸ But if that wicked servant says to himself, 'My master is delayed,' ⁴⁹ and begins to beat his fellow servants, and eats and drinks with the drunken, ⁵⁰ the master of that servant will come on a day when he does not expect him and at an hour he does not know, ⁵¹ and will punish him, and put him with the hypocrites; there men will weep and gnash their teeth.

REVELATION 20:1-15

1 Then I saw an angel coming down from heaven, holding in his hand the key of the bottomless pit and a great chain. ² And he seized the dragon, that ancient serpent, who is the Devil and Satan, and bound him for a thousand years, ³ and threw him into the pit, and shut it and sealed it over him, that he should deceive the nations no more, till the thousand years were ended. After that he must be loosed for a little while.

4 Then I saw thrones, and seated on them were those to whom judgment was committed. Also I saw the souls of those who had been beheaded for their testimony to Jesus and for the word of God, and who had not worshiped the beast or its image and had not received its mark on their foreheads or their hands. They came to life, and reigned with Christ a thousand years. ⁵ The rest of the dead did not come to life until the thousand years were ended. This is the first resurrection. ⁶ Blessed and holy is he who shares in the first resurrection! Over such the second death has no power, but they shall be priests of God and of Christ, and they shall reign with him a thousand years.

7 And when the thousand years are ended, Satan will be loosed from his prison ⁸ and will come out to deceive the nations which are at the four corners of the earth, that is, Gog and Magog, to gather them for battle; their number is like the sand of the sea. ⁹ And they marched up over the broad earth and surrounded the camp of the saints and the beloved city; but fire came down from heaven and consumed them, ¹⁰ and the devil who had deceived them was thrown into the lake of fire and brimstone where the beast and the false prophet were, and they will be tormented day and night for ever and ever.

11 Then I saw a great white throne and him who sat upon it; from his presence earth and sky fled away, and no place was found for them. ¹² And I saw the dead, great and small, standing before the throne, and books were opened. Also another book was opened, which is the book of life. And the dead were judged by what was written in the books, by what they had done. ¹³ And the sea gave up the dead in it, Death and Hades gave up the dead in them, and all were judged by what they had done. ¹⁴ Then Death and Hades were thrown into the lake of fire. This is the second death, the lake of fire; ¹⁵ and if any one's name was not found written in the book of life, he was thrown into the lake of fire.

The Church and the Empire

The Christian Church was first subjected to official Imperial persecution in the year 64 A.D. under the Emperor Nero. Christianity, illegal by the late first century, suffered sporadic persecution until 250, when the Emperor Decius initiated the first systematic and universal persecution of Christians in the Empire. The usual charges against the Christians were atheism and treason: atheism because they refused to worship the old gods; and treason because they would not participate in emperor-worship. The persecution ended when the Emperor Constantine, after his conversion to Christianity in 312, issued the Edict of Milan which gave complete freedom to Christianity. The following selections are taken from the writings of Eusebius of Caesarea, a church historian who was contemporary to these events. Eusebius' description of Constantine's conversion is followed by the Edict of Milan.

EUSEBIUS—CONVERSION OF CONSTANTINE

CHAPTER XXVII

That after reflecting on the Downfall of those who had worshiped Idols, he made Choice of Christianity.

Being convinced, however, that he needed some more powerful aid than his military forces could afford him, on account of the wicked and magical enchantments which were so diligently practiced by the tyrant, he sought Divine assistance, deeming the possession of arms and a numerous soldiery of secondary importance, but believing the co-operating power of Deity invincible and not to be shaken. He considered, therefore, on what God he might rely for protection and assistance. While engaged in this enquiry, the thought occurred to him, that, of the many emperors who had preceded him, those who had rested their hopes in a multitude of gods, and served them with sacrifices and offerings, had in the first place been deceived by flattering predictions, and oracles which promised them all prosperity, and at last had met with an unhappy end, while not one of their gods had stood by to warn them of the impending wrath of heaven; while one alone who had pursued an entirely opposite course, who had condemned their error, and honored the one Supreme God during his whole life, had found him to be the Saviour and Protector of his empire, and the Giver of every good thing. Reflecting on this, and well weighing the fact that they who had trusted in many gods had also fallen by manifold forms of death, without leaving behind them either family or offspring, stock, name, or memorial among men: while the God of his father had given to him, on the other hand, manifestations of his power and very many tokens: and considering farther that those who had already taken arms against the tyrant, and had marched to the battle-field under the protection of a multitude of gods, had met with a dishonorable end (for one of them had shamefully retreated from the contest without a blow, and the other, being slain in the midst of his own troops, became, as it were, the mere sport of death); reviewing, I say, all these considerations, he judged it to be folly indeed to join in the idle worship of those who were no gods, and, after such convincing evidence, to err from the truth; and therefore felt it incumbent on him to honor his father's God alone.

CHAPTER XXVIII

How, while he was praying, God sent him a Vision of a Cross of Light in the Heavens at Mid-day, with an Inscription admonishing him to conquer by that.

Accordingly he called on him with earnest prayer and supplications that he would reveal to him who he was, and stretch forth his right hand to help him in his present difficulties. And while he was thus praying with fervent entreaty, a most marvelous sign appeared to him from heaven, the account of which it might have been hard to believe had it been related by any other person. But since the victorious emperor himself long afterwards declared it to the writer of this history, when he was honored with his acquaintance and society, and confirmed his statement by an oath, who could hesitate to accredit the relation, especially since the testimony of after-time has established its truth? He said that about noon, when the day was already beginning to decline, he saw with his own eyes the trophy of a cross of light in the heavens, above the sun, and bearing the inscription, **CONQUER BY THIS.** At this sight he himself was struck with amazement, and his whole army also, which followed him on this expedition, and witnessed the miracle.

CHAPTER XXIX

How the Christ of God appeared to him in his Sleep, and commanded him to use his Wars a Standard made in the Form of the Cross.

He said, moreover, that he doubted within himself what the import of this apparition could be. And while he continued to ponder and reason on its meaning, night suddenly came on; then in his sleep the Christ of God appeared to him with the same sign which he had seen in the heavens, and commanded him to make a likeness of that sign which he had seen in the heavens, and to use it as a safeguard in all engagements with his enemies.

CHAPTER XXX

The Making of the Standard of the Cross.

At dawn of day he arose and communicated the marvel to his friends: and then, calling together the workers in gold and precious stones, he sat in the midst of them, and described to them the figure of the sign he had seen, bidding them represent it in gold and precious stones. And this representation I myself have had an opportunity of seeing.

CHAPTER XXXI

A Description of the Standard of the Cross, which the Romans now call the Labarum.

Now it was made in the following manner. A long spear, overlaid with gold, formed the figure of the cross by means of a transverse bar laid over it. On the top of the whole was fixed a wreath of gold and precious stones; and within this, the symbol of the Saviour's name, two letters indicating the name of Christ by means of its initial characters, the letter P being intersected by X in its centre: and these letters the emperor was in the habit of wearing on his helmet at a later period. From the cross-bar of the spear was suspended a cloth, a royal piece, covered with a profuse embroidery of most brilliant precious stones; and which, being also richly interlaced with gold, presented an indescribable degree of beauty to the beholder. This banner was of a square form, and the upright staff, whose lower section was of great length, bore a golden half-length portrait of the pious emperor and his children on its upper part, beneath the trophy of the cross, and immediately above the embroidered banner.

The emperor constantly made use of this sign of salvation as a safeguard against every adverse and hostile power, and commanded that others similar to it should be carried at the head of all his armies.

CHAPTER XXXII

How Constantine received Instruction, and read the Sacred Scriptures.

These things were done shortly afterwards. But at the time above specified, being struck with amazement at the extraordinary vision, and resolving to worship no other God save Him who had appeared to him, he sent for those who were acquainted with the mysteries of His doctrines, and enquired who that God was, and what was intended by the sign of the vision he had seen.

They affirmed that He was God, the only begotten Son of the one and only God: that the sign which had appeared was the symbol of immortality, and the trophy of that victory over death which He had gained in time past when sojourning on earth. They taught him also the causes of His advent, and explained to him the true account of His incarnation. Thus he was instructed in these matters, and was impressed with wonder at the divine manifestation which had been presented to his sight. Comparing, therefore, the heavenly vision with the interpretation given, he found his judgment confirmed; and, in the persuasion that the knowledge of these things had been imparted to him by Divine teaching, he determined thenceforth to devote himself to the reading of the Inspired writings.

Moreover, he made the priests of God his counselors, and deemed it incumbent on him to honor the God who had appeared to him with all devotion. And after this, being fortified by well-grounded hopes in Him, he hastened to quench the threatening fire of tyranny.

EUSEBIUS—EDICT OF MILAN

"Perceiving long ago that religious liberty ought not to be denied, but that it ought to be granted to the judgment and desire of each individual to perform his religious duties according to his own choice, we had given orders that every man, Christians as well as others, should preserve the faith of his own sect and religion. But since in that rescript, in which such liberty was granted them, many and various conditions seemed clearly added, some of them, it may be, after a little retired from such observance. When I, Constantine Augustus, and I, Licinius Augustus, came under favorable auspices to Milan and took under consideration everything which pertained to the common weal and prosperity, we resolved among other things, or rather first of all, to make such decrees as seemed in many respects for the benefit of every one; namely, such as should preserve reverence and piety toward the deity. We resolved, that is, to grant both to the Christians and to all men freedom to follow the religion which they choose, that whatever heavenly divinity exists may be propitious to us and to all that live under our government. We have, therefore, determined, with sound and upright purpose, that liberty is to be denied to no one, to choose and to follow the religious observances of the Christians, but that to each one freedom is to be given to devote his mind to that religion which he may think adapted to himself, in order that the Deity may exhibit to us in all things his accustomed care and favor. It was fitting that we should write that this is our pleasure, that those conditions being entirely left out which were contained in our former letter concerning the Christians which was sent to your devotedness, everything that seemed very severe and foreign to our mildness may be annulled, and that now every one who has the same desire to observe the religion of the Christians may do so without molestation. We have resolved to communicate this most fully to thy care, in order that thou mayest know that we have granted to these same Christians freedom and full liberty to observe their own religion. Since this has been granted freely by us to them, thy devotedness perceives that liberty is granted to others also who may wish to follow their own religious observances; it being clearly in accordance with the tranquillity of our times, that each one should have the liberty of choosing and worshiping whatever deity he pleases. This has been done by us in order that we might not seem in any way to discriminate against any rank or religion. And we decree still further in regard to the Christians, that their places, in which they were formerly accustomed to assemble, and concerning which in the former letter sent to thy devotedness a different command was given, if it appear that any have bought them either from our treasury or from any other person, shall be restored to the said Christians, without demanding money or any other equivalent, with no delay or hesitation. If any happen to have received the said places as a gift, they shall restore them as quickly as possible to these same Christians: with the understanding that if those who have bought these places, or those who have received them as a gift, demand anything from our bounty, they may go to the judge of the district, that provision may be made for them by our clemency. All these things are to be granted to the society of Christians by your care immediately and without any delay. And since the said Christians are known to have possessed not only those places in which they were accustomed to assemble, but also other places, belonging not to individuals among them, but to the society as a whole, that is, to the society of Christians, you will command that all these, in virtue of the law which we have above stated, be restored, without any hesitation, to these same Christians; that is, to their society and congregation: the above-mentioned provision being of course observed, that those who restore them without price, as we have before said, may expect indemnification from our bounty. In all these things, for the behoof of the aforesaid society of Christians, you are to use the utmost diligence, to the end that our command may be speedily fulfilled, and that in this also, by our clemency, provision may be made for the common and public tranquillity. For by this means, as we have said before, the divine favor toward us which we have already experienced in many matters will continue sure through all time. And that the terms of this our gracious ordinance may be known to all, it is expected that this which we have written will be published everywhere by you and brought to the knowledge of all, in order that this gracious ordinance of ours may remain unknown to no one."

Shortly after the Edict of Milan, a serious theological controversy threatened to destroy the unity of the Church. The issue involved the person of Christ. The one party, led by Arius, taught that Christ, although God, was a created being. He was a lower God, neither fully God nor fully man. The other party, led by Bishop Alexander, insisted that the Son was uncreated, eternal and of the same essence as the Father. The bitterness of the controversy led Constantine to assemble a general council of the Church at Nicea in 325. This is considered the most important council in the history of the Church. Bishop Alexander prevailed at the council, as is evident in the Nicene Creed.

NICENE CREED

We believe in one God, the Father, the Almighty, maker of heaven and earth, of all that is seen and unseen. We believe in one Lord, Jesus Christ, the only Son of God, eternally begotten of the Father, God from God, Light from Light, true God from True God, begotten, not made, one in Being with the Father. Through him all things were made. For us men and for our salvation he came down from heaven: by the power of the Holy Spirit he was born of the Virgin Mary, and became man. For our sake he was crucified under Pontius Pilate; he suffered, died, and was buried. On the third day he rose again in fulfillment of the Scriptures; he ascended into heaven and is seated at the right hand of the Father. He will come again in glory to judge the living and the dead, and his kingdom will have no end. We believe in the Holy Spirit, the Lord, the giver of life, who proceeds from the Father and the Son. With the Father and the Son he is worshiped and glorified. He was spoken through the Prophets. We believe in one holy catholic and apostolic Church. We acknowledge one baptism for the forgiveness of sins. We look for the resurrection of the dead, and the life of the world to come. Amen.

Augustine (354-430) was one of the great thinkers of the Christian tradition. Not only did he adapt Platonism to Christianity for his own age, but he continued to influence western Christian thought for centuries. His theology and philosophy became both the cornerstone of medieval thought and the basis for much of the Protestant theology of the Reformation. The first selection is excerpts from his **Confessions**, *his spiritual autobiography, written about 400.*

ST. AUGUSTINE: CONFESSIONS

He deplores the wickedness of his youth.

I will now call to mind my past foulness, and the carnal corruptions of my soul, not because I love them, but that I may love Thee, O my God. For love of Thy love do I it, recalling, in the very bitterness of my remembrance, my most vicious ways, that Thou mayest grow sweet to me,—Thou sweetness without deception! Thou sweetness happy and assured!—and re-collecting myself out of that my dissipation, in which I was torn to pieces, while, turned away from Thee the One, I lost myself among many vanities. For I even longed in my youth formerly to be satisfied with worldly things, and I dared to grow wild again with various and shadowy loves; my form consumed away, and I became corrupt in Thine eyes, pleasing myself, and eager to please in the eyes of men.

He commits theft with his companions, not urged on by poverty, but from a certain distaste of well-doing.

Theft is punished by Thy law, O Lord, and by the law written in men's hearts, which iniquity itself cannot blot out. For what thief will suffer a thief? Even a rich thief will not suffer him who is driven to it by want. Yet had I a desire to commit robbery, and did so, compelled neither by hunger, nor poverty, but through a distaste for well-doing, and a lustiness of iniquity. For I pilfered that of which I had already sufficient, and much better. Nor did I desire to enjoy what I pilfered, but the theft and sin itself. There was a pear-tree close to our vineyard, heavily laden with fruit, which was tempting neither for its colour nor its flavour. To shake and rob this some of us wanton young fellows went, late one night (having, according to our disgraceful habit, prolonged our games in the streets until them), and carried away great loads, not to eat ourselves, but to fling to the very swine, having only eaten some of them; and to do this pleased us all the more because it was not permitted. Behold my heart, O my God; behold my heart, which Thou hadst pity upon when in the bottomless pit. Behold, now, let my heart tell Thee what it was seeking there, that I should be gratuitously wanton, having no inducement to evil but the evil itself. It was foul, and I loved it. I loved to perish. I loved my own error—not that for which I erred, but the error itself. Base soul, falling from Thy firmament to utter destruction—not seeking aught through the shame but the shame itself!

Concerning the motives to sin, which are not in the love of evil, but in the desire of obtaining the property of others.

There is a desirableness in all beautiful bodies, and in gold, and silver, and all things; and in bodily contact sympathy is powerful, and each other sense hath his proper adaptation of body. Worldly honour hath also its glory, and the power of command, and of overcoming; whence proceeds also the desire for revenge. And yet to acquire all these, we must not depart from Thee, O Lord, nor deviate from Thy law. The life which we live here hath also its peculiar attractiveness, through a certain measure of comeliness of its own, and harmony with all things here below. The friendships of men also are endeared by a sweet bond, in the oneness of many souls. On account of all these, and such as these, is sin committed; while through an inordinate preference for these goods of a lower kind, the better and higher are neglected,—even Thou, our Lord God, Thy truth, and Thy law. For these meaner things have their delights, but not like unto my God, who hath created all things; for in Him doth the righteous delight, and He is the sweetness of the upright in heart.

When, therefore, we inquire why a crime was committed, we do not believe it, unless it appear that there might have been the wish to obtain some of those which we designated meaner things, or else a fear of losing them. For truly they are beautiful and comely, although in comparison with those higher and celestial goods they be abject and contemptible. A man hath murdered another; what was his motive? He desired his wife or his estate; or would steal to support himself; or he was afraid of losing something of the kind by him; or, being injured, he was burning to be revenged. Would he commit murder without a motive, taking delight simply in the act of murder? Who would credit it? For as for that savage and brutal man, of whom it is declared that he was gratuitously wicked and cruel, there is yet a motive assigned. "Lest through idleness," he says, "hand or heart should grow inactive." And to what purpose? Why, even that, having once got possession of the city through that practice of wickedness, he might attain unto honours, empire, and wealth, and be exempt from the fear of the laws, and his difficult circumstances from the needs of his family, and the consciousness of his own wickedness. So it seems that even Catiline himself loved not his own villanies, but something else, which gave him the motive for committing them.

Why he delighted in that theft, when all things which under the appearance of good invite to vice are true and perfect in God alone.

What was it, then, that I, miserable one, so doted on in thee, thou theft of mine, thou deed of darkness, in that sixteenth year of my age? Beautiful thou wert not, since thou wert theft. But art thou saying, that so I may argue the case with thee? Those pears that we stole were fair to the sight, because they were Thy creation, Thou fairest of all, Creator of all, Thou good God—God, the highest good, and my true good. Those pears truly were pleasant to the sight; but it was not for them that my miserable soul lusted, for I had abundance of better, but those I plucked simply that I might steal. For, having plucked them, I threw them away, my sole gratification in them being my own sin, which I was pleased to enjoy. For if any of these pears entered my mouth, the sweetner of it was my sin in eating it. And now, O Lord my God, I ask what it was in that theft of mine that caused me such delight; and behold it hath no beauty in it—not such, I mean, as exists in justice and wisdom; nor such as is in the mind, memory, senses, and animal life of man; nor yet such as is the glory and beauty of the stars in their courses; or the earth, or the sea, teeming with incipient life, to replace, as it is born, that which decayeth; nor, indeed, that false and shadowy beauty which pertaineth to deceptive vices.

For thus doth pride imitate high estate, whereas Thou alone art God, high above all. And what does ambition seek but honours and renown, whereas Thou alone art to be honoured above all, and renowned for evermore? The cruelty of the powerful wishes to be feared; but who is to be feared but God only, out of whose power what can be forced away or withdrawn—when, or where, or whither, or by whom? The enticements of the wanton would fain be deemed love; and yet is naught more enticing than Thy charity, nor is aught loved more healthfully than that, Thy truth, bright and beautiful above all. Curiosity affects a desire for knowledge, whereas it is Thou who supremely knowest all things. Yea, ignorance and foolishness themselves are concealed under the names of ingenuousness and harmlessness, because nothing can be found more ingenuous than Thou; and what is more harmless, since it is a sinner's own works by which he is harmed? And sloth seems to long for rest; but what sure rest is there besides the Lord? Luxury would fain be called plenty and abundance; but Thou art the fulness and unfailing plenteousness of unfading joys. Prodigality presents a shadow of liberality; but Thou art the most lavish giver of all good. Covetousness desires to possess much; and Thou art the Possessor of all things. Envy contends for excellence; but what so excellent as Thou? Anger seeks revenge; who avenges more justly than Thou? Fear starts at unwonted and sudden chances which threaten things beloved, and is wary for their security; but what can happen that is unwonted or sudden to Thee? or who can deprive Thee of what Thou lovest? or where is there unshaken security save with Thee? Grief languishes for things lost in which desire had delighted itself, even because it would have nothing taken from it, as nothing can be from Thee.

Thus doth the soul commit fornication when she turns away from Thee, and seeks without Thee what she cannot find pure and untainted until she returns to Thee. Thus all pervertedly imitate Thee who separate themselves far from Thee and raise themselves up against Thee. But even by thus imitating Thee they acknowledge Thee to be the Creator of all nature, and so that there is no place whither they can altogether retire from Thee. What, then, was it that I loved in that theft? And wherein did I, even corruptedly and pervertedly, imitate my Lord? Did I wish, if only by artifice, to act contrary to Thy law, because by power I could not, so that, being a captive, I might imitate an imperfect liberty by doing with impunity things which I was not allowed to do, in obscured likeness of Thy omnipotency? Behold this servant of Thine, fleeing from his Lord, and following a shadow! O rottenness! O monstrosity of life and profundity of death! Could I like that which was unlawful only because it was unlawful?

Whatever things the good God has created are very good.

And it was made clear unto me that those things are good which yet are corrupted, which, neither were they supremely good, nor unless they were good, could be corrupted; because if supremely good, they were incorruptible, and if not good at all, there was nothing in them to be corrupted. For corruption harms, but, unless it could diminish goodness, it could not harm. Either, then, corruption harms not, which cannot be; or, what is most certain, all which is corrupted is deprived of good. But if they be deprived of all good, they will cease to be. For if they be, and cannot be at all corrupted, they will become better, because they shall remain incorruptibly. And what more monstrous than to assert that those things which have lost all their goodness are made better? Therefore, if they shall be deprived of all good, they shall no longer be. So long, therefore, as they are, they are good; therefore whatsoever is, is good. That evil, then, which I sought whence it was, is not any substance; for were it a substance, it would be good. For either it would be an incorruptible substance, and so a chief good, or a corruptible substance, which unless it were good it could not be corrupted. I perceived, therefore, and it was made clear to me, that Thou didst make all things good, nor is there any substance at all that was not made by Thee; and because all that Thou hast made are not equal, therefore all things are; because individually they are good, and altogether very good, because our God made all things very good.

It is meet to praise the Creator for the good things which are made in heaven and earth.

And to Thee is there nothing at all evil, and not only to Thee, but to Thy whole creation; because there is nothing without which can break in, and mar that order which Thou hast appointed it. But in the parts thereof, some things, because they harmonize not with others, are considered evil; whereas those very things harmonize with others, and are good, and in themselves are good. And all these things which do not harmonize together harmonize with the inferior part which we call earth, having its own cloudy and windy sky concordant to it. Far be it from me, then, to say, "These things should not be." For should I see nothing but these, I should indeed desire better; but yet, if only for these, ought I to praise Thee; for that Thou art to be praised is shown from the "earth, dragons, and all deeps; fire, and hail; snow, and vapours; stormy winds fulfilling Thy word; mountains, and all hills; fruitful trees, and all cedars; beasts, and all cattle; creeping things, and flying fowl; kings of the earth, and all people; princes, and all judges of the earth; both young men and maidens; old men and children," praise Thy name. But when, "from the heavens," these praise Thee, praise Thee, our God, "in the heights," all Thy "angels," all Thy "hosts," "sun and moon," all ye stars and light, "the heavens of heavens," and the "waters that be above the heavens;" praise Thy name. I did not now desire better things, because I was thinking of all; and with a better judgment I reflected that the things above were better than those below, but that all were better than those above alone.

Being displeased with some part of God's creation, he conceives of two original substances.

There is no wholeness in them whom aught of Thy creation displeaseth; no more than there was in me, when many things which Thou madest displeased me. And, because my soul dared not be displeased at my God, it would not suffer aught to be Thine which displeased it. Hence it had gone into the opinion of two substances, and resisted not, but talked foolishly. And, returning thence, it had made to itself a god, through infinite measures of all space; and imagined it to be Thee, and placed it in its heart, and again had become the temple of its own idol, which was to Thee an abomination. But after Thou hadst fomented the head of me unconscious of it, and closed mine eyes lest they should "behold vanity," I ceased from myself a little, and my madness was lulled to sleep; and I awoke in Thee, and saw Thee to be infinite, though in another way; and this sight was not derived from the flesh.

Whatever is, owes its being to God.

And I looked back on other things, and I perceived that it was to Thee they owed their being, and that they were all bounded in Thee; but in another way, not as being in space, but because Thou holdest all things in Thine hand in truth: and all things are true so far as they have a being; nor is there any falsehood, unless that which is not is thought to be. And I saw that all things harmonized, not with their places only, but with their seasons also. And that Thou, who only art eternal, didst not begin to work after innumerable spaces of time; for that all spaces of times, both those which have passed and which shall pass, neither go nor come, save through Thee, working and abiding.

Evil arises not from a substance, but from the perversion of the will.

And I discerned and found it no marvel, that bread which is distasteful to an unhealthy palate is pleasant to a healthy one; and that the light, which is painful to sore eyes, is delightful to sound ones. And Thy righteousness displeaseth the wicked; much more the viper and little worm, which Thou hast created good, fitting in with inferior parts of Thy creation; with which the wicked themselves also fit in, the more in proportion as they are unlike Thee, but with the superior creatures, in proportion as they become like to Thee. And I inquired what iniquity was, and ascertained it not to be a substance, but a perversion of the will, bent aside from Thee, O God, the Supreme Substance, towards these lower things, and casting out its bowels, and swelling outwardly.

Above his changeable mind, he discovers the unchangeable author of truth.

And I marvelled that I now loved Thee, and no phantasm instead of Thee. And yet I did not merit to enjoy my God, but was transported to Thee by Thy beauty, and presently torn away from Thee by mine own weight, sinking with grief into these inferior things. This weight was carnal custom. Yet was there a remembrance of Thee with me; nor did I any way doubt that there was one to whom I might cleave, but that I was not yet one who could cleave unto Thee; for that the body which is corrupted presseth down the soul, and the earthly dwelling weigheth down the mind which thinketh upon many things. And most certain I was that Thy "invisible things from the creation of the world are clearly seen, being understood by the things that are made, even Thy eternal power and Godhead." For, inquiring whence it was that I admired the beauty of bodies whether celestial or terrestrial, and what supported me in judging correctly on things mutable, and pronouncing, "This should be thus, this not,"—inquiring, then, whence I so judged, seeing I did so judge, I had found the unchangeable and true eternity of Truth, above my changeable mind. And thus, by degrees, I passed from bodies to the soul, which makes use of the senses of the body to perceive; and thence to its inward faculty, to which the bodily senses represent outward things, and up to which reach the capabilities of beasts; and thence, again, I passed on to the reasoning faculty, unto which whatever is received from the senses of the body is referred to be judged, which also, finding itself to be variable in me, raised itself up to its own intelligence, and from habit drew away my thoughts, withdrawing itself from the crowds of contradictory phantasms; that so it might find out that light by which it was besprinkled, when, without all doubting, it cried out, "that the unchangeable was to be preferred before the changeable;" whence also it knew that unchangeable, which, unless it had in some way known, it could have had no sure ground for preferring it to the changeable. And thus, with the flash of a trembling glance, it arrived at that which is. And then I saw Thy invisible things understood by the things that are made. But I was not able to fix my gaze thereon; and my infirmity being beaten back, I was thrown again on my accustomed habits, carrying along with me naught but a loving memory thereof, and an appetite for what I had, as it were, smelt the odour of, but was not yet able to eat.

Jesus Christ, the mediator, is the only way of safety.

And I sought a way of acquiring strength sufficient to enjoy Thee; but I found it not until I embraced that "Mediator between God and man, the man Christ Jesus," "who is over all, God blessed for ever," calling unto me, and saying, "I am the way, the truth, and the life," and mingling that food which I was unable to receive with our flesh. For "the Word was made flesh," that Thy wisdom, by which Thou createdst all things, might provide milk for our infancy. For I did not grasp my Lord Jesus,—I, though humbled, grasped not the humble One; nor did I know what lesson that infirmity of His would teach us. For Thy Word, the Eternal Truth, pre-eminent above the higher parts of Thy creation, raises up those that are subject unto Itself; but in this lower world built for Itself a humble habitation of our clay, whereby He intended to abase from themselves such as would be subjected and bring them over unto Himself, allaying their swelling, and fostering their love; to the end that they might go on no further in self-confidence, but rather should become weak, seeing before their feet the Divinity weak by taking our "coats of skins;" and wearied, might cast themselves down upon It, and It rising, might lift them up.

He does not fully understand the saying of John, that "the Word was made flesh."

But I thought differently, thinking only of my Lord Christ as of a man of excellent wisdom, to whom no man could be equalled; especially for that, being wonderfully born of a virgin, He seemed, through the divine care for us, to have attained so great authority of leadership,—for an example of contemning temporal things for the obtaining of immortality. But what mystery there was in, "The Word was made flesh," I could not even imagine. Only I had learnt out of what is delivered to us in writing of Him, that He did eat, drink, sleep, walk, rejoice in spirit, was sad, and discoursed; that flesh alone did not cleave unto Thy Word, but with the human soul and body. All know thus who know the unchangeableness of Thy Word, which I now knew as well as I could, nor did I at all have any doubt about it. For, now to move the limbs of the body at will, now not; now to be stirred by some affection, now not; now by signs to enunciate wise sayings, now to keep silence, are properties of a soul and mind subject to change. And should these things be falsely written of Him, all the rest would risk the imputation, nor would there remain in those books any saving faith for the human race. Since, then, they were written truthfully, I acknowledged a perfect man to be in Christ—not the body of a man only, nor with the body a sensitive soul without a rational, but a very man; whom, not only as being a form of truth, but for a certain great excellency of human nature and a more perfect participation of wisdom, I decided was to be preferred before others. But Alypius imagined the Catholics to believe that God was so clothed with flesh, that, besides God and flesh, there was no soul in Christ, and did not think that a human mind was ascribed to Him. And, because He was thoroughly persuaded that the actions which were recorded of Him could not be performed except by a vital and rational creature, he moved the more slowly towards the Christian faith. But, learning afterwards that this was the error of the Apollinarian heretics, he rejoiced in the Catholic faith, and was conformed to it. But somewhat later it was, I confess, that I learned how in the sentence, "The Word was made flesh," the Catholic truth can be distinguished from the falsehood of Photinus. For the disapproval of heretics makes the tenets of Thy Church and sound doctrine to stand out boldly. For there must be also heresies, that the approved may be made manifest among the weak.

He rejoices that he proceeded from Plato to the Holy Scriptures, and not the reverse.

But having then read those books of the Platonists, and being admonished by them to search for incorporeal truth, I saw Thy invisible things, understood by those things that are made; and though repulsed, I perceived what that was, which through the darkness of my mind I was not allowed to contemplate,—assured that Thou wert, and wert infinite, and yet not diffused in space finite or infinite; and that Thou truly art, who art the same ever, varying neither in part nor motion; and that all other things are from Thee, on this most sure ground alone, that they are. Of these things was I indeed assured, yet too weak to enjoy Thee. I chattered as one well skilled; but had I not sought Thy way in Christ our Saviour, I would have proved not skilful, but ready to perish. For now, filled with my punishment, I had begun to desire to seem wise; yet mourned I not, but rather was puffed up with knowledge. For where was that charity building upon the "foundation" of humility, "which is Jesus Christ"? Or, when would these books teach me it? Upon these, therefore, I believe, it was Thy pleasure that I should fall before I studied Thy Scriptures, that it might be impressed on my memory how I was affected by them; and that afterwards when I was subdued by Thy books, and when my wounds were touched by Thy healing fingers, I might discern and distinguish what a difference there is between presumption and confession,—between those who saw whither they were to go, yet saw not the way, and the way which leadeth not only to behold but to inhabit the blessed country. For had I first been moulded in Thy Holy Scriptures, and hadst Thou, in the familiar use of them, grown sweet unto me, and had I afterwards fallen upon those volumes, they might perhaps have withdrawn me from the solid ground of piety; or, had I stood firm in that wholesome disposition which I had thence imbibed, I might have thought that it could have been attained by the study of those books alone.

What he found in the sacred books which are not to be found in Plato.

Most eagerly, then, did I seize that venerable writing of Thy Spirit, but more especially the Apostle Paul; and those difficulties vanished away, in which he at one time appeared to me to contradict himself, and the text of his discourse not to agree with the testimonies of the Law and the Prophets. And the face of that pure speech appeared to me one and the same; and I learned to "rejoice with trembling." So I commenced, and found that whatsoever truth I had there read was declared here with the recommendation of Thy grace; that he who sees may not so glory as if he had not received not only that which he sees, but also that he can see (for what hath he which he hath not received?); and that he may not only be admonished to see Thee, who art ever the same, but also may be healed, to hold Thee; and that he who from afar off is not able to see, may still walk on the way by which he may reach, behold, and possess Thee. For though a man "delight in the law of God after the inward man," what shall he do with that other law in his members which warreth against the law of his mind, and bringeth him into captivity to the law of sin, which is in his members? For Thou art righteous, O Lord, but we have sinned and committed iniquity, and have done wickedly, and Thy hand is grown heavy upon us, and we are justly delivered over unto that ancient sinner, the governor of death; for he induced our will to be like his will, whereby he remained not in Thy truth. What shall "wretched man" do? "Who shall deliver him from the body of this death," but Thy grace only, "through Jesus Christ our Lord," whom Thou hast begotten co-eternal, and createdst in the beginning of Thy ways, in whom the Prince of this world found nothing worthy of death, yet killed he Him, and the handwriting which was contrary to us was blotted out? This those writings contain not. Those pages contain not the expression of this piety,—the tears of confession, Thy sacrifice, a troubled spirit, "a broken and a contrite heart," the salvation of the people, the espoused city, the earnest of the Holy Ghost, the cup of our redemption. No man sings there, Shall not my soul be subject unto God? For of Him cometh my salvation, for He is my God and my salvation, my defender, I shall not be further moved. No one there hears Him calling, "Come unto me all ye that labour." They scorn to learn of Him because He is meek and lowly of heart; for "Thou hast hid those things from the wise and prudent, and hast revealed them unto babes." For it is one thing, from the mountain's wooded summit to see the land of peace, and not to find the way thither,—in vain to attempt impassable ways, opposed and waylaid by fugitives and deserters, under their captain the "lion" and the "dragon;" and another to keep to the way that leads thither, guarded by the host of the heavenly general, where they rob not who have deserted the heavenly army, which they shun as torture. These things did in a wonderful manner sink into my bowels, when I read that "least of Thy apostles," and had reflected upon Thy works, and feared greatly.

Augustine's greatest treatise was his City of God, written between 412 and 426. It was both an answer to the pagans, who blamed the sack of Rome in 410 on the teachings of the Christians, and an explication of his philosophy of history. Augustine's great theory of history prevailed in the West until modern times. He argued that there have been two categories of men, or two cities, since the first rebellion of man against God. The Earthly City, founded by Cain, is characterized by love of self and contempt of God. It is represented by the civil state. Nevertheless, it is a relative good, for the state represses disorder in the world. The City of God, founded by Abel, is composed of the elect, those whom God has chosen for salvation. Thus the City of God, as it exists on earth, is the visible, organized Church, which will more and more rule the world. As the City of God grows, the Earthly City will eventually disappear. Then the Kingdom of God will be complete.

ST. AUGUSTINE: CITY OF GOD

Preface, explaining his design in undertaking this work.

The glorious city of God is my theme in this work, which you, my dearest son Marcellinus, suggested, and which is due to you by my promise. I have undertaken its defence against those who prefer their own gods to the Founder of this city,—a city surpassingly glorious, whether we view it as it still lives by faith in this fleeting course of time, and sojourns as a stranger in the midst of the ungodly, or as it shall dwell in the fixed stability of its eternal seat, which it now with patience waits for, expecting until "righteousness shall return unto judgment," and it obtain, by virtue of its excellence, final victory and perfect peace. A great work this, and an arduous; but God is my helper.

What subjects are to be handled in the following discourse.

But I have still some things to say in confutation of those who refer the disasters of the Roman republic to our religion, because it prohibits the offering of sacrifices to the gods. For this end I must recount all, or as many as may seem sufficient, of the disasters which befell that city and its subject provinces, before these sacrifices were prohibited; for all these disasters they would doubtless have attributed to us, if at that time our religion had shed its light upon them, and had prohibited their sacrifices. I must then go on to show what social well-being the true God, in whose hand are all kingdoms, vouchsafed to grant to them that their empire might increase. I must show why He did so, and how their false gods, instead of at all aiding them, greatly injured them by guile and deceit. And, lastly, I must meet those who, when on this point convinced and confuted by irrefragable proofs, endeavor to maintain that they worship the gods, not hoping for the present advantages of this life, but for those which are to be enjoyed after death. And this, if I am not mistaken, will be the most difficult part of my task, and will be worthy of the loftiest argument; for we must then enter the lists with the philosophers, but the most renowned, who in many points agree with ourselves, as regarding the immortality of the soul, and that the true God created the world, and by His providence rules all He has created. But as they differ from us on other points, we must not shrink from the task of exposing their errors, that, having refuted the gainsaying of the wicked with such ability as God may vouchsafe, we may assert the city of God, and true piety, and the worship of God, to which alone the promise of true and everlasting felicity is attached. Here, then, let us conclude, that we may enter on these subjects in a fresh book.

Of this part of the work, wherein we begin to explain the origin and end of the two cities.

The city of God we speak of is the same to which testimony is borne by that Scripture, which excels all the writings of all nations by its divine authority, and has brought under its influence all kinds of minds, and this not by a casual intellectual movement, but obviously by an express providential arrangement. For there it is written, "Glorious things are spoken of thee, O city of God." And in another psalm we read, "Great is the Lord, and greatly to be praised in the city of our God, in the mountain of His holiness, increasing the joy of the whole earth." And, a little after, in the same psalm, "As we have heard, so have we seen in the city of the Lord of hosts, in the city of our God. God has established it for ever." And in another, "There is a river the streams whereof shall make glad the city of our God, the holy place of the tabernacles of the Most High. God is in the midst of her, she shall not be moved." From these and similar testimonies, all of which it were tedious to cite, we have learned that there is a city of God, and its Founder has inspired us with a love which makes us covet its citizenship. To this Founder of the holy city the citizens of the earthly city prefer their own gods, not knowing that He is the God of gods, not of false, *i.e.*, of impious and proud gods, who, being deprived of His unchangeable and freely communicated light, and so reduced to a kind of poverty-stricken power, eagerly grasp at their own private privileges, and seek divine honors from their deluded subjects; but of the pious and holy gods, who are better pleased to submit themselves to one, than to subject many to themselves, and who would rather worship God than be worshipped as God. But to the enemies of this city we have replied in the ten preceding books, according to our ability and the help afforded by our Lord and King. Now, recognizing what is expected of me, and not unmindful of my promise, and relying, too, on the same succor, I will endeavor to treat of the origin, and progress, and deserved destinies of the two cities (the earthly and the heavenly, to wit), which, as we said, are in this present world comingled, and as it were entangled together. And, first, I will explain how the foundations of these two cities were originally laid, in the difference that arose among the angels.

That the disobedience of the first man would have plunged all men into the endless misery of the second death, had not the grace of god rescued many.

We have already stated in the preceding books that God, desiring not only that the human race might be able by their similarity of nature to associate with one another, but also that they might be bound together in harmony and peace by the ties of relationship, was pleased to derive all men from one individual, and created man with such a nature that the members of the race should not have died, had not the two first (of whom the one was created out of nothing, and the other out of him) merited this by their disobedience; for by them so great a sin was committed, that by it the human nature was altered for the worse, and was transmitted also to their posterity, liable to sin and subject to death. And the kingdom of death so reigned over men, that the deserved penalty of sin would have hurled all headlong even into the second death, of which there is no end, had not the undeserved grace of God saved some therefrom. And thus it has come to pass, that though there are very many and great nations all over the earth, whose rites and customs, speech, arms, and dress, are distinguished by marked differences, yet there are no more than two kinds of human society, which we may justly call two cities, according to the language of our Scriptures. The one consists of those who wish to live after the flesh, the other of those who wish to live after the spirit; and when they severally achieve what they wish, they live in peace, each after their kind.

Of the nature of the two cities, the earthly and the heavenly.

Accordingly, two cities have been formed by two loves: the earthly by the love of self, even to the contempt of God; the heavenly by the love of God, even to the contempt of self. The former, in a word, glories in itself, the latter in the Lord. For the one seeks glory from men; but the greatest glory of the other is God, the witness of conscience. The one lifts up its head in its own glory; the other says to its God, "Thou art my glory, and the lifter up of mine head." In the one, the princes and the nations it subdues are ruled by the love of ruling; in the other, the princes and the subjects serve one another in love, the latter obeying, while the former take thought for all. The one delights in its own strength, represented in the persons of its rulers; the other says to its God, "I will love Thee, O Lord, my strength." And therefore the wise men of the one city, living according to man, have sought for profit to their own bodies or souls, or both, and those who have known God "glorified Him not as God, neither were thankful, but became vain in their imaginations, and their foolish heart was darkened; professing themselves to be wise,"—that is, glorying in their own wisdom, and being possessed by pride,—"they became fools, and changed the glory of the incorruptible God into an image made like to corruptible man, and to birds, and four-footed beasts, and creeping things." For they were either leaders or followers of the people in adoring images, "and worshipped and served the creature more than the Creator, who is blessed for ever." But in the other city there is no human wisdom, but only godliness, which offers due worship to the true God, and looks for its reward in the society of the saints, of holy angels as well as holy men, "that God may be all in all."

Of the two lines of the human race which from first to last divide it.

Of the bliss of Paradise, of Paradise itself, and of the life of our first parents there, and of their sin and punishment, many have thought much, spoken much, written much. We ourselves, too, have spoken of these things in the foregoing books, and have written either what we read in the Holy Scriptures, or what we could reasonably deduce from them. And were we to enter into a more detailed investigation of these matters, an endless number of endless questions would arise, which would involve us in a larger work than the present occasion admits. We cannot be expected to find room for replying to every question that may be started by unoccupied and captious men, who are ever more ready to ask questions than capable of understanding the answer. Yet I trust we have already done justice to these great and difficult questions regarding the beginning of the world, or of the soul, or of the human race itself. This race we have distributed into two parts, the one consisting of those who live according to man, the other of those who live according to God. And these we also mystically call the two cities, or the two communities of men, of which the one is predestined to reign eternally with God, and the other to suffer eternal punishment with the devil. This, however, is their end, and of it we are to speak afterwards. At present, as we have said enough about their origin, whether among the angels, whose numbers we know not, or in the first two human beings, it seems suitable to attempt an account of their career, from the time when our two first parents began to propagate the race until all human generation shall cease. For this whole time or world-age, in which the dying give place and those who are born succeed, is the career of these two cities concerning which we treat.

Of these two first parents of the human race, then, Cain was the first-born, and he belonged to the city of men; after him was born Abel, who belonged to the city of God. For as in the individual the truth of the apostle's statement is discerned, "that is not first which is spiritual, but that which is natural, and afterward that which is spiritual," whence it comes to pass that each man, being derived from a condemned stock, is first of all born of Adam evil and carnal, and becomes good and spiritual only afterwards, when he is grafted into Christ by regeneration: so was it in the human race as a whole. When these two cities began to run their course by a series of deaths and births, the citizen of this world was the first-born, and after him the stranger in this world, the citizen of the city of God, predestinated by grace, elected by grace, by grace a stranger below, and by grace a citizen above. By grace,—for so far as regards himself he is sprung from the same mass, all of which is condemned in its origin: but God, like a potter (for this comparison is introduced by the apostle judiciously, and not without thought), of the same lump made one vessel to honor, another to dishonor. But first the vessel to dishonor was made, and after it another to honor. For in each individual, as I have already said, there is first of all that which is reprobate, that from which we must begin, but in which we need not necessarily remain; afterwards is that which is well-approved, to which we may by advancing attain, and in which, when we have reached it, we may abide. Not, indeed, that every wicked man shall be good, but that no one will be good who was not first of all wicked; but the sooner any one becomes a good man, the more speedily does he receive this title, and abolish the old name in the new. Accordingly, it is recorded of Cain that he built a city, but Abel, being a sojourner, built none. For the city of the saints is above, although here below it begets citizens, in whom it sojourns till the time of its reign arrives, when it shall gather together all in the day of the resurrection; and then shall the promised kingdom be given to them, in which they shall reign with their Prince, the King of the ages, time without end.

Of the conflict and peace of the earthly city.

But the earthly city, which shall not be everlasting (for it will no longer be a city when it has been committed to the extreme penalty), has its good in this world, and rejoices in it with such joy as such things can afford. But as this is not a good which can discharge its devotees of all distresses, this city is often divided against itself by litigations, wars, quarrels, and such victories as are either life-destroying or short-lived. For each part of it that arms against another part of it seeks to triumph over the nations through itself in bondage to vice. If, when it has conquered, it is inflated with pride, its victory is life-destroying; but if it turns its thoughts upon the common casualties of our mortal condition, and is rather anxious concerning the disasters that may befall it than elated with the successes already achieved, this victory, though of a higher kind, is still only short-lived; for it cannot abidingly rule over those whom it has victoriously subjugated. But the things which this city desires cannot justly be said to be evil, for it is itself, in its own kind, better than all other human good. For it desires earthly peace for the sake of enjoying earthly goods, and it makes war in order to attain to this peace; since, if it has conquered, and there remains no one to resist it, it enjoys a peace which it had not while there were opposing parties who contested for the enjoyment of those things which were too small to satisfy both. This peace is purchased by toilsome wars; it is obtained by what they style a glorious victory. Now, when victory remains with the party which had the juster cause, who hesitates to congratulate the victor, and style it a desirable peace? These things, then, are good things, and without doubt the gifts of God. But if they neglect the better things of the heavenly city, which are secured by eternal victory and peace never-ending, and so inordinately covet these present good things that they believe them to be the only desirable things, or love them better than those things which are believed to be better,—if this be so, then it is necessary that misery follow and ever increase.

Of the fratricidal act of the founder of the earthly city, and the corresponding crime of the founder of Rome.

Thus the founder of the earthly city was a fratricide. Overcome with envy, he slew his own brother, a citizen of the eternal city, and a sojourner on earth. So that we cannot be surprised that this first specimen, or, as the Greeks say, archetype of crime, should, long afterwards, find a corresponding crime at the foundation of that city which was destined to reign over so many nations, and be the head of this earthly city of which we speak. For of that city also, as one of their poets has mentioned, "the first walls were stained with a brother's blood," or, as Roman history records, Remus was slain by his brother Romulus. And thus there is no difference between the foundation of this city and of the earthly city, unless it be that Romulus and Remus were both citizens of the earthly city. Both desired to have the glory of founding the Roman republic, but both could not have as much glory as if one only claimed it; for he who wished to have the glory of ruling would certainly rule less if his power were shared by a living consort. In order, therefore, that the whole glory might be enjoyed by one, his consort was removed; and by this crime the empire was made larger indeed, but inferior, while otherwise it would have been less, but better. Now these brothers, Cain and Abel, were not both animated by the same earthly desires, nor did the murderer envy the other because he feared that, by both ruling, his own dominion would be curtailed,—for Abel was not solicitous to rule in that city which his brother built,—he was moved by that diabolical, envious hatred with which the evil regard the good, for no other reason than because they are good while themselves are evil. For the possession of goodness is by no means diminished by being shared with a partner either permanent or temporarily assumed; on the contrary, the possession of goodness is increased in proportion to the concord and charity of each of those who share it. In short, he who is unwilling to share this possession cannot have it; and he who is most willing to admit others to a share of it will have the greatest abundance to himself. The quarrel, then, between Romulus and Remus shows how the earthly city is divided against itself; that which fell out between Cain and Abel illustrated the hatred that subsists between the two cities, that of God and that of men. The wicked war with the wicked; the good also war with the wicked. But with the good, good men, or at least perfectly good men, cannot war; though, while only going on towards perfection, they war to this extent, that every good man resists others in those points in which he resists himself. And in each individual "the flesh lusteth against the spirit, and the spirit against the flesh." This spiritual lusting, therefore, can be at war with the carnal lust of another man; or carnal lust may be at war with the spiritual desires of another, in some such way as good and wicked men are at war; or, still more certainly, the carnal lusts of two men, good but not yet perfect, contend together, just as the wicked contend with the wicked, until the health of those who are under the treatment of grace attains final victory.

What produces peace, and what discord, between the heavenly and earthly cities.

But the families which do not live by faith seek their peace in the earthly advantages of this life; while the families which live by faith look for those eternal blessings which are promised, and use as pilgrims such advantages of time and of earth as do not fascinate and divert them from God, but rather aid them to endure with greater ease, and to keep down the number of those burdens of the corruptible body which weigh upon the soul. Thus the things necessary for this mortal life are used by both kinds of men and families alike, but each has its own peculiar and widely different aim in using them. The earthly city, which does not live by faith, seeks an earthly peace, and the end it proposes, in the well-ordered concord of civic obedience and rule, is the combination of men's wills to attain the things which are helpful to this life. The heavenly city, or rather the part of it which sojourns on earth and lives by faith, makes use of this peace only because it must, until this mortal condition which necessitates it shall pass away. Consequently, so long as it lives like a captive and a stranger in the earthly city, though it has already received the promise of redemption, and the gift of the Spirit as the earnest of it, it makes no scruple to obey the laws of the earthly city, whereby the things necessary for the maintenance of this mortal life are administered; and thus, as this life is common to both cities, so there is a harmony between them in regard to what belongs to it. But, as the earthly city has had some philosophers whose doctrine is condemned by the divine teaching, and who, being deceived either by their own conjectures or by demons, supposed that many gods must be invited to take an interest in human affairs, and assigned to each a separate function and a separate department,—to one the body, to another the soul; and in the body itself, to one the head, to another the neck, and each of the other members to one of the gods; and in like manner, in the soul, to one god the natural capacity was assigned, to another education, to another anger, to another lust; and so the various affairs of life were assigned,—cattle to one, corn to another, wine to another, oil to another, the woods to another, money to another, navigation to another, wars and victories to another, marriages to another, births and fecundity to another, and other things to other gods: and as the celestial city, on the other hand, knew that one God only was to be worshipped, and that to Him alone was due that service which the Greeks call λατρεια, and which can be given only to a god, it has come to pass that the two cities could not have common laws of religion, and that the heavenly city has been compelled in this matter to dissent, and to become obnoxious to those who think differently, and to stand the brunt of their anger and hatred and persecutions, except in so far as the minds of their enemies have been alarmed by the multitude of the Christians and quelled by the manifest protection of God accorded to them. This heavenly city, then, while it sojourns on earth, calls citizens out of all nations, and gathers together a society of pilgrims of all languages, not scrupling about diversities in the manners, laws, and institutions whereby earthly peace is secured and maintained, but recognizing that, however various these are, they all tend to one and the same end of earthly peace. It therefore is so far from rescinding and abolishing these diversities, that it even preserves and adopts them, so long only as no hindrance to the worship of the one supreme and true God is thus introduced. Even the heavenly city, therefore, while in its state of pilgrimage, avails itself of the peace of earth, and, so far as it can without injuring faith and godliness, desires and maintains a common agreement among men regarding the acquisition of the necessaries of life, and makes this earthly peace bear upon the peace of heaven; for this alone can be truly called and esteemed the peace of the reasonable creatures, consisting as it does in the perfectly ordered and harmonious enjoyment of God and of one another in God. When we shall have reached that peace, this mortal life shall give place to one that is eternal, and our body shall be no more this animal body which by its corruption weighs down the soul, but a spiritual body feeling no want, and in all its members subjected to the will. In its pilgrim state the heavenly city possesses this peace by faith; and by this faith it lives righteously when it refers to the attainment of that peace every good action towards God and man; for the life of the city is a social life.

Of the eternal felicity of the city of God, and of the Perpetual Sabbath.

How great shall be that felicity, which shall be tainted with no evil, which shall lack no good, and which shall afford leisure for the praises of God, who shall be all in all! For I know not what other employment there can be where no lassitude shall slacken activity, nor any want stimulate to labor. I am admonished also by the sacred song, in which I read or hear the words, "Blessed are they that dwell in Thy house, O Lord; they will be still praising Thee." All the members and organs of the incorruptible body, which now we see to be suited to various necessary uses, shall contribute to the praises of God; for in that life necessity shall have no place, but full, certain, secure, everlasting felicity. For all those parts of the bodily harmony, which are distributed through the whole body, within and without, and of which I have just been saying that they at present elude our observation, shall then be discerned; and, along with the other great and marvellous discoveries which shall then kindle rational minds in praise of the great Artificer, there shall be the enjoyment of a beauty which appeals to the reason. What power of movement such bodies shall possess, I have not the audacity rashly to define, as I have not the ability to conceive. Nevertheless I will say that in any case, both in motion and at rest, they shall be, as in their appearance, seemly; for into that state nothing which is unseemly shall be admitted. One thing is certain, the body shall forthwith be wherever the spirit wills, and the spirit shall will nothing which is unbecoming either to the spirit or to the body. True honor shall be there, for it shall be denied to none who is worthy, nor yielded to any unworthy; neither shall any unworthy person so much as sue for it, for none but the worthy shall be there. True peace shall be there, where no one shall suffer opposition either from himself or any other. God Himself, who is the Author of virtue, shall there be its reward; for, as there is nothing greater or better, He has promised Himself. What else was meant by His word through the prophet, "I will be your God, and ye shall be my people," than, I shall be their satisfaction, I shall be all that men honorably desire,—life, and health, and nourishment, and plenty, and glory, and honor, and peace, and all good things? This, too, is the right interpretation of the saying of the apostle, "That God may be all in all." He shall be the end of our desires who shall be seen without end, loved without cloy, praised without weariness. This outgoing of affection, this employment, shall certainly be, like eternal life itself, common to all. . . .

This Sabbath shall appear still more clearly if we

count the ages as days, in accordance with the periods of time defined in Scripture, for that period will be found to be the seventh. The first age, as the first day, extends from Adam to the deluge; the second from the deluge to Abraham, equalling the first, not in length of time, but in the number of generations, there being ten in each. From Abraham to the advent of Christ there are, as the evangelist Matthew calculates, three periods, in each of which are fourteen generations,—one period from Abraham to David, a second from David to the captivity, a third from the captivity to the birth of Christ in the flesh. There are thus five ages in all. The sixth is now passing, and cannot be measured by any number of generations, as it has been said, "It is not for you to know the times, which the Father hath put in His own power." After this period God shall rest as on the seventh day, when He shall give us (who shall be the seventh day) rest in Himself. But there is not now space to treat of these ages; suffice it to say that the seventh shall be our Sabbath, which shall be brought to a close, not by an evening, but by the Lord's day, as an eighth and eternal day, consecrated by the resurrection of Christ, and prefiguring the eternal repose not only of the spirit, but also of the body. There we shall rest and see, see and love, love and praise. This is what shall be in the end without end. For what other end do we propose to ourselves than to attain to the kingdom of which there is no end?

I think I have now, by God's help, discharged my obligation in writing this large work. Let those who think I have said too little, or those who think I have said too much, forgive me; and let those who think I have said just enough join me in giving thanks to God. Amen.

THE MIDDLE AGES

Feudalism

Feudalism was the major political system in central and western Europe and in England during the late Middle Ages. It developed out of necessity and experience and not from any basic theory. However a rather complicated system of homage, vassalage, rights and justice eventually developed which became so complicated it helped kill the system it was intended to perpetuate. Here are some selections of oaths of fealty and mutual duties of vassals and lords which help explain some basic premises of feudalism. The final selection demonstrates how the feudal law was upheld.

FEUDALISM

1. THE CEREMONY OF HOMAGE AND FEALTY

Homage and Fealty to Count of Flanders, A.D. 1127

Through the whole remaining part of the day those who had been previously enfeoffed by the most pious count Charles, did homage to the count, taking up now again their fiefs and offices and whatever they had before rightfully and legitimately obtained. On Thursday the seventh of April, homages were again made to the count being completed in the following order of faith and security.

First they did their homage thus. The count asked if he was willing to become completely his man, and the other replied, "I am willing;" and with clasped hands, surrounded by the hands of the count, they were bound together by a kiss. Secondly, he who had done homage gave his fealty to the representative of the count in these words, "I promise on my faith that I will in future be faithful to count William, and will observe my homage to him completely against all persons in good faith and without deceit," and thirdly, he took his oath to this upon the relics of the saints. Afterward, with a little rod which the count held in his hand, he gave investitures to all who by this agreement had given their security and homage and accompanying oath ...

2. MUTUAL DUTIES OF VASSALS AND LORDS

Letter from Bishop Fulbert of Chartres, A.D. 1020

To William most glorious duke of the Aquitanians, bishop Fulbert the favor of his prayers.

Asked to write something concerning the form of fealty, I have noted briefly for you on the authority of the books the things which follow. He who swears fealty to his lord ought always to have these six things in memory; what is harmless, safe, honorable, useful, easy, practicable. Harmless, that is to say that he should not be injurious to his lord in his body; safe, that he should not be injurious to him in his secrets or in the defences through which he is able to be secure; honorable, that he should not be injurious to him in his justice or in other matters that pertain to his honor; useful, that he should not be injurious to him in his possessions; easy or practicable, that that good which his lord is able to do easily, he make not difficult, nor that which is practicable he make impossible to him.

However, that the faithful vassal should avoid these injuries is proper, but not for this does he deserve his holding; for it is not sufficient to abstain from evil, unless what is good is done also. It remains, therefore, that in the same six things mentioned above he should faithfully counsel and aid his lord, if he wishes to be looked upon as worthy of his benefice and to be safe concerning the fealty which he has sworn.

The lord also ought to act toward his faithful vassal reciprocally in all these things. And if he does not do this he will be justly considered guilty of bad faith, just as the former, if he should be detected in the avoidance of or the doing of or the consenting to them, would be perfidious and perjured.

I would have written to you at greater length, if I had not been occupied with many other things, including the rebuilding of our city and church which was lately entirely consumed in a great fire;

Reprinted from Translations and Reprints from the *Original Sources of European History*, Vol. IV., No. 3 (1897). Published by the Department of History of the University of Pennsylvania.

from which loss though we could not for a while be diverted, yet by the hope of the comfort of God and of you we breathe again. . . .

3. FEUDAL JUSTICE

To every lord it is allowed to summon his man that he may be at right to him in his court; and even if he is resident at the most distant manor of that honor from which he holds, he shall go to the plea if his lord summons him. If his lord holds different fiefs the man of one honor is not compelled by law to go to another plea, unless the cause belongs to the other to which his lord has summoned him.

If a man holds from several lords and honors, however much he holds from others, he owes most and will be subject for justice to him of whom he is the liege man.

Every vassal owes to his lord fidelity concerning his life and members and earthly honor and keeping of his counsel in what is honorable and useful saving the faith of God and of the prince of the land. Theft, however, and treason and murder and whatever things are against the Lord and the catholic faith are to be required of or performed by no one; but faith shall be held to all lords, saving the faith of the earlier, and the more to the one of which he is the liege. And let permission be given him, if any of his men seek another lord for himself. . . .

4. CONDEMNATION BY A FEUDAL COURT

Raymond by the grace of God count of Toulouse, marquis of Provence, to the nobleman Arnold Atton, viscount of Lomagne, greeting.

Let it be known to your nobility, by the tenor of these presents what has been done in the matter of the complaints which we have made about you before the court of Agen; that you have not taken the trouble to keep or fulfil the agreements sworn by you to us, as is more fully contained in the instrument drawn up there, sealed with our seal by the public notary; and that you have refused contemptuously to appear before the said court for the purpose of doing justice; and otherwise committed multiplied and great delinquencies against us. As your faults have required, the aforesaid court of Agen has unanimously and concordantly pronounced sentence against you, and for these matters has condemned you to hand over and restore to us the chateau of Auvillars and all that land which you hold from us in fee, to be had and held by us by right of the obligation by which you have bound it to us for fulfilling and keeping the said agreements.

Likewise it has declared that we are to be put into possession of the said land and that it is to be handed over to us, on account of your contumacy, because you have not been willing to appear before the same court on the days which were assigned to you. Moreover, it has declared that you shall be held and required to restore the said land in whatsoever way we wish to receive it, with few or many, in peace or in anger, in our own person, by right of lordship. Likewise it has declared that you shall restore to us all the expenses which we have incurred or the court itself has incurred on those days which were assigned to you or because of those days, and has condemned you to repay these to us.

Moreover, it has declared that the nobleman Gerald d'Armagnac, whom you hold captive, you shall liberate, and deliver him free to us. We will, moreover, by right of our lordship that you liberate him.

We call, therefore, upon your discretion in this matter, strictly requiring you and commanding that you obey the aforesaid sentences in all things and fulfil them in all respects and in no way defer the fulfilment of them. For making the announcement, the demand and the reception of these things, we have appointed as our representatives our beloved and faithful noblemen Gaston de Gontaud and R. Bernard de Balencs, promising that whatever shall be done by them in the aforesaid matters, we will hold as settled and firm forever. In testimony of which we have caused these present letters to be corroborated by the strength of our seal. Similar letters, divided through the alphabet, for a perpetual memory of this matter we have caused to be retained with us. Given at Agen, the third of the Kalends of July, A.D. 1249.

St. Anselm of Canterbury

St. Anselm was born in northern Italy in 1033. While still in his teens, after the death of his mother, Anselm left Italy and in the next three years wandered to northern France where he became a monk in a monastery at Bec. At age 30 he was chosen to be the second Abbot of the monastery. In 1093 he was appointed Archbishop of Canterbury in the reign of William Rufus. During his stormy tenure of office, he was twice in exile because he supported papal claims over the claims of the king of England. Anselm was completely embroiled in one of the greatest issues of his age, the investiture controversy, which was finally resolved by a compromise in the year 1106. However, Anselm is known also for his great contribution to scholastic thought, claiming a place among the greatest thinkers of the western world. When Anselm died in 1109 at age 76, he left behind a reputation for sanctity and great learning. Here we have some excerpts dealing with Anselm's arguments concerning the existence of God, one of the major philosophical and theological problems not only of the Middle Ages, but of every age.

PROSLOGIUM

CHAPTER II

Truly there is a God, although the fool hath said in his heart
  There is no God.

And so, Lord, do thou, who dost give understanding to faith, give me, so far as thou knowest it to be profitable, to understand that thou art as we believe; and that thou art that which we believe. And, indeed, we believe that thou art a being than which nothing greater can be conceived. Or is there no such nature, since the fool hath said in his heart, there is no God? (Psalms xiv. I). But, at any rate, this very fool, when he hears of this being of which I speak—a being than which nothing greater can be conceived—understands what he hears, and what he understands is in his understanding; although he does not understand it to exist.

For, it is one thing for an object to be in the understanding, and another to understand that the object exists. When a painter first conceives of what he will afterwards perform, he has it in his understanding, but he does not yet understand it to be, because he has not yet performed it. But after he has made the painting, he both has it in his understanding, and he understands that it exists, because he has made it.

Hence, even the fool is convinced that something exists in the understanding, at least, than which nothing greater can be conceived. For, when he hears of this, he understands it. And whatever is understood, exists in the understanding. And assuredly that, than which nothing greater can be conceived, cannot exist in the understanding alone. For, suppose it exists in the understanding alone: then it can be conceived to exist in reality; which is greater.

Therefore, if that, than which nothing greater can be conceived, exists in the understanding alone, the very being, than which nothing greater can be conceived, is one, than which a greater can be conceived. But obviously this is impossible. Hence, there is no doubt that there exists a being, than which nothing greater can be conceived, and it exists both in the understanding and in reality....

CHAPTER III

God cannot be conceived not to exist.—God is that, than which nothing greater can be conceived.—That which can be conceived not to exist is not God.

And it assuredly exists so truly, that it cannot be conceived not to exist. For, it is possible to conceive of a being which cannot be conceived not to exist; and this is greater than one which can be

Reprinted from *Saint Anselm Basic Writings,* Second Ed. Translated by S. W. Deane with introduction by Charles Hartshorne. Open Court Publishing Company, LaSalle, Illinois, 1962. Used by permission.

conceived not to exist. Hence, if that, than which nothing greater can be conceived, can be conceived not to exist, it is not that, than which nothing greater can be conceived. But this is an irreconcilable contradiction. There is, then, so truly a being than which nothing greater can be conceived to exist, that it cannot even be conceived not to exist; and this being thou art, O Lord, our God.

So truly, therefore, dost thou exist, O Lord, my God, that thou canst not be conceived not to exist; and rightly. For, if a mind could conceive of a being better than thee, the creature would rise above the Creator; and this is most absurd. And, indeed, whatever else there is, except thee alone, can be conceived not to exist. To thee alone, therefore, it belongs to exist more truly than all other beings, and hence in a higher degree than all others. For, whatever else exists does not exist so truly, and hence in a less degree it belongs to it to exist. Why, then, has the fool said in his heart, there is no God (Psalms xiv. I), since it is so evident, to a rational mind, that thou dost exist in the highest degree of all? Why, except that he is dull and a fool?

CHAPTER IV

How the fool has said in his heart what cannot be conceived.—A thing may be conceived in two ways: (1) when the word signifying it is conceived; (2) when the thing itself is understood. As far as the word goes, God can be conceived not to exist; in reality he cannot.

But how has the fool said in his heart what he could not conceive; or how is it that he could not conceive what he said in his heart? since it is the same to say in the heart, and to conceive.

But, if really, nay, since really, he both conceived, because he said in his heart; and did not say in his heart, because he could not conceive; there is more than one way in which a thing is said in the heart or conceived. For, in one sense, an object is conceived, when the word signifying it is conceived; and in another, when the very entity, which the object is, is understood.

In the former sense, then, God can be conceived not to exist; but in the latter, not at all. For no one who understands what fire and water are can conceive fire to be water, in accordance with the nature of the facts themselves, although this is possible according to the words. So, then, no one who understands what God is can conceive that God does not exist; although he says these words in his heart, either without any or with some foreign, signification. For, God is that than which a greater cannot be conceived. And he who thoroughly understands this, assuredly understands that this being so truly exists, that not even in concept can it be non-existent. Therefore, he who understands that God so exists, cannot conceive that he does not exist.

I Thank thee, gracious Lord, I thank thee; because what I formerly believed by thy bounty, I now so understand by thine illumination, that if I were unwilling to believe that thou dost exist, I should not be able not to understand this to be true.

Peter Abelard

Peter Abelard (1079-1142), a brilliant theologian and philosopher, was one of the most important thinkers of the Middle Ages. An eloquent and provocative teacher, he established Paris as the great European center of learning in the twelfth century. His greatest contribution to medieval thought was his method, with its emphasis on methodical doubt and rational inquiry. This is most evident in his famous *Sic et Non*, in which he exposed theological issues to rational and logical examination, thus becoming an important figure in the development of the scholastic method. He selected one hundred and fifty-eight points of theology, and supplied arguments for and against each proposition from the greatest Church authorities. The following is a summarized segment from *Sic et Non*, plus several examples of the questions Abelard dealt with in the treatise.

SIC ET NON

There are many seeming contradictions and even obscurities in the innumerable writings of the church fathers. Our respect for their authority should not stand in the way of an effort on our part to come at the truth. The obscurity and contradictions in ancient writings may be explained upon many grounds, and may be discussed without impugning the good faith and insight of the fathers. A writer may use different terms to mean the same thing, in order to avoid a monotonous repetition of the same word. Common, vague words may be employed in order that the common people may understand; and sometimes a writer sacrifices perfect accuracy in the interest of a clear general statement. Poetical, figurative language is often obscure and vague.

Not infrequently apocryphal works are attributed to the saints. Then, even the best authors often introduce the erroneous views of others and leave the reader to distinguish between the true and the false. Sometimes, as Augustine confesses in his own case, the fathers ventured to rely upon the opinions of others.

Doubtless the fathers might err; even Peter, the prince of the apostles, fell into error; what wonder that the saints do not always show themselves inspired? The fathers did not themselves believe that they, or their companions, were always right. Augustine found himself mistaken in some cases and did not hesitate to retract his errors. He warns his admirers not to look upon his letters as they would upon the Scriptures, but to accept only those things which, upon examination, they find to be true.

All writings belonging to this class are to be read with full freedom to criticize, and with no obligation to accept unquestioningly; otherwise the way would be blocked to all discussion, and posterity be deprived of the excellent intellectual exercise of debating difficult questions of language and presentation. But an explicit exception must be made in the case of the Old and New Testaments. In the Scriptures, when anything strikes us as absurd, we may not say that the writer erred, but that the scribe made a blunder in copying the manuscripts, or that there is an error in interpretation or that the passage is not understood. The fathers make a very careful distinction between the Scriptures and later works. They advocate a discriminating, not to say suspicious, use of the writings of their own contemporaries.

In view of these considerations, I have ventured to bring together various dicta of the holy fathers, as they came to mind, and to formulate certain questions which were suggested by the seeming contradictions in the statements. These questions ought to serve to excite tender readers to a zealous inquiry into truth and so sharpen their wits. The master key of knowledge is, indeed, a persistent and frequent questioning. Aristotle, the most clear-sighted of all the philosophers, was desirous above all things else to arouse this questioning spirit, for in his *Categories* he exhorts a student as follows: "It may well be difficult to reach a positive conclusion in these matters unless they be frequently discussed. It is by no means fruitless to be doubtful on particular points." By doubting we come to examine, and by examining we reach the truth.

. . . .

Should human faith be based upon reason, or no?
Is God one, or no?
Is God a substance, or no?
Does the first Psalm refer to Christ, or no?
Is sin pleasing to God, or no?
Is God the author of evil, or no?
Is God all-powerful, or no?
Can God be resisted, or no?
Has God free will, or no?
Was the first man persuaded to sin by the devil, or no?
Was Adam saved, or no?
Did all the apostles have wives except John, or no?
Are the flesh and blood of Christ in very truth and essence present in the sacrament of the altar, or no?
Do we sometimes sin unwillingly, or no?
Does God punish the same sin both here and in the future, or no?
Is it worse to sin openly than secretly, or no?

From *Readings in European History,* Vol. I by James Harvey Robinson, 1904, Ginn and Company, Boston.

University Life

Universities first began to appear in Europe in the middle twelfth century. Although in many ways the life of the medieval student differed greatly from that of the modern student, there are some striking similarities. The following poems, written by medieval university students, give us some insight into their lives and interests.

THE CONFESSION OF GOLIAS

BOILING in my spirit's veins
   With fierce indignation,
From my bitterness of soul
   Springs self-revelation:
Framed am I of flimsy stuff,
   Fit for levitation,
Like a thin leaf which the wind
   Scatters from its station.

While it is the wise man's part
   With deliberation
On a rock to base his heart's
   Permanent foundation,
With a running river I
   Find my just equation,
Which beneath the self-same sky
   Hath no habitation.

Carried am I like a ship
   Left without a sailor,
Like a bird that through the air
   Flies where tempests hale her;
Chains and fetters hold me not,
   Naught avails a jailer;
Still I find my fellows out
   Toper, gamester, railer.

To my mind all gravity
   Is a grave subjection;
Sweeter far than honey are
   Jokes and free affection.
All that Venus bids me do,
   Do I with erection,
For she ne'er in heart of man
   Dwelt with dull dejection.

Down the broad road do I run,
   As the way of youth is;
Snare myself in sin, and ne'er
   Think where faith and truth is;

Eager far for pleasure more
   Than soul's health, the sooth's is,
For this flesh of mine I care,
   Seek not ruth where ruth is.

Prelate, most discreet of priests,
   Grant me absolution!
Dear's the death whereof I die,
   Sweet my dissolution;
For my heart is wounded by
   Beauty's soft suffusion;
All the girls I come not nigh,
   Mine are in illusion.

'Tis most arduous to make
   Nature's self surrender;
Seeing girls, to blush and be
   Purity's defender!
We young men our longings ne'er
   Shall to stern law render,
Or preserve our fancies from
   Bodies smooth and tender.

Who, when into fire he falls,
   Keeps himself from burning?
Who within Pavia's walls
   Fame of chaste is earning?
Venus with her finger calls
   Youths at every turning,
Snares them with her eyes, and thralls
   With her amorous yearning.

If you brought Hippolitus
   To Pavia Sunday,
He'd not be Hippolitus
   On the following Monday;
Venus there keeps holiday
   Every day as one day;

From *Wine, Women, and Song: Medieval Latin Students' Songs Now First Translated into English Verse with an Essay by John Addington Symonds,* Chatto and Winders Publishers, London, 1907.

THE MIDDLE AGES

'Mid these towers in no tower dwells
    Venus Verecunda.

In the second place I own
    To the vice of gaming:
Cold indeed outside I seem,
    Yet my soul is flaming:
But when once the dice-box hath
    Stripped me to my shaming,
Make I songs and verses fit
    For the world's acclaiming.

In the third place, I will speak
    Of the tavern's pleasure;
For I never found nor find
    There the least displeasure;
Nor shall find it till I greet
    Angels without measure,
Singing requiems for the souls
    In eternal leisure.

In the public-house to die
    Is my resolution;
Let wine to my lips be nigh
    At life's dissolution:
That will make the angels cry,
    With glad elocution,
"Grant this toper, God on high,
    Grace and absolution!"

With the cup the soul lights up,
    Inspirations flicker;
Nectar lifts the soul on high
    With its heavenly ichor:
To my lips a sounder taste
    Hath the tavern's liquor
Than the wine a village clerk
    Waters for the vicar.

Nature gives to every man
    Some gift serviceable;
Write I never could nor can
    Hungry at the table;
Fasting, any stripling to
    Vanquish me is able;
Hunger, thirst, I liken to
    Death that ends the fable.

Nature gives to every man
    Gifts as she is willing;
I compose my verses when
    Good wine I am swilling,
Wine the best for jolly guest
    Jolly hosts are filling;
From such wine rare fancies fine
    Flow like dews distilling.

Such my verse is wont to be
    As the wine I swallow;
No ripe thoughts enliven me
    While my stomach's hollow;
Hungry wits on hungry lips
    Like a shadow follow,
But when once I'm in my cups,
    I can beat Apollo.

Never to my spirit yet
    Flew poetic vision
Until first my belly had
    Plentiful provision;
Let but Bacchus in the brain
    Take a strong position,
Then comes Phoebus flowing in
    With a fine precision.

There are poets, worthy men,
    Shrink from public places,
And in lurking-hole or den
    Hide their pallid faces;
There they study, sweat, and woo
    Pallas and the Graces,
But bring nothing forth to view
    Worth the girls' embraces.

Fasting, thirsting, toil the bards,
    Swift years flying o're them;
Shun the strife of open life,
    Tumults of the forum;
They, to sing some deathless thing,
    Lest the world ignore them,
Die the death, expend their breath,
    Drowned in dull decorum.

Lo! my frailties I've betrayed,
    Shown you every token,
Told you what your servitors
    Have against me spoken;
But of those men each and all
    Leave their sins unspoken,
Though they play, enjoy to-day,
    Scorn their pledges broken.

Now within the audience-room
    Of this blessed prelate,
Sent to hunt out vice, and from
    Hearts of men expel it;
Let him rise, nor spare the bard,
    Cast at him a pellet:
He whose heart knows not crime's smart,
    Show my sin and tell it!

I have uttered openly
    All I knew that shamed me,

And have spued the poison forth
   That so long defamed me;
Of my old ways I repent,
   Now life hath reclaimed me;
God beholds the heart—'twas man
   Viewed the face and blamed me.

Goodness now hath won my love,
   I am wroth with vices;
Made a new man in my mind,
   Lo, my soul arises!
Like a babe new milk I drink—
   Milk for me suffices,
Lest my heart should longer be
   Filled with vain devices.

Thou Elect of fair Cologne,
   Listen to my pleading!
Spurn not thou the penitent;
   See, his heart is bleeding!
Give me penance! what is due
   For my faults exceeding
I will bear with willing cheer,
   All thy precepts heeding.

Lo, the lion, king of beasts,
   Spares the meek and lowly;
Toward submissive creatures he
   Tames his anger wholly.
Do the like, ye powers of earth,
   Temporal and holy!
Bitterness is more than's right
   When 'tis bitter solely.

PHYLLIS

THINK no evil, have no fear,
   If I play with Phyllis;
I am but the guardian dear
   Of her girlhood's lilies,
Lest too soon her bloom should swoon
   Like spring's daffodillies.

All I care for is to play,
   Gaze upon my treasure,
Now and then to touch her hand,
   Kiss in modest measure;
But the fifth act of love's game,
   Dream not of that pleasure!

For to touch the bloom of youth
   Spoils its frail complexion;
Let the young grape gently grow
   Till it reach perfection;
Hope within my heart doth glow
   Of the girl's affection.

Sweet above all sweets that are
   Tis to play with Phyllis;
For her thoughts are white as snow,
   In her heart no ill is;
And the kisses that she gives
   Sweeter are than lilies.

Love leads after him the gods
   Bound in pliant traces;
Harsh and stubborn hearts he bends,
   Breaks with blows of maces;
Nay, the unicorn is tamed
   By a girl's embraces.

Love leads after him the gods,
   Juniper with Juno;
To his waxen measure treads
   Masterful Neptune O!
Pluto stern to souls below
   Melts to this one tune O!

Whatsoe'er the rest may do,
   Let us then be playing:
Take the pastime that is due
   While we're yet a-Maying;
I am young and young are you;
   'Tis the time for playing.

BACCHIC FRENZY

TOPERS in and out of season!
'Tis not thirst but better reason
   Bids you tope on steadily!—
   Pass the wine-cup, let it be
   Filled and filled for bout on bout!
      Never sleep!
   Racy jest and song flash out!
      Spirits leap!

Those who cannot drink their rations,
Go, begone from these ovations!
   Here's no place for bashful boys;
   Like the plague, they spoil out joys.—
   Bashful eyes bring rustic cheer
      When we're drunk,
   And a blush betrays a drear
      Want of spunk.

If there's here a fellow lurking
Who his proper share is shirking,
   Let the door to him be shown,
   From our crew we'll have him thrown;—
   He's more desolate than death,
      Mixed with us;
   Let him go and end his breath!
      Better thus!

THE MIDDLE AGES

When your heart is set on drinking,
Drink on without stay or thinking,
   Till you cannot stand up straight,
   Nor one word articulate!—
But herewith I pledge to you
     This fair health:
May the glass no mischief do,
     Bring you wealth!

Wed not you the god and goddess,
For the god doth scorn the goddess;
   He whose name is Liber, he
   Glories in his liberty.
All her virtue in the cup

     Runs to waste,
And wine wedded yieldeth up
     Strength and taste.

Since she is the queen of ocean,
Goddess she may claim devotion:
   But she is no mate to kiss
   His superior holiness.
Bacchus never deigned to be
     Watered, he!
Liber never bore to be
     Christened, he!

St. Thomas Aquinas

St. Thomas Aquinas (1225-1274) was the leading philosopher and theologian of medieval scholasticism. Born of a noble family in Italy, Thomas quite early entered the service of the church, becoming a Dominican monk at the age of 19. After he had attended the University in Naples where he came into contact with the philosophy of Averroes, he was sent to the University of Paris. His teacher there was Albert the Great who recognized the intelligence of his student, but his fellow students looked upon him as rather stupid; in fact, his nickname for a time was "the dumb ox." Thomas, however, soon amazed everyone with his brilliance, quite early evidencing his preference for Aristotelian philosophy. Thomas's greatest work was the *Summa Theologica.* In this work Thomas raised 631 questions, then answered each one of them by quoting from various authorities, and then dealt with almost 10,000 objections to his conclusions. When he died in 1274 the manuscript was as yet uncompleted but it was finished by his teacher, St. Albert. Today Thomas is known as the official theologian of the church, but in his own day he was not accepted by all medieval theologians. In fact, he was looked upon as a radical, a rebel and an innovator. Nevertheless, he was canonized in 1323 and in 1567 was made a Doctor of the Church. Then in 1879 Pope Leo XIII ordered all Catholic schools to teach Thomas's position as the true philosophy. Thomas's great contribution was his attempt to reconcile reason and faith. He felt it was possible to support the essential doctrines of Christian theology by reason. In the selections here from the *Summa Theologica,* the wide range of the thought of St. Thomas is evident. The one selection on usury was an attempt to bring the church into line with the changes in the economic situation of his day. Then his five proofs on the existence of God demonstrate his attempt to bring reason to bear on the great truths of Christianity. Thomas saw man as a creature of great dignity; indeed, in Thomism (the philosophy of St. Thomas) man is the logical center of the universe. The synthesis of theology and philosophy attempted by St. Thomas is probably the greatest work ever done for the church by any one man. "There have probably been greater minds among . . . theologians, but there has been no man who came nearer to writing a synthesis of Christian belief."

SUMMA THEOLOGICA

QUESTION LXXVIII

Of the Sin of Usury That Is Committed in Loans

ARTICLE I.—*Is it a sin to take usury for the lending of money?*

R. To take usury for the lending of money is in itself unjust, because it is a case of selling what is non-existent; and that is manifestly the setting up of an inequality contrary to justice. In evidence of this we must observe that there are certain things, the use of which is the consumption of the thing; as we consume wine by using it to drink, and we consume wheat by using it for food. Hence in such things the use of the thing ought not to be reckoned apart from the thing itself; but whosoever has the use granted to him, has thereby granted to him the thing; and therefore in such things lending means the transference of ownership. If therefore any vendor wanted to make two separate sales, one of the wine and the other of the use of the wine, he would be selling the same thing twice over, or selling the non-existent: hence clearly he would be committing the sin of injustice. And in like manner he commits injustice, who lends wine or wheat, asking a double recompense to be given him, one a return of an equal commodity, another a price for the use of the commodity, which price of use is called *usury*. But there are things the use of which is not the consuming of the thing: thus the use of a house is inhabiting it, not destroying it. In such things ownership and use may be made the matter of separate grants. Thus one may grant to another the ownership of a house, reserving to himself the use of it for a time; or grant the use and reserve the ownership. And therefore a man may lawfully take a price for the use of a house, and besides demand back the house which he has lent, as we see in the hiring and letting of houses. Now according to the Philosopher, money was invented principally for the effecting of exchanges; and thus the proper and principal use of money is the consumption or disbursal of it, according as it is expended on exchanges.

§ 2. To the text, "Thou shalt not lend to thy brother money to usury, nor corn, nor any other thing, but to the stranger,"[1] it is to be said that from its being prohibited to the Jews to take usury from their brethren, that is, from other Jews, we are to understand that taking usury of any man is simply evil; for we ought to regard every man as a neighbour and a brother, especially in the Gospel state, to which all are called. As for their taking usury of strangers, that was not granted them as a thing lawful, but permitted for the avoidance of a greater evil, that their avarice might not lead them to take usury of Jews, the worshippers of God.

§ 5. To the objection, that a man may take a price for what he is not bound to do; but a man with money is not in every case bound to lend it,—it is to be said that he who is not bound to lend may receive compensation for what he has done in lending, but ought not to exact more. But compensation is given him according to the equality of justice, if the exact amount is returned to him that he has lent. Hence if he exacts more for the use of a thing that has no other use than the consumption of the substance, he exacts a price for that which has no existence, and so the exaction is unjust.

§ 6. The principal use of silver vessels is not the consumption of them; and so the use of them can be sold while the ownership is reserved. But the principal use of silver money is the disbursal of the money on exchanges. Hence it is not lawful to sell the use of it, while at the same time claiming to have back the original sum lent. There may be a secondary use of money, for show, or to pledge, and such a use of money a man may lawfully sell.

§ 7. To the objection, that any one may lawfully take a thing that the owner voluntarily hands over to him; and that the borrower voluntarily hands over the usury,—it is to be said that he who gives usury does not give it as an absolutely voluntary payment, but under some stress of necessity, inasmuch as he needs to borrow money, which the possessor will not lend without usury.

ARTICLE VI.—*Is there any case in which it is lawful to kill an innocent man?*

R. A man may be looked at in two ways, in himself, and in reference to some other being. Looked at in himself, it is lawful to slay no man; because in every man, even in the sinner, we ought to love the nature which God has made, and which is destroyed by killing. But the slaying of the sinner becomes lawful in reference to the good of the community that is destroyed by sin. On the other hand, the life of the just makes for the preservation and promotion of the good of the community, seeing that they are the chiefer part of the people. And therefore it is nowise lawful to slay the innocent.

§ 3. If a judge knows that a party is innocent, whose guilt is being evidenced by false witnesses,

From *Aquinas Ethicus* or *The Moral Teaching of St. Thomas*, Vol. II with notes by Joseph Rickaby, S. J. London, Burns and Oates, Limited, Granville Mansions W., 1892.

1. Deut. xxiii. 19,20.

he ought to examine the witnesses more diligently, to find occasion of discharging the unoffending party, as Daniel did. If he cannot do that, he ought to leave him to the judgment of a higher court. If he cannot do that either, he does not sin by passing sentence according to the evidence before him; because it is not he that slays the innocent, but they who assert him to be guilty. But whoever is charged to carry out the sentence of a judge that condemns the innocent, ought not to obey, if the sentence contains intolerable error; otherwise the executioners who put the martyrs to death would be excused. but if the sentence does not involve manifest injustice, he does not sin in doing as he is bid: because it is not his business to discuss the sentence of his superior; nor is it he that slays the innocent, but the judge whose officer he is.

ARTICLE VII.—*Is it lawful to slay a man in self-defence?*

R. There is nothing to hinder one act having two effects, of which one only is in the intention of the agent, while the other is beside his intention. But moral acts receive their species from what is intended, not from what is beside the intention, as that is accidental. From the act therefore of one defending himself a twofold effect may follow, one the preservation of his own life, the other the killing of the aggressor. Now such an act, in so far as the preservation of the doer's own life is intended, has no taint of evil about it, seeing that it is natural to everything to preserve itself in being as much as it can. Nevertheless, an act coming of a good intention may be rendered unlawful, if it be not in proportion to the end in view. And therefore, if any one uses greater violence than is necessary for the defence of his life, it will be unlawful. But if he repels the violence in a moderate way, it will be a lawful defence: for according to the Civil and Canon Laws it is allowable "to repel force by force with the moderation of a blameless defence." Nor is it necessary to salvation for a man to omit the act of moderate defence in order to avoid the killing of another; because man is more bound to take thought for his own life than for the life of his neighbour. But because to kill a man is not allowable except by act of public authority for the common good, it is unlawful for a man to intend to kill another man in order to defend himself, unless he be one who has public authority, who intending to kill a man in order to his own defence, refers this to the public good, as does a soldier fighting against the enemy, or an officer of justice fighting against robbers, though these two sin if they are moved by lust of private vengeance.

ARTICLE VIII.—*Is the guilt of homicide incurred by killing a man accidentally?*

R. According to the Philosopher, chance is a cause that acts beside the intention. And therefore the events of chance, absolutely speaking, are not intended nor voluntary. And because every sin is voluntary, consequently the events of chance, as such, are not sins. Sometimes however what is not actually and in itself willed or intended, is willed or intended incidentally, inasmuch as what removes an obstacle is called an *incidental cause*. Hence he who does not remove the conditions from which homicide follows, supposing it to be his duty to remove them, incurs in a manner the guilt of wilful homicide; and this in two ways: in one way when, being engaged upon unlawful actions which he ought to avoid, he incurs homicide; in another way when he does not observe due precaution. And therefore, according to the Civil and Canon Laws, if one is engaged upon a lawful action, taking due care therein, and homicide follows from it, he does not incur the guilt of homicide. But if he is engaged upon an unlawful one, neglects to observe due precaution therein, he does not escape the charge of homicide, if the death of a man follows from his doing.

QUESTION XLVI

Of Stupidity

ARTICLE II.—*Is stupidity a sin?*

R. Stupidity implies a dulness of perception in judging, particularly about the Highest Cause, the Last End and Sovereign Good. This may come of natural incapacity, and that is not a sin. Or it may come of man burying his mind so deep in earthly things as to render his perceptions unfit to grasp the things of God, according to the text: "The sensual man perceiveth not these things that are of the Spirit of God;" and such stupidity is a sin.

§ 2. Though no one wishes to be stupid, still people do wish for what leads to stupidity, by withdrawing their thoughts from things spiritual and burying them in things of earth. So it is also with other sins: for the lustful man wants the pleasure, to which the sin is attached, though he does not absolutely wish for the sin; for he would like to enjoy the pleasure without the sin.

From *Aquinas Ethicus* or *The Moral Teaching of St. Thomas* with notes by Joseph Rickaby, S. J. London: Burns and Oates, Limited, Granville Mansions W., 1892.

ST. THOMAS AQUINAS: ON THE EXISTENCE OF GOD[1]

The existence of God can be proved in five ways.

The first and more manifest way is the argument from motion. It is certain and evident to our senses that some things are in motion. Whatever is in motion is moved by another, for nothing can be in motion except it have a potentiality for that towards which it is being moved; whereas a thing moves inasmuch as it is in act. By "motion" we mean nothing else than the reduction of something from a state of potentiality into a state of actuality. Nothing, however, can be reduced from a state of potentiality into a state of actuality, unless by something already in a state of actuality. Thus that which is actually hot as fire, makes wood, which is potentially hot, to be actually hot, and thereby moves and changes it. It is not possible that the same thing should be at once in a state of actuality and potentiality from the same point of view, but only from different points of view. What is actually hot cannot simultaneously be only potentially hot; still, it is simultaneously potentially cold. It is therefore impossible that from the same point of view and in the same way anything should be both moved and mover, or that it should move itself. Therefore, whatever is in motion must be put in motion by another, and that by another again. But this cannot go on to infinity, because then there would be no first mover; as the staff only moves because it is put in motion by the hand. Therefore it is necessary to arrive at a First Mover, put in motion by no other; and this everyone understands to be God.

The second way is from the formality of efficient causation. In the world of sense we find there is an order of efficient causation. There is no case known (neither is it, indeed, possible) in which a thing is found to be the efficient cause of itself; for so it would be prior to itself, which is impossible. In efficient causes it is not possible to go on to infinity, because in all efficient causes following in order, the first is the cause of the intermediate cause, and the intermediate is the cause of the ultimate cause, whether the intermediate cause be several, or one only. To take away the cause is to take away the effect. Therefore, if there be no first cause among efficient causes, there will be no ultimate cause, nor any intermediate. If in efficient causes it is possible to go on to infinity, there will be no first efficient cause, neither will there be an ultimate effect, nor any intermediate efficient causes; all of which is plainly false. Therefore it is necessary to put forward a First Efficient Cause, to which everyone gives the name of God.

The third way is taken from possibility and necessity, and runs thus. We find in nature things that could either exist or not exist, since they are found to be generated, and to corrupt; and, consequently, they can exist, and then not exist. It is impossible for these always to exist, for that which can one day cease to exist must at some time have not existed. Therefore, if everything could cease to exist, then at one time there could have been nothing in existence. If this were true, even now there would be nothing in existence, because that which does not exist only begins to exist by something already existing. Therefore, if at one time nothing was in existence, it would have been impossible for anything to have begun to exist; and thus even now nothing would be in existence — which is absurd. Therefore, not all beings are merely possible, but there must exist something the existence of which is necessary. Every necessary thing either has its necessity caused by another, or not. It is impossible to go on to infinity in necessary things which have their necessity caused by another, as has been already proved in regard to efficient causes. Therefore we cannot but postulate the existence of some being having of itself its own necessity, and not receiving it from another, but rather causing in others their necessity. This all men speak of as God.

The fourth way is taken from the gradation to be found in things. Among beings there are some more and some less good, true, noble, and the like. But "more" and "less" are predicated of different things, according as they resemble in their different ways something which is in the degree of "most," as a thing is said to be hotter according as it more nearly resembles that which is hottest; so that there is something which is truest, something best, something noblest, and consequently, something which is uttermost being; for the truer things are, the more truly they exist. What is most complete in any genus is the cause of all in that genus; as fire, which is the most complete form of heat, is the cause whereby all things are made hot. Therefore, there must also be something which is to all beings the cause of their being, goodness, and every other perfection; and this we call God.

The fifth way is taken from the governance of the world; for we see that things which lack intelligence, such as natural bodies, act for some purpose, which fact is evident from their acting always, or nearly always, in the same way, so as to obtain the best result. Hence it is plain that not fortuitously, but designedly, do they achieve their purpose. Whatever lacks intelligence cannot fulfil some purpose unless it be directed by some being endowed with intelligence and knowledge; as the arrow is shot to its mark by the archer. Therefore some intelligent being exists by whom all natural things are ordained towards a definite purpose; and this being we call God.

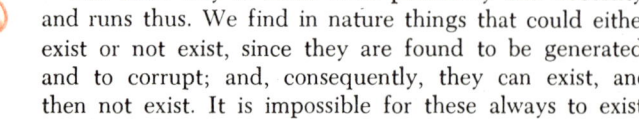

---

[1] From the *Summa Theologica* of St. Thomas Aquinas, tr. by the Fathers of the English Domincan Province (New York, 1911), Part I, First Number Q. II, 19-27. Reprinted by permission of Benziger Brothers, Inc.

William of Ockham

William of Ockham (c. 1300-1349) was an English Franciscan who studied at Oxford and taught in Paris. From 1324 until his death he was in trouble with the papacy. In 1328 he accepted the protection of Louis of Bavaria, then at odds with the papacy, and for the rest of his life he vigorously defended the independence of the state from the Church. It was Ockham who sounded the death note for medieval scholasticism. Dissatisfied with the Thomist synthesis of faith and reason, he denied that theological truth could be demonstrated by human reason. This resulted directly from his position on universals. The realists, such as Anselm and Thomas Aquinas, had argued that universals or concepts have a real existence independent from the particular things which appear to the senses. Ockham, however, was a nominalist, claiming that universals are simply names or symbols which exist only as convenient labels created by men. They have no independent existence. Men can know only what they experience through their senses, and reality can only be found in individual things. The following selection is Ockham's argument on universals.

EPISTEMOLOGICAL PROBLEMS

[A universal is an act of the intellect]

There could be another opinion,[1] according to which a concept is the same as the act of knowing. This opinion appears to me to be the more probable one among all the opinions which assume that these concepts really exist in the soul as a subject, like true qualities of the soul; so I shall first explain this opinion in its more probable form.

I maintain, then, that somebody wishing to hold this opinion may assume that the intellect apprehending a singular thing performs within itself a cognition of this singular only. This cognition is called a state of mind, and it is capable of standing for this singular thing by its very nature. Hence, just as the spoken work 'Socrates' stands by convention for the thing it signifies, so that one who hears this utterance, 'Socrates is running', does not conceive that this word, 'Socrates', which he hears, is running, but rather that the thing signified by this word is running; so likewise one who knew or understood that something was affirmatively predicated of this cognition of a singular thing would not think that the cognition was such and such, but would conceive that the thing to which the cognition refers is such and such. Hence, just as the spoken word stands by convention for a thing, so the act of intellect, by its very nature, and without any convention, stands for the thing to which it refers.

Beside this intellectual grasp of a singular thing the intellect also forms other acts which do not refer more to one thing than to another. For instance, just as the spoken word 'man' does not signify Socrates more than Plato, and hence does not stand more for Socrates than Plato, so it would be with an act of intellect which does not relate to Socrates any more than to Plato or any other man. And in like manner there would be also a knowledge whereby this animal is not more known than that animal; and so with other notions.

To sum up: The mind's own intellectual acts are called states of mind. By their nature they stand for the actual things outside the mind or for other things in the mind, just as the spoken words stand for them by convention....

... By such a common or confused intellection, singular things outside the mind are known. For instance, to say that we have a confused intellection of man, means that we have a cognition by which we do not understand one man rather than another, but that by such a cognition we have cognition of a man rather than a donkey. And this amounts to saying that such a cognition, by some kind of assimilation, bears a greater resemblance to a donkey, but does not resemble one man rather than another. In consequence of the aforesaid, it seems necessary to say that an infinity of objects can be known by such a confused cognition. Still this seems no more untenable than that an infinity of objects can be liked or desired by the same act of liking or desiring. Yet the latter does not seem

From *Ockham, Philosophical Writings* by Philotheus Bochner, O.F.M., Thomas Nelson and Sons LTD, Publishers, 1957. Used by permission.

1. [Different from those opinions concerning the nature of universals previously criticized by Ockham.]

to be untenable. For a man may like all the parts of a continuous thing, which are infinite in number, or he may desire that all these parts remain in existence. Now in such a case, what was desired would simply be a part of the continuous thing, but not one part rather than another; therefore all parts must be desired; these parts, however, are infinite in number. Likewise, somebody can desire the existence of all men who can exist. Now these are infinite in number, since an infinity of men can be generated.

And so it could be said that one and the same cognition refers to an infinite number of singulars without being a cognition proper to any one of them, and this is so because of some specific likeness between these individuals that does not exist between others. However, no singular thing can be distinguished from another by such a cognition.

Dante

Dante Alighieri was born in Florence in 1265 and died in 1321 in Ravenna, while in exile from his beloved city of Florence. Although little is known of his early life, we know that he studied the literature and philosophy of his time and that he admired the Greek and Roman writers, especially Vergil. He was also engaged in the political life of Florence and it was because of this activity that, in 1302, Dante was sent into exile.

One strange aspect of Dante's early life is his relationship with a woman named Beatrice. It appears that Dante fell in love with her the first time he saw her when he was nine years old, and from all we can gather he saw her only two times before she died. Yet to Dante this woman was the object of what we know as chivalric love, which was most important in the Middle Ages. It is Beatrice who sends Vergil to conduct Dante through the Inferno and it is Beatrice who guides Dante through Paradise.

Dante's first major work, the *La Vita Nuova* (New Life), probably written in 1292, tells the story of Dante's love for Beatrice, who had died in 1290. But Dante's greatest work is his *Comedy,* named by the people of Renaissance Italy the *Divine Comedy,* as it has been known ever since. This work is a description of a trip through Hell, Purgatory and Paradise. Here we have only a few selections from the first part, the trip through Hell, known as the "Inferno." The entire poem is one of great importance in this particular period of time, since it presents a synthesis of the philosophy, science, religion and ethics of the High Middle Ages. The theme of the entire poem is the salvation of mankind through reason and grace. Several important points should be noted. First, the poem was not written in Latin but in the vernacular Italian. Also the poem shows that Dante firmly believed that there was a Hell and that man's soul had a chance to go either to Heaven or to Hell. It should also be noted that Dante describes with great detail the geography of Hell and also the particular types of sinners found at the various levels. Dante felt that sins of the flesh received a less severe punishment than treason or betrayal of ones friends. The poem is not only full of symbolism and allegory, but also has exceedingly literal descriptions of the punishment in Hell of specific people who had once lived on earth. Note as you read the various Cantos the names of people with whom you are familiar, the position which Dante gives them in Hell and the punishment which he feels should be meted out to them for their sins.

THE NEW LIFE

IN that part of the book of my memory before the which is little that can be read, there is a rubric, saying, *Incipit Bita Nova,* "Here beginneth the new life." Under such rubric I find written many things; and among them the words which I purpose to copy into this little book; if not the whole of them, at the least their substance.

Nine times since my birth had the heaven of light returned to the selfsame point almost, as concerns its own revolution, when first the glorious Lady of my mind was made manifest to mine eyes; even she who was called Beatrice by many who knew not wherefore.* She had been in this life for so long that, within her time, the starry heaven had

From *The New Life* by Dante Alighieui. Translated by Dante Gabriel Rossetti. Copyright 1907 by The National Alumni.

*In reference to the meaning of the name: "She who confers blessing." We learn from Boccaccio that this first meeting took place at a May Feast, given in 1274 by Folco Portinari, father of Beatrice, who ranked among the principal citizens of Florence; to which feast Dante accompanied his father, Alighiero Alighieri.

moved toward the Eastern quarter one of the twelve parts of a degree; so that she appeared to me at the beginning of her ninth year almost, and I saw her almost at the end of my ninth year. Her dress, on that day, was of the most noble color, a subdued and goodly crimson, girdled and adorned in such sort as best suited with her very tender age. I say most truly that at that moment the spirit of life, which hath its dwelling in the secretest chamber of the heart, began to tremble so violently that the least pulses of my body shook therewith; and in trembling it said these words: *Ecce deus fortior me, qui veniens dominabitur mihi,* ("Here is a deity stronger than I; who, coming, shall rule over me.") At that moment the animate spirit, which dwelleth in the lofty chamber whither all the senses carry their perceptions, was filled with wonder, and speaking more especially unto the spirits of the eyes, said these words. *Apparuit jam beatitudo vestra,* ("Your beatitude hath not been made manifest unto you"). At that moment the natural spirit, which dwelleth there where our nourishment is administered, began to weep, and in weeping said these words: *Heu miser! quia frequenter impeditus ero deinceps,* ("Woe is me! for that often I shall be disturbed from this time forth!").

I say that, from that time forward, Love quite governed my soul; which was immediately espoused to him, and with so safe and undisputed a lordship (by viture of strong imagination) that I had nothing left for it but to do all his bidding continually. He often commanded me to seek whether I might see this youngest of the angels; wherefore I in my boyhood often went in search of her, and found her so noble and praiseworthy that certainly of her might have been said those words of the poet Homer: "She seemed not to be the daughter of a mortal man, but of a god."(*Iliad,* xxiv. 258.) And albeit her image, which was with me always, was an exultation of Love to subdue me, it was yet of so perfect a quality that it never allowed me to be overruled by Love without the faithful counsel of reason, whensoever such counsel was useful to be heard. But seeing that were I to dwell overmuch on the passions and doings of such early youth, my words might be counted something fabulous, I will therefore put them aside; and passing many things that my be conceived by the pattern of these, I will come to such as are writ in my memory with a better distinctness.

After the lapse of so many days that nine years exactly were completed since the above-written appearance of this most gracious being, on the last of those days it happened that the same wonderful lady appeared to me dressed all in pure white, between two gentle ladies elder than she. And passing through a street, she turned her eyes thither where I stood sorely abashed: and by her unspeakable courtesy, which is now guerdoned in the Great Cycle, she saluted me with so virtuous a bearing that I seemed then and there to behold the very limits of blessedness. The hour of her most sweet salutation was exactly the ninth of that day; and because it was the first time that any words from her reached mine ears, I came into such sweetness that I parted thence as one intoxicated. And betaking me to the loneliness of mine own room, I fell to thinking of this most courteous lady, thinking of whom I was overtaken by a pleasant slumber, wherein a marvelous vision was presented to me: for there appeared to be in my room a mist of the color of fire, within the which I discerned the figure of a lord of terrible aspect to such as should gaze upon him, but who seemed therewithal to rejoice inwardly that it was a marvel to see. Speaking, he said many things, among the which I could understand but few; and of these, this: *Ego dominus tuus* ("I am thy master"). In his arms it seemed to me that a person was sleeping, covered only with a blood-colored cloth; upon whom looking very attentively, I knew that it was the lady of the salutation who had deigned the day before to salute me. And he who held her held also in his hand a thing that was burning in flames; and he said to me, *Vide cor tuum,* ("Behold thy heart"). But when he had remained with me a little while, I thought that he set himself to awaken her that slept; after the which he made her to eat that thing which flamed in his hand; and she ate as one fearing. Then, having waited again a space, all his joy was turned into most bitter weeping; and as he wept he gathered the lady into his arms, and it seemed to me that he went with her up toward heaven: whereby such a great anguish came upon me that my light slumber could not endure through it, but was suddenly broken. And immediately having considered, I knew that the hour wherein this vision had been made manifest to me was the fourth hour (which is to say, the first of the nine last hours) of the night.

Inferno

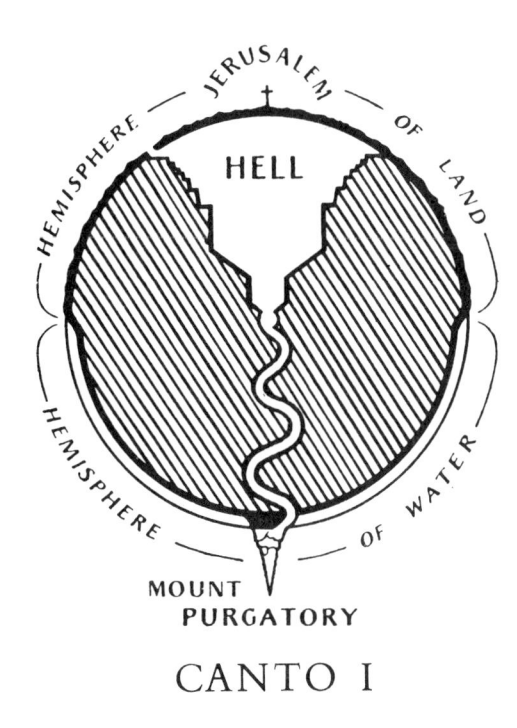

CANTO I

THE STORY. *Dante finds that he has strayed from the right road and is lost in a Dark Wood. He tries to escape by climbing a beautiful Mountain, but is turned aside, first by a gambolling Leopard, then by a fierce Lion, and finally by a ravenous She-Wolf. As he is fleeing back into the Wood, he is stopped by the shade of Vergil, who tells him that he cannot hope to pass the Wolf and ascend the Mountain by that road. One day a Greyhound will come and drive the Wolf back to Hell; but the only course at present left open to Dante is to trust himself to Vergil, who will guide him by a longer way, leading through Hell and Purgatory. From there, a worthier spirit than Vergil (Beatrice) will lead him on to see the blessed souls in Paradise. Dante accepts Vergil as his "master, leader, and lord", and they set out together.*

    Midway this way of life we're bound upon,
      I woke to find myself in a dark wood,
      Where the right road was wholly lost and gone.

4   Ay me! how hard to speak of it – that rude
      And rough and stubborn forest! the mere breath
      Of memory stirs the old fear in the blood;

7   It is so bitter, it goes nigh to death;
      Yet there I gained such good, that, to convey
      The tale, I'll write what else I found therewith.

10   How I got into it I cannot say,
      Because I was so heavy and full of sleep
      When first I stumbled from the narrow way;

13   But when at last I stood beneath a steep
      Hill's side, which closed that valley's wandering maze
      Whose dread had pierced me to the heart-root deep,

16   Then I looked up, and saw the morning rays
      Mantle its shoulder from that planet bright
      Which guides men's feet aright on all their ways;

19   And this a little quieted the affright
      That lurking in my bosom's lake had lain
      Through the long horror of that piteous night.

22   And as a swimmer, panting, from the main
      Heaves safe to shore, then turns to face the drive
      Of perilous seas, and looks, and looks again,

25   So, while my soul yet fled, did I contrive
      To turn and gaze on that dread pass once more
      Whence no man yet came ever out alive.

28   Weary of limb I rested a brief hour,
      Then rose and onward through the desert hied,
      So that the fixed foot always was the lower;

31   And see! not far from where the mountain-side
      First rose, a Leopard, nimble and light and fleet,
      Clothed in a fine furred pelt all dapple-dyed,

34   Came gambolling out, and skipped before my feet,
      Hindering me so, that from the forthright line
      Time and again I turned to beat retreat.

37   The morn was young, and in his native sign
      The Sun climbed with the stars whose glitterings
      Attended on him when the Love Divine

40   First moved those happy, prime-created things:
      So the sweet reason and the new-born day
      Filled me with hope and cheerful augurings

43   Of the bright beast so speckled and so gay;
      Yet not so much but that I fell to quaking
      At a fresh sight – a Lion in the way.

46   I saw him coming, swift and savage, making
      For me, head high, with ravenous hunger raving
      So that for dread the very air seemed shaking.

49   And next, a Wolf, gaunt with the famished craving
      Lodged ever in her horrible lean flank,
      The ancient cause of many men's enslaving; –

52   She was the worst – at that dread sight a blank
      Despair and whelming terror pinned me fast,
      Until all hope to scale the mountain sank.

55   Like one who loves the gains he has amassed,
      And meets the hour when he must lose his loot,
      Distracted in his mind and all aghast,

58   Even so was I, faced with that restless brute
      Which little by little edged and thrust me back,
      Back, to that place wherein the sun is mute.

61   Then, as I stumbled headlong down the track,
      Sudden a form was there, which dumbly crossed
      My path, as though grown voiceless from long lack

From *The Search for Personal Freedom* by Neal M. Cross, Leslie Dae Lindou and Robert C. Lamm, Wm. C. Brown Co. Publishers, Dubuque, Iowa, 1968.

64   Of speech; and seeing it in that desert lost,
       "Have pity on me!" I hailed it as I ran,
       "Whate'er thou art – or very man, or ghost!"

67   It spoke: "No man, although I once was man;
       My parents' native land was Lombardy
       And both by citizenship were Mantuan.

70   *Sub Julio* born, though late in time, was I,
       And lived at Rome in good Augustus' days,
       When the false gods were worshipped ignorantly.

73   Poet was I, and tuned my verse to praise
       Anchises' righteous son, who sailed from Troy
       When Ilium's pride fell ruined down ablaze.

76   But thou – oh, why run back where fears destroy
       Peace? Why not climb the blissful mountain yonder,
       The cause and first beginning of all joy?"

79   "Canst thou be Virgil? thou that fount of splendour
       Whence poured so wide a stream of lordly speech?"
       Said I, and bowed my awe-struck head in wonder;

82   "Oh honour and light of poets all and each,
       Now let my great love stead me – the bent brow
       And long hours pondering all thy book can teach!

85   Thou art my master, and my author thou,
       From thee alone I learned the singing strain,
       The noble style, that does me honour now.

88   See there the beast that turned me back again –
       Save me from her, great sage – I fear her so,
       She shakes my blood through every pulse and vein."

91   "Nay, by another path thou needs must go
       If thou wilt ever leave this waste," he said,
       Looking upon me as I wept, "for lo!

94   The savage brute that makes thee cry for dread
       Lets no man pass this road of hers, but still
       Trammels him, till at last she lays him dead.

97   Vicious her nature is, and framed for ill;
       When crammed she craves more fiercely than before;
       Her raging greed can never gorge its fill.

100   With many a beast she mates, and shall with more,
       Until the Greyhound come, the Master-hound,
       And he shall slay her with a stroke right sore.

103   He'll not eat gold nor yet devour the ground;
       Wisdom and love and power his food shall be,
       His birthplace between Feltro and Feltro found;

106   Saviour he'll be to that low Italy
       For which Euryalus and Nisus died,
       Turnus and chaste Camilla, bloodily.

109   He'll hunt the Wolf through cities far and wide,
       Till in the end he hunt her back to Hell,
       Whence Envy first of all her leash untied.

112   But, as for thee, I think and deem it well
       Thou take me for thy guide, and pass with me
       Through an eternal place and terrible

115   Where thou shalt hear despairing cries, and see
       Long-parted souls that in their torments dire
       Howl for the second death perpetually.

118   Next, thou shalt gaze on those who in the fire
       Are happy, for they look to mount on high,
       In God's good time, up to the blissful quire;

121   To which glad place, a worthier spirit than I
       Must lead thy steps, if thou desire to come,
       With whom I'll leave thee then, and say good-bye;

124   For the Emperor of that high Imperium
       Wills not that I, once rebel to His crown,
       Into that city of His should lead men home.

127   Everywhere is His realm, but there His throne,
       There is His city and exalted seat:
       Thrice-blest whom there He chooses for His own!"

130   Then I to him: "Poet, I thee entreat,
       By that great God whom thou didst never know,
       Lead on, that I may free my wandering feet

133   From these snares and from worse; and I will go
       Along with thee, St Peter's Gate to find,
       And those whom thou portray'st as suffering so."

136   So he moved on; and I moved on behind.

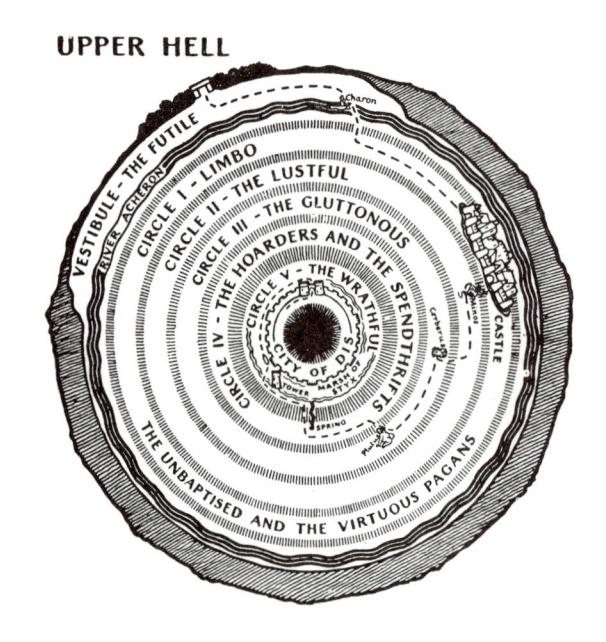

UPPER HELL

Dante continues to follow Vergil but soon loses his purpose and hesitates. Vergil tells him that he must continue because he cannot come to divine love unaided; reason must lead him. He also tells Dante that Beatrice had come to Limbo to ask him to save Dante. Dante, therefore, continues and the two pass through the Gate of Hell over which is written several sentences, the last of which says, "Abandon all hope you who enter here." The first souls Dante sees are those of the opportunists who in life only thought of themselves and never took a side for good or for evil. Dante & Vergil then come to the river Acheron where, after a short argument, they are ferried across by Charon. Before getting into the boat Dante faints and does not revive until he reaches the other side.

THE MIDDLE AGES

CANTO IV

THE STORY. *Recovering from his swoon, Dante finds himself across Acheron and on the edge of the actual Pit of Hell. He follows Vergil into the First Circle – the Limbo where the Unbaptized and the Virtuous Pagans dwell "suspended", knowing no torment save exclusion from the positive bliss of God's presence. Vergil tells him of Christ's Harrowing of Hell, and then shows him the habitation of the great men of antiquity – poets, heroes, and philosophers.*

A heavy peal of thunder came to waken me
   Out of the stunning slumber that had bound me,
   Startling me up as though rude hands had shaken me.

4 I rose, and cast my rested eyes around me,
   Gazing intent to satisfy my wonder
   Concerning the strange place wherein I found me.

7 Hear truth: I stood on the steep brink whereunder
   Runs down the dolorous chasm of the Pit,
   Ringing with infinite groans like gathered thunder.

10 Deep, dense, and by no faintest glimmer lit
   It lay, and though I strained my sight to find
   Bottom, not one thing could I see in it.

13 "Down must we go, to that dark world and blind,"
   The poet said, turning on me a bleak
   Blanched face; "I will go first – come thou behind."

16 Then I, who had marked the colour of his cheek:
   "How can I go, when even thou art white
   For fear, who art wont to cheer me when I'm weak?"

19 But he: "Not so; the anguish infinite
   They suffer yonder paints my countenance
   With pity, which thou takest for affright;

22 Come, we have far to go; let us advance."
   So, entering, he made me enter, where
   The Pit's first circle makes circumference.

25 We heard no loud complaint, no crying there,
   No sound of grief except the sound of sighing
   Quivering for ever through the eternal air;

28 Grief, not for torment, but for loss undying,
   By women, men, and children sighed for so,
   Sorrowers thick-thronged, their sorrows multiplying.

31 Then my good guide: "Thou dost not ask me who
   These spirits are," said he, "whom thou perceivest?
   Ere going further, I would have thee know

34 They sinned not; yet their merit lacked its chiefest
   Fulfilment, lacking baptism, which is
   The gateway to the faith which thou believest;

37 Or, living before Christendom, their knees
   Paid not aright those tributes that belong
   To God; and I myself am one of these.

40 For such defects alone – no other wrong –
   We are lost; yet only by this grief offended:
   That, without hope, we ever live, and long."

43 Grief smote my heart to think, as he thus ended,
   What souls I knew, of great and sovran
   Virtue, who in that Limbo dwelt suspended.

46 "Tell me, sir – tell me, Master," I began
   (In hope some fresh assurance to be gleaning
   Of our sin-conquering Faith), "did any man

49 By his self-merit, or on another leaning,
   Ever fare forth from hence and come to be
   Among the blest?" He took my hidden meaning.

52 "When I was newly in this state," said he,
   "I saw One come in majesty and awe,
   And on His head were crowns of victory.

55 Our great first father's spirit He did withdraw,
   And righteous Abel, Noah who built the ark,
   Moses who gave and who obeyed the Law,

58 King David, Abraham the Patriarch,
   Israel with his father and generation,
   Rachel, for whom he did such deeds of mark,

61 With many another of His chosen nation;
   These did He bless; and know, that ere that day
   No human soul had ever seen salvation."

64 While he thus spake, we still made no delay,
   But passed the wood – I mean, the wood (as 'twere)
   Of souls ranged thick as trees. Being now some way –

67 Not far – from where I'd slept, I saw appear
   A light, which overcame the shadowy face
   Of gloom, and made a glowing hemisphere.

70 'Twas yet some distance on, yet I could trace
   So much as brought conviction to my heart
   That persons of great honour held that place.

73 "O thou that honour'st every science and art,
   Say, who are these whose honour gives them claim
   To different customs and a sphere apart?"

76 And he to me: "Their honourable name,
   Still in thy world resounding as it does,
   Wins here from Heaven the favour due to fame."

79 Meanwhile I heard a voice that cried out thus:
   "Honour the most high poet! his great shade,
   Which was departed, is returned to us."

82 It paused there, and was still; and lo! there made
   Toward us, four mighty shadows of the dead,
   Who in their mien nor grief nor joy displayed.

85 "Mark well the first of these," my master said,
   "Who in his right hand bears a naked sword
   And goes before the three as chief and head;

88 Homer is he, the poets' sovran lord;
   Next, Horace comes, the keen satirical;
   Ovid the third; and Lucan afterward.

91 Because I share with these that honourable
   Grand title the sole voice was heard to cry
   They do me honour, and therein do well."

94 Thus in their school assembled I, even I,
   Looked on the lords of loftiest song, whose style
   O'er all the rest goes soaring eagle-high.

97 When they had talked together a short while
   They all with signs of welcome turned my way,
   Which moved my master to a kindly smile;

100 And greater honour yet they did me – yea,
　　Into their fellowship they deigned invite
　　And make me sixth among such minds as they.

103 So we moved slowly onward toward the light
　　In talk 'twere as unfitting to repeat
　　Here, as to speak there was both fit and right.

106 And presently we reached a noble seat –
　　A castle, girt with seven high walls around,
　　And moated with a goodly rivulet

109 O'er which we went as though upon dry ground;
　　With those wise men I passed the sevenfold gate
　　Into a fresh green meadow, where we found

112 Persons with grave and tranquil eyes, and great
　　Authority in their carriage and attitude,
　　Who spoke but seldom and in voice sedate.

115 So here we walked aside a little, and stood
　　Upon an open eminence, lit serene
　　And clear, whence one and all might well be viewed.

118 Plain in my sight on the enamelled green
　　All those grand spirits were shown me one by one –
　　It thrills my heart to think what I have seen!

121 I saw Electra, saw with her anon
　　Hector, Aeneas, many a Trojan peer,
　　And hawk-eyed Caesar in his habergeon;

124 I saw Camilla and bold Penthesilea,
　　On the other hand; Latinus on his throne
　　Beside Lavinia his daughter dear;

127 Brutus, by whom proud Tarquin was o'erthrown,
　　Marcia, Cornelia, Julia, Lucrece – and
　　I saw great Saladin, aloof, alone.

130 Higher I raised my brows and further scanned,
　　And saw the Master of the men who know
　　Seated amid the philosophic band;

133 All do him honour and deep reverence show;
　　Socrates, Plato, in the nearest room
　　To him; Diogenes, Thales and Zeno,

136 Democritus, who held that all things come
　　By chance; Empedocles, Anaxagoras wise,
　　And Heraclitus, him that wept for doom;

139 Dioscorides, who named the qualities,
　　Tully and Orpheus, Linus, and thereby
　　Good Seneca, well-skilled to moralize;

142 Euclid the geometrician, Ptolemy,
　　Galen, Hippocrates, and Avicen,
　　Averroës who made the commentary –

145 Nay, but I tell not all that I saw then;
　　The long theme drives me hard, and everywhere
　　The wondrous truth outstrips my staggering pen.

148 The group of six dwindles to two; we fare
　　Forth a new way, I and my guide withal,
　　Out from that quiet to the quivering air,

151 And reach a place where nothing shines at all.

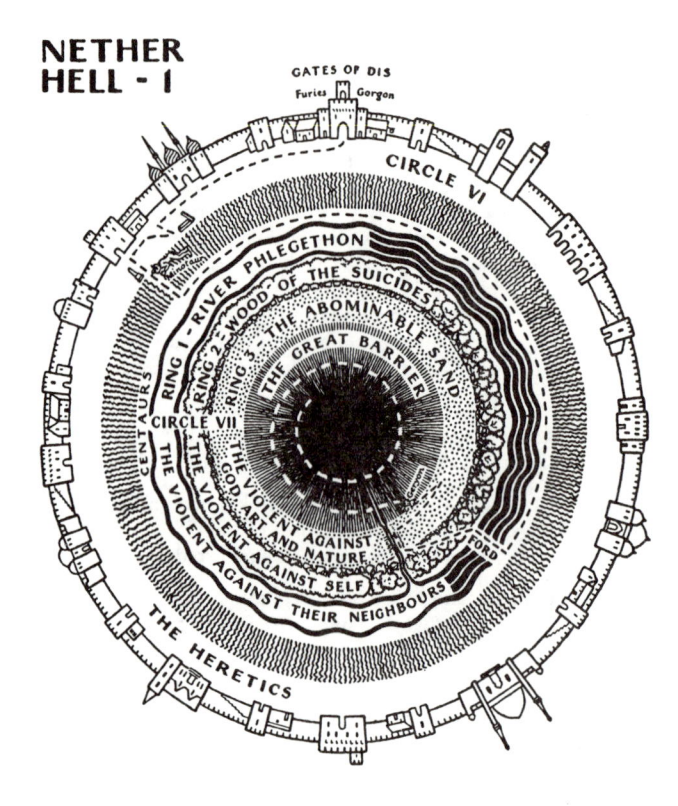

NETHER HELL – 1

Dante and Vergil continue into the next circle which contains the souls of the carnal who betrayed reason to their appetite. Here Dante sees many famous people such as Cleopatra, Achilles and Tristan. Next they pass through the third circle where they see the gluttons, then the hoarders and the wasters, and on past the wrathful. At circle six Dante sees the fallen angels who guard the city of Dis which is the capital of Hell. The rest of Hell according to Dante lies within the walls of this city which separates upper and lower hell as can be seen from the sketch. The poets now pass by the heretics and move into circle seven where they see those who were violent against their neighbors. Generally, these are the great war-makers, tyrants, robbers, all of whom are living in a river of boiling blood. Dante notices among them Alexander the Great and Attila the Hun. Next they pass by those who were violent against God, nature and art—committing such sins as blasphemy, sodomy and usury. The poets now arrive at circle eight which is divided into ten trenches and as can be seen from the next sketch it contains many different sinners. They stop for a moment in the third trench or bowge where those guilty of the sin of simony are found.

CANTO XIX

THE STORY. *In the Third Bowge of Malbowges, Dante sees the Simoniacs, plunged head-downwards in holes of the rock, with flames playing upon their feet. He talks to the shade of Pope Nicholas III, who prophesies that two of his successors will come to the same bad end as himself. Dante rebukes the avarice of the Papacy.*

　　O Simon Magus! O disciples of his!
　　　Miserable pimps and hucksters, that have sold
　　　The things of God, troth-plight to righteousness,

THE MIDDLE AGES

4 Into adultery for silver and gold;
   For you the trump must sound now – you are come
   To the bag: the third bowge has you in its hold.

7 Already we'd mounted over the next tomb,
   Scaling the cliff until we reached that part
   Whence a dropped line would hit the centre plumb.

10 O most high Wisdom, how exact an art
   Thou showest in heaven and earth and hell's profound;
   How just thy judgments, righteous as thou art!

13 I saw the gulley, both its banks and ground,
   Thickset with holes, all of the selfsame size,
   Pierced through the livid stone; and each was round,

16 Seeming nor more nor less wide to mine eyes
   Than those in my own beautiful St John,
   Made for the priests to stand in, to baptize;

19 Whereof, not many years back, I broke up one,
   To save a stifling youngster jammed in it;
   And by these presents be the true facts known.

22 From each hole's mouth stuck out a sinner's feet
   And legs up to the calf; but all the main
   Part of the body was hid within the pit.

25 The soles of them were all on fire, whence pain
   Made their joints quiver and thrash with such strong throes,
   They'd have snapped withies and hempen ropes in twain.

28 And as on oily matter the flame flows
   On the outer surface only, in lambent flashes,
   So did it here, flickering from heels to toes.

31 "Master, who is that writhing wretch, who lashes
   Out harder than all the rest of his company,"
   Said I, "and whom a ruddier fire washes?"

34 "If thou wouldst have me carry thee down," said he,
   "By the lower bank, his own lips shall afford
   News of his guilt, and make him known to thee."

37 "Thy pleasure is my choice; for thou art lord,"
   Said I, "and knowest I swerve not from thy will;
   Yea, knowest my heart, although I speak no word."

40 So to the fourth brink, and from thence downhill,
   Turning to the left, we clambered; and thus passed
   To the narrow and perforate bottom, my dear lord still

43 Loosing me not from his side, until at last
   He brought me close to the cleft, where he who made
   Such woeful play with his shanks was locked up fast.

46 "Oh thou, whoever thou art, unhappy shade,
   Heels over head thus planted like a stake,
   Speak if thou canst." This opening I essayed

49 And stood there like the friar who leans to take
   Confession from the treacherous murderer
   Quick-buried, who calls him back for respite's sake.

52 He cried aloud: "Already standing there?
   Art standing there already, Boniface?
   Why then, the writ has lied by many a year.

55 What! so soon sated with the gilded brass
   That nerved thee to betray and then to rape
   The Fairest among Women that ever was?"

58 Then I became like those who stand agape,
   Hearing remarks which seem to make no sense,
   Blank of retort for what seems jeer and jape.

61 But Virgil now broke in: "Tell him at once:
   'I am not who thou think'st, I am not he'";
   So I made answer in obedience.

64 At this the soul wrenched his feet furiously,
   Almost to spraining; then he sighed, and wept,
   Saying: "Why then, what dost thou ask of me?

67 Art so concerned to know my name, thou'st leapt
   These barriers just for that? Then truly know
   That the Great Mantle once my shoulders wrapped.

70 Son of the Bear was I, and thirsted so
   To advance the ursine litter that I pouched
   Coin up above, and pouched myself below.

73 Dragged down beneath my head lie others couched,
   My predecessors who simonized before,
   Now in the deep rock-fissures cowering crouched.

76 I too shall fall down thither and make one more
   When he shall come to stand here in my stead
   Whom my first sudden question took thee for.

79 But already have I been planted in this bed
   Longer with baked feet and thus topsy-turvy
   Than he shall stand flame-footed on his head;

82 For after him from the west comes one to serve ye
   With uglier acts, a lawless Shepherd indeed,
   Who'll cover us both – fit end for soul so scurvy;

85 He'll be another Jason, as we read
   The tale in Maccabees; as that controlled
   His king, so this shall bend France like a reed."

88 I know not whether I was here too bold,
   But in this strain my answer flowed out free:
   "Nay, tell me now how great a treasure of gold

91 Our Lord required of Peter, ere that He
   Committed the great Keys into his hand;
   Certes He nothing asked save 'Follow Me.'

94 Nor Peter nor the others made demand
   Of silver or gold when, in the lost soul's room,
   They chose Matthias to complete their band.

97 Then bide thou there; thou hast deserved thy doom;
   Do thou keep well those riches foully gained
   That against Charles made thee so venturesome.

100 And were it not that I am still constrained
    By veneration for the most high Keys
    Thou barest in glad life, I had not refrained

103 My tongue from yet more grievous words than these;
    Your avarice saddens the world, trampling on worth,
    Exalting the workers of iniquities.

106 Pastors like you the Evangelist shewed forth,
    Seeing her that sitteth on the floods committing
    Fornication with the kings of the earth;

109 Her, the seven-headed born, whose unremitting
    Witness uplifted in her ten horns thundered,
    While she yet pleased her Spouse with virtues fitting.

112 You deify silver and gold; how are you sundered
   In any fashion from the idolater,
   Save that he serves one god and you an hundred?

115 Ah, Constantine! what ills were gendered there –
   No, not from thy conversion, but the dower
   The first rich Pope received from thee as heir!"

118 While I thus chanted to him, such a sour
   Rage bit him – or perhaps his conscience stirred –
   He writhed and jerked his feet with all his power.

121 I think my guide approved of what he heard –
   I think so, since he patiently attended
   With a pleased smile to each outspoken word;

124 And after took me in both arms extended,
   And, when he had clasped me close upon his breast,
   Climbed back by the same road he had descended,

127 Nor wearied of the load that he embraced
   Till he had borne me to the arch's crown
   Linking the fourth and fifth banks; on that crest

130 He set at length his burden softly down,
   Soft on the steep, rough crag where even a goat
   Would find the way hard going; here was thrown

133 Open the view of yet another moat.

The Simoniacs. Simony is the sin of trafficking in holy things, e.g. the sale of sacraments or ecclesiastical offices. The sinners who thus made money for themselves out of what belongs to God are "pouched" in fiery pockets in the rock, head-downwards, because they reversed the proper order of things and subordinated the heavenly to the earthly. The image here is ecclesiastical: we need not, however, suppose that, allegorically, the traffic in holy things is confined to medieval people or even to modern clergymen. A mercenary marriage, for example, is also the sale of a sacrament.

The only image here is that of Hell itself. Dante's classification of sins is based chiefly on Aristotle, with a little assistance from Cicero. Aristotle divided wrong behaviour into three main kinds: (A) *Incontinence* (uncontrolled appetite); (B) *Bestiality* (perverted appetite); (C) *Malice* or *Vice* (abuse of the specifically human faculty of reason). Cicero declared that all injurious conduct acted by either (a) *Violence* or (b) *Fraud*. Combining these two classifications, Dante obtains three classes of sins: I. *Incontinence*; II *Violence* (or *Bestiality*); III. *Fraud* (or *Malice*). These he subdivides and arranges in 7 Circles: 4 of Incontinence, 1 of Violence, and 2 of Fraud.

To these purely ethical categories of wrong *behaviour* he, as a Christian, adds 2 Circles of wrong *belief*: 1 of *Unbelief* (Limbo) and 1 of *Mischief* (the Heretics), making 9 Circles in all. Finally, he adds the Vestibule of the Futile, who have neither faith nor works; this, not being a Circle, bears no number.

Thus we get the 10 main divisions of Hell. In the other books of the *Comedy* we shall find the same numerical scheme of 3, made up by subdivision to 7; plus 2 (= 9); plus 1 (= 10). Hell, however, is complicated by still further subdivision. The Circle of *Violence* is again divided into 3 Rings; the Circle of Fraud Simple into 10 Bowges; and the Circle of Fraud Complex into 4 Regions. So that Hell contains a grand total of 24 divisions. (See section map.)

The two now move on through several other trenches until they come to the sixth trench where they find the hypocrites.

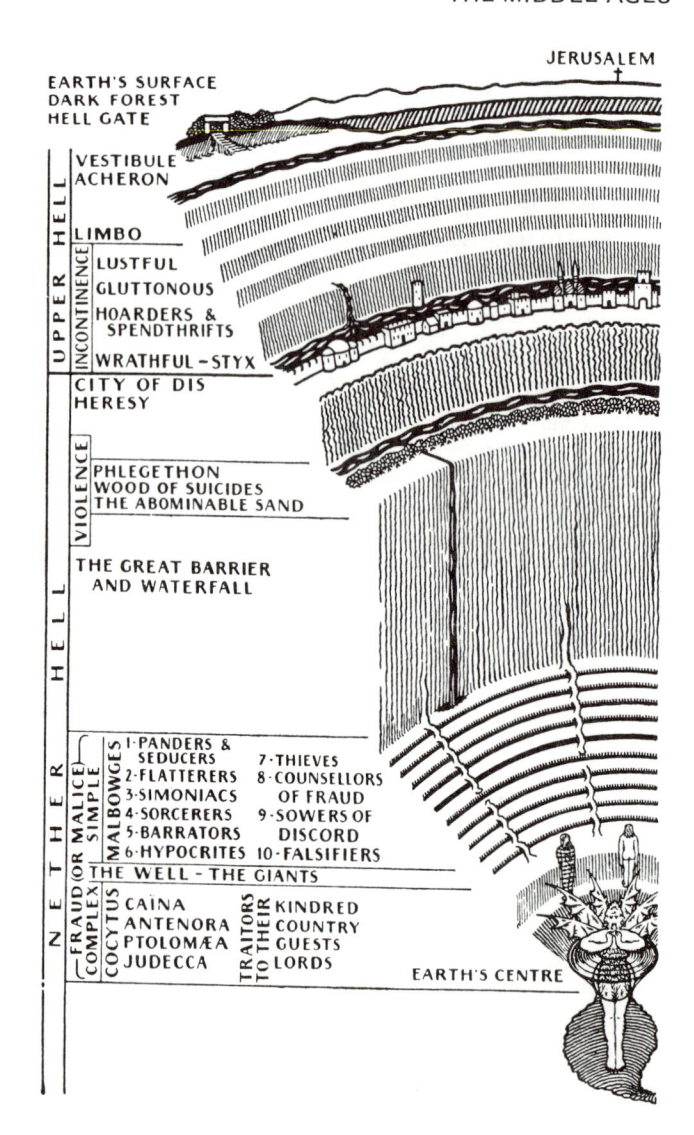

CANTO XXIII

THE STORY. *The angry demons pursue the Poets, who are forced to escape by scrambling down the upper bank of Bowge vi. Here they find the Hypocrites, walking in Gilded Cloaks lined with lead. They talk to two Jovial Friars from Bologna, and see the shade of Caiaphas crucified upon the ground.*

Silent, apart, companionless we went,
   One going on before and one behind,
   Like Friars Minor on a journey bent.

4 And Aesop's fable came into my mind
   As I was pondering on the late affray –
   I mean the frog-and-mouse one; for you'll find

6 That if with an attentive mind you lay
   Their heads and tails together, the two things
   Are just as much alike as Yes and Yea.

10 And, as one fancy from another springs
   Sometimes, this started a new train of thought
   Which doubled my first fears and flutterings.

THE MIDDLE AGES

13 I argued thus: "These demons have been brought,
   Through us, to a most mortifying plight –
   Tricked, knocked about, made fools of, set at naught;

16 If rage be added to their natural spite
   They'll come for us, pursuing on our heel
   Like greyhounds on the hare, teeth bared to bite."

19 I kept on looking backward, and could feel
   My hair already bristling on my head;
   "Master," said I, "unless thou canst conceal

22 Thyself and me, I'm very much afraid
   Of the Hellrakers; they're after us; I see
   And imagine it so, I can hear them now," I said.

25 "If I were made of looking-glass," said he,
   "My outward image scarce could mirror thine
   So jump as I mirror thine image inwardly.

28 Even now thy mind came entering into mine,
   Its living likeness both in act and face;
   So to one single purpose we'll combine

31 The two; if on our right-hand side this place
   So slopes that we can manage to descend
   To the next bowge, we'll flee the imagined chase."

34 Thus he resolved. He'd hardly made an end,
   When lo! I saw them, close at hand, and making
   To seize us, swooping on wide wings careened.

37 Then my master caught me up, like a mother, waking
   To the roar and crackle of fire, who sees the flare,
   And snatches her child from the cradle and runs, taking

40 More thought for him than herself, and will not spare
   A moment even so much as to cast a shift
   About her body, but flees naked and bare;

43 And over the flinty ridge of the great rift
   He slithered and slid with his back to the hanging spill
   Of the rock that walls one side of the next cleft.

46 Never yet did water run to the mill
   So swift and sure, where the head-race rushes on
   Through the narrow sluice to hit the floats of the wheel,

49 As down that bank my master went at a run,
   Carrying me off, hugged closely to his breast,
   Truly not like a comrade, but a son.

52 And his foot had scarce touched bottom, when on the crest
   Above us, there they were! But he, at large
   In the other chasm, could set his fears at rest;

55 For that high provident Will which gave them charge
   Over the fifth moat, curbs them with constraint,
   So that they have no power to pass its verge.

58 And now we saw a people decked with paint,
   Who trod their circling way with tear and groan
   And slow, slow steps, seeming subdued and faint.

61 They all wore cloaks, with deep hoods forward thrown
   Over their eyes, and shaped in fashion quite
   Like the great cowls the monks wear at Cologne;

64 Outwardly they were gilded dazzling-bright,
   But all within was lead, and, weighed thereby,
   King Frederick's copes would have seemed feather-light.

67 O weary mantle for eternity!
   Once more we turned to the left, and by their side
   Paced on, intent upon their mournful cry.

70 But crushed 'neath that vast load those sad folk plied
   Such slow feet that abreast of us we found
   Fresh company with every changing stride.

73 Wherefore: "Try now to find some soul renowned
   In name or deed, and as we forward fare,"
   I begged my guide, "pray cast thine eyes around."

76 And, hearing the Tuscan tongue, some one, somewhere
   Behind us cried: "Stay, stay now! slack your speed,
   You two that run so fast through this dark air,

79 And I, maybe, can furnish what you need."
   My guide looked round, and then to me said: "Good!
   Wait here, and then at his own pace proceed."

82 I stopped, and saw two toiling on, who showed,
   By looks, much haste of mind to get beside me,
   Though cumbered by the great load and strait road.

85 But when at length they reached us, then they eyed me
   Askance for a long time before they spoke;
   Then turned to each other, saying, while still they spied me:

88 "That one seems living – his throat moves to the stroke
   Of the breath and the blood; besides, if they are dead,
   What favour exempts them from the heavy cloak?"

91 And then to me: "O Tuscan, strangely led
   To the sad college of hypocrites, do not scorn
   To tell us who thou art," the spirits said.

94 I answered them: "I was bred up and born
   In the great city on Arno's lovely stream,
   And wear the body that I've always worn.

97 But who are you, whose cheeks are seen to teem
   Such distillation of grief? What comfortless
   Garments of guilt upon your shoulders gleam?"

100 And one replied: "Our orange-gilded dress
    Is leaden, and so heavy that its weight
    Wrings out these creakings from the balances.

103 Two Jovial Friars were we; our city-state
    Bologna; Catalano was my name,
    His, Loderingo; we were designate

106 By thine own city, to keep peace and tame
    Faction, as one sole judge is wont to do;
    What peace we kept, Gardingo can proclaim."

109 "Friars," I began, "the miseries that you –"
    But broke off short, seeing one lie crucified
    There on the ground, with three stakes stricken through;

112 Who, when he saw me, writhed himself, and sighed
    Most bitterly in his beard; and seeing me make
    A questioning sign, Friar Catalan replied:

115 "He thou dost gaze on, pierced by the triple stake,
    Counselled the Pharisees 'twas expedient
    One man should suffer for the people's sake.

118 Naked, transverse, barring the road's extent,
    He lies; and all who pass, with all their load
    Must tread him down; such is his punishment.

121 In this same ditch lie stretched in this same mode
    His father-in-law, and all the Sanhedrim
    Whose counsel sowed for the Jews the seed of blood."

124 Then I saw Virgil stand and marvel at him
    Thus racked for ever on the shameful cross
    In the everlasting exile. He to them

127	Turning him, then addressed the Friars thus: "May it so please you, if your rule permit, To tell us if, on this right side the fosse,
130	Be any gap to take us out of it, That we need not compel any of the Black Angels to extricate us from this pit."
133	"Nearer than thou hop'st," the Friar answered back, "There lies a rock, part of the mighty spur That springs from the great wall, and makes a track
136	O'er all the cruel moats save this, for here The arch is down; but you could scale the rock, Whose ruins are piled from the floor to the barrier."
139	My guide stood with bent head and downward look Awhile; then said: "He gave us bad advice, Who spears the sinners yonder with his hook."
142	And the Friar: "I heard the devil's iniquities Much canvassed at Bologna; among the rest 'Twas said, he was a liar and father of lies."
145	My guide with raking steps strode off in haste, Troubled in his looks, and showing some small heat Of anger; so I left those spirits oppressed,
148	Following in the prints of the belovèd feet.

Now the poets pass on through the other trenches of circle eight seeing thieves, evil councillors, sowers of discord and the falsifiers. Finally they arrive at the ninth and last circle of Hell which is the Well. Around this Well stand the giants who are visible only from the waist up above its rim. These men are symbols of the earth and one of them, Antaeus takes the poets in his hand and lowers them gently to the final floor of hell. Here Dante finds those who are guilty of being treacherous to their relatives, treacherous to their country, treacherous to their guests and hosts, and finally in Canto thirty-four those who were treacherous to their masters.

CANTO XXXIV

THE STORY. *After passing over the region of Judecca, where the Traitors to their Lords are wholly immersed in the ice, the Poets see Dis (Satan) devouring the shades of Judas, Brutus, and Cassius. They clamber along his body until, passing through the centre of the Earth, they emerge into a rocky cavern. From here they follow the stream of Lethe upwards until it brings them out on the island of Mount Purgatory in the Antipodes.*

	"*Vexilla regis prodeunt inferni* Encountering us; canst thou distinguish him, Look forward," said the master, "as we journey."
4	As, when a thick mist breathes, or when the rim Of night creeps up across our hemisphere, A turning windmill looms in the distance dim,
7	I thought I saw a shadowy mass appear; Then shrank behind my leader from the blast, Because there was no other cabin here.
10	I stood (with fear I write it) where at last The shades, quite covered by the frozen sheet, Gleamed through the ice like straws in crystal glassed;
13	Some lie at length and others stand in it, This one upon his head, and that upright, Another like a bow bent face to feet.
16	And when we had come so far that it seemed right To my dear master, he should let me see That creature fairest once of the sons of light,
19	He moved him from before me and halted me, And said: "Behold now Dis! behold the place Where thou must steel thy soul with constancy."
22	How cold I grew, how faint with fearfulness, Ask me not, Reader; I shall not waste breath Telling what words are powerless to express;
25	This was not life, and yet it was not death; If thou hast wit to think how I might fare Bereft of both, let fancy aid thy faith.
28	The Emperor of the sorrowful realm was there, Out of the girding ice he stood breast-high, And to his arm alone the giants were
31	Less comparable than to a giant I; Judge then how huge the stature of the whole That to so huge a part bears symmetry.
34	If he was once as fair as now he's foul, And dared outface his Maker in rebellion, Well may he be the fount of all our dole.
37	And marvel 'twas, out-marvelling a million, When I beheld three faces in his head; The one in front was scarlet like vermilion;
40	And two, mid-centred on the shoulders, made Union with this, and each with either fellow Knit at the crest, in triune junction wed.
43	The right was of a hue 'twixt white and yellow; The left was coloured like the men who dwell Where Nile runs down from source to sandy shallow.
46	From under each sprang two great wings that well Befitted such a monstrous bird as that; I ne'er saw ship with such a spread of sail.
49	Plumeless and like the pinions of a bat Their fashion was; and as they flapped and whipped Three winds went rushing over the icy flat
52	And froze up all Cocytus; and he wept From his six eyes, and down his triple chin Runnels of tears and bloody slaver dripped.
55	Each mouth devoured a sinner clenched within, Frayed by the fangs like flax beneath a brake; Three at a time he tortured them for sin.
58	But all the bites the one in front might take Were nothing to the claws that flayed his hide And sometimes stripped his back to the last flake.
61	"That wretch up there whom keenest pangs divide Is Judas called Iscariot," said my lord, "His head within, his jerking legs outside;
64	As for the pair whose heads hang hitherward: From the black mouth the limbs of Brutus sprawl – See how he writhes and utters never a word;
67	And strong-thewed Cassius is his fellow-thrall. But come; for night is rising on the world Once more; we must depart; we have seen all."
70	Then, as he bade, about his neck I curled My arms and clasped him. And he spied the time And place; and when the wings were wide unfurled

73 Set him upon the shaggy flanks to climb,
    And thus from shag to shag descended down
    'Twixt matted hair and crusts of frozen rime.

76 And when we had come to where the huge thigh-bone
    Rides in its socket at the haunch's swell,
    My guide, with labour and great exertion,

79 Turned head to where his feet had been, and fell
    To hoisting himself up upon the hair,
    So that I thought us mounting back to Hell.

82 "Hold fast to me, for by so steep a stair,"
    My master said, panting like one forspent,
    "Needs must we quit this realm of all despair."

85 At length, emerging through a rocky vent,
    He perched me sitting on the rim of the cup
    And crawled out after, heedful how he went.

88 I raised my eyes, thinking to see the top
    Of Lucifer, as I had left him last;
    But only saw his great legs sticking up.

91 And if I stood dumbfounded and aghast,
    Let those thick-witted gentry judge and say,
    Who do not see what point it was I'd passed.

94 "Up on thy legs!" the master said; "the way
    Is long, the road rough going for the feet,
    And at mid-terce already stands the day."

97 The place we stood in was by no means fit
    For a king's palace, but a natural prison,
    With a vile floor, and very badly lit.

100 "One moment, sir," said I, when I had risen;
    "Before I pluck myself from the Abyss,
    Lighten my darkness with a word in season.

103 Kindly explain; what's happened to the ice?
    What's turned him upside-down? or in an hour
    Thus whirled the sun from dusk to dawning skies?"

106 "Thou think'st," he said, "thou standest as before
    Yon side the centre, where I grasped the hair
    Of the ill Worm that pierces the world's core.

109 So long as I descended, thou wast there;
    But when I turned, then was the point passed by
    Toward which all weight bears down from everywhere.

112 The other hemisphere doth o'er thee lie –
    Antipodal to that which land roofs in,
    And under whose meridian came to die

115 The Man born sinless and who did no sin;
    Thou hast thy feet upon a little sphere
    Of whose far side Judecca forms the skin.

118 When it is evening there, it's morning here;
    And he whose pelt our ladder was, stands still
    Fixt in the self-same place, and does not stir.

121 This side the world from out high Heaven he fell;
    The land which here stood forth fled back dismayed,
    Pulling the sea upon her like a veil,

124 And sought our hemisphere; with equal dread,
    Belike, that peak of earth which still is found
    This side, rushed up, and so this void was made."

127 There is a place low down there underground,
    As far from Belzebub as his tomb's deep,
    Not known to sight, but only by the sound

130 Of a small stream which trickles down the steep,
    Hollowing its channel, where with gentle fall
    And devious course its wandering waters creep.

133 By that hid way my guide and I withal,
    Back to the lit world from the darkened dens
    Toiled upward, caring for no rest at all,

136 He first, I following; till my straining sense
    Glimpsed the bright burden of the heavenly cars
    Through a round hole; by this we climbed, and thence

139 Came forth, to look once more upon the stars.

Judecca. The region of the Traitors to sworn allegiance is called Judecca after Judas, who betrayed Our Lord. Here, cut off from every contact and every means of expression, those who committed the final treason lie wholly submerged.

Judas, Brutus and Cassius. Judas, obviously enough, is the image of the betrayal of God. To us, with our minds dominated by Shakespeare and by "democratic" ideas, the presence here of Brutus and Cassius needs some explanation. To understand it, we must get rid of all political notions in the narrow sense. We should notice, first, that Dante's attitude to Julius Caesar is ambivalent. *Personally*, as a pagan, Julius is in Limbo (Canto IV. 123). *Politically*, his rise to power involved the making of civil war, and Curio, who advised him to cross the Rubicon, is in the Eighth Circle of Hell (Canto XXVIII. 97-102 and note). But, although Julius was never actually Emperor, he was the founder of the Roman Empire, and *by his function*, therefore, he images that institution which, in Dante's view, was divinely appointed to govern the world. Thus Brutus and Cassius, by their breach of sworn allegiance to Caesar, were Traitors to the Empire, i.e. to World-order. Consequently, just as Judas figures treason against God, so Brutus and Cassius figure treason against Man-in-Society; or we may say that we have here images of treason against the Divine and the Secular government of the world.

Dis, so Virgil calls him; Dis, or Pluto, being the name of the King of the Classical Underworld. But to Dante he is Satan or Lucifer or Beelzebub – or, as we say, the Devil. "He can see it now – that which monotonously resents and repels, that which despairs. ... Milton imagined Satan, but an active Satan; this is beyond it, this is passive except for its longing. Shakespeare imagined treachery; this is treachery raised to an infinite cannibalism. Treachery gnaws treachery, and so inevitably. It is the imagination of the freezing of every conception, an experience of which neither life nor death can know, and which is yet quite certain, if it is willed." (Charles Williams: *The Figure of Beatrice*, p. 144.)

Geoffrey Chaucer

Geoffrey Chaucer (c. 1345-1400) is the greatest poet of the English Middle Ages. His *Canterbury Tales* is one of the best known poems of all literature. Although little is known of the early life of Chaucer, it is certain that quite early he was a page in a household of royal rank, and it appears that he did quite well for himself, progressing through various jobs connected with the royal family until he became the Controller of Customs. By his marriage, his fortunes became tied quite closely to the House of Lancaster. Chaucer also took several trips to Italy, thus becoming familiar with Italian literature of his day in addition to his knowledge of French and Latin literature. In the "Prologue," Chaucer, an acute observer of his fellow man, presents an entire portrait of late medieval English society. Included are almost all ranks and vocations, all trades and professions. In Chaucer's day, it was quite customary for people to go on a pilgrimage to a shrine of a great saint, and one of the greatest shrines in England was the tomb of St. Thomas a Becket, an Archbishop of Canterbury murdered in the Cathedral in 1170. In this particular group of pilgrims, Chaucer says, there were twenty-nine, including Chaucer but not the Host. (Probably only one priest accompanied the Prioress, not three who would make the group number thirty-one.)

THE CANTERBURY TALES

THE PROLOGUE[1]

When April with his sweet showers has pierced the drouth of March to the root, and bathed every vein in liquor such that by virtue of it the flower is engendered; when, also, Zephyrus with his sweet breath has inspired the tender shoots in every holt and heath, and the young sun has run his half-course in the Ram; and small birds that sleep all night with their eyes open make melody—Nature so goads them in their hearts; then folk long to go on pilgrimages, and palmers, in order to seek strange shores, long to go to ancient shrines known in sundry lands; and especially from the end of every shire of England do they go to Canterbury to seek the holy, blessed martyr who has helped them when they were sick.

It happened that one day in that season, as I was stopping at the *Tabard* in Southwark, ready to go with fully devout heart on my pilgrimage to Canterbury, there came at night into that hostelry a company of twenty-nine folk, fallen by chance into fellowship; and they were all pilgrims who wished to ride to Canterbury. The chambers and the stables were spacious; and we enjoyed the greatest comfort. And shortly, when the sun was down, I had so spoken to every one of them that I was taken into their fellowship. And we prepared to rise early to set out, as I will describe to you.

But, nevertheless, while I have time and space, it seems to me to be reasonable to tell you the characteristics of each of them, who they were, and of what degree, and also how they were arrayed; and I will begin with the knight.

A KNIGHT there was, a worthy man, who, from the time he first went on a military expedition, loved chivalry, fidelity, honor, liberality, and courtesy. He was very worthy in his lord's war, in which he had ridden farther than any man, both in Christendom and in heathen lands, and always he was honored for his worthiness. He was at Alexandria when it was taken. Many times he sat at the head of the table above knights of other nations in Prussia.... And though he was brave he was prudent, and carried himself as modestly as a young girl. In all his life he had never spoken a villainous word to any sort of person. He was a true, perfect, noble knight. But to tell you of his dress and accoutrements—his horses were good, but he was not showily dressed; he wore a doublet of coarse cloth soiled by his coat-of-mail, for he had recently come from his expedition, and had gone at once to make his pilgrimage.

---

1. Translated by Robert Thackaberry; reprinted by permission of the copyright owner, Don A. Keister.

With him was his son, a young SQUIRE, a lusty lover and a candidate for knighthood, with locks curled as though they had been laid in a press. He was about twenty years old, I suppose; he was of moderate height, wonderfully agile, and of great strength. He had been on raids in Flanders, Artois, and Picardy; and in that short time he had conducted himself well in hopes of gaining his lady's favor. He was embroidered as though he were a meadow full of fresh red and white flowers. All day he sang or played the flute; he was as fresh as the month of May. His gown was short with long, wide sleeves. He was an expert horseman. He knew how to compose both words and music for songs, joust, dance, and draw well, and write. He was so much in love that at night he slept no more than a nightingale. He was courteous, humble, willing to serve, and at table he carved for his father.

The Knight had with him a YEOMAN, who was a forester, and no other servants. . . .

There was also a NUN, a PRIORESS, who was very simple and shy in her smiling; her greatest oath was "by Saint Loy"; and she was called Madame Eglentyne. She sang the divine service very well, intoning it becomingly through her nose; and she spoke French very suitably and handsomely—after the school of Stratford-at-Bow, for the French of Paris was unknown to her. At table she was very well mannered; she let no morsel fall from her lips, nor did she wet her fingers in her sauce; for she knew how to carry morsels nicely to her mouth and prevent any drop from falling on her breast—she had set her heart on being courtly. She wiped her upper lip so clean that no blob of grease was seen in her cup when she put it down; she reached for her meat very prettily. And certainly she was very merry, completely pleasant, and lovable in her behavior; she took trouble to imitate the ways of court and to be stately of manner and to be considered worthy of reverence. But to speak of her sensibilities—she was so charitable and full of pity that she would weep if she saw a mouse caught in a trap, if it was dead or bleeding. She had some small dogs that she fed with roast meat or milk and fine bread; she wept sorely if one of them died or if anybody struck one of them sharply with a stick. And all was sensitiveness and tender heart. Her wimple was very handsomely pleated; her nose well formed, her eyes grey as glass; she had a beautiful brow—I swear it was almost a span in breadth—for she was scarcely undersized. About her arm she wore a string of small coral beads, with greed gauds, on which hung a brooch engraved with an A, above which was a crown, and then the motto *Amor vincit omnia.*

With her she had another NUN, her chaplain, and three priests.

A MONK there was, fit to be a man of authority, licensed to ride outside the monastery, who loved hunting: a man's man, the right sort to be an abbot. He kept many dainty horses in his stable, and when he rode you could hear his bridle jingling in the wind as clear and loud as the chapel bell of that cell of the monastic house which this lord has charge of. The rule of St. Maurus and St. Benedict, because it was old and somewhat strict—this monk let old things go, and meanwhile did according to the new ways. He didn't give a plucked hen for the text which says that hunters are not holy men, or for the one saying that a monk who is reckless about discipline is like a fish out of water—that is to say, a monk out of his monastery. He thought that text not worth an oyster. And I said his opinion was right; why should he study and drive himself mad by always poring over a book in a cloister, or work with his hands, as Augustine advised? How shall the world be served? Let Augustine have his labor saved for him. Therefore he was a hard rider indeed. He had greyhounds as swift as birds in flight; his delight was all in tracking and hunting the hare, and he didn't spare the expense. I saw his sleeves bordered at the cuffs with grey fur, the finest in the country; and to fasten his hood under his chin he had a curious pin of wrought gold, with a love knot in the larger end. His head was bald and shone like a mirror, and his face shone as if it had been annointed; he was a lord as fat as if ready for market; his prominent eyes, rolling in his head, gleamed like a furnace under a cauldron. His boots were supple, his horse in good condition. Now, certainly he was a fine prelate. He wasn't pale like a tormented ghost—the roast he loved best was a fat swan. And his palfrey was as brown as a berry.

A FRIAR there was, a wanton and merry fellow, licensed to beg within a limited area, an impressive man. In all the Four Orders no one knew so much about dalliance and pretty speeches. He had performed the marriage ceremony for many young women free of charge. He was a noble pillar of his order, beloved of and familiar with the franklins of his territory, and with the respectable and well-to-do women of the town; for, as he said himself, he had more power to hear confession than a curate, for he was a licenciate of his order. He heard confessions sweetly, and his absolution was pleasant; he imposed an easy penance when he knew he would be well requited, for to give to a poor order is a sign that a man is well shriven, for if a man gave money, this friar dared assert that he knew the man to be repentant. Many a man is so hard of heart that he cannot weep, even though he is sorely grieved; therefore, instead of weeping and saying prayers, they ought to give silver to poor friars. His cape was full of knives and pins for presents for young wives. He certainly had a merry voice and knew how to sing and play on a rote. His neck was as white as a lily. Besides, he was as strong as a champion. He was known in every tavern in town, and he knew every innkeeper and barmaid better than he knew the lepers or beggers, for according to his official position it was not fitting for so worthy a man as he to have dealings with such lazars. It is not honorable—it is not advantageous—to have dealings with such paupers, but only with the rich and the sellers of victuals. Wherever it might be profitable, he was courteous and humbly willing to serve. There was no man anywhere so capable—he was the best beggar in his religious house; for though a widow didn't have a shoe, his *In principio* was so charming that he would be given a farthing before he left—what he picked up came to more than his regular income. He was as frolicsome as a puppy, for he was not like a cloistered monk with a threadbare cloak, nor like a poor scholar, but like a lord or a pope. His outer cape was of double worsted and smoothly pressed. He lisped a little, as an affectation, to make his English sweet upon his tongue. And as he played the harp, after he had finished singing, his eyes twinkled in his head like stars on a frosty night. . . .

There was a MERCHANT, in figured cloth, with a forked beard, sitting high on his horse, wearing a beaver hat in the Flemish style; the clasps on his boots were handsome and fashionable. He made his remarks very pompously, always managing to mention his profits. He wished the sea were kept clear of pirates between Middlebury in Flanders, and Orwell in England. He knew how to profiteer in foreign exchange—this honorable man could make use of his wits! So dignified was he in his financial deals and in his borrowing and lending, that nobody knew he was in debt.

There was also a CLERK from Oxford, who had long since advanced to the study of logic. His horse was as skinny as a rake, and he himself wasn't exactly fat, but looked hollow and grave. His outer coat was exceedingly threadbare, for he hadn't yet got a benefice and he was not so worldly as to accept secular employment. For he would rather have twenty books of Aristotle's philosophy, bound in red and black, at the head of his bed, than rich robes or a fiddle or a psaltery. . . . He had little money, but whatever he might obtain from his friends he spent on books and on his learning, and then prayed busily for the souls of those who gave him the wherewithal for his schooling. His greatest concern was for his studies; he never spoke a word more than necessary, and what he said formally, respectfully, shortly, and quickly, was full of high seriousness. His speech tended always to be concerned with moral virtue; and gladly would he learn and gladly teach.

There was also a SERGEANT OF LAW, canny and wise . . . a man of great excellence. He was discreet and greatly to be revered—or he seemed so, his words were so wise. He had often been appointed justice of the assizes. Because of his wide knowledge and great reputation he had received many fees and gifts. No one ever got his hands on so much land as he did; and regardless of the terms of the land's tenure he always gained absolute ownership. Nowhere was there a man so busy as he—and yet he seemed busier than he was. He knew accurately all the cases and decisions from the time of William the Conqueror, . . . and all the statutes by heart. He dressed simply in a figured coat and silk sash.

With him was a FRANKLIN with a beard as white as a daisy. He was sanguine of complexion. In the morning he loved a bit of bread in wine. It was his custom to live very pleasurably, for he was a true son of Epicurus, who held that complete pleasure is complete happiness. He was a great landowner and the St. Julian, the patron saint of hospitality, of his district. His bread and ale were uniformly fine, and no one ever had a better wine cellar. His house was never without baked fish and flesh in such plenteous quantities that it snowed meat and drink in his house—all the dainties in season that you could think of. He had many a fat partridge in his coops, many a fish in his ponds. His cook had better watch out if his sauce wasn't spicy and sharp, and his table stood set up for eating at all times in his hall. He was justice of the local court and had often been knight of the shire as its appointed representative in Parliament. From his belt, as white as morning milk, hung a dagger and a silk purse.

A HABERDASHER, a CARPENTER, a WEAVER, a DYER, a TAPESTRY-MAKER—all dressed in the uniform of a solemn and great fraternal order. Each of them seemed fit to be a burgess and sit on a dias in a guildhall, each so wise as to make a suitable alderman; for they had enough property and income, and besides their wives would have readily agreed to it, or else they were certainly to be blamed—it's very pleasant to be addressed *Madame* and be first in line at vigils and have a train to be carried like royalty.

They had a COOK with them for the journey, a good cook, but it seemed to me too bad that he had a running sore on his shin, for the dish he made best was blanc-mange.

There was a SHIPMAN from the West, perhaps Dartmouth, riding a hired horse as best he could, with a daggar in his belt, just under his hand. He was all browned by the sun, and he was certainly a fine rascal. While the merchant slept on the voyage from Bordeaux, this fellow stole drinks of wine. He didn't care for fine feelings: if his ship was attacked and he won, he sent his attackers home by water. But between Hull and Cartagena none knew more about sailing than he; he was an expert in knowledge of tides, currents, the phases of the moon, the waters of harbors, and all the details of pilotage. He knew all the havens from Gotland to the Cape of Finisterre, and every creek in Brittany and Spain. He called his ship the *Magdalen*.

With us there was a DOCTOR OF PHYSIC. There was none like him in all the world—if you're talking of medicine and surgery. He was learned in astronomy and, by using natural magic, he treated his patient according to the astrological hours favorable to the treatment. He was skilful in ascertaining the advantageous time for making charms. He knew the cause of every malady—whether hot, moist, and by which humor. He was a true, perfect practitioner. Having learned the cause of the trouble he gave the sick man the remedy at once. He had his apothecaries ready to send him drugs and prescriptions, for each brought profit to the other—their friendship was not unprecedented. He knew well the medical authorities: Aesculapius, Dioscorides, Rufus of Ephesus, Hippocrates, Hali ibn el Abbas, Galen, Serapion, Rhazes of Bagdad, Avicenna, Averroes, Damascenus, Constantinus Afer, Bernard Gordon, John of Gatesden, and Gilbertus Anglicus. His diet was moderate, nourishing and digestible. His study was but little on the Bible. He was clad in dark red and blue, lined with taffeta and silk; yet he was slow to spend money and kept the large profits he made during the pestilence. For gold has medicinal properties: therefore, he loved gold especially.

There was a GOOD WIFE from near Bath. She was somewhat deaf, which was a pity. She had such a knack at cloth-making that she surpassed the weavers of Ypres and Ghent. No wife in the parish might precede her to the offering, or if any did she was so wroth that she was quite out of patience. The kerchiefs which made up her elaborate Sunday head-dress were of fine texture, but so intricately fashioned that I swear they weighed ten pounds. Her hose were of fine scarlet and tied straight, and her shoes were moist and new. Her face was bold, fair and red. All her life she had been a worthy woman. She had married five husbands at the church door, not to speak of other companions in her youth. But we needn't talk about that now. She had been three times to Jerusalem; she had crossed many strange rivers and been at Rome, at Boulogne, at the shrine of St. James at Compostello, and at Cologne. She knew the fine art of dawdling by the way. And, truly, she was gap-toothed. She sat easily upon her ambler, well wimpled and with a hat as big as a buckler or a target; she had a short outer shirt about her large hips and sharp spurs on her feet. She knew very well how to laugh and talk in fellowship. She knew, *by chance*, the cures for love, for she understood that art—that old, old dance.

There was a good man of religion, a poor PARSON of a town; but he was rich in holy thought and works. He was also a learned man, a clerk who wished truly to preach the gospel of Christ; he wanted devoutly to teach his parishoners. He was benign, extremely diligent, very patient in adversity, as he had proved long since. He was very loathe to threaten excommunication for nonpayment of tithes, but he would doubtless rather share his own offerings and sustenance with his poor parish folk. His parish was large and the houses far apart, but bad weather did not keep him from visiting the most distant houses when there was sickness or trouble, no matter whether the person was important or not; and he went on foot with a staff in his hand. He gave his noble example to his sheep, that "first he did and afterwards he taught" according to the gospel, and he added this figure, "If gold rust, what shall iron do?" ... A priest ought well to be an example, by his own cleanliness, of how his sheep should live. He didn't hire someone else to do the work of his benefice and run to London to gain the income from a chauntery of souls at St. Paul's or be employed as chaplain by a guild, but dwelt at home and kept his flock. ... He was a shepherd, not a mercenary. Though holy and virtuous himself he was not hateful to sinners or haughty in his speech, but discreet and benign, trying to lead folk to heaven by fairness and good example; an obstinate person, however, whether of high or low estate, he rebuked.... He demanded no pomp and reverence, nor was he overparticular in minor matters. He taught the lesson of Christ and the Apostles, but first followed it himself.

With him was a PLOWMAN, his brother.... He was a true worker and a good one, living in peace and perfect charity. He loved God with his whole heart and at all times, and his neighbor as himself. For the sake of Christ, he would without pay thresh and ditch for every poor person, if it lay in his power. He paid his tithes fairly and well both in the labor required of him and in chattels. He wore a tabard and rode on a mare.

The MILLER was a stout fellow, brawny and big-boned. At wrestling he always won the ram. He was short-necked, thick-shouldered. There was no door that he couldn't knock off the hinges or break by running and butting it with his head. His beard was red like a sow or a fox and broad as a spade. On the top of his nose he had a wart on which grew a tuft of hairs as red as the bristles in a sow's ear. His nostrils were black and wide. He wore a sword and a buckler. His mouth was as big as a furnace. He was a chatterer and a coarse talker—mostly about sin and harlotries. He knew how to steal corn and charge the price three times over; and I swear he had a thumb of gold. He wore a white coat and a blue hood. He had a bagpipe, which he played well, and with that he piped us out of town.

There was a gentle MAUNCIPLE of a Temple, from whom buyers of provisions might learn how to buy victuals wisely, for whether he paid or bought on credit he always came out ahead. Now isn't it a mark of God's grace that this ignorant man, whose master's were thirty experts in law, a dozen of whom were worthy of being stewards of the estate for any lord in England and able to make the lord live within his income—that this Maunciple outwitted them and made a profit off them?

The REEVE was a slender, choleric man, close-shaven, with his short hair docked, like a priest's, in front. His legs were long and skinny. He knew how to manage a granary or a bin so that no auditor could catch up with him. His lord's lands and chattels had been in the Reeve's control since his lord was twenty. No man could catch him in arrears. He knew the dishonesties and trickeries of all the bailiffs and the serfs, and they dreaded him like death. His dwelling place was on a fair heath with green tress shading it. He knew how to acquire goods better than his lord, and he was secretly well off. He could please his lord so cagily that he could lend him the lord's own goods and be thanked and given a gown and hood besides. In youth he had learned a good mystery—he was a wright, a carpenter. He rode a good stallion, and was always the hindmost of our company.

There was a SUMMONER who had a fire-red face like a cherub's for he was pimpled, with narrow eyes. He was as hot and lecherous as a sparrow, his black eyebrows scaly and his beard scanty. Children were afraid of his face. No medicine could cleanse the white pustules and the knobs on his cheeks. He loved garlic, onions, and leeks, and he drank strong wine as red as blood. And then he would speak and shout as though he was crazy, and when he was very drunk he would speak nothing but Latin. He knew two or three terms which he had picked up from some decree—no wonder, he heard Latin all day, and you know that a jay can learn to say "Wat" as well as a pope. But if anyone questioned him or tested him further, then his learning was exhausted, and he would cry, "Ay, questio quid juris." He was a kind and gentle rogue—you couldn't find a better one. For a quart of wine he'd let a good fellow have his concubine for a year and excuse him fully. He knew how to cheat a victim, and if he found another good rascal, he'd teach him, in like circumstances, to have no fear of the archdeacon's curse, unless the man's soul was in his purse, for he'd be punished in his purse: "Purse is the archdeacon's hell," he said. But I knew he lied, for a guilty man ought to dread excommunication. Excommunication will kill just as absolution will save. He had the young people of the diocese at his mercy, knew their secrets and gave them advice. On his head he had set a garland big enough for an ale stake, and he carried a cake for a buckler.

With him was a noble PARDONER from Rouncivale, his friend and comrade, who had just come from the curia at Rome. Loudly he sang, "Come hither, love, to me." The summoner accompanied him in bass—no trumpet was ever so loud. The pardoner had hair as yellow as wax, which hung down in stringy locks and spread thinly over his shoulders. Out of jollity he wore no hood, but carried it in his knapsack. It seemed to him that he rode in the latest fashion. He had glaring eyes like those of a hare. He had a vernicle sewed on his cap. His knapsack lay on his lap in front of him, brimful of pardons hot from Rome. He had a small voice like a goat's. He had no beard and never would have; his face was as smooth as though he had just shaved—I think he was a gelding or a mare. From

Berwick to Ware there was no pardoner who knew the business better than he. In his pack he had a pillowcase which he said was the veil of Our Lady, and he said that he had a piece of the sail that St. Peter used before Christ called him to be a disciple. He had a latten cross, full of stones, and pig bones in a glass. When he found a poor parson dwelling in his parish, this pardoner made more money in a day from these relics than the parson made in two months. He made fools of the parson and the people with feigned flattery and jokes. But truly, in church he was a noble ecclesiastic. He knew how to interpret the Scripture, but best of all he sang the offertory, for he well knew that, when that song was sung, he must preach and make his talk smooth so that he would gain silver—as he knew how to do. Therefore he sang loudly and merrily.

Chaucer now says that he will tell what happened on the pilgrimage. After supper Harry Bailey, the Host of the Tabard, *proposed that the pilgrims amuse themselves by telling stories on the way to Canterbury and back. The pilgrim who told the most moral and entertaining story would be treated, back at the* Tabard, *to a meal paid for by the others. Harry Bailey decided to go along as guide and as referee in the story-contest, and whoever disobeyed Harry's orders would have to pay for the whole pilgrimage. Chaucer says that he will tell all the stories in the very words of each of the pilgrims—though some of them used fairly foul language. He jokingly excuses himself for doing this by saying that, if he didn't use their words, he wouldn't be telling the truth.*

THE NUN'S PRIEST'S TALE
[Translated by Robert Thackaberry.]

During the pilgrimage, the Knight interrupts the Monk's dull recital of a series of brief tragedies, and the Host calls upon the Nun's Priest for a story. The Priest tells a mock-heroic epic—that is a barnyard story told as if it were the Iliad, *the* Odyssey, *or the* Aeneid. *Part of the joke comes from our awareness of the wide discrepancy between the description and the reality, as when the Priest tells us that the cock, walking on tiptoe, is regal or kinglike; another part comes from the shifting back and forth in tone between the seemingly serious and the plainly ridiculous, as when the hen cites a "learned authority" at one point and then recommends that the cock take a digestive of worms.*

Once upon a time there was a poor old widow who lived in a small cottage beside a grove standing in a dale. This widow, since the day that she was last a wife, lived patiently a very simple life because her goods and her income were small. By handling thriftily what God sent her she supported herself and also her two daughters. She had three large sows, no more, three cows, and a sheep called Malle. Her "bower" and her "hall" in which she ate many a scanty meal were very sooty. [The words "bower" and "hall" are appropriate to the mansion or palace of a nobleman. We learn that the widow's hovel was a single room which also included the roosting place for the chickens.] She didn't need a spicy sauce; no dainty morsel passed through her throat. Her meals were appropriate to her clothing. Over-eating never made her sick. An abstemious diet was her medicine—that, and exercise and contentment at heart. Gout didn't keep her from dancing. Apoplexy didn't hurt her head. She drank no wine, neither red or white. Her table was served mostly with white and black—milk and black bread with which she found no fault, broiled bacon and, sometimes, an egg or two, for she was a sort of dairy woman.

She had a yard enclosed with dry sticks outside of which was a dry ditch. In the yard she had a cock named Chantecleer [clear singer]. No one in all the land was his equal in crowing. His voice was merrier than the merry organ played in the church on mass-days. His crowing in his "lodge" [again, upperclass] was more exact than any clock or any abbey's horologe. By nature he knew the ascension of the equinoctial [celestial equator] in that town; for each time it ascended 15 degrees he crowed; no one could indicate the hour more correctly.

His comb was redder than fine coral and battlemented like a castle wall. His bill was as black and shiny as jet. His legs and his toes were like azure; his nails whiter than the lily-flower. His feathers were colored like burnished gold.

This noble cock had in his governance seven hens to do what gave him pleasure. They were his sisters and his paramours. They were wonderously like him in color. The one of them who had the most beautifully colored throat was named lovely Demoiselle Pertelote. She was courteous, discreet, meek, and companionable [words appropriate in praise of a noblewoman]. Since the day when she was seven nights old, she behaved so beautifully that she had Chantecleer's heart completely in her power. He loved her so much that all went well with him. When the bright sun arose, what a joy it was to hear them sing in sweet accord, "My beloved has gone to the country!" For in that time, as I understand it, birds and beasts knew how to talk and sing.

One dawn it happened that, as Chantecleer among all his wives sat on the porch, which was in the hall (and lovely Pertelote sat closest to him), he began to groan in his throat like a man who is sorely troubled in a dream. When Pertelote heard him roar in this way, she was aghast and said, "Dear heart, what is wrong with you that you groan like that. You are usually a good sleeper. Shame on you."

And he answered, "Madame, I pray you, don't take it amiss. By God, I dreamed right now that I was in such trouble that even now my heart is badly frightened. Now, for God's sake, interpret my dream favorably and keep my body out of a foul prison. I dreamed that I roamed up and down in our yard, and there I saw a beast, rather like a dog, who wanted to seize me and kill me. His color was between yellow and red, and his tail and both ears were tipped with black. His snout was small, and his two eyes were glowing. I still almost die from fear when I think of his looks. No doubt, this caused my groaning."

"For shame, coward," she said, "for shame. Alas, by God above, now you have lost my heart and all my love. I cannot love a coward, by my faith. For certainly, whatever any woman may say, we all desire, if it is possible, to have husbands who are brave, wise, generous, and discreet, and not a stingy man, nor a fool, nor one who is aghast at every weapon, nor a braggart, by God above! How dare you say—for shame—to your beloved that anything could make you afraid? You don't have a man's heart even though you have a beard. Alas, can you be aghast of dreams? God knows, a dream is nothing but empty illusions. Dreams are caused by over-eating, and by fumes and mixtures when bodily fluids [humors] are too abundant in a person. Certainly, the dream you dreamed last night comes from a superfuity of red bile [choler]. It causes people in their dreams to dread arrows, and fires with red flames, red beasts and to fear that they will bite, also conflict and big and little whelps. In the same way the fluid melancholy [the humor black bile] causes many a man to cry out in his sleep for fear of black bears and black bulls or else black devils which want to seize them. I could tell about other humors, too, which cause distress to many a man in his sleep. But I'll pass over all that as lightly as possible."

"Consider Cato, who was so wise a man, didn't he say this: 'Pay no attention to dreams'? [Cato was the author of a Latin primer or first reading book.]"

"Now, sire, when you fly down from the beams, for the love of God, take a laxative. May my soul and life be in peril if I am not giving you the best possible advice. I wouldn't lie to you in saying that you should purge yourself both of choler and melancholy. And so that you won't delay, though there is no pharmacist in this town, I myself will teach you what will be best for your health and benefit, and I will find in our yard those herbs which by nature have the power to purge you below and also above. For love of God, don't forget this: You are very choleric in your mixture of humors. Beware lest the sun in rising should find you filled with hot humors. Because, if you do, I would dare to bet a penny that you will have a tertian fever or an ague that may cause your death. For a day or two you will take digestives of worms before you take your laxatives of spurge-laurel, centaury, and fumitory, or else of hellebore, which grows there, or caper berry or gaiter berry, or pleasant herb-ivy growing in our yard. Peck them right up where they grow and eat them. Be merry, husband; dread no dream. I can tell you no more."

"Madame," he said, "Many thanks for your learned advice. But, nevertheless, concerning Lord Cato, who has such great renown for wisdom, though he told us not to dread dreams, by God, men may read in old books about many a man of more authority than Cato ever had, so help me, who say the very reverse of this advice, and who have well found by experience that dreams are significations both of joy and of tribulations which people endure in this present life. There is no need to devise arguments about this; the real proof is revealed in the event."

"One of the greatest authorities whom men read says this: Once upon a time two men, with very good intentions, went on a pilgrimage, and it so happened that they came to a town where there was such a congregation of people and so few rooms for sleeping that they couldn't find so much as a cottage in which they might both be lodged for the night. For that night they must necessarily separate. Each went to his hostelry and took such lodging as befell him. One of them was lodged far away in a yard with plow-oxen; the other was lodged well enough as was his chance or fortune which commonly governs all of us."

"It so happened that, long before day, the second man dreamed where he lay in his bed that his fellow pilgrim called to him and said, 'Alas, tonight I shall be murdered where I lie in an ox's stall. Help me, dear brother, or I'll die. In all haste, come to me'. Because of fear the man roused abruptly from his sleep, but when he was wholly awake, he turned over and took no heed. It seemed to him that his dream was only foolishness. He had the same dream a second time. In his third dream, it seemed to him that his companion came to him and said, 'I have now been slain. Look at my bloody wounds, deep and wide. Get up early in the morning, and at the west gate of the town you will see a cart load of dung in which my corpse is secretly hidden. Have that cart stopped by the authorities. To tell the truth, my gold caused me to be murdered'. And with a pitiful, pale face he told him every detail of how he had been killed. Now believe me, the man who dreamed found that his dream was entirely true, for in the morning, at daybreak, he took his way to his companion's inn, and when he came to the ox's stall, he began to call his companion."

"The innkeeper answered him right away saying, 'Sire, your companion has gone. As soon as it was day, he went out of town'. The traveler, remembering his dream, became suspicious and went without hesitation to the town's west gate and found there a dung-cart going out as if to manure the land—a cart just like the one the dead man had described. He began boldly to cry for vengeance and justice on this felony. 'My companion was murdered during the night and lies dead in this cart. I call upon the authorities who rule this city, Harrow! [This cry—a legal one—announced to all who heard it that a crime was being committed. Everyone who heard the cry was duty bound to help capture the felon.] Here my companion lies slain.'"

"What more should I say. The people came out, overturned the cart, and found the newly murdered man in the middle of the dung."

"O blessed God, who art so just and true, thou revealest murder always. Murder will out, we see that day after day. Murder is so loathsome and abominable to God, who is so just and reasonable, that He will not suffer it to remain concealed though it may remain unknown for a year or two. Murder will out; this is my conclusion."

"And immediately the officers of the town seized the carter and the hosteler and put them to torture so that they confessed their wicked deed and were hanged by the neck."

"Thus may men see that dreams are to be feared. And indeed, in the next chapter of the same book I read—I'm not lying, so help me—that two men wanted for a certain purpose, to cross the sea to a far country. But the wind was contrary and made them stay in the city which stood on the side of a harbor. Then a few days later toward evening the wind changed and blew in exactly the way they wanted. Cheerful and glad they went to bed, determined to sail early next morning. But a great marvel happened to one of them. As he lay sleeping, he dreamed, near dawn, a wondrous dream. It seemed to him that a man stood beside his bed and commanded him to remain in the city and said to him, 'If you sail tomorrow, you will be drowned'. The traveler awoke and told his dream to his companion and begged him to give up his voyage, for that day at least. His companion, who lay by his bed side, laughed and made fun of him. 'No dream', he said, 'can so frighten me as to cause me to give up my plans. I wouldn't give a straw for your dream. Dreams are only illusions and deceits. Men dream constantly of owls and apes and many other illusions. Men dream of things that never have been nor ever will be. But since I see that you are determined to remain here and wilfully miss your tide, God knows, it makes me sorry, but still goodbye'. And thus he took his leave and went away. But before he had sailed fully half his course—I don't know why or what bad luck fell upon it, but by chance the ship's bottom split open, and man and ship sank in the sight of nearby ships which had sailed with it on the same tide."

"And, therefore, dear lovely Pertelote, from such examples you may learn that no man should be too careless about dreams, for I tell you certainly that many a dream is greatly to be feared."

"Consider the 'Life of St. Kenelm', the son of Kenulfus, the noble king of Mercia. In Kenelm's 'Life' I read that a little before he was murdered he saw his own murder in a dream. His nurse expounded to him every detail of his dream and told him to take great care against treason; but he was only seven years old and, therefore gave little importance to any dream; he was so holy at heart. By God, I'd give my shirt for you to have read this legend as I have."

"Madame Pertelote, truly, Macrobius who wrote about the 'Dream of Scipio' asserts the validity of dreams and says that they are warnings of things which will be seen in the future. And, furthermore,

I beg you to consider Daniel, in the Old Testament, whether he believed that dreams were illusions. Read there about Joseph, too, and you will see that dreams are sometimes—I don't say all dreams—warnings of future events. Consider Lord Pharaoh, the king of Egypt, and his baker and his butler, too, whether they didn't experience the effects of dreams. Whoever studies the histories of various kingdoms will read many wondrous things about dreams. For example, Croesus, king of Lydia, didn't he have a dream that he sat in a tree which signified that he would be hanged? Another example, Andromache, Hector's wife: The night before the day when Hector was to lose his life, she dreamed that he would be killed if he went into battle that day. She warned him but could not prevail upon him to stay. He went out to fight and was at once slain by Achilles. But that is too long a story to tell. Besides it is nearly day, and I must not remain here. But briefly, in conclusion, I say that I will have some misfortune from my dream. And furthermore, I say that I don't put any trust in laxatives because I know very well that they are poisonous. I repudiate them. I don't like them at all."

"But let's speak of pleasant things and stop all this. Madame Pertelote, by heaven, God has shown me much favor in one thing: When I see the beauty of your face, you are so scarlet red around your eyes that it makes me dread to die. It is certainly true, *In principio, mulier est hominis confusio.* [In the beginning, woman is the ruination of man.] Madame, the meaning of this Latin is: Woman is man's joy and all his happiness. For when at night I feel your soft side—even though I cannot tread you because, alas, our perch is too narrow—I am so full of comfort and joy that I defy both dream and vision."

And with that word, they—and all his other hens—flew down from the beam because it was day. And with a cluck he began to call them because he had found a kernel of wheat which lay in the yard. He was very regal; he was no longer afraid. He feathered and trod Pertelote twenty times before it was fully daylight. He looked as if he were a grim lion as he roamed up and down on his toes: he didn't deign to set his foot to the ground. He clucks every time he finds a kernel, and all his wives run to him. Thus as royal as a prince in his great hall, I leave Chantecleer in his pasture, and later I will tell his adventure.

When March—the month the world began and in which God made man—when March was over and one day more, it happened that Chantecleer, in all his pride, his seven hens walking beside him, cast up his eyes to the bright sun which had passed through 21° and a little more in the sign of Taurus, and Chantecleer knew by nature, not by any learning, that it was the third hour of the day, he crowed with a cheerful sound and said, "The sun has climbed 21° and more in the heavens. Madame Pertelote, joy of my world, listen to the happy birds—how they sing! And look at the fresh flowers—how they bloom! My heart is full of merriment and comfort."

But suddenly a terrible thing happened to him: for happiness always turns into grief. Worldly happiness, God knows, is soon gone. And if a rhetorician really knew how to write well, he could write it in a chronicle as a most noteworthy truth. Now let everyone listen to me because this story is as true as *The Book of Lancelot de Lac*, which women admire so greatly. Now I will return to my theme.

A fox, full of crafty wickedness, who had lived in that grove for three years, on that very night (as the great vision had foretold) broke through the hedge into the yard where handsome Chantecleer and his wives were accustomed to walk. The fox lay still in a bed of cabbages, waiting for a time to fall upon Chantecleer, as eagerly as do all murderers who lie in wait to murder men.

O false murderer, lurking in your den! O, new Judas Iscariot, new Ganelon [who betrayed Charlemagne and Roland], false dissembler! O, Greek Sinon who brought Troy to utter ruin!

O, Chantecleer! May the morning be accursed on which you flew from the beam into the yard! You had been warned by your dreams that this day would be perilous for you. But what God foreknows must be—according to the opinion of certain learned men. Any great scholar will tell you that in the universities there has been great altercation and great disputation on this subject, and it has involved a hundred thousand men. But I am not able to sift it to the bran [get down to the bare truth] as the holy doctor Augustine is able to, or Boethius, or Bishop Bradwardine—whether God's foreknowledge forces men of necessity to do a thing. By "necessity" I mean *simple necessity;* or whether I have been given free choice to do that thing or not do it, even though God foreknew it before it was done. Or whether his foreknowledge does not force it at all except by *conditional necessity.*

I don't want to have anything to do with that question. My story is about a cock, as you are about to hear, who, to his sorrow, took his wife's advice to walk in the yard on the morning when he had dreamed that dream I told you of. Women's advice is very often harmful; a woman's advice first brought mankind to woe, and made Adam leave Paradise where he had been happy and wholly at ease. But because I don't know whom I might displease if I blame the advice of women, forget it; I said it as a joke. Read the authorities where they deal with this subject, and you will learn what they say about women. These are the cock's words, not mine. I can't discern any harm in any woman.

Lovely Pertelote lies in the sun pleasantly bathing herself in the sand, and all her sisters near her. And Chantecleer freely sings more merrily than the mermaids in the sea; for *Physiologos* [*The Beastiary*] says that they sing very well and merrily. And it so happened that as Chantecleer glanced at a butterfly among the cabbages, he became aware of the fox who lay very close to the ground. He didn't in the least wish to crow then, but immediately cried out, "Cock, cock!" and startled like a man frightened to the heart; because an animal by nature desires to flee from his natural enemy if he should see him. Chantecleer, the moment he spied the fox, wanted to flee, but quickly the fox said, "Noble sire, alas, where do you want to go? Are you afraid of me? I am your friend. Indeed, I would be worse than a friend if I wanted to do any harm or injury to you. I haven't come to spy out your private affairs. But truly the only cause of my coming was to listen to you sing. My lord, your father—God bless his soul—and also your mother (bless her for her gentility) have both been in my house to my great pleasure. And certainly, sire, I would gladly please you. For when people talk about singing, I always say—may I lose my eyes if I'm lying—that, except for you, I never heard any man sing the way your father used to in the morning. Surely, all he sang was from the heart. And to make his voice stronger he would shut both his eyes very tightly, and stand on his tiptoes, and stretch his neck out until it was long and small around. And also he was so perceptive that no man anywhere could surpass him in singing or in wisdom. I have read among the verses of the book *Lord Burnel the Ass,* that there was a cock who, when he was young and ignorant, was injured in the leg by a priest's son. In revenge, the cock made the priest's son lose his benefice [appointment to a church office]. [The cock didn't wake him on the day he was to receive the office.] But certainly there is no comparison between the subtlety of this cock and the wisdom and discretion of your father. Now sing, sire, for the love of heaven, and let's see if you are able to imitate your father."

Chantecleer began to beat his wings like a man who cannot espy treachery; he was too carried away by the flattery.

Alas, O noble lords, how many false flatterers and liars are in your courts who please you much more, believe me, than any man who tells you the truth. Read *Ecclesiastes* on flatterers, and beware, lords, of their treachery.

Chantecleer stood high on his toes, stretched out his neck, kept his eyes tightly closed, and began to crow his very loudest crow. Lord Russell the fox immediately leapt up, grabbed Chantecleer by the neck, threw him over his back, and started to carry him off toward the woods because, as yet, no one pursued him.

O destiny which no one can escape! Alas that Chantecleer flew down from the roost. Alas that his wife denied the significance of dreams. And all this misfortune happened on a Friday.

O Venus, goddess of pleasure, since Chantecleer was your devout worshiper and did all in his power to serve you (more for sensual delight than for procreation), how could you let him die on your day?

O Godfrey, dear sovereign master [of rhetoric], when your worthy King Richard was slain, how exquisitely you lamented his death. Why don't I have your skill and learning so that I could reproach Friday, as you did because your king was killed on a Friday? Then I would show you how ably I would lament for Chantecleer's fear and pain.

When Troy was captured and Pyrrhus seized Priam by the beard and killed him, as the *Aeneid* says, the ladies of the city never made half such a cry and lamentation as the hens of the yard made when they saw what was happening to Chantecleer. But Madame Pertelote shrieked most sovereignly, much louder than Hasdrubal's wife shrieked when the Romans killed her husband and burned Carthage. She was so full of grief and despair that she rushed into the fire and burned herself with a steadfast heart. O woeful hens, you cried out exactly as, when Nero burned Rome, the wives of the senators cried out because their husbands had lost their lives, for Nero, though they were guiltless, had them slain.

Now, I'll return to my story.

The simple widow and her two daughters at once rushed outdoors when they heard the hens cry out in their grief. The women saw the fox going toward the grove carrying the cock away on his back; they cried, "Out! Harrow!" and "Weilawey! Look! Look! the fox," and they ran after him. Many men with staves ran with them. The dogs took up the chase—Colle, Talbot, and Garland, and also Malkyn with a distaff in her hand. There ran also the cow, the calf, and even the hogs—they were so frightened by the barking of the dogs and the shouting of the men and women that the hogs ran as if to break their hearts. They yowled like fiends in hell. The ducks cried out as if they were being killed; out of fear the geese flew over the trees; out of the hive came a swarm of bees. The noise was so hideous—surely Jack Straw [leader of the great Peasant Revolt, 1381] and all his followers never made shouts so shrill, when they were killing a Fleming as that day were made against the fox. Men brought trumpets of brass, wood, horn, and bone upon which they blew and tooted; the others shrieked and whooped. It seemed as if the heavens might fall.

Now, good men, I pray you all, listen. Behold how Fortune reverses suddenly the hope and pride of her enemy! The cock, lying upon the fox's back, though deeply frightened, spoke to the fox and said, "Sire, God help me, if I were you, I'd say, 'Turn back, all you proud louts! May a pestilence fall upon you! Now that I have reached the edge of the woods, the cock will stay here, and indeed I will eat him right away.'"

The fox answered, "That's just what I'll do." And as he spoke those words, the cock quickly escaped from the fox's mouth and flew immediately up to the branch of a tree.

When the fox realized that the cock was gone, he said, "Alas, Chantecleer, I did you a wrong by making you afraid when I seized you and carried you out of the yard. But, sire, I didn't do it with any wicked intention. Come down, and I will tell you what I meant to do. I'll tell you the truth, God help me."

"No," said the cock, "then I would say, 'A curse on both of us', but first a curse on me, my blood, and my bones, if I let you trick me more than once. Never again with your flattery will you cause me to sing and close my eyes, for the man who wilfully closes his eyes when he should keep them open—may God never let him prosper."

"No," the fox said, "may God give great misfortune to the man who controls himself so badly that he yaks when he should shut up."

Notice well what happens when one is reckless and careless and puts his trust in flattery.

But you who think this tale is some foolishness—all about a cock and a hen, consider instead the moral lesson in the story, for St. Paul says that every thing that is written is indeed written for our instruction. Take the wheat and throw away the chaff.

And now, O God, if it be thy will, as Our Lord says, make us all good men and bring us into the bliss of heaven. Amen.

St. Francis of Assisi

St. Francis (c. 1181-1226), the son of a wealthy merchant of Assisi, gave up his worldly goods to follow Christ's teachings in 1208. St. Francis, with a few friends, founded the Friars Minor, known as the Franciscans; in 1210 they received approval from the Pope for their order. The life of St. Francis is a complete contrast to the wealth and splendor of medieval Christianity. St. Francis devoted his life to the preaching of poverty, simple devotion to Christ and service to mankind. He had a simple profound love of every creature, not just human beings but all creatures, and took great delight in the beauty of the world about him because it had come from God. He has been described as the most Christ-like man who ever lived. However, the Franciscan order, founded as it was on such ascetic principals as Francis put forth, could not continue in this world without some change, since few people were of the make-up of St. Francis. Therefore, the Franciscans inevitably changed in their outlook, although St. Francis remained their guiding spirit. The following prayer, composed by St. Francis is often called one of the most perfect prayers ever written. In addition, it seems to state St. Francis' aim in life. The will of St. Francis gives to all his brothers the rules which they should follow after his death.

PRAYER OF ST. FRANCIS

O Lord, make me an instrument of Thy peace.
Where there is hatred, let me sow love.
Where there is injury, pardon.
Where there is darkness, light.
Where there is sadness, joy.
Where there is doubt, faith
And where there is despair, hope.

O divine Master, grant that I may not so much seek
To be consoled as to console.
To be understood as to understand.
To be loved as to love.

For it is in giving that we receive,
It is in forgiving that we are pardoned,
And it is in dying that we are born to Eternal Life.

WILL OF ST. FRANCIS

... God gave it to me, Brother Francis, to begin to do penance in the following manner: when I was yet in my sins it did seem to me too bitter to look upon the lepers, but the Lord himself did lead me among them, and I had compassion upon them. When I left them, that which had seemed to me bitter had become sweet and easy.

A little while after I left the world, and God gave me such faith that I would kneel down with simplicity in any of his churches, and I would say, "We adore thee, Lord Jesus Christ, here and in all thy churches which are in the world, and we bless thee that by thy holy cross thou hast ransomed the world."

Afterward the Lord gave me, and still gives me, so great a faith in priests who live according to the form of the holy Roman Church, because of their sacerdotal character, that even if they persecuted me I would have recourse to them, and even though I had all the wisdom of Solomon, if I should find poor secular priests, I would not preach in their parishes against their will. I desire to respect them like all the others, to love them and honor them as my lords. I will not consider their sins, for in them I see the Son of God, and they are my lords. I do this because here below I see nothing, I perceive nothing corporeally of the most high Son of God, except his most holy body and blood, which the priests receive and alone distribute to others.

I desire above all things to honor and venerate all these most holy mysteries and to keep them precious. Wherever I find the sacred names of Jesus, or his words, in unsuitable places, I desire to take them away and put them in some decent place; and I pray that others may do the same. We ought to honor and revere all the theologians and

From *Readings in European History*, Vol. I by James Harvey Robinson, 1904, Ginn and Company, Boston.

those who preach the most holy word of God, as dispensing to us spirit and life.

When the Lord gave me the care of some brothers, no one showed me what I ought to do, but the Most High himself revealed to me that I ought to live according to the model of the holy gospel. I caused a short and simple formula to be written, and the lord pope confirmed it for me.

Those who presented themselves to follow this kind of life distributed all they might have to the poor. They contented themselves with one tunic, patched within and without, with the cord and breeches, and we desired to have nothing more. The clerics said the office like other clerics, and the laymen repeated the paternoster.

We loved to live in poor and abandoned churches, and we were ignorant, and were submissive to all. I worked with my hands and would still do so, and I firmly desire also that all the other brothers work, for this makes for goodness. Let those who know no trade learn one, but not for the purpose of receiving the price of their toil, but for their good example and to flee idleness. And when we are not given the price of our work, let us resort to the table of the Lord, begging our bread from door to door. The Lord revealed to me the salutation which we ought to give: "God give you peace!"

Let the brothers take great care not to accept churches, habitations, or any buildings erected for them, except as all is in accordance with the holy poverty which we have vowed in the Rule; and let them not live in them except as strangers and pilgrims. I absolutely interdict all the brothers, in whatsoever place they may be found, from asking any bull from the court of Rome, whether directly or indirectly, in the interest of church or convent, or under pretext of preaching, nor even for the protection of their bodies. If they are not received anywhere, let them go of themselves elsewhere, thus doing penance with the benediction of God.

I firmly desire to obey the minister general of this brotherhood, and the guardian whom he may please to give me. I desire to put myself entirely into his hands, to go nowhere and do nothing against his will, for he is my lord. Though I be simple and ill, I would, however, have always a clerk who will perform the office, as it is said in the Rule. Let all the other brothers also be careful to obey their guardians and to do the office according to the Rule.

If it come to pass that there are any who do not the office according to the Rule, and who desire to make any other change, or if they are not Catholics, let all the brothers, wherever they may be, be bound by obedience to present them to the nearest custodian. Let the custodians be bound by obedience to keep such a one well guarded, like a man who is in bonds, day and night, so that he may not escape from their hands until they personally place him in the minister's hands. And let the minister be bound by obedience to send him, by brothers who will guard him as a prisoner day and night, until they shall have placed him in the hands of the lord bishop of Ostia, who is the lord protector, and the corrector of all the brotherhood.

And let the brothers not say, "This is a new Rule"; for this is only a reminder, a warning, an exhortation; it is my last will and testament, that I, little Brother Francis, make for you, my blessed brothers, in order that we may observe in a more Catholic way the Rule which we promised the Lord to keep.

Let the ministers general, all the other ministers, and the custodians be held by obedience to add nothing to and take nothing away from these words. Let them always keep this writing near them beside the Rule; and in all the assemblies which shall be held, when the Rule is read, let these words be read also.

I interdict absolutely by obedience all the brothers, clerics and laymen, to introduce comments in the Rule, or in this will, under pretext of explaining it. But since the Lord has given me to speak and to write the Rule and these words in a clear and simple manner, so do you understand them in the same way without commentary, and put them in practice until the end.

And whoever shall have observed these things, may he be crowned in heaven with the blessings of the heavenly Father, and on earth with those of his well-beloved Son and of the Holy Spirit, the Consoler, with the assistance of all the heavenly virtues and all the saints.

And I, little Brother Francis, your servitor, confirm to you, so far as I am able, this most holy benediction. Amen.

Heresies

Many medieval people were not satisfied by the formal religion of the Church. Especially was this true in the towns and cities in the twelfth and thirteenth centuries, where large numbers turned either to sects which emphasized a personal religion or to some form of heresy. The following selections concern two popular movements which were considered heretical by the medieval Church. The first, an excerpt from an anonymous chronicle written about 1218, describes the conversion of Peter Waldo, the founder of the Waldensians. The second is a description of the Albigensians by an experienced inquisitor of the early fourteenth century.

PETER WALDO

And during the same year, that is the 1173d since the Lord's Incarnation, there was at Lyons in France a certain citizen, Waldo by name, who had made himself much money by wicked usury. One Sunday, when he had joined a crowd which he saw gathered around a troubadour, he was smitten by his words and, taking him to his house, he took care to hear him at length. The passage he was reciting was how the holy Alexis died a blessed death in his father's house. When morning had come the prudent citizen hurried to the schools of theology to seek counsel for his soul, and when he was taught many ways of going to God, he asked the master what way was more certain and more perfect than all others. The master answered him with this text: "If thou wilt be perfect, go and sell all that thou hast," etc.

Then Waldo went to his wife and gave her the choice of keeping his personal property or his real estate, namely, what he had in ponds, groves and fields, houses, rents, vineyards, mills, and fishing rights. She was much displeased at having to make this choice, but she kept the real estate. From his personal property he made restitution to those whom he had treated unjustly; a great part of it he gave to his two little daughters, who, without their mother's knowledge, he placed in the convent of Font Evrard; but the greatest part of his money he spent for the poor. A very great famine was then oppressing France and Germany. The prudent citizen, Waldo, gave bread, with vegetables and meat, to every one who came to him for three days in every week from Pentecost to the feast of St. Peter's bonds.

At the Assumption of the blessed Virgin, casting some money among the village poor, he cried, "No man can serve two masters, God and mammon." Then his fellow-citizens ran up, thinking he had lost his mind. But going on to a higher place, he said: "My fellow-citizens and friends, I am not insane, as you think, but I am avenging myself on my enemies, who made me a slave, so that I was always more careful of money than of God, and served the creature rather than the Creator. I know that many will blame me that I act thus openly. But I do it both on my own account and on yours; on my own, so that those who see me henceforth possessing any money may say that I am mad, and on yours, that you may learn to place hope in God and not in riches."

On the next day, coming from the church, he asked a certain citizen, once his comrade, to give him something to eat, for God's sake. His friend, leading him to his house, said, "I will give you whatever you need as long as I live." When this came to the ears of his wife, she was not a little troubled, and as though she had lost her mind, she ran to the archbishop of the city and implored him not to let her husband beg bread from any one but her. This moved all present to tears.

[Waldo was accordingly conducted into the presence of the bishop.] And the woman, seizing her husband by the coat, said, "Is it not better, husband, that I should redeem my sins by giving you alms than that strangers should do so?" And from that time he was not allowed to take food from any one in that city except from his wife.

From *Readings in European History,* Vol. I by James Harvey Robinson, 1904, Ginn and Company, Boston.

ALBIGENSIANS

It would take too long to describe in detail the manner in which these same Manichaean heretics preach and teach their followers, but it must be briefly considered here.

In the first place, they usually say of themselves that they are good Christians, who do not swear, or lie, or speak evil of others; that they do not kill any man or animal, nor anything having the breath of life, and that they hold the faith of the Lord Jesus Christ and his gospel as Christ and his apostles taught. They assert that they occupy the place of the apostles, and that, on account of the above-mentioned things, they of the Roman Church, namely the prelates, clerks, and monks, and especially the inquisitors of heresy, persecute them and call them heretics, although they are good men and good Christians, and that they are persecuted just as Christ and his apostles were by the Pharisees.

Moreover they talk to the laity of the evil lives of the clerks and prelates of the Roman Church, pointing out and setting forth their pride, cupidity, avarice, and uncleanness of life, and such other evils as they know. They invoke, with their own interpretation and according to their abilities, the authority of the Gospels and the Epistles against the condition of the prelates, churchmen, and monks, whom they call Pharisees and false prophets, who say, but do not.

Then they attack and vituperate, in turn, all the sacraments of the Church, especially the sacrament of the eucharist, saying that it cannot contain the body of Christ, for had this been as great as the largest mountain Christians would have entirely consumed it before this. They assert that the host comes from straw, that it passes through the tails of horses, to wit, when the flour is cleaned by a sieve (of horse hair); that, moreover, it passes through the body and comes to a vile end, which, they say, could not happen if God were in it.

Of baptism, they assert that water is material and corruptible, and is therefore the creation of the evil power and cannot sanctify the soul, but that the churchmen sell this water out of avarice, just as they sell earth for the burial of the dead, and oil to the sick when they anoint them, and as they sell the confession of sins as made to the priests.

Hence they claim that confession made to the priests of the Roman Church is useless, and that, since the priests may be sinners, they cannot loose nor bind, and, being unclean themselves, cannot make others clean. They assert, moreover, that the cross of Christ should not be adored or venerated, because, as they urge, no one would venerate or adore the gallows upon which a father, relative, or friend had been hung. They urge, further, that they who adore the cross ought, for similar reasons, to worship all thorns and lances, because as Christ's body was on the cross during the passion, so was the crown of thorns on his head and the soldier's lance in his side. They proclaim many other scandalous things in regard to the sacraments.

Moreover they read from the Gospels and the Epistles in the vulgar tongue, applying and expounding them in their favor and against the condition of the Roman Church in a manner which it would take too long to describe in detail; but all that relates to this subject may be read more fully in the books they have written and infected, and may be learned from the confessions of such of their followers as have been converted.